MEANING-BASED TRANSLATION

A Guide to Cross- Language Equivalence

Second Edition

Mildred L. Larson

University Press of America,® Inc.
Lanham • New York • Oxford

Copyright © 1998 by
University Press of America,® Inc.
4720 Boston Way
Lanham, Maryland 20706

12 Hid's Copse Rd.
Cummor Hill, Oxford OX2 9JJ

Co-published by arrangement with the Summer Institute of
Linguistics. Inc.

Previous edition © 1984
Volume editor: Bonnie Brown

Library of Congress Cataloging-in-Publication Data

Larson, Mildred L.
Meaning-based translation : a guide to cross-language equivalence /
Mildred L. Larson. —2nd ed.
p.   cm.
Includes bibliographical references and index.
l. Translating and interpreting.   I. Title.
P306.L34   1997   418'.02—DC21   97-44626 CIP

ISBN 0-7618-0970-8 (cloth: alk. ppr.)
ISBN 0-7618-0971-6 (pbk: alk. ppr.)

ACKNOWLEDGMENTS

The author wishes to express appreciation to the following authors and publishers for granting permission to quote from their materials in this book: Samson Negbo Abangma from *The Use of Modes in Denya Discourse* (1987); Katharine Barnwell from her two textbooks *Bible Translation* (1975) and *Introduction to Semantics and Translation* (1980); Chicago Linguistic Society from *Papers from the Eighth Regional Meeting*; Ellis W. Deibler and A. J. Taylor from *Translation Problems* (1977); Carl D. Dubois from his article *Connectives in Sarangani Manobo*; Ilah Fleming from her *Field Guide for Communication Situation, Semantic and Morphemic Analysis* (1977); Ellen M. Jackson from *Real and Rhetorical Questions in Tikar* (1982); Kenneth and Evelyn Pike for permission to use the example on pages 49–50 of their book *Grammatical Analysis* (1977); the Summer Institute of Linguistics for permission to quote from *Notes on Translation*, *Notes on Linguistics*, John Beekman and John Callow, *Translating the Word of God* (1974), Kathleen Callow, *Discourse Considerations in Translating the Word of God* (1974), Mildred Larson, *A Manual for Problem Solving in Bible Translation* (1975) and John Beekman, John Callow, and Michael Kopesec, *The Semantic Structure of Written Communication* (1981); The United Bible Societies from *The Bible Translator*, particularly the articles by Barclay Newman (1977) and David Fox (1959); Western Publishing Company from *Universal History of the World* Vol. 2 by James L. Steffensen (1966); and James Wheatley from his articles *Knowledge, Authority, and Individualism among the Cura (Bacairi)* (1970) and *Pronouns and Nominal Elements in Bacairi Discourse* (1973).

CONTENTS

FOREWORD

In the last thirty years a body of literature on translation theory, strongly influenced by modern linguistics, has appeared to support and give academic respectability to the new profession of the nonliterary translator. Some of these books, notably written by West or East Germans, have been too philosophical and abstract to relate at all closely to the translator's mundane problems. Some have leaned towards contrastive linguistics. Others have tended to tie translation too closely to a linguistic theory.

Nida's were the first to deal at all practically with the cultural as well as the manifold linguistic problems of translation. Dr. Mildred Larson has here produced the first textbook designed to be used in the classroom, as a basis for course work.

I am pleased and flattered to be invited to write a foreword for her textbook of translation method. The book's purpose is first to make the Summer Institute of Linguistics' translation principles and study procedures widely known, and secondly, to offer a textbook which will be generally useful to translation courses in universities and colleges of further and higher education throughout the world, particularly in the third world countries, where good English textbooks are much in demand.

This book includes translation examples from a remarkably wide range of languages, particularly Asian, African, and Amerindian languages, ranging from the semantics of words, collocations and proposition to that of texts, ending each chapter with a useful set of practical exercises which are also a back-up for learning English. Her treatment of collocations is the most thorough and illuminating that I know. Metaphor and simile have an important place in the book; the semantic distortions of literal translation are well handled.

Dr. Larson is continuously exercised to explain and illustrate the interplay of syntax, semantics, and communicative force through stress and variations of word order in the composition of a text. She makes good use of the still fairly recently established principles of text-linguistics.

The emphasis of the book is on the value of idiomatic and unconstrained language. The abundant and subtle resources of the English language are described and exemplified here with a pervasive verve and enthusiasm. The book is exceptionally well planned, with a comprehensive index and bibliography, and I have no doubt that every teacher and self-teaching student of translation and of English will find much in it which they can use with profit.

Peter Newmark
Polytechnic of Central London and Universities of Bradford and Surrey, U.K.

PREFACE

More and more universities around the world are adding courses in translation to their curriculum; however, the textbooks available for such courses are few. This volume has been written with these courses in mind. The desire of the author is to make available the principles of translation which have been learned through personal experience in translation and consultation, and through interaction with colleagues involved in translation projects in many parts of the world.

A pedagogical style of presentation has been deliberately adopted. Repetition is regularly used; frequently use is made of examples; and each chapter concludes with exercises to be carried out by the student. Since it is assumed that many of the students will be speakers of minority languages, many of these exercises involve translating from or into their mother tongue. The material is presented in such a way that it can be used in a self-teaching situation or in a classroom. An attempt has been made to keep technical terms to a minimum. When technical vocabulary is used, every effort is made to clarify the meaning of such vocabulary. This has been done so that the book can be used by any translator, even though his exposure to linguistic and translation theory has been minimal. However, some of the theory is complex and no attempt has been made to oversimplify it. But the author has sought to use an uncomplicated straightforward style in order to make it easy for the user to grasp the principles being presented.

This is an introductory textbook. The first five chapters give an overview presenting the fundamental principles of translation and the rest of the book expands and illustrates these principles. The overriding principle is that translation is meaning-based rather than form-based. Once the translator has identified the meaning of the source text, his goal is to express that same meaning in the receptor language with forms which may be very different from those of the source text. Many examples of cross-language equivalence are used to illustrate this principle.

The author is deeply indebted to the late John Beekman, from whom she learned much of what is included in this book. The material presented here borrows heavily from his writings and those of John Callow, Kathleen Callow, Katharine Barnwell, and Eugene Nide. This book simply takes the translation principles expounded by them and puts these principles into a new framework as a textbook for prospective translators, especially speakers of the many minority languages of the world.

I also wish to thank Dr. Peter Newmark for reviewing the manuscript and writing the foreword. Dr. Newmark is visiting Professor at the Polytechnic of Central London and Universities of Bradford and Surrey, U.K., with considerable experience in training translators. His 1981 book, *Approaches to Translation*, was especially helpful to me in the preparation of this text book.

Many persons have helped in the preparation of this book. The author is especially grateful to her colleagues, members of the Summer Institute of Linguistics, who reviewed the manuscript, making many helpful suggestions, and to those who helped in many ways in the preparation of the manuscript. The list of those who contributed is very long and each is greatly appreciated.

MLL
September 1997

OVERVIEW OF THE TRANSLATION TASK

Chapter 1
Form and Meaning

What is translation?

Translation, by dictionary definition, consists of changing from one state or **form** to another, to turn into one's own or another's language (The Merriam-Webster Dictionary 1974). Translation is basically a change of **form**. When we speak of the **form** of a language, we are referring to the actual words, phrases, clauses, sentences, paragraphs, etc., which are spoken or written. These **forms** are referred to as the **surface structure** of a language. It is the structural part of language which is actually seen in print or heard in speech. In translation the **form** of the source language is replaced by the **form** of the receptor (target) language. But how is this change accomplished? What determines the choices of **form** in the translation?

The purpose of this text is to show that translation consists of transferring the **meaning** of the source language into the receptor language. This is done by going from the **form** of the first language to the **form** of a second language by way of semantic structure. It is **meaning** which is being transferred and must be held constant. Only the **form** changes. The **form** from which the translation is made will be called the SOURCE LANGUAGE and the **form** into which it is to be changed will be called the RECEPTOR LANGUAGE. Translation, then, consists of studying the lexicon, grammatical structure, communication situation, and cultural context of the source language text, analyzing it in order to determine its meaning, and then reconstructing this same meaning using the lexicon and grammatical structure which are appropriate in the RECEPTOR LANGUAGE and its cultural context. The process may be diagrammed as shown in Display 1.1.

Let us look at an example. Assume that we are translating the Spanish sentence "*Tengo sueño*," into the Aguaruna language of Peru. This Spanish form consists of the verb form *teng-* 'have', the suffix *-o* 'first person', and the word *sueño* 'sleep.' The combination means that "a person, the speaker, is in the state of being sleepy." To convey this same meaning in Aguaruna one would use "*Kajang pujawai*,"

3

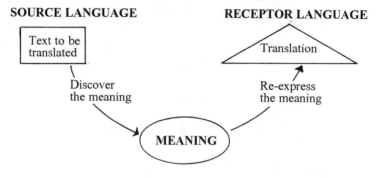

Display 1.1

which consists of the noun *kaja-* 'sleep', the suffix *-ng* 'my', and the verb *puja* 'live' with the suffix *-wai* 'third person indicative'. A very literal translation of the Spanish into English would be "I have sleep," and of the Aguaruna *"My sleep lives."* Neither of these would be a good English translation. The appropriate English translation would be *"I am sleepy,"* (*I* 'first person,' *am* 'be', and an adjective *sleepy*). The three languages use different grammatical forms and different lexical selections to signal the same meaning (see Display 1.2).

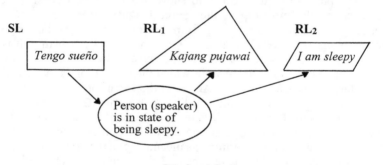

Display 1.2

It is true that persons who know both the SOURCE LANGUAGE and the RECEPTOR LANGUAGE well can often make the transfer from one **form** to the other very rapidly, without thinking about the semantic structure overtly. However, for complicated texts, and when the translators may not be equally fluent in the two languages (if they are mother-tongue speakers of only one), the study of the principles to be presented here will enable them to make a more adequate translation.

Even if one is able to make an adequate translation without detailed analysis, it should be of interest to all translators to study the process of translating by semantic analysis.

It is relatively easy to handle the transfer for simple sentences used in everyday conversation. For example, one easily learns such differences as the following:

English: *What is your name?*

Spanish: *Como se llama?*
(literally "how yourself you-call?")

Aguaruna: *Amesh yaitpa?*
(literally "you-doubt who-are-you?")

It is not simply a matter of different word choices, but of different grammatical structures as well. We expect greetings to have varying **forms**. But notice the following additional example of the **forms** used to express the **meaning** that "a person, who is the speaker, possesses money": English uses *I have money*; Japanese and Latin use **forms** which literally say *to me there is money*; Arabic and Russian use **forms** which literally say *with me there is money*; and Aguaruna and Turkish use **forms** which say *my money exists*.

Translators will almost never have problems with these common expressions. They hardly think about the fact that the grammatical form and the lexical choices are so different. But as they move into unfamiliar material or into higher levels of syntactic structure with complicated sentences and discourses, there is a tendency for choices of lexical items and grammatical forms in the receptor language to be unduly influenced by the lexical items and grammatical forms of the source language. The result will be forms which sound strange and "foreign" to speakers of the receptor language. For example, a German speaker may say in English, "*The child has* **fever, it** *is ill*," instead of "*The child has* **a fever,** *he/she is ill*," because of the influence of the German, "*Das Kind hat* **Fieber, es** *ist krank.*" In English there needs to be an article, *a*, before *fever*; and *child* is referred to by a masculine or feminine pronoun rather than the neuter pronoun, *it*.

We are familiar with the kinds of mistakes non-native speakers of a language make. If analyzed, these errors almost always reflect the lexical and grammatical forms of the person's mother-tongue. He has translated literally the **form** from his own language (the source language) and, therefore, his speech in the receptor language is unnatural. For example, a brochure used in an advertisement for tourists in Belem, Brazil says, "*We glad to you an unforgettable trip by fantastic Marajó Island*," meaning "We offer you an unforgettable trip to fantastic Marajo Island." In another place the brochure says, *"Beyond all those things, enjoy of delicious that your proper mind can create. Marajó is inspiration,"* meaning "And above all, enjoy the delights which your own mind will create. Marajo will inspire you." A look at the Portuguese on the other side of the brochure shows that the unnatural English was the result of following the form of the Portuguese source language in making the English receptor language translation. To do effective translation one must discover the **meaning** of the source language and use receptor language **forms** which express this meaning in a natural way.

It is the purpose of this book to familiarize the reader with the basic linguistic and sociolinguistic factors involved in translating a text from a SOURCE LANGUAGE into a second language, i.e., the RECEPTOR LANGUAGE, and to give them enough practice in the translation process for the development of skills in cross-language transfer. The underlying premise upon which the book is based is that the best translation is the one which (1) uses the normal language forms of the receptor language, (2) communicates, as much as possible, to the receptor language speakers the same meaning that was understood by the speakers of the source language, and (3) maintains the dynamics of the original source language text. Maintaining the "dynamics" of the original source text means that the translation is presented in such a way that it will, hopefully, evoke the same response as the source text attempted to evoke.

Characteristics of language which affect translation

There are certain characteristics of languages which have a very direct bearing on principles of translation. First, let us look at the characteristics of meaning components. **Meaning components** are "packaged" into lexical items, but they are "packaged" differently in one language than in another. In most languages there is a **meaning component** of *plurality*, for example the English *-s*. This often occurs in the grammar as a suffix on the nouns or verbs or both. In Aguaruna, however, **plurality** is a component of the verb stem itself and cannot be separated out for many of the more common verbs. If the actor is **singular**, the first form will be used, if **plural**, the second.

1. *tupikau*	he runs	2. *pisaju*	they run
1. *eketu*	he sits	2. *pekemsau*	they sit
1. *weu*	he went	2. *shiaku*	they went

A study of any dictionary will indicate the amazing "packaging" of meaning components in lexical items. In Otomí (Mexico), one single word means *watch sheep by night*. All of those components are in a single lexical item. In Vietnamese, there is a word which means *someone leaves to go somewhere and something happens at home so that he has to go back home*. Many times a single word in the source language will need to be translated by several words. For example, a *projector* was called *the thing that shows pictures on the wall* by the Chipaya of Bolivia.

Second, it is characteristic of languages that the same meaning component will occur in several surface structure lexical items (forms). In English, the word *sheep* occurs. However, the words *lamb, ram*, and *ewe* also include the meaning *sheep*. They include the additional meaning components of *young* (in *lamb*), *adult* and *male* (in *ram*), and *adult* and *female* (in *ewe*). In Huambisa (Peru), *lamb* would need to be translated by "sheep its child," *ram* by "sheep big," and *ewe* by "sheep its woman."

Third, it is further characteristic of languages that one **form** will be used to represent several alternative **meanings**. This again is obvious from looking in any good dictionary. For example, the Reader's Digest Great Encyclopedic Dictionary gives fifty-four meanings for the English word *run*. Most words have more than one meaning. There will be a primary meaning – the one which usually comes to mind when the word is said in isolation – and secondary meanings – the additional meanings which a word has in context with other words. In English, we can say *the boy runs*, using *run* in its primary meaning. We can also say *the motor runs, the river runs*, and *his nose runs*, using *run* in secondary senses, i.e., with different meanings. But notice the following comparison with Spanish. Motors and noses do not *run* in all languages.

ENGLISH	SPANISH
The boy runs.	El niño corre (runs).
The motor runs.	El motor funciona (functions).
The clock runs.	El reloj anda (walks).
His nose runs.	Su naríz chorrea (drips).

This principle is not limited to lexical items for it is also true that the same grammatical pattern may express several quite different meanings. For example, the English possessive phrase *my house* may mean "the house I own," "the house I rent," "the house I live in," "the house I built," or "the house for which I drew up the plans." Only the larger context determines the meaning. Notice the following possessive phrases and the variety of meanings:

my car	ownership
my brother	kinship
my foot	part-whole (part of my body)
my singing	actor-activity (I sing)
my book	ownership or authorship (the book I own, or, the book I wrote)
my village	residence (the village where I live)
my train	use (the train I ride on)

Whole sentences may also have several functions. A question **form** may be used for a nonquestion. For example, the question *"Mary, why don't you wash the dishes?"* has the **form** of a question, and may in some context be asking for information, but it is often used with the **meaning** of command (or suggestion), rather than a real question. It is then a rhetorical question. (The matter of translating questions will be discussed in chapter 22.) A simple English sentence like *"He made the bed,"* may mean either "He made (as a carpenter would make) the bed," or "He put the sheets, blanket, and pillow in neat order on the bed."

Just as words have primary and secondary meanings, so grammatical markers have their primary function and often have other secondary functions. The preposition *on* is used in English to signal a variety of meanings. Compare the following uses of *on* with the corresponding form used in Spanish.

John found a book *on* the floor.	Juan encontró un libro *en* (on) el suelo.
John found a book *on* mathematics.	Juan encontró un libro *sobre/de* (about) matemáticas.
John found a book *on* Tuesday.	Juan encontró un libro *el* (the) martes.
John found a book *on* sale.	Juan encontró un libro *a* (at) la venta (en rebaja, en baratillo).

Compare also the following uses of *by*:

> John was stopped *by* the policeman.

> John stopped *by* the bookstand.

In the first, *by* is used to signal the meaning that the policeman is the *agent* of the action. In the second, *by* signals that the bookstand is the *location*.

In the Acholi language of Sudan, the word *oto* has various meanings depending on the words with which it occurs. Notice the following:

Latin *oto*.	The child *is dead*.
Agulu *oto*.	The pot *is broken*.
Mac *oto*.	The fire *is gone out*.

We have seen that one **form** may express a variety of **meanings**. On the other hand, another characteristic of languages is that a single **meaning** may be expressed in a variety of **forms**. For example, the meaning "the cat is black" may be expressed by the following: *the cat is black, the black cat,* and *the cat, which is black,* depending on how that meaning relates to other meanings. In addition, the meanings of "*Is this place taken?*" "*Is there anyone sitting here?*" and "*May I sit here?*" are essentially the same. The speaker is indicating a desire to sit in a certain seat. In Pidgin, the meaning "He gave me a book" stays essentially the same whether one says "*em i givim wanpela buk long mi*" or "*em i givim mi wanpela buk.*" Also, the meaning is essentially the same in the following English sentences (example from K.L. Pike):

> Others blamed John because of the difficulty.

> Others blamed John for the difficulty.

> Others blamed the difficulty on John.

> Others said John was responsible for the difficulty.

> Others accused John of being responsible for the difficulty.

We have seen that even within a single language there are a great variety of ways in which form expresses meaning. Only when a form is being used in its **primary meaning** or function is there a one-to-one correlation between form and meaning. The other meanings are **secondary meanings** or **figurative meanings**. Words have these extended meanings and in the same way grammatical forms have extended usages (secondary and figurative functions).

This characteristic of "skewing," that is, the diversity or the lack of one-to-one correlation between **form** and **meaning**, is the basic reason that translation is a complicated task. If there were no skewing, then all lexical items and all grammatical forms would have only one meaning; and a literal word-for-word and grammatical structure-for-grammatical structure translation would be possible. But the fact is that a language is a complex set of skewed relationships between **meaning** (semantics) and **form** (lexicon and grammar). Each language has its own distinctive **forms** for representing the **meaning**. Therefore, in translation the same **meaning** may have to be expressed in another language by a very different **form**. To translate the **form** of one language literally according to the corresponding **form** in another language would often change the **meaning**, or at least result in a form which is unnatural in the second language. **Meaning** must, therefore, have priority over **form** in translation. It is **meaning** which is to be carried over from the source language to the receptor language, not the linguistic **forms**. For example, to translate the English phrase *he is cold hearted*, i.e., *his heart is cold* (meaning "he is unfeeling, has no emotional sympathy") literally into Mambila (Nigeria) would be understood to mean *he is peaceful, not quick-tempered*, and if translated literally into Cinyanja (Zambia), it would mean *he is afraid* (Barnwell 1980:12). In this case, it is not a secondary meaning but a figurative meaning which is causing the difference.

Unless the source language and the receptor language are closely related languages, from the same language family, it is not likely that there will be much correspondence of form between the source text and the translation. The nature of language is that each language uses different forms and these forms have secondary and figurative meanings which add further complications. A "word-for-word" translation which follows closely the **form** of the source language is called a **literal translation**. A **literal translation** is useful if one is studying the structure of the source text as in an interlinear translation, but a **literal translation** does not communicate the **meaning** of the source text. It is generally no more than a string of words intended to help someone read a text in its original language. It is unnatural and hard to understand, and may even be quite meaningless, or give a wrong meaning in the receptor language. It can hardly be called a translation.

The goal of a translator should be to produce a receptor language text (a translation) which is **idiomatic**; that is, one which has the **same meaning** as the source language but is expressed in the **natural form** of the receptor language. The **meaning**, not the **form**, is retained.

The following is a literal translation of a story first told in the Quiché language of Guatemala (Fox 1959:174):

> *It is said that being one man not from here, not known where the his or the he comes where. One day these things he walks in a plantation or in them the coastlands, he saw his appearance one little necklace, or he thought that a little necklace the very pretty thrown on the ground in the road. He took the necklace this he threw in his mouth for its cause that coming the one person another to his behindness, for his that not he encounters the one the following this way in his behindness, not he knows and that the necklace the he threw in his mouth this one snake and the man this one died right now because not he knows his appearance the snake or that the he ate this not this a necklace only probably this snake.*

Now compare the above with the following less literal translation of the same story:

> *It is said that there once was a man (not from here, and I do not know his town or where he came from), who one day was walking in a plantation (or in the coastlands). He saw a little necklace, or rather, what he thought was a very pretty little necklace, lying on the road. He grabbed this necklace and threw it into his mouth because there was someone coming along behind him, and he did not want the other person to see it. Well, he did not know that the necklace which he threw into his mouth was really a snake. The man died in short order, because he did not recognize from its appearance that it was a snake. He did not know that what he had put in his mouth was not a necklace, but rather a snake.*

In the first, each Quiché word was replaced by the nearest English equivalent. The result was nonsense. In the second translation, the natural **forms** of English lexicon and grammar were used to express the **meaning** of the Quiché story. Below the story is again rewritten in a more idiomatic English style:

> *I'm told that there once was a stranger from some other town who was walking in a plantation along the coast. As he walked*

along he suddenly saw a very pretty little necklace lying on the road. He snatched up the necklace and threw it into his mouth because there was another person walking behind him and he didn't want him to see the necklace. The stranger didn't know that the necklace was really a snake. He died immediately. He died because he didn't realize that it was a snake; he didn't know he put a snake into his mouth, rather than a necklace.

Anything which can be said in one language can be said in another. It is possible to translate. The goal of the translator is to keep the **meaning** constant. Wherever necessary, the receptor language **form** should be changed in order that the source language **meaning** not be distorted. Since a **meaning** expressed by a particular **form** in one language may be expressed by quite a different **form** in another language, it is often necessary to change the **form** when translating.

EXERCISES – Form and Meaning

A. Identifying change of **meaning** versus change of **form**. Some of the following pairs of sentences differ in their **form**. Some differ in **meaning**. Indicate if the primary change is in the **form** or in the **meaning**.

> Ex. They robbed the old man.
> The old man was robbed by them.
> Answer: Change of form

1. The students like to study semantics.
    The students like studying semantics.

2. I bought a pair of horseshoes.
    I bought a pair of leather shoes.

3. He saw the bird.
    She heard the cat.

4. Phillip went walking.
    Phillip took a walk.

5. Go to bed.
    I want you to go to bed.

6. I came; I saw; I conquered.
   I came, saw, and conquered.

7. Two weeks later he came.
   After two weeks he came.

8. There is a table in the book.
   There is a book on the table.

9. The young man had a Greek grammar book stolen.
   A Greek grammar book was stolen from the young man.

10. He was awakened by a thunderclap.
    A thunderclap awakened him.

B. List as many grammatical **forms** as you can which realize the **same meaning** as the one given below. Then put the **same meaning** into a language other than English in as many **forms** as you can.

> Ex. the cat is black
> the black cat
> the cat, which is black

1. the water jug

2. John bought a car

3. a hot day

4. mother's long blue dress

5. Peter's house

C. All of the following have the same grammatical form. With the change of lexical items, there is a change of meaning which is signaled by that lexical item, apart from the referential meaning of the word itself. What meaning is signaled in each of the following possessive phrases? Answer by restating. How can that meaning best be expressed in another language which you speak?

> Ex. the man's car - the man owns the car
> the man's eye - the eye is part of the man

1. the doctor's office

2. the doctor's patient

3. the doctor's book

4. the doctor's brother

5. the doctor's hand

6. the doctor's house

D. (Adapted from Barnwell 1986:24 –5.) For each pair of sentences, state whether the two sentences are (1) the same in meaning or (2) different in meaning.

1. (a) It rained all night.
   (b) Rain fell all night.

2. (a) There is a book on the table.
   (b) There is a table in the book.

3. (a) John was very surprised when he heard the news.
   (b) The news very much amazed John when he heard it.

4. (a) It was a hot day.
   (b) The day was hot.

5. (a) Peter's house.
   (b) The house that belongs to Peter.

6. (a) He remained silent.
   (b) He did not say anything.

7. (a) I bought cloth to make Mary a new dress.
   (b) I bought a new dress for Mary.

8. (a) I bought vegetables in the market.
   (b) I bought tomatoes and onions in the market.

9. (a) My parents are well.
   (b) My mother and father are well.

10. (a) John is ill; he has a bad case of malaria.
    (b) John is very ill indeed.

11. (a) There are four rooms in the house.
    (b) The house has four rooms and a kitchen at the back.

12. (a) In my opinion, the government is doing well and making many improvements in the country. But there are many people who do not agree that this is so.
    (b) Opinions are divided concerning the government. Some say they are doing well and making many improvements in the country. Others do not agree.

Chapter 2
Kinds of Translations

Literal versus idiomatic

Because a given text has both form and meaning, as discussed in the previous chapter, there are two main kinds of translations. One is form-based and the other is meaning-based. Form-based translations attempt to follow the form of the source language and are known as **literal translations**. Meaning-based translations make every effort to communicate the meaning of the source language text in the natural forms of the receptor language. Such translations are called **idiomatic translations**.

An interlinear translation is a completely **literal translation**. For some purposes, it is desirable to reproduce the linguistic features of the source text, as for example, in a linguistic study of that language. Although these **literal translations** may be very useful for purposes related to the study of the source language, they are of little help to speakers of the receptor language who are interested in the meaning of the source language text. A **literal translation** sounds like nonsense and has little communication value. For example:

Chuave (Papua New Guinea): *kan daro*

Literal translation: your-name call!

This **literal translation** makes little sense in English. The appropriate translation would be *What is your name?*

If the two languages are related, the literal translation can often be understood, since the general grammatical form may be similar. However, the literal choice of lexical items makes the translation sound foreign. The following bilingual announcement was overheard at an airport (Barnwell 1980:18).

Literal English: *Madame Odette, passenger with destination Douala, is demanded on the telephone.*

17

This English version is a **literal translation** of the French.

> **French:** *Madame Odette, passager à destination de Douala, est demandée au téléphone.*

An **idiomatic translation** into English would be:

> **Idiomatic English:** Ms. Odette, passenger for Douala, you are wanted on the phone.

Except for interlinear translations, a truly literal translation is uncommon. Most translators who tend to translate literally actually make a partially **modified literal translation.** They modify the order and grammar enough to use acceptable sentence structure in the receptor language. However, the lexical items are translated literally. Occasionally, these are also changed to avoid complete nonsense or to improve the communication. However, the result still does not sound natural. Notice the following example from a language in Papua New Guinea:

ro	ahombo	ngusifu	pamariboyandi	
I	her	heart	I-fastened-her	(literal)
I fastened her in my heart.				(modified literal)

The **modified literal translation** changes the order into English structure. However, the sentence still does not communicate in clear English. An **idiomatic translation** would have used the form: "I never forgot her," or "I've kept her memory in my heart."

A person who translates in a **modified literal** manner will change the grammatical forms when the constructions are obligatory. However, if he has a choice, he will follow the form of the source text even though a different form might be more natural in the receptor language. **Literal** and **modified literal translations** consistently err in that they choose literal equivalents for the words, i.e., the lexical items being translated. **Literal translations** of words, idioms, figures of speech, etc., result in unclear, unnatural, and sometimes nonsensical translations. In a **modified literal translation**, the translator usually adjusts the translation enough to avoid real nonsense and wrong meanings, but the unnaturalness still remains.

Idiomatic translations use the natural forms of the receptor language, both in the grammatical constructions and in the choice of lexical items. A truly **idiomatic translation** does not sound like a translation. It sounds like it was written originally in the receptor language. Therefore, a good translator will try to translate idiomatically. This is his goal. However, translations are often a mixture of a **literal** transfer of the grammatical units along with some **idiomatic translation** of the meaning of the text. It is not easy to consistently translate idiomatically. A translator may express some parts of his translation in very natural forms and then in other parts fall back into a literal form. Translations fall on a continuum from very literal, to literal, to modified literal, to near idiomatic, to idiomatic, and then may even move on to be **unduly free** (see Display 2.1).

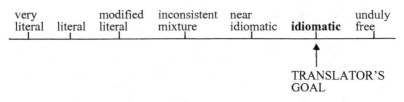

Display 2.1

Unduly free translations are not considered acceptable translations for most purposes. Tranlations are **unduly free** if they add extraneous information not in the source text, if they change the meaning of the source language, or if they distort the facts of the historical and cultural setting of the source language text. Sometimes **unduly free translations** are made for purposes of humor or to bring about a special response from the receptor language speakers. However, they are not acceptable as normal translations. The emphasis is on the reaction of those reading or hearing it and the meaning is not necessarily the same as that of the source language.

In one translation, the source text said, "*I was glad when Stephanas, Fortunatus and Achaicus arrived, because they have supplied what was lacking from you. For they refreshed my spirit and yours also. Such men deserve recognition.*" It was translated, "It sure is good to see Steve, Lucky and 'Big Bam'. They sorta make up for your not being here. They're a big boost to both me and you all. Let's give them a big hand." The purpose of the translation was to make an ancient text seem contemporary, but the result is an **unduly free translation.**

The translator's goal should be to reproduce in the receptor language a text which communicates the same message as the source language but using the natural grammatical and lexical choices of the receptor language. His goal is an **idiomatic translation**. In the chapters which follow, the many details involved in producing such a translation will be discussed. The basic overriding principle is that an

idiomatic translation reproduces the meaning of the source language (that is, the meaning intended by the original communicator) in the natural form of the receptor language.

However, there is always the danger of interference from the form of the source language. The study of many translations shows that in order to translate idiomatically a translator will need to make many adjustments in form. Some examples of the kinds of adjustment which will need to be made are discussed below as general background to show the need for the more detailed study which follows in later chapters.

Translating grammatical features

Parts of speech are language specific. Each language has its own division of the lexicon into classes such as nouns, verbs, adjectives, etc. Different languages will have different classes and subclasses. It will not always be possible to translate a source language noun with a noun in the receptor language. For example, Indo-European languages have many nouns which really refer to actions. Most languages will prefer to express actions as verbs rather than nouns.

A translator in Papua New Guinea (from Deibler and Taylor 1977:1060) was asked by a patrol officer to translate the Eight-Point Improvement Plan for Papua New Guinea (Papua New Guinea: Central Planning Office 1973). One of the points reads, "Decentralization of economic activity, planning and government spending, with emphasis on agricultural development, village industry, better internal trade, and more spending channeled through local and area bodies." Such sentences are very difficult for translators who want to translate into the indigenous languages of the country. Word such as *decentralization, activity, planning, government spending, emphasis, development,* and *trade* would have to be rendered by verbs in most languages. When verbs are used, then, the appropriate subject and object of the verb may need to be made explicit also. The form in the receptor language is very different from the source language form and yet this kind of adjustment, using verbs rather than nouns, must be made in order to communicate the message. An idiomatic translation was made which used verbs as in the following:

> The government wants to decrease the work it does for businesses and what it plans, and the money it spends in the capital, and wants to increase what people and groups in local areas do to help farmers and small businesses whose owners live in villages, and help people in this country buy and sell things made in this country, and to help local groups spend the government's money.

Most languages have a class of words which may be called pronouns. Pronominal systems vary greatly from language to language, and the translator is obliged to use the forms of the receptor language even though they may have very different meanings from the pronouns of the source language. For example, if one is translating into Kiowa (USA), the pronouns will have to indicate a difference between singular, dual, and plural person even though the source language does not make this three-way distinction. Or if a translator is translating into Balinese (Swellengrebel 1963:158), he must distinguish degrees of honor even though nothing in the source language indicates these distinctions. He will need to understand the culture of the Balinese and the cultural context of the text he is translating in order to choose correctly.

In English, the first person plural pronoun *we* is often used when the real meaning is second person *you*. The reason for the use of *we* is to show empathy and understanding. The nurse says to the sick child, "It's time for *us* to take *our* medicine now." Or the teacher says, "*We*'re not going to shout, *we*'ll walk quietly to *our* places." Clearly, the pronouns do not refer to the nurse or the teacher but to the children whom she is addressing, *you*. In translating these pronouns into another language, a literal translation with first person plural would probably distort the meaning. The translator would need to look for the natural way to communicate second person, and the feeling of empathy carried by the source language sentences.

Grammatical constructions also vary between the source language and the receptor language. The order, for example, may be completely reversed. The following simple sentence from Gahuku (Papua New Guinea) is given with a morpheme-by-morpheme literal translation underneath (data from Deibler):

muli	*mako*	*al-it-ove*	*loko*	*taoni-loka*	*v-it-ove.*
lemons	some	get-will-I	saying	town-to	go-will-I

It will readily be seen that a somewhat understandable translation into English requires a complete reversal of the order: *I will go to town saying, "I will get some lemons."* A more idiomatic translation would read: *I will go to town to get some lemons.* In order to have an understandable English form, the order must be changed completely and follow English grammatical patterns. In addition, the direct quote which signaled purpose in Gahuku must be changed to the equivalent English form for purpose clauses.

It is not uncommon that passive constructions will need to be translated with an active construction or vice versa, depending on the natural form of the receptor language. In Japanese (Wallace 1977:1-2), there is a passive form with the suffix *-(r)are-*. Notice the two sentences below:

Active: *Sensei*   *wa*   *Taro*   *o*   *sikatta.*
           Teacher   topic   Taro   accusative   scold-perfect.

           The teacher scolded Taro.

Passive: *Taro*   *wa*   *sensei*   *ni*   *sikarareta.*
           Taro   topic   teacher   dative   scold-passive-perfect.

           Taro was scolded by the teacher.

However, it is not simply that there are two forms and so translations into Japanese may use either. The passive sentences are used primarily when "the subject is portrayed as suffering" (Wallace 1977:2). In traditional Japanese style, this is the only use of the passive verb with *-(r)are-*. Many source language passives cannot be translated into Japanese with a passive since this would give the wrong meaning, the idea of suffering. Grammatical choices in the translation must be based on the function of the grammatical construction in the receptor language, not on a literal rendition of a source language form.

The above are only examples to show some types of grammatical adjustments which will result if a translator translates idiomatically. Seldom will a text be translated with the same form as that which occurs in the source language. Certainly, there will be times when by coincidence they match, but a translator should translate the meaning and not concern himself with whether the forms turn out the same or not.

Translating lexical features

Each language has its own idiomatic way of expressing meaning through lexical items (words, phrases, etc.). Languages abound in idioms, secondary meanings, metaphors, and other figurative meanings. For example, notice the following ways in which *a fever* is referred to (literal translations are given to show the source language form):

     Greek: *The fever left him.*

     Aguaruna: *He cooled.*

     Ilocano: *The fever was no more in him.*

The English translation of all three would be: *His fever went down,* or *His temperature returned to normal.*

All languages have **idioms,** i.e., a string of words whose meaning is different than the meaning conveyed by the individual words. In English to say that someone is *bull-headed* means that the person is "stubborn." The meaning has little to do with *bull* or *head.* Languages abound in such **idioms.** The following are a few English idioms using *into* and *in: run into debt, rush into print, step into a practice, fly into a passion, spring into notice, jump into a fight, dive into a book, wade into adversity, break into society, stumble into acquaintance, glide into intimacy, fall in love.* In spite of all these combinations, one cannot say the following: *break into debt, fall into print, wade into practice,* etc. The combinations are fixed as to form and their meaning comes from the combination. A literal word-for-word translation of these **idioms** into another language will not make sense. The form cannot be kept, but the receptor language word or phrase which has the equivalent meaning will be the correct one to use in the translation.

The following **idioms** occur in the Apinayé language of Brazil (Ham 1965:2). In the first column is a **literal translation** from Apinayé. In the second is an **idiomatic translation.** The literal English is misleading.

LITERAL	IDIOMATIC
I don't have my eye on you.	I don't remember you.
I've already buried my eye.	I'm already ready to go.
I'll pull your eyelid.	I'll ask a favor of you.
My eye is hard on you.	I remember you.
I'll do it with my head.	I'll do it the way I think it should be done.
His ear is rotten.	He is spoiled.

Translators who want to make a good idiomatic translation often find figures of speech especially challenging. A literal translation of *blind as a bat* might sound really strange in a language where the comparison between a *blind person* and a *bat* has never been used as a figure of speech. In Aguaruna it would be more natural to say *blind as a fox.* There is a legend in which the sun borrowed the fox's eyes and then returned to heaven taking the fox's good eyes with him and leaving the fox with the sun's inferior eyes. That is why they say, when the fox is trying to see, he stretches back his head and looks with his throat. Figures of speech are often based on stories or historical incidents. Many times, the origin of the figure is no longer apparent.

Names of animals are used metaphorically in most languages. But the comparison is often different and so the figure will be misunderstood unless some adjustment is made. For example, when someone is called a *pig* in English, it usually means he is dirty or a greedy eater. In languages of Mexico, it has different meanings. In Mixteco, it means the person is stupid; in Tzeltal, that he sleeps on the ground; in Aztec, that he is drunk; and in Otomí, that the person is immoral. Care would need to be taken if *pig* were used metaphorically or a wrong meaning might result in the receptor language.

In some languages, certain words can only be expressed by the use of a quotation and the verb *say*. For example, the Waiwai of Guyana do not have a special word for *promise, praise, deny,* and other similar words. These must be translated by the word *say* and a quotation as follows (Hawkins 1962:164):

ENGLISH	WAIWAI
You promised to come.	"I will certainly come," you said.
He praised the canoe.	"It's a wonderful canoe," he said.
He denied that he took it.	"I didn't take it," he said.

In Aguaruna the only way to express *believe* is with a quotation:

English: *I believe you.*

Aguaruna: *"It is true," I say to you.*

Some lexical combinations of the source language may be ambiguous. The meaning is not clear. For example, *"It is too hot to eat,"* could mean any of the following: The food is too hot to eat; the weather is too hot for us to feel like eating; the horse is too hot after running a race and doesn't want to eat. It would be hard to translate this sentence into another language and still have it mean all three. In the process of making an idiomatic translation, such ambiguities must often be resolved and only the intended meaning communicated.

Conclusion

Translation is a complicated process. However, a translator who is concerned with transferring the meaning will find that the receptor language has a way in which the desired meaning can be expressed, even though it may be very different from the source language form. In the early days, men like Cicero and Horace insisted that one must translate the general sense and force of the language. Literal translations are laughed out of court. Horace stated that a faithful translator will not translate word-for-word. Jerome said that two things are necessary for a good translation – an adequate understanding of the original language (the source language) and an adequate command of the language into which one is translating (the receptor language).

But considering the complexity of language structures, how can a translator ever hope to produce an adequate translation? Literalisms can only be avoided by careful analysis of the source language; by, first of all, understanding clearly the message to be communicated. A translator who takes the time to study carefully the source language text, to write a semantic analysis of it, and then to look for the equivalent way in which the same message is expressed naturally in the receptor language, will be able to provide an adequate, and sometimes brilliant, translation. His goal must be to avoid literalisms and to strive for a truly idiomatic receptor language text. He will know he is successful if the receptor language readers do not recognize his work as a translation at all, but simply as a text written in the receptor language for their information and enjoyment.

EXERCISES – Kinds of Translations

A. In each of the following pairs of sentences, decide which is more idiomatic English, a or b? How would the meaning be expressed idiomaticaly in a second language which you speak?

   1. (a) The storekeeper said that we will refund your money.
      (b) The storekeeper promised to refund our money.

   2. (a) A certain boy told me this little story at a party.
      (b) He is one boy. He told the one little story. This in a game he said.

   3. (a) An International Alphabet would inevitably bring about a spelling reform as well. How many children have shed hot tears about spelling!

(b) An International Alphabet would inevitably bring about a spelling reform, too. And how many hot children's tears have not been shed on spelling!

4. (a) He then reported his misfortune to the police, who are searching diligently for the thief.

(b) He then his mishap reported to the police, who are the thief intensively searching.

B. Look for **literalisms** in the following translations into English and underline the words or phrases that do not sound natural in English. Suggest a more **idiomatic** way of saying it. (All of these examples are from published translated material. References are not given so as not to embarrass the translator.)

1. We offers as attractions horse trip or car by fields and forests. (Tourist Brochure)

2. To move the cabin push button of wishing floor. If cabin should enter more persons, each one should press number of wishing floor. (Instructions in elevator/lift)

3. The archeological matters in Egypt indicated that the princesses in those days had used natural cosmetic to polish their beauty. (Newspaper)

4. Since 1976, the women has joined the popular army, and has been permitted to join the armed forces and to acquire an equal military rank. Other laws have extended the mother's leave before and after delivery, and granted the mother an additional two-year leave to take care of her child under four years of age. (Newspaper)

5. A hold-up (robbery) took place of a motorcycle rider at Kampung early yesterday morning. (Newspaper)

6. When you feel cold, because of the climate, or you feel something had in your bones, please rub Param Kocok Super Kecil. Shake well the solution before use. (Directions with medicine)

7. Guatemala City is always full of surprises. It has a delicious climate, for reasons of its altitude–1500 meters–but not so high as to affect people from low-lying areas. (Magazine of an airline)

8. Villagers spend most of their energies in producing corn and beans for their families. Those are the principle products, including coffee, greens and fruit. (Magazine of an airline)

C. The following are sentences written by Sudanese who are not yet fluent English speakers. The form used shows examples of how their mother-tongue language structures have been carried over into English. The same information is then given in parenthesis in idiomatic English. What changes were made in correcting the English? These changes point out some of the differences between Sudanese languages and English.

1. Sir, the problems of before don't forget.
   (Sir, please don't forget the problems we discussed before.)

2. If there is any means, send me a letter to Riwoto.
   (If there is any way to do so, send a letter to me at Riwoto.)

3. I will think you time to time day and day.
   (I will be thinking about you often every day.)

4. I am very grateful to inform you with this letter.
   (I am very happy to be able to send/write you this letter.)

5. I am a man who has been to Juba for 15 years.
   (I have now lived in Juba for 15 years.)

Chapter 3
The Semantic Structure of Language

Deep and surface structure

Another way of looking at **form** and **meaning** is to think of them as **surface structure** and **deep structure**. One of the basic assumptions of this text is that there is a valid distinction between the **deep** (semantic) and the **surface** (grammatical, lexical, phonological) structures of languages. An analysis of the **surface structure** of a language does not tell us all that we need to know about the language in order to translate. Behind the **surface structure** is the **deep structure**, the meaning. It is this **meaning** that serves as the base for translation into another language.

A second basic assumption is that meaning is structured. It is not just an inaccessible mass. It can be analyzed and represented in ways that are useful to the translator. It is not ordered in the same way in which the **surface structure** must be ordered. It is a network of semantic units and the relations between these units. These units and relations may be represented in various ways. The conventions which will be used in this text have been chosen for practical reasons. The aim of the book is not to argue linguistic theory but to present tools which will help translators. Nevertheless, it is important to note that the procedures are based on the two assumptions given above.

Semantic structure is more nearly universal than **grammatical structure**. That is, types of units, the features, and the relationships are essentially the same for all languages. All have **meaning components** which can be classified as THINGS, EVENTS, ATTRIBUTES, or RELATIONS, for example. But not all languages have the same **surface structure** grammatical classes–some have conjunctions, others do not, some have prepositional phrases, others do not. Word classes differ from language to language. The four semantic classes listed above occur in all languages. Any concept occurring in any language will refer to either a THING, EVENT, ATTRIBUTE, or RELATION.

Semantic **propositions** occur in all languages. They consist of **concepts** (groupings of meaning components) related to one another with an EVENT, THING, or ATTRIBUTE as the central **concept**. Many different ways could be used to represent a **proposition**. For example, the three concepts – JOHN, HIT, and BALL – and the roles – **agent** (the one who does the action) and **affected** (the one affected by the action) – might be indicated by saying:

the **agent**, JOHN, HIT the **affected**, BALL

or a diagram could be made as follows:

JOHN...**agent**...HIT...**affected**...BALL

The order does not matter. The meaning is not changed if the diagram were as follows:

BALL...**affected**...HIT...**agent**...JOHN

There are all sorts of conventions which could be used. Another would be to set up a formula like this:

agent: JOHN   **activity**: HIT   **affected**: BALL

For simplicity in presentation, we have chosen to express **propositions** with English **surface structure** forms, i.e., John hit the ball. This convention will be used throughout this text. For example, it is used in the following four propositions which are in sequential relation to one another.

DEEP STRUCTURE

John met Bill on the corner.

John and Bill talked.

Bill left.

John left.

These four propositions can be encoded in any language with the **surface structures** of that language. In English, a number of alternate **surface structure** forms might be used:

SURFACE STRUCTURE

1. *John met Bill on the corner. They talked. Bill left. Then John left, too.*

2. *John met Bill on the corner and they talked. Then Bill left and John did too.*

3. *John met Bill on the corner. After they talked, Bill left and then John left.*

4. *John and Bill met on the corner to talk. When they finished talking, Bill left first and then John also left.*

In semantic structure the only ordering is chronological. However, this chronological order does not need to match the order of words in the grammatical structure and is often different (skewed). The above **propositions** could also be expressed in the following English form:

5. *John left last, after he and Bill had met on the corner, talked, and Bill had left.*

Any one of the above would be considered an acceptable **surface structure** form with which to represent the four **propositions.** (It should be realized that this is a simplification of the matter in order to get across the general idea of the difference between **deep** and **surface structure.**)

Semantic units

The lexicon of the surface structure of a language is classified by distribution in the grammar. The classification and number of word classes will depend on the distribution which the words have as the subject, predicate, object, etc., in the sentence. For example, if we say, *"The work is difficult,"* the word *work* would be classified as a noun in English grammar. This is simply because it is being used as the subject of a grammatical construction. *Work*, however, is something that one does; it is an EVENT which is an action. There is, therefore, a skewing between semantic classes and grammatical classes at this point.

The sentence *"The dog treed the cat"* is grammatically a subject, predicate, object (SPO) sentence concerning its order of grammatical units. But the semantic structure is considerably more complicated. The translation into another language may not be a simple one-clause sentence. The reason is that the verb *treed* is another example of skewing between grammar and semantics. *Tree*, which is a THING, is being used as a verb. The EVENT which took place is *caused to go up*. The meaning of the sentence is that *the dog caused the cat to go up into a tree or the dog chased the cat; therefore, the cat went up into a tree*. There is a great deal of skewing between the grammar and the semantics. The grammars of languages use various alternatives to express the semantic structure. Throughout this text we will discuss the kinds of skewing which a translator needs to watch for as he translates.

The smallest unit in the semantic structure is a **meaning component**. **Meaning components** group together to form **concepts**. (These terms are defined more carefully in chapter 6.) **Meaning components** and **concepts** are classified semantically into four principle groups– THINGS, EVENTS, ATTRIBUTES, and RELATIONS. THINGS include all animate beings, natural and supernatural, and all inanimate entities *(boy, ghost, angel, stone, galaxy, idea, blood)*. EVENTS include all actions, changes of state (process), and experiences *(eat, run, think, melt, stretch, smile)*. ATTRIBUTES include all those attributes of quality and quantity ascribed to any THING or EVENT *(long, thick, soft, rough, slowly, suddenly, few, all)*. Finally, RELATIONS include all those relations posited between any two of the above semantic units *(with, by, because, since, and, therefore, after, or)*.

In the examples given above, you will notice that for the English examples, only nouns are used to illustrate THINGS, only verbs to illustrate EVENTS, only modifiers to illustrate ATTRIBUTES, and RELATIONS are illustrated by prepositions and conjunctions. In other words, in all of the examples given above there was a one-to-one correlation between the semantic and grammatical structures. There was no occurrence of "skewing."

Boy, which is a THING, is a single lexical item in English. However, it is made up of several **meaning components** – HUMAN BEING, MALE, and YOUNG. (HUMAN BEING belongs to the semantic class THINGS. MALE and YOUNG belong to the class ATTRIBUTES.) Some languages also have a word which includes these three **meaning components** in a single lexical item. However, other languages do not. Ndogo (Sudan) has a word *dako* which includes the **meaning components** MALE and HUMAN BEING. The word *vi* means YOUNG and, therefore, *vi dako* would be equivalent to the English word *boy*. In Chinantec (Mexico), each **meaning component** would be a separate word *jiuung dsea nu'*. The three words mean YOUNG (CHILD), HUMAN, and MALE. The three words are equivalent to the English word *boy*. How languages organize the **meaning components** into words and phrases is a characteristic of each language.

Generally speaking, the nouns and pronouns of the grammar refer to THINGS in the semantic structure, the verbs of the grammar to EVENTS, etc. If there were no skewing, the relationship would be as follows:

THINGS . . . . . . nouns, pronouns

EVENTS . . . . . . verbs

ATTRIBUTES . . adjectives, adverbs

RELATIONS . . . conjunctions, prepositions, particles, enclitics, etc.

In a simple sentence like, *John called Mary*, JOHN and MARY belong to the semantic class THINGS and are nouns in this particular sentence; CALLED is an EVENT semantically and a verb grammatically. The structure of the sentence indicates that *John*, the **agent**, is the subject and *Mary*, the **affected**, is the object. There is no skewing between surface structure and semantic structure (presupposing that the unskewed form would have **agent** as subject and **affected** as object).

But in the surface structures of languages, there is a great deal of skewing. For example, in the sentence, *"I heard John's call,"* call is a noun in the surface structure. But in this particular sentence, it represents a semantic EVENT, *call*. Semantically, there are two EVENTS and two PROPOSITIONS which are represented in the surface form *"I heard John's call."* The first proposition is *John called* and the second, *I heard*. It is possible to represent these two propositions in English by saying, *"John called me and I heard him."* This would not be skewed. However, if one says, *"I heard John's call,"* thus, expressing the two propositions in a single clause rather than in two clauses, there is skewing. Discovering the semantic structure includes removing the skewing between semantic classes and grammatical classes.

Semantic hierarchy

In surface structure, units are grouped into increasingly larger units in a **hierarchy** of grammatical structures. Morphemes (roots and affixes) unite to form words, words unite to form phrases, phrases unite into clauses, clauses into a sentence, sentences into a paragraph, paragraphs into discourse units of various kinds, and these unite to form a text–story, letter, sermon, or whatever.

Although semantic structure is more of a network of configurations, each being part of a larger configuration, for the practical purposes of this book we will look at semantic structure **hierarchically** also. The smallest unit is a *meaning component*. Meaning components unite into *concepts*, concepts into *propositions*, propositions into *propositional clusters*, propositional clusters into *semantic para-graphs*, semantic paragraphs into *episodes*, episodes into *episode clusters*, and these units unite to form *larger units of the discourse*. The structure is one of smaller groupings, uniting to form larger groupings. If there were no skewing between the semantic configurations and the grammatical structures then the relationship would be as follows:

meaning component . . .	morpheme (roots and affixes)
concept	word
complex concept (concept cluster) . . .	phrase
proposition.	clause
propositional cluster . . .	sentence
semantic paragraph . . .	paragraph
episode	section
episode cluster	division
semantic part	part
discourse	text

The above would be the units for a narrative type discourse. Different labels would be needed for the units above the propositional cluster for other discourse types. How many levels of structure will depend on the text. A book may have several parts; whereas, a shorter text will consist only of a single **episode**.

As has already been mentioned, and as we will point out in much more detail later, there is considerable skewing between semantic and surface structures and that is, of course, what makes translation a challenge. The translator must study the surface structure of the source language to find the **concepts, propositions**, etc., of the semantic structure. Then, he has the task of reconstructing meaning from the semantic structure into the surface structure of the receptor language. To do that he must have also studied the skewing of the receptor language grammar in relation to the semantic structure and know how to use this skewing to reconstruct meaning in a natural way in the receptor language.

The communication situation

One helpful way to look at the distinction between meaning and form (between deep and surface) is the way that Grimes states it (1975:114):

...it is desirable to make a distinction between those things in language over which the speaker can exercise choice and over which no choice is available to him. The former reflect meaning; as many linguists have pointed out, meaning is possible only when a speaker could choose to say something else instead. The latter are the more mechanical components of language, the implementation process by which the results of the speaker's choices are expressed in a conventional form that permits communication with someone else.

The **meaning** which is chosen will be influenced by the **communication situation**, e.g., by who the speaker is, who the audience is, the traditions of the culture, etc. (This will be discussed in detail in chapter 33.) The speaker (or writer), basing his choices on many factors in the **communication situation**, chooses what he wishes to communicate. Once he has determined the **meaning**, he is limited to use the **forms** (grammatical, lexical, phonological) of the language in which he wishes to communicate that **meaning**. He may choose one form over another in order to give a certain **emotive meaning** in addition to the information he wishes to convey. He may choose one **form** over another because he wishes to make some part more prominent than another, to add some focus to a part of the message.

For example, a mother who is angry with her son for not doing his part of the family chores, may desire to tell him to *empty the garbage*. She has told him to do it before, so he knows it is his duty. She will want to convey all of this meaning–the command to empty the garbage and the emotion she feels about it. To do so, she might not use a surface structure command form but rather a question (see Larson 1979), e.g., a *when* question–*When are you going to empty the garbage?* If he had never been told to do it before, and if she were not angry or exasperated, she would have probably used a command form such as "Please empty the garbage for me." Here, because of the **emotive meaning** being communicated, we have a skewing of form and meaning in that a question form signals a command. Many languages do not use questions in this way, so a different form will be used in the translation. However, whichever form is chosen, it should communicate both the information and the emotion of the source language.

The information content is:

        agent: I . . . . . . **activity**: COMMAND

        agent: YOU . . . **activity**: EMPTY . . . **affected**: GARBAGE

Before the form is chosen from the possibilities in the surface structure, sociolinguistic and psycholinguistic matters which affect meaning must be taken into account; and the speaker's purpose, which in this case is not just to command but to show frustration and insistence, must be included. A question form using *when* indicates this sociolinguistic and psycholinguistic information.

The Aguaruna translation of *"When are you going to take out the garbage?"* would say: *Wamak, wamak. ¿Wa aniáme? Wamak tsuwat ajapata.* A very literal translation back into English would be "Quickly, quickly. Why are you like that? Quickly garbage you-throw-out!" The form would be completely different from idiomatic English, *"When are you going to take out the garbage?"* But the same information and emotive meaning would be communicated. Every translator desires to be faithful to the original. To do this, he must communicate not only the same information, but he must also attempt to evoke the same emotional response as the writers of the original text attempted to evoke.

For the translation to have the same dynamics as the original, it will need to be natural and easy to understand so that the readers will find it easy to grasp the message, including both the information and the emotional effect intended by the source language writer. Each source language text is written in a specific historical setting, in a specific cultural setting, and with a purpose, i.e., the intent of the author. These matters must also be taken into consideration if a faithful translation is to result. When ancient manuscripts are being translated into today's languages, there may be tension between trying to be faithful to the historical setting and trying to be faithful to the intent of the author. In order to get across the author's purpose, the translator may be tempted to update the historical material and "modernize" the translation. Such changes make the translation less faithful.

When a source language text is from a culture very different from the culture in which the receptor language is spoken, it is often difficult to translate in such a way that the results will communicate the same message. Details of how the communication situation and the culture affect translation are discussed in chapter 33.

EXERCISES – The Semantic Structure of Language

A. In each of the following there is at least one example of **skewing** between the deep (semantic) and surface (grammatical) structure. Underline the words which represent this **skewing**. Then rewrite the sentence so that the **skewing** is eliminated:

> Ex. Forgiveness is important.
> *Forgiveness* is important.
> It is important to forgive.
> (or, It is important that we forgive people.)

1. The sheep was taken to the slaughter.

2. They were told of the death of Susan.

3. Suddenly there was a great earthquake.

4. Her singing is too loud.

5. Eating is very necessary.

6. The man knifed him to death.

7. Length is unimportant.

8. Prayer comes first each day.

B. The grammatical form may change without effectively changing the meaning. Below, a paragraph is given first with the grammar and semantics nearly matching. Here every event is realized by a finite verb, every participant by a noun, every relation by an overt marker, etc. Then three possible surface structures are given, keeping the meaning constant.

DEEP (SEMANTIC) STRUCTURE

Yesterday John went to town. Next John bought a car. Next John drove the car home. Next John showed the car to Mary. Therefore, Mary was very happy.

SURFACE (GRAMMATICAL) STRUCTURES

(1) Yesterday John went to town and bought a car. He drove it home and showed it to Mary, who was very happy.

(2) John bought a car yesterday when he went to town. Driving it home he showed Mary the car, which made her very happy.

(3) John bought a car in town yesterday. Mary was very happy when he brought it home and showed it to her.

In the example above, the paragraph is first written with all the concepts, propositions, and propositional clusters given in full. Then the three surface structures which follow are used to communicate the same meaning. In these three different rewrites:

   a. What surface forms (specific words) are used to refer to the concept *John?*

   b. What surface forms are used to refer to the concept *car?*

   c. What surface forms are used to express the proposition *Next John drove the car home?*

   d. What surface forms are used to express the proposition *Yesterday John went to town?*

   e. What surface forms are used to show the relationship between the two propositions *John showed the car to Mary* and *Mary was very happy?*

C. Using the deep structure propositions in B above, translate the information into a language other than English. Rewrite in two or three different forms, keeping the meaning the same.

D. Rewrite the following in English, changing the form but keeping the meaning as constant as possible. Rewrite the paragraph several times. Use natural, clear English sentences. (Such rewrites are called paraphrases because the same thing is being said in a different way in the same language. A paraphrase changes the form but not the meaning.)

The day was beautiful. It was 10 o'clock. Jane left the house. The house belonged to Jane. Next Jane drove the car to the post office. Next Jane stopped the car. Next Jane got out. Next Jane took a hold of the doorknob. The doorknob was on the door. The door was part of the post office. The door was locked. Therefore, Jane was frustrated. But Jane was not angry. Rather Jane was concerned. Jane wondered: Is Mr. Smith sick?

E. Using the information given in the paragraph in D above, translate this story into a language other than English. Rewrite the paragraph several times using different forms each time.

Chapter 4
Implicit Meaning

Translation, then, is communicating the same meaning in a second language as was communicated in the first. But to do so adequately, one must be aware of the fact that there are various kinds of meaning. Not all of the meaning which is being communicated is stated overtly in the forms of the source language text. Discovering the meaning of the text to be translated includes consideration of both **explicit** and **implicit information.** The purpose of this chapter is to give an overview of the importance of **implicit** meaning to the translator. The matter of implicit meaning will be mentioned many times throughout this book.

Kinds of meaning

People usually think of meaning as something to which a word or sentence refers. For example, the word *apple* refers to the fruit produced by a certain tree. People know the meaning of *apple* because they have seen an apple and learned to call it *apple*. This kind of meaning is called REFERENTIAL MEANING because the word refers to a certain thing, event, attribution, or relation which a person can perceive or imagine. A sentence has meaning because it refers to something that happened, or may happen, or is imagined as happening. REFERENTIAL MEANING is what the communication is about. It is the information content.

The REFERENTIAL MEANING is organized into a semantic structure. The information bits are "packaged"; that is, they are put together and expressed by a variety of combinations. As they are "packaged" into larger and larger units there is ORGANIZATIONAL MEANING in the discourse which must also be taken into account in the translation. For example, if *apple* has been referred to in the text and then *apple* is referred to again, the fact that it is the same *apple* is part of the ORGANIZATIONAL MEANING of the text. Certain information may be old information, some new; certain information may be the topic (what is being talked about) of the discourse, other information

41

commenting on the topic; and some information may be more central to the message, that is, more important or more prominent. It is the ORGANIZATIONAL MEANING that puts the referential information together into a coherent text. ORGANIZATIONAL MEANING is signaled by deictics, repetition, groupings, and by many other features in the grammatical structure of a text.

The two propositions *Mary peeled an apple* and *Mary ate an apple* include MARY as the **agent** and APPLE as the **affected** in both propositions. MARY and APPLE are both referred to twice (REFERENTIAL MEANING). But in order to form a correct grammatical structure, we must also know if the ORGANIZATIONAL MEANING includes the fact that there is only one MARY and only one APPLE or if there are two MARYS or two APPLES. If they are the same, the surface structure in English would be a form like *Mary peeled an apple, and then she ate it.* After the first proposition is given, MARY and APPLE are both old information and so pronominal forms are used.

If, however, there are references to two MARYS and only one APPLE, then the grammatical form would need to indicate this with something like *Mary peeled an apple, and then the other Mary ate it.* All languages have ways of signaling the ORGANIZATIONAL MEANING, but these may be very different from language to language. For example, pronominal forms are not used in the same way in all languages, but all languages will have a formal way to indicate that certain information is old information.

Besides the REFERENTIAL MEANING and the ORGANIZATIONAL MEANING, there is also SITUATIONAL MEANING which is crucial to the understanding of any text. The message is produced in a given communication situation. The relationship between the writer or speaker and the addressee will affect the communication. Where the communication takes place, when it takes place, the age, sex, and social status of the speaker and hearer, the relationship between them, the presuppositions that each brings to the communication, the cultural background of the speaker and the addressee, and many other situational matters result in SITUATIONAL MEANING.

For example, the very same person may be referred to by various lexical items. A man named *John Smith* may be referred to as *John, Mr. Smith, Professor Smith,* etc., depending on the situation. This choice carries SITUATIONAL MEANING. It may indicate whether the situation is formal or informal. A friend who refers to him as *John* as he greets him in the morning may later in the day call him *Professor Smith* when introducing him at a university seminar. Different lexical forms will be chosen to indicate SITUATIONAL MEANING.

A text may be completely unintelligible to someone who does not know the culture in which the language is spoken because there is so much SITUATIONAL MEANING. When translating into another language, the original SITUATIONAL MEANING may need to be included in a more overt form if the same total meaning is to be communicated to the readers.

The range of implications for translation which grow out of these three kinds of meaning will be discussed in detail throughout the remaining chapters. However, there is one matter which is very basic to translating and is directly related to these three kinds of meaning; that is, the fact that in every text there is meaning which is expressed **explicitly** and there is meaning which is left **implicit**. The translator must be aware of these two kinds of information. There is **explicit** and **implicit** information communicating all three kinds of meaning.

Implicit and explicit information

As stated above, the translator must be aware of the **implicit** and **explicit** information which is being communicated. When people speak or write, the amount of information included in the text will depend on the amount of shared information that already exists between the speaker (writer) and the addressee. When we talk about something, we leave out some of the information because the addressee already knows these facts and might even be insulted if they were included. It might imply that they were stupid or uninformed. And so in every communication, some information which is being communicated is left **implicit** in conversation or written text.

For example, news broadcasters in the United States will make statements like, *"The Reagan tax bill passed in the Senate today."* If the announcer said, *"The tax bill proposed by the President of the United States, Ronald Reagan, was passed in the Senate of the United States today,"* people would soon stop listening to this announcer. He is wasting their time telling them things they know. It is shared information.

All communication is based on shared information. It may include shared language structures, culture, previous conversations, having read the same material, a common experience, etc. In every text that one may want to translate, there will be information which is **implicit**; that is, it is not stated in an **explicit** form in the text itself. Some information, or meaning, is left **implicit** because of the structure of the source language; some because it has already been included elsewhere in the text, and some because of shared information in the communication situation. However, the **implicit** information is part of the meaning which is to be communicated by the translation, because it is part of the meaning intended to be understood by the original writer.

Explicit information, then, is the information which is overtly stated by lexical items and grammatical forms. It is a part of the surface structure form. The **implicit** information is that for which there is no form but the information is part of the total communication intended or assumed by the writer.

There may be **implicit** information which is REFERENTIAL, ORGANIZATIONAL, and/or SITUATIONAL. That is, all three kinds of meaning may be either **explicit** or **implicit**.

Implicit referential meaning

In any text, the reference to certain THINGS, EVENTS, ATTRIBUTES, and RELATIONS will be left **implicit**. The meaning is there but not expressed **explicitly**. For example, if someone asks, *"How many people came?"* the person asked may answer, *"Ten."* In this context it is clear that *"ten"* means *"Ten people came."* The reference to *people* and *came* is left **implicit** in the answer.

All languages have grammatical forms which are obligatory, but languages differ in what is obligatory. For example, in English, it is obligatory to make **explicit** whether a noun is singular or plural. One cannot say, *"I saw dog walking down street."* One must say, *"I saw some dogs walking down the street,"* or *"I saw a dog walking down the street."* Number must be made **explicit** in English, but in many languages it can be left **implicit**.

Nouns which refer to EVENTS contain **implicit** information. Since a noun form is used, there is no indication of who the **agent** and **affected** are. The sentence *"Help will come,"* has no subject or object (the **agent** and **affected** are **implicit**), but in a language which uses verbs to describe this EVENT, the subject and object would need to be supplied; that is, a form something like the following: *Someone will come and he/they will help us.* No new REFERENTIAL MEANING has been added. The information has simply been made **explicit** rather than left **implicit**.

Pidgin (Papua New Guinea) has no difference in grammatical forms for *masculine* and *feminine*, but when translating from Pidgin into some languages of Papua New Guinea, it is obligatory to make this information **explicit**. To translate this same material into English, it would be obligatory to distinguish *masculine, feminine,* and *neuter,* even though the original text in Pidgin left this **implicit**.

Which referential meaning is **implicit** and which is **explicit** will depend on the individual language. Since languages differ greatly in this matter, many adjustments will need to be made in translation. These will be discussed in more detail later in the book.

The fact that some information is left **implicit** in certain grammatical constructions leads to ambiguities. For example, *the shooting* *of the hunters* is ambiguous in English, It has two different semantic structures. If the **implicit** information is made **explicit**, it may mean either *someone shot the hunters* or *the hunters shot something*. In one case, the **agent** is left **implicit**; in the other, the **affected**. In translating such ambiguous forms, the ambiguity is often resolved since the receptor language will make **explicit** the **implied** information. However, for translation, it is important to note that **implicit** information and ambiguity are sometimes related.

Implicit information and organizational meaning

A text is a unit. It is organized in some logical way. It is characterized by cohesion, continuity, grouping, and patterns of prominence. There is a flow of old and new information, redundancy which helps signal the unity, and various ways to indicate the topic or theme of the text, but languages differ in how these matters are indicated. One language may use pronominal forms a great deal and another may have an abundance of pro-verbal forms. One may have clear markers of which EVENTS make up the backbone of the story. Another may rely on chronological order.

In many languages, leaving some information **implicit** is one feature used to signal ORGANIZATIONAL MEANING. Part of the information which occurs in the semantic structure is left **implicit** in the grammar in order to indicate old information, in order to add cohesion, and, in some cases, even to mark theme or focus.

In the Hebrew, the description of creation in Genesis 1 uses the **explicit** name of God thirty-two times in this rather short text because God is the **agent** of the many actions described. But in other languages, God, once introduced at the beginning of the translation, would need to be left **implicit** throughout the rest of the story. Pronouns would be used in some languages to retain a part of the meaning, but in some languages only verb affixes indicating THIRD PERSON would occur. Some of the information would be left **implicit** in the sentences of this text in order to add cohesion to the story. No information is lost; it is simply made **implicit**. In translating from Hebrew into Aguaruna, for example, the equivalent form for God in Aguaruna would be made **explicit** only at the beginning when the **agent** is new information, and then, because it is old information, would not be repeated **explicitly** but would be left **implicit** throughout the rest of the text. If it were repeated **explicitly** again and again, the Aguaruna reader would be very confused and think there were many gods involved in creation rather than one.

Some languages use passive constructions to indicate focus. By using a passive construction, some of the meaning is left **implicit** since the agent need not be indicated. For example, *the school was founded in 1902* might be used to put *the school* in focus, but to do this, the information of who founded the school has to be left **implicit**. The information left **implicit** is REFERENTIAL MEANING, but it is left **implicit** to signal ORGANIZATIONAL MEANING; that is, that *school* is in focus. The semantic proposition would be *(someone) founded the school in 1902*. In one language, focus is indicated by a passive grammatical form. In another language, a completely different form may be needed to indicate focus and the passive would not occur. In this case, the **agent** of the action would need to be made **explicit**. In Aguaruna, for example, it would need to be translated *(the community) founded a school*. The ORGANIZATIONAL MEANING of focus would need to be indicated by a special suffix on the word *school* marking focus.

Less **explicit** forms are often used to signal ORGANIZATIONAL MEANING. For example, pronouns, pro-verbs, and other substitute words are less explicit than the nouns and verbs to which they refer. It is important that the translator be aware of the need to adjust these in translation. Some languages will require that the receptor language translation be **more explicit** than the source language. At other times, the translation may need to be **less explicit**. The translator expects to find differences between languages in the matter of how much information must be stated **explicitly**.

Implicit situational meaning

Information which is left **implicit** when talking to one person might be made **explicit** when talking to another. A woman might say to her husband, *"Peter is sick."* In reporting the same information to the doctor she would say, *"My son Peter is sick,"* or *"My son is sick."* The information *my son* was not needed to identify *Peter* when talking to her husband who knew very well who *Peter* was.

Often in normal conversation, there is much which is going on in the situation which makes it possible to understand exactly what is meant without using many words. For example, a mother, seeing her child about to put his hand in the fire, cries out, *"No!"* The child understands the message, *"Don't put your hand in the fire!"* All of this information is carried by one word, *"No,"* because of the situation. In a different situation *"No!"* might mean something very different, as when used to answer the question, *"Did you go to town today?"* In that case, the implied information is not found in the situation but in the question which had been asked; that is, in the linguistic context.

It is quite possible for a person from one culture to read a story written about a happening in another culture and not understand the story at all because so much information is left **implicit**. For example, Richards (1979), working with speakers of Waurá (Brazil), was attempting to translate one of their stories into Portuguese. But she found it very difficult because the text itself did not identify the various participants in the story. The storyteller had not made this information **explicit** because everyone in the culture knew who did what at the festival he was describing. The language structure did not make it necessary to include this information, and since the common culture supplied it to his audience, it was left **implicit**. However, a translation into Portuguese required that the information be made **explicit** if the story was to be understood. In order to adequately determine the meaning of the text, one must know the situational setting of the communication.

One of the challenges facing a translator is knowing when to supply the information which is **implicit** in the text. The author may have written for people with the same culture and same experiences as his. But the translator, or those whom he would like to read his translation, may not have this background and may not know much of this **implied** information. They may not be able to understand his translation unless he makes some of this **implicit** information from the communication situation **explicit**.

As will be discussed in much more detail later, the translator does not want to add information which is not part of the text he is translating. There is a difference between **implicit** information and information which is simply **absent** and never intended to be part of the communication. For instance, in the example *"My son Peter is sick,"* the mother did not say, *"Peter has brown hair and is ten years old."* This is not **implied**. It is **absent**. It is not part of the communication and, therefore, should not be added.

If a person wrote, *"John made the Queen's list,"* he is assuming that the readers know that the Queen of England is indicated. However, for an audience that did not know this fact and had never heard of the *Queen*, much less her *list*, the **implied** information would need to be added. It is not **absent**, it is **implied**, and part of the communication situation. The translation may have to be so **explicit** as to state, *"John made the Queen of England's yearly Honors list."* **Implicit** information needs to be added only when it is necessary to communicate correct meaning or to insure naturalness of form in the receptor language translation. It will sometimes need to be made **explicit** because the source language writer and his audience shared information which is not shared by the receptor language audience.

EXERCISES – Implicit Meaning

A. Identify and make **explicit** any **implicit** THINGS or EVENTS in the following:

> Example: After counting the books, Peter said "There are 57."

> *Books* is left implicit in the quotation.
> After counting the books, Peter said, "There are 57 *books*."

1. Forgiveness was difficult for some people.

2. The people of Nigeria are hard workers.

3. It is a country where there are vineyards to give wine and grain for making bread.

4. Testing has been going on at depths of more than 18,000 feet.

5. Women generally get up well before dawn and long before their husbands to relight the fire and begin making breakfast.

B. In the following, a proposition, or part of a proposition, is left **implicit**. Identify and make **explicit** the **implicit** proposition. (See chapter 3 for a definition.)

> Example: The next day John decided to go to town. He saw the judge and had the matter taken care of.

> Implicit information: *John went to town, he arrived in town.*
> The text says that "he decided to" but does not say that he actually did so.

1. The King summoned his wise men and asked them to interpret his dream.

2. But I never did have to chop it with an axe because I had brothers; I only had to use a long knife.

3. Then my mother told me to make myself a little head covering, that she would show me how.

4. No time. Let's handle it with a telephone call.

5. I didn't teach after all because Mr. Jones arrived.

C. The following paragraph is a rather literal translation from Baka (Sudan, data from Wanda Pace). The **implicit organizational** and **situational information** makes the paragraph difficult for a non-Baka speaker to understand. First the paragraph is given, then the added information as supplied by a Baka speaker is given. Rewrite the paragraph into English that will be easily understood by someone outside the Baka culture. Then translate this same paragraph into a second language which you speak.

> *When they have finished bride negotiations, they return home. Then they appoint a day for them. Then they prepare themselves to go for marriage.*

Added information: The negotiations are carried on by the suitor's relatives. This is done at the home of the bride. The bride's relatives are the ones who decide on the date for the marriage. However, it is the suitor's relatives who make the preparations for the marriage ceremonies.

D. The following story is a modified literal translation from Kalinga (Philippines). A person who does not know Kalinga culture would not understand the story. The words and phrases which are in italics contain **implied information**. At the end of the story, an explanation is given for each of these phrases. Study them carefully and then rewrite the story in good idiomatic English (or your mother-tongue).

Kalinga Headhunting Story
(transcribed by Hart Wiens)

The people from upriver who came from Malaya, it is said, built their houses at the confluence where the river meets the *pool with no sides*. They were happy because they were free and they did not allow themselves to be conquered by their fellow-man for their men were very big, very strong, and very brave, and they were fearless warriors for whenever they went *headhunting* each one carried a *pot* and they went singing on their way. Whenever they arrived at the *entrance of the village*, when they *shouted*, the *shouts of the women* resounded in answer to the *men's shouts*. So then nothing could be heard for the drums *um-um-um-ed* and there was no *cutting off of it*.

But the *changed ones* who lived around them went and had them captured by the *red-eyed ones* for *they* hindered *their* work whenever their headhunting instinct came. So then the *whites* arrived firing their guns and the upriver people were terrified, *for* they just stood there staring and easily captured the *ones with patterned clothes* for they were their fearless warriors.

Notes

the pool with no sides: the ocean

headhunting: the act of killing one's enemy and then removing the head and preserving it as a trophy.

pot: a metaphorical use, a euphemism for disembodied heads.

entrance of the village: refers to their own village at the entrance of which there is a split bamboo pole with a cup on it where the guardian spirit of the village lives. (Notice that the whole raid is left implicit, the story tells how they left to go on the raid and then what happened when they came back to their village.)

shouted: indicates victory or they would not have shouted

shouts of the women: who were left in the village when the men went on the raid, shouting to answer the men's shouts of victory

um-um-um-ed: the sound of the drum which indicates victory

cutting off of it: went on without stopping

changed ones: Kalinga who lived in the lowlands and had taken on European customs

red-eyed ones: white people

they: warring Kalinga

their: lowlanders who had taken on European customs.

whites: white people

for: this was evident because...

ones with patterned clothes: the warriors who had killed many people. Each time they killed someone another tatoo was made adding to the pattern of tatoos on their bodies.

Chapter 5
Steps in a Translation Project

The purpose of the first section of this book has been to give an overview of the main aspects of translation. We have dealt with what translation is, the kinds of translations, and some of the aspects of the relationship between grammar and semantics which affect the translation process. In order to complete this overview, we turn now to a general discussion of the steps in a translation project. Before beginning any actual translation, it is important to have in mind the total translation project and what is involved in producing a good translation. Each of these steps will be elaborated on in more detail in the last section of the book.

Establishing the project

Before one considers beginning a translation project, there are a number of matters which need to be clearly understood by all who will be involved. These can be summarized under four T's–the **text**, the **target**, the **team**, and the **tools**.

The **text** refers to the source language document which is to be translated. The desirability of translating a particular text must be determined. Texts are chosen to be translated for various reasons. Most often it is to communicate certain information to people speaking another language, or it may be to share the enjoyment of the source text. The translator should examine his reasons for choosing the text and the potential for its use by the receptor language audience.

The **target** refers to the audience. For whom is the translation being prepared? The form of the translation will be affected by questions of dialect, educational level, age level, bilingualism, and people's attitudes towards their languages. Will it be used in school, in business, or read orally in church and at home? The question of alphabet is also very important. The attitude of the target audience towards the proposed alphabet should be determined before the translation begins. Some excellent translations have been rejected because those who read them did not like, or could not read, the alphabet.

51

Team refers to the people who will be involved in the project. If a person is a competent speaker of both the source language and the receptor language, it may be that the project can be done completely by one person. But even so there should be others available for evaluation and consultation. Most translation projects require a team, a number of people who are going to contribute to the translation at some stage in the project. The working relationship between these people needs to be established before the project gets underway. It may, however, also change as the project moves along and new factors come into focus.

There are certain essentials to any translation project. Not all of these need to be found in one person. There are various kinds of programs which may be set up depending on the abilities and backgrounds of those who will be involved. The team may consist of (1) co-translators, where one is a specialist in the source language and the other a specialist in the receptor language, (2) a translator with capability to handle both source language and receptor language matters and an advisor or consultant, or (3) a committee working together with specific responsibilities delegated to each one. Which kind of a program is developed will depend on who is available and qualified to determine the meaning of the source language, who is most skilled at drafting in the receptor language, and who has an understanding of translation principles. The team may include the translator(s), a consultant, testers and reviewers, and technical people to do typing and proofreading. The publisher and distributor are also part of the team. Before the program is far along it is important to know who will perform these different functions. (For details see chapter 35.) The various members of the team may need special training in order to do their part. This training may need to be taken before the project begins.

Tools refers to the written source materials which will be used by the translators as helps. These include, in addition to the document to be translated, any dictionaries, lexicons, grammars, cultural descriptions, etc., of both the source language and receptor language which are available. The team will want as much information available as possible while translating. All of these tools should be brought to the translation site in preparation for the project. For some projects, there will be a wealth of materials that can be used to help in interpreting the source language text and in finding equivalents in the receptor language. For other projects, there may be a scarcity of such material, but whatever is available should be there to make the work easier. Equipment and finances are also tools needed to carry on an effective program.

Once the matters of the text, the target audience, and the team relationships are cared for, and the tools needed made available, the project is ready to begin. The project will follow a series of steps which include preparation, analysis, transfer, initial draft, reworking the initial draft, testing, polishing, and preparing the manuscript for the publisher. These steps are discussed in detail in chapters 36 and 37.

Exegesis

Exegesis is used to refer to the process of discovering the meaning of the source language text which is to be translated. It is the step which includes the preparation and analysis which must be done before anything at all can be written in the receptor language. The text must be understood completely. This is the process which takes place in moving from the source language form to the semantic structure, i.e., to the meaning of the text.

The translator(s) should begin by reading the text several times, then by reading other materials that may help in understanding the culture or language of the source text. As he reads the text, he will be looking for the author's purpose and the theme of the text. He will look for larger groupings or sections. He may want to outline the text. The purpose is to understand the text as a whole. Once he has done this, he is ready to work on the material a section at a time.

The analysis of the source text will include resolving ambiguity, identifying implicit information, studying key words, interpreting figurative senses, recognizing when words are being used in a secondary sense, when grammatical structures are being used in a secondary function, etc. It will involve doing the kind of analysis which this book is all about. The goal of **exegesis** is to determine the meaning which is to be communicated in the receptor language text. The translator carefully studies the source language text and, using all the available tools, determines the content of the source language message, the related communication situation matters, and all other factors which will need to be understood in order to produce an equivalent translation.

Transfer and initial draft

After a careful analysis of the source language text, as indicated above, the translator begins drafting piece by piece, section by section. The **transfer** results in the **initial draft**. In preparing this draft, the translator is transferring from the source language into the receptor language. As he does so, he must always keep his target audience in mind.

Before any extensive drafting can be done, the key terms must be determined. Every text has a set of words which are crucial to the content and correct communication of the theme. These need to be decided upon and may need to be checked with other speakers of the receptor language.

There are two ways of approaching the **transfer** and **initial draft**. Some translators prefer to do a quick rough translation so that the material flows naturally. Then they go back and tighten up the details to be sure that there is no wrong information and no omissions or additions. In this way, the receptor language text is more apt to be in the natural style of the receptor language. Others prefer to prepare a proposition-like semantic draft, being sure that all the information is accounted for, and then reword it for naturalness; that is, reword it in the idiomatic form of the receptor language. Either method will lead to an idiomatic translation if careful work is done.

It may be necessary to rework the **initial draft** several times before the team is satisfied that all the adjustments needed have been made, that no information is wrong or omitted, that the text communicates clearly in the receptor language, and that the form chosen will communicate to the desired audience. While making and reworking this draft, the audience must always be kept in mind. Once the translation team has sufficiently reworked the **initial draft,** they arrange for copies to be made so that adequate evaluation can be carried on.

Evaluation

The purpose of **evaluation** is threefold: accuracy, clearness, and naturalness. The questions to be answered are (1) Does the translation communicate the **same meaning** as the source language? (2) Does the audience for whom the translation is intended understand it **clearly**? and (3) Is the form of the translation easy to read and **natural** receptor language grammar and style? Those helping with the **evaluation** should be mother-tongue speakers of the receptor language. There are a number of kinds of **evaluations** which need to be done. (These are discussed in more detail in chapter 37.)

The translator will want to compare the translation with the source text at several points during the translation process to be sure no additions, deletions, or change of information have crept in. Others may help with this work. It is especially advantageous to have a consultant check over the material. The translator will want to have receptor language speakers read the text and then tell back what the text communicated to them. As they read, there will be parts that are hard to read or hard to understand. Any time there is an indication of a problem in reading, this should be noted for further checking. Another way to check is by asking questions of those who read the text or to whom it is read. Questions need to be carefully formed so that they bring out the theme, the author's purpose, and the relevant facts of the text. Any wrong understanding should be noted and then checked with others as well. It is best to have someone who has not worked on the translation, but knows both the source language and the receptor language, translate back from the receptor language into the source language without reference to the original source language text. Does the back translation carry the same information as the original source language text? Any difference will need to be checked further.

It is very important that sufficient time and effort be given to **evaluation**. If many of the people who will eventually be using the receptor language text can be involved in the **evaluation** process, this will also create interest in the translated material when it is finally published.

Revised draft

After evaluation is done carefully, there will need to be a **revised draft** made on the basis of the feedback received. Those with whom the translator has checked may have suggested many rewordings, may have expressed misunderstanding, etc. The translation team now works through this material, honestly accepting the evaluation, and rewording the material accordingly. If any key words are changed, the text will need to be checked carefully for consistency in the change made. If some parts were hard for people to read, they may need to be made easier by more redundancy (or less redundancy in another language), by adding more information to clarify participants or theme, or whatever. How much re-drafting will be needed will vary depending on the results of the evaluation.

Consultation

In many translation projects, there are advisors or consultants who are willing to help the translator. The translator(s) will expect that the consultant is interested in three matters: (1) accuracy of content, (2) naturalness of style, and (3) effect on the receptor language audience.

It is important that translators check their materials with a trained consultant after completing a section or two of a long document. If they continue, and do large amounts of translation work without this kind of a check, they will miss out on the training which a consultant can give as they go over the material together. Asking a consultant to work through the material with him will give the translator insights which will not only help his final draft of the material being worked on, but will help him do better transfer drafts on the sections of the document remaining to be done.

The consultant will want to know how the exegesis and initial draft was done and what tools were used. In early meetings, if he was not in on the planning, he may ask about the project as a whole, i.e., all four T's. Questions may deal with linguistic matters and with cultural matters. The goal of the consultant is to evaluate the quality of the translation as to meaning, naturalness, and its potential acceptance by the receptor language audience. In addition to evaluation, he is also interested in training and helping the translator improve and learn to make even more adequate translations.

Final draft

The translator incorporates into the translated text the suggestions made by the consultant, checks them again with mother-tongue speakers to be sure they are warranted, and makes any other minor changes which have come to his attention. However, before he prepares the **final draft**, decisions about format need to be discussed with the whole translation team, the consultant, the potential publisher, and those who will promote distribution.

Some matters may need special testing before the **final draft** is prepared. If the publication is to include pictures, these will need evaluation. If a special size of print is being recommended, it will need to be tested. A final editing for spelling and punctuation will need to be made. When all matters are cared for, a number of copies should be prepared and distributed for proofreading by various people before the actual printing takes place. Every translator wants his final copy to be as accurate as possible. The time spent in careful checking and preparation of the final draft will improve quality and will make the translation more acceptable to the audience for whom it is being prepared.

EXERCISES – Steps in a Translation Project

A. Name and discuss the four T's of a translation project.

B. Explain what is meant by exegesis.

C. What are the goals of the translator as he prepares the initial draft?

D. What is the purpose of the evaluation?

E. What kinds of evaluation checks can be made?

F. How is the revision draft different from the initial draft?

G. What is the consultant concerned about when he checks a translation?

H. How will the final draft be different from the revision draft done earlier?

THE LEXICON

Chapter 6
Words as "Bundles" of Meaning

As discussed in the previous chapters, the aim of the translator is to communicate clearly the meaning of the source text in the translation. In chapter 1, characteristics of language which affect how a translator does this are listed. The first characteristic mentioned was that meaning components are combined into lexical items but that they are "packaged" differently in one language from another. A word is a "bundle" of **meaning components**. The translator needs to be able to analyze the lexical items (words) of the source text in order to translate them. This means being able to "unpack" words in order to show the **meaning** that is represented by the lexical **form**. Dictionaries "unpack" the meanings of words. That is why a good translator will use all the dictionaries and lexicons available in his study of the source language text. He wants to be sure he knows the meaning of each word. Since languages combine meanings differently, there will be many words which will not have an exact one-word equivalent in the receptor language.

Concepts

In chapter 3, where the structure of meaning was discussed, it was pointed out that **meaning components** and **concepts** are classified semantically as THINGS, EVENTS, ATTRIBUTES, and RELATIONS. THINGS are defined as all animate beings and all inanimate entities. EVENTS include all actions, processes, and experiences. ATTRIBUTES include all attributes of quality and quantity ascribed to THINGS or EVENTS. And RELATIONS include all those relations posited between any two semantic units.

Concept is used in this text to refer not to the form (word) but only to the meaning content. A **concept** is a recognizable unit of meaning in any given language. These **concepts** may be broken down into a number of meaning components (bits of information). For example, the **concept** *ram* can be broken down into SHEEP, MALE, and ADULT. A **concept** is a bundle of components of meaning. Since each language has its own unique inventory of **concepts**, how can **concepts** be identified? Concerning this, Barnwell (1980:141) says:

> In a given language, the concept unit usually, but by no means always, is represented by a word; it may also be represented by a morpheme, or by an idiomatic expression, or by tone, or by word order. Concepts are identified in a given language on the principle of *contrast and comparison* within the system of that language. Each concept is associated with a particular area of meaning which is distinct from that of other concepts in the language; its function is to refer to some specific area of meaning.

In chapter 8, the matter of contrast and comparison will be discussed and exemplified. As mentioned above, all languages have **concepts** but not the same **concepts**. There will be words in the source language and receptor language which are very similar in content (contain the same meaning components), but not all will match by any means. Not all language communities have the same ideas. Reality is conceptualized differently in different communities. The phenomena of reality around us are "bundled" together differently by different communities and labeled (given a name, i.e., lexicalized). As will be pointed out in chapters 7 and 8, even physical phenomena are classified and "bundled" differently. Social phenomena are themselves diverse in different communities and so give rise to diverse labels (words). (For more information on concepts see Nida and Taber 1969:37–55; Barnwell 1980:141-43; and Beekman, Callow, and Kopesec 1981:16–17.)

The first step, then, in the analysis of words is to determine whether the word is referring primarily to a THING **concept**, an EVENT **concept**, an ATTRIBUTE **concept**, or a RELATION **concept**. What is the **central concept** of the word? Many words are easily classified. For example, *stone* is a THING, *eat* is an ACTION, *green* is an ATTRIBUTE, and *on* is a RELATION. However, many words are not that easily classified. They are more difficult to classify because there is a skewing between the semantic classification and the grammatical classification. Some words are made up of more than one **concept**.

When we define such a word, we make explicit the **concepts** which are combined together in that word. For example, we might define *runner* by saying *a person who runs*. We have made explicit the fact that *runner* is used to refer to a PERSON, and that that person *runs. Runner* is a word in the English language. The central **concept** is PERSON and the **concept** RUNS serves to define more concisely (to restrict) PERSON. The word *runner* is talking about a THING, that is a PERSON, but it is also talking about an EVENT, RUN.

The combining of a number of meanings into a single word reflects the principle of language economy. In surface structure lexicons, several **concepts** may be represented by a single lexical item. Common THINGS and EVENTS are usually identified by a single word, even though they may consist of a number of **concepts**. For example, most languages have the words for *see, hear,* and *smell.* The **concept** *perceive* is restricted by other **concepts** – *with eyes, with ears,* and *with nose,* so that in each case English has a single word carrying the complex meaning. However, in Kabba-kaka of Chad there is a basic root meaning *perceive,* and HEAR and SEE can only be distinguished by adding *eyes* and *ears* (Nida 1964:51).

For pastoral cultures, it is not uncommon to have a single word meaning *taking care of at night,* where the ACTIVITY of *taking care of* and the TIME, *night,* are both included as the meaning of a single word. For example, in Quiché of Guatemala, the concepts *taking care of* and *at night* have been lexicalized in one form or word, *kwrax.* The word for *take care of,* without the **concept** of *night* is *kutstsxix.* Otomí of Mexico does not have a word for *island.* What meaning is packaged in the English word *island*? An *island* is a THING. It is *land* surrounded by *water.* The **central concept** is *land,* but this is further restricted by *surrounded (encircled) by water.*

The Quiché word *kwrax* would need to be "unpacked" to be translated into English. English does not combine *take care of* and *at night* into a single word. The English word *island* would have to be unpacked to translate into Otomí.

Translating concepts

A translator will often find that there is no exact equivalent between the words of one language and the words of another. There will be words which have some of the **meaning components** combined in them matching a word which has these components with some additional ones. There will be overlap, but there is seldom a complete match between languages. Because of this, it is often necessary to translate one word of the source language by several words in the receptor language in order to give the same meaning. Sometimes the opposite will also be true. Several words in the source language may be translated by a single word. For example, the Trique word *ó* would be translated into English by the sentence *"We are shelling corn."* The Aguaruna word *dakumjukmaukait* would be translated by the sentence *"Is it a picture of me?"* in English. On the other hand, the English word *sad* can be translated into Aguaruna with only the phrase *stomach being-broken feeling.*

In order to analyze the meaning of a word in preparation for translation, one must first think of what the **central concept** is and in what way this is limited. It may then be possible to translate with a word in the receptor language which is equivalent to the **central concept** and use a phrase to add the further definition. Note the following examples from Aguaruna:

wilderness -   *aents*   *atsamaunum*
            people   where-they-are-not-place

(a place where there are no people)

theater -   *jega*   *muun*   *jegamkamunum*   *aents*   *tuwaka*
        house   big   that-built-place   people   diverting

ijunbaunum
where-they-gather-place

(a big house where people gather for diversion)

Skewing of classifications

The same form may also be used as two different parts of speech. For example, notice the use of *blue* in the phrases *blue sky* and *sky blue*. In the first, *blue* is used as an adjective to describe the *sky*, and in the second, *sky* is used as an adjective to describe *blue*. In the first, there is no **skewing** because *blue* is an ATTRIBUTE used as an adjective and *sky* is a THING used as a noun. In the second, however, a THING, the *sky* is used as an adjective to modify *blue* which is an ATTRIBUTE used as a noun. Whenever there is **skewing** of this kind, there is likely to have to be some kind of adjustment in translation. The **skewing** between the grammar and the semantic categories must be taken into consideration in finding the underlying meaning. Translators must be aware of this **skewing** in the source language. Once the meaning is clear, they can think about how to reconstruct the meaning in the receptor language.

The translator must guard against trying to match parts of speech from language to language, since each language has its own system for arranging concepts into different parts of speech. There is little guarantee that what is a noun in one language is best translated by a noun in another language. It is interesting, however, that in contrasting languages one often notes a fairly consistent correlation between two different parts of speech. Where one language is using the verb with some degree of frequency, another language may be expressing the very same meanings by means of the verbal noun. Such observations about the natural differences between languages can be very useful to the translator. Translating from a language which uses many verbs into a language which uses many verbs will be easier than from a language which uses many nouns into a language which uses mostly verbs.

The **skewing** between semantic classes and parts of speech occurs frequently. Many languages have special forms which make it possible to use an EVENT **concept** as a noun in the grammar. For example, in English, *knowledge* is a noun based on the EVENT **concept** *know*. *Ability* is a noun based on the **concept** *to be able* and *full report* is a noun phrase based on the **concept** *to report fully*. In some languages, there are forms which modify nouns that refer to EVENT **concepts**, as, for example, *falling* in *falling star*. Since *falling* refers to an EVENT **concept**, the semantic structure would be *a star which is falling*. In the phrase *starry eyes* the adjective *starry* refers to THINGS, stars, and so the semantic structure would be *eyes which look like stars*. There is skewing between the grammar and the semantic structure.

There are various reasons why nominalizing, for example, occurs. One of the main reasons in English, and some other languages, is so that the topic under discussion can be introduced by a noun. If the topic is an EVENT, then a noun form, often called an abstract noun, will be used. For example, the noun *salvation* may be used to talk about the EVENT *to save* or the noun *height* may be used to talk about the ATTRIBUTE *high* or the noun *the reason* may be used to talk about the RELATION **reason-result** if it is the topic of the sentence. Skewing of this kind is used for pointing out the topic of the sentence or paragraph.

If there were no skewing, the text would sound very monotonous and uninteresting. Skewing by nominalization, verbalization, and adjectivization adds dynamics and "life" to the text. They are part of the style which makes a given text a work of art. But if translated literally into a second language, they will sound strange and not accomplish the purpose which they had in the source text.

A translator will find it helpful to analyze the source language by comparing the part of speech with the semantic classification. In the following examples, the labels above the words indicate their grammatical classification and the labels underneath indicate their semantic class. Notice the **skewing**:

	1. Pronoun	Verb	Noun
	our	*beloved*	*ruler*
	THING	EVENT	THING-EVENT

	2. Noun	Prep	Noun
	the death	*of*	*the dancer*
	EVENT	RELATION	THING-EVENT

	3. Noun	Prep	Noun
	a carpenter	*from*	*Abidjan*
	THING-EVENT	EVENT-RELATION	THING

In order to restate a noun in semantic structure, it may be necessary to "unpack" the words and at the same time eliminate the **skewing** of classification by using verbs for EVENTS and nouns for THINGS. When this is done, the restatement will be closer to semantic structure. The above examples could be unpacked and rewritten as follows:

1. We love him. He rules us.

2. The person who danced died.

3. He is a person who works with wood and who lives in Abidjan.

Notice that sometimes a word represents several concepts and it may even represent a proposition, as in the examples above.

Restatement

A translator who is having difficulty analyzing the source text which he wants to translate may be greatly benefited by rewriting the material in semantic structure before beginning to think about how to translate it in the receptor language. In the following example, the paragraph is first given as it occurred in English. Below that is a restatement which reflects more exactly the semantic structure because the **skewing** between the grammar and the semantics has been eliminated. That is, THINGS are represented by nouns, EVENTS by verbs, ATTRIBUTES by adjectives or adverbs, and RELATIONS by relationals.

ENGLISH PARAGRAPH

Word and reading games can sometimes be used for motivation and reading readiness. Some of these are also useful for additional drills when more normal instruction begins. They may actually teach the pupil his first words while he thinks he is only playing. They make good relief from concentrated study. (From Gudschinsky 1957:13)

RESTATEMENT

Playing games in which the pupils use words and read can sometimes motivate them and prepare them to read. Persons who teach may also use some of these games to drill the pupils more when they are later instructing them in regular classes. The games actually teach the pupil his first words while he thinks he is only playing. They relieve/relax pupils who have been concentrating as they study.

A **restatement** of this kind is usually not good English style, but it helps the translator identify the meaning and matches the grammatical categories with the semantic categories, thus eliminating most of the skewing and making it easier to translate into a more verbal language.

The process of "unpacking" the semantic structure of a word is sometimes called **restatement. Restatement**, used in a technical way, means to say the same thing in another way. In this kind of **restating**, there should be no change in the semantic components; that is, there should be no additions or deletions, but the same meaning should be carried by the **restatement** as much as possible. The idea is simply to restate by means of semantic concepts and/or propositions. Restating in this way through a **restatement** draws to the attention of the translator all of the meanings of the source language. As he eliminates the skewing between the grammar and the semantics, he will need to make each concept explicit, and in this way all of the meaning is brought out. Notice the following **restatements**. These are literal English equivalents of the translation of phrases occurring in *Matias Talks About Government* (Hoffman 1969) which are taken from the translation into Gahuku (Deibler and Taylor 1977:1061).

ENGLISH	GAHUKU
hum of an engine	the thing that hummed put its sound
the long wait	that he kept waiting a long time
happy meeting	they met and were happy
decisions	we will say-cut (decide)
keep a diary of appointments	you will burn a carving about people saying, "we want to see the Administrator man"
many requests	the people are continually requesting

Deibler and Taylor state:

It should be noted that whereas in the highlands of Papua New Guinea it is often impossible to render verbal nouns literally, it is possible to do so in the Austronesian type languages. But here again it has been found that changing them to verbs in translation greatly increases the intelligibility of the translation.

One of the concomitant difficulties arising from the necessity to render verbal nouns as verbs in Papua New Guinea is that a decision must be made as to how the resultant clause relates to the context; i.e., exactly what logical or temporal relationship to use as a connector. Often the translator succeeds in removing the noun and substituting a verb, only to use the wrong conjunction to relate the clause to the rest of the sentence.

(These matters of relationship will be discussed in later chapters.)

When a word is **restated** to indicate its full meaning, it is important to be aware of which concept in the **restatement** is the central component. In the example of *island* given above, the paraphrase given was *land surrounded by water*. *Land* is the central or nuclear component of meaning and *surrounded by water* delimits or defines more clearly which *land*. It distinguishes it from other *land* which may take the form of a *desert, plain,* or *mountain*.

Notice that the English word *teacher* includes both a THING, that is, the *person,* and an EVENT, that is, the action *teach*. A *teacher* is *a person who teaches*. A single word may consist of both a THING and an EVENT. *Person* is the nuclear concept in *teacher* and *who teaches* describes the *person*. In the same way *help* may be restated as *someone who can help* for the sentence *Help is coming. Help* includes both a THING, *someone*, and an EVENT, the action *help*.

Some words represent a nuclear concept plus additional concepts and some words represent whole semantic propositions. Words are generally semantically complex and consist of a number of concepts which may further be divided into semantic components. The classification of the nuclear component, that is deciding whether it is a THING, EVENT, ATTRIBUTE, or RELATION, determines the semantic class or classes included in the word.

As we noted in chapter 3, the smallest unit of meaning is the meaning component. Meaning components unite to form concepts and concepts form propositions. Often a word represents a single concept which is made up of meaning components but more often a word represents a concept cluster; that is, a number of concepts, or even a proposition, as we have noted above. In restating, it is not always important to analyze down to the smallest meaning component. However, when there is more than one concept included in the word, the **restatement** will make explicit each concept of the concept cluster or of the proposition which is represented by the word.

For example, a word like *centurion* may be restated by a concept cluster–*a man who commands one hundred soldiers*. Words in this **restatement** like "soldiers" could again be broken down into meaning components, but it is not to the advantage of the translator to try to break down every word into basic structure of meaning components. It is, however, very helpful to **restate** words by indicating all of the concepts which are included. Analysis by paraphrase should be done only to eliminate the skewing between grammar and semantics and to clarify the concepts in complex words. Concepts peculiar to one culture will have a word in that language, but may only be translatable by unpacking, i.e., by a **restatement** using several words.

EXERCISES – Words as "Bundles" of Meaning

A. The following English lexical items are semantically complex. What components are found in each lexical item? Which is central? Rewrite in such a way that semantic and grammatical classes match and only relevant components are included.

> Example: martyr – human being who is killed because he refuses to renounce what he believes.
>
> The central component is *human being*

1. skater
2. legislation
3. pilot
4. distributor (of a book)
5. doctor
6. to whiten
7. to ensnare
8. to dive
9. to stone
10. to justify (a person)
11. to tree
12. running (water)
13. falling (star)
14. glutton
15. deny
16. substitution
17. truth
18. communication
19. postpone
20. postponement

B. Rewrite the following so that there is **no skewing** between the semantic and grammatical classes:

> Example: It took a lot of judgment to find a solution.
>
> Someone judged well and solved something.

1. I cried when they told me of the death of my mother.
2. The love of our country is very important.
3. Envy is not good.
4. Did you like your grandfather's gift?
5. He is a liar.
6. Nobody respects a cheat.

7. Success spoiled him.
8. Dishonesty is bad.
9. The wealthy live here.
10. He's here on a visit.

C. Rewrite the following paragraph so that there is **no skewing** between the semantic and the grammatical classes. You do not need to break lexical items down into meaning components unless this is necessary to match the semantic and grammatical classes (i.e., *hunter* could be *a man who was hunting*, without giving the components of *human* and *being* since by separating *man* and *hunting* we now have a THING, *man*, as a noun and an EVENT, *was hunting*, as a verb, and there is, therefore, no skewing.)

> *The hunter saw a snow white swan gliding along in the rushing brook. The beauty of the bird stopped him from shooting. He watched its disappearance around the next bend and then continued his hunt.*

D. In each of the following, the forms of several languages are given with a literal translation into English of this form. What would the idiomatic English equivalent be for each set?

1. **Aguaruna (Peru):** kajág pujáwai - my-sleep it-exists
   Spanish: tengo sueño - I-have sleepiness
   English:
   Another language you speak:

2. **Maxakali (Brazil):** ukura yum ka'ak - heart sits firmly in
   Aguaruna (Peru): "dekaskeapi," tawai- "it-is-surely-true," he says
   Spanish: lo cree - it he-believes
   Apinaye (Brazil): kot amaxpẽr - thinks with
   English:
   Another language:

3. **Maxakali (Brazil):** kãm ãktux rex - put away words
   Aguaruna (Peru): "dutikatajai," tiu - "I-will-do-thus," he-said
   Spanish: dió su promesa - gave his promise
   English:
   Another language:

4. **Mundurukú (Brazil):** ĩguycũg̃ ikẽrẽat kug̃ puye - he-is-sad
because he-has-ugliness (sin)
Aguaruna (Peru): anentái yapajiáwai - his-heart changes
Canela (Brazil): ihken mã hikra - lets-go-of his sin
English:
Another language:

E. In each of the following translations into English the italicized
words have been translated literally and may or may not be
idiomatic or correct. Evaluate the italicized words as translations.
As an exercise, change the part of speech of the word (or main
word, if more than one word is involved) in the italicized
construction to some other part of speech to see whether you can
improve upon the translation of the sentence as a whole. Do not
change the meaning of the sentences, but substitute words and, if
necessary, change grammatical structures.

1. Before *departure*, I gave them some instructions.

2. If costs *change* in any way prior to *delivery* of the equipment,
the *rent* will likewise be changed in equal proportion.

3. It is common *knowledge* that the U.S. share in the foreign trade
has shown a *tendency* toward *reduction* in recent years.

4. *A complete elimination* of the general *decline* in economic
activity seems almost impossible.

5. The *government* is taking all necessary steps for *a defense* of
the borders.

6. The United States is committed to *a ceaseless striving* for *the
attainment* of a genuine *disarmament*.

7. He could not incite his men to *mutiny*. That would be *a crime*.

8. He *rises* early.

9. With *my knowledge* of Hungary's past, I can review the past
it has traversed and assess its present *development*.

10. Today *leaders* and *rank and file laborers* are more united than
at any time in the past.

Chapter 7
Some Relationships between Lexical Items

Generic-specific

In chapter 1, it was noted that the same meaning components may occur in several lexical items (words) of a language. The example was given of the word *sheep*. The meaning SHEEP is also found in the words *lamb, ram,* and *ewe.* This is true because the word *sheep* is a **generic word** which includes the more **specific words** *ram, ewe,* and *lamb.* Every language has whole areas of vocabulary with this kind of relationship between the words. Notice Display 7.1 which shows the semantic content of some English vocabulary.

		SHEEP	HORSE	CHICKEN	DOG	DEER
ADULT	MALE	*ram*	*stallion*	*rooster*	*dog*	*buck*
	FEMALE	*ewe*	*mare*	*hen*	*bitch*	*doe*
YOUNG		*lamb*	*colt/foal*	*chick*	*puppy*	*fawn*

Display 7.1

Note that across the top, the **generic words** SHEEP, HORSE, CHICKEN, DOG, and DEER occur. Then, on the left hand side, the additional meaning components, which are part of the words in the squares of the display, are given; that is, ADULT, MALE, FEMALE, and YOUNG. (Note that there is no specific word in English for ADULT, MALE DOG.) When looking at vocabulary this way, one sees how the kinds of restating presented in the last chapter could be arrived at for each of the words on the display. A *ram* is an ADULT, MALE SHEEP; a *ewe* is an ADULT, FEMALE SHEEP; and a *lamb* is a YOUNG SHEEP. We

71

could do the same kind of restating for the other words. Looking at the display this way, we are looking at the meaning components which make up each of the words in the display, and this is also what we were doing in the previous chapter.

It is also possible to look at this same set of words in another way and draw a tree as seen in Display 7.2. At the top of the tree, occurs the word *animal* which is even more **generic** than *sheep, horse, chicken,* or *dog*. One can then be more specific by choosing between *sheep, horse, chicken,* and *dog*. Once one has decided to talk about *sheep*, it is possible to be even more **specific** and talk about a *ram*, a *ewe*, or a *lamb*.

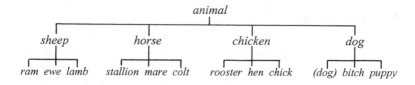

Display 7.2

Within a given language, words have various kinds of relationships to other words of that language. The relationship of one word as being more **generic** and another as being a **specific** of that **generic** word is common to all languages. Those who have studied botany are familiar with these kinds of relationships between words. These relationships are called *taxonomies*. The concept of **specific-generic** can be very helpful in analyzing the vocabulary of both the source language and the receptor language. It is also a very helpful tool when one is looking for equivalents in translation.

In speaking of **generic** vocabulary, we are referring to the manner in which certain words are grouped together in a language and given a class name; that is, a more **generic word** which includes all of a set of words. This **generic term** is a class word, the meaning of which is also found in two or more different words which are more **specific**. More **specific words** have additional components of meaning as well as the meaning of the **generic term**. For example, a *dog* is more **specific** than *animal* because the word *animal* is used to define *dog*; that is, a *dog* is an *animal* which has certain **specific** characteristics. Words may be related to one another in that one word has a general meaning which is included in the meaning of the more **specific word**. We can say that a *collie* is a *dog*, an *animal*, and a *thing*. Each word is more **generic** than the previous one. Notice the following diagram of a taxonomy beginning with the **generic** word *plant* (data from Litteral 1975). *Plants* may be divided into *flowers, shrubs, trees, grass, ferns,* and so forth. At the next level down in the taxonomy, *trees* are subdivided into *palm, pine, gum, oak, birch,* and so forth. Then *palms* are divided more specifically into *betelnut, coconut, sego, limbum,* and so forth. In cultures where there are a variety of coconuts, there will no doubt be more **specific words** subdividing coconut palms (see Display 7.3).

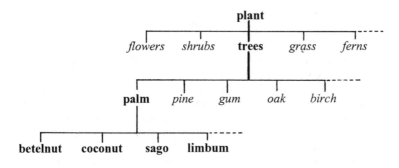

Display 7.3

    A taxonomy comprises different sets of contrasting categories at successive levels, the categories at any one level being included in a category of the next higher level. These can be looked at in two dimensions. If one reads across horizontally, one sees that there is discrimination; that is, a *palm* is different from a *pine*, different from a *gum*, different from an *oak*, and different from a *birch*. On the next level, *betelnut* is different from *coconut*, different from *sago*, and different from *limbum*. However, if one reads vertically, then the relationship is one of general and specific, the item at the top being **generic** and the one at the bottom being most **specific**. The **specific** *coconut* is a *palm*, which is a *tree*, which is a *plant*.

    There are also many occurrences within languages where the same word, that is the same form, is used at several levels within the vertical **generic-specific** line. Note, for example, Display 7.4, which begins with the generic *animal*, distinguishes *man* from *animal* at the next level of specificity, then subdivides *man* into more specific *man* versus *woman*, and next subdivides *man* into the more specific *man* versus *boy*. At the last, more specific level, some additional components of meaning are added to delineate the more **generic** term.

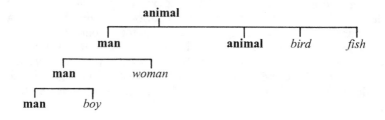

Display 7.4

It is important to realize that the same word can be used sometimes in a very **generic** way and other times in a very **specific** way. Since the generic relationships of any two languages are usually quite different, it is unlikely that a second language would use one form for all of these occurrences of *man*. In the Philippines, *rice* is the generic term for all grain. A possible way to translate *wheat* might be *a rice called wheat.*

It is also important to realize that EVENT words, that is, words which are standing for a semantic EVENT, may also be arranged in **generic-specific** relationships in a language. Notice Display 7.5.

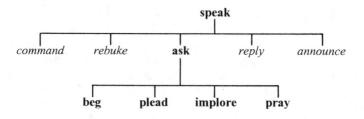

Display 7.5

The word *speak* has a very general meaning, while *command, rebuke, ask, reply,* and *announce* are more specific. That is, they have added components of meaning. The central component of meaning, *speak,* occurs in all of them, but there are additional components of meaning that distinguish them one from the other. At another level, *ask* can be delineated by additional components of meaning resulting in *beg, plead, implore,* and *pray.*

Notice, also, Display 7.6 where *prepare* is the most **generic** and one way of *preparing* is to *cook,* and *cooking* can be done in several **specific** ways; that is, by *roasting, broiling, boiling,* or *frying.*

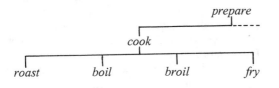

Display 7.6

A translator needs to know about the **generic** and **specific** relationships of words because this may help him find a good lexical equivalent which might be hard to find if he were not aware of this possibility. For example, he may be able to use a generic word in the receptor language which would include the source language word and then add a descriptive phrase in order to make clear the restricting components of meaning of the source language word. For example, if *wolf* did not occur in the receptor language, the generic term *animal* plus a descriptive phrase like *fierce/wild* might need to be used as was done in a translation into Tepehua of Mexico. *Centurion* was translated into Mazahua of Mexico by using the generic term *man* and the additional descriptive phrase *who commands 100 soldiers*.

Sometimes, the translator will have difficulty in translating a source language word which represents a concept which is unfamiliar to the receptor language speakers. He may need to borrow a word from the source language, but in order to insure that it will be understood, he will want to use a generic class word along with the loan word in order to make it very clear what is being talked about. The Aguaruna are tropical forest people who have never seen a *camel*. The word *camel* was translated into Aguaruna as *an animal called camello*, using the Spanish loan word *camello* and identifying the generic class of *animal*.

It is important to notice that languages tend to differ most in **generic** terminology, rather than in **specific**. When translating relatively **specific** words, it is usually easier it find a close equivalent. **Specific** vocabulary is more likely to correspond between two languages. But when one is translating **generic** words, it may be more difficult. **Generic** vocabulary in one language will be quite different from that of another and there will be no exact equivalent. For example, in the Aguaruna language, there is no word equal to English *bird*. The word *pishak* means "small bird," the word *chigki* means "game bird," and the word *chiwag* means "big nongame bird," such a as *buzzard*. It is possible to say "flying things," but this would include insects, airplanes, etc. When one is looking for equivalent **generic** words, these cannot be found by simply asking for the equivalent words of the source language. If one were to ask for *bird* in Aguaruna, the native speaker would probably choose at random either *pishak* or *chigki*. However, this is not equivalent to the English word *bird*. When all kinds of birds are referred to, all three of the Aguaruna words need to be included. For example: Then God created the *pishak*, the *chigki*, and also the *chiwag*. The Munduruku (Brazil, data from Marjorie Crofts) language has a generic word *umayu*, meaning literally *high up ones*, which includes *monkeys* and *birds*. There is no **generic** word for *monkeys* apart from this word which includes *birds*, and there is no **generic** word for *birds* apart from this word which includes *monkeys*.

Most languages will have quite close equivalents for **specific** words like *murder, steal,* and *lie*, but it may be very hard to find equivalent **generic** words for *bad*. The Gueaca language of Venezuela has a contrast of three **generic** words *good, bad,* and *taboo*.

> *Good* includes desirable food, killing enemies, chewing dope in moderation, putting fire on one's wife to teach her to obey, and stealing from any person not belonging to the same band... *Bad* includes rotten fruit, any object with a blemish, murdering a person of the same band, stealing from a member of the extended family, and lying... *Taboo* includes incest, being too close to one's mother-in-law, a married woman's eating tapir before the birth of the first child, and a child's eating rodents. (Nida 1964:79)

The translation of abstract or more **generic** terms is often very complex, especially if the cultural contexts of the two languages are quite different. A translator will want to know what the specifics are which are included in a generic term, both in the source language and the receptor language, in order to find a good translation equivalent. The two systems will not match exactly, but a careful analysis will help determine what equivalent can best be used.

Substitute words

The generic words that we have been discussing so far are **indefinite**; that is, they are referring to a generic class and do not specify a particular THING or EVENT. However, it is important to notice that generic words may also be used in a **definite** generic way to refer to something that is already being discussed in the text. These are quite different from the general **indefinite** vocabulary, although they may include many of the same words. We will distinguish between these two usages by calling the latter **substitute words** and the former **generic words**. To illustrate **substitute words**, notice how the same thing is referred to by several different terms in the following:

"My old *Plymouth* broke down again. *It* has been a good *car*. But it is time to get rid of the old *thing*."

In this paragraph, *Plymouth* has been referred to by *it, car*, and *thing*. These are all **substitute words** for the antecedent *Plymouth*. A **substitute word** refers to something already introduced to the context. Sometimes the **substitute word** will be a more generic word as, for example, *car* is a more generic word than *Plymouth*, and *thing* is more generic than *car*. However, *it*, which is a pronoun, is a **substitute word** which may substitute for any noun. A pet may be referred to as *the cat, my pet, pussy,* or *Blacky*. These are **substitute words** all referring to the same THING, but are not necessarily part of a generic-specific hierarchy. Some languages have pro-verbs. English has the verbs *do* and *make* which substitute for verbs. **Substitute words** will be discussed more as we discuss the cohesion of a text in chapter 30.

In the Aguaruna language of Peru, there are a number of *pro-verbs*. These verbs stand for sets of actions just like *he, she*, and *it* stand for sets of objects. Since the discourse structure of the text makes it necessary to connect sentences by pro-verbs, it is very important to know which actions are specifics of which pro-verbs. One pro-verb includes as specifics all transitive verbs and another pro-verb includes as specifics all intransitive verbs. A third pro-verb includes all verbs of "saying." It is very important to know how **substitute words** are used in the receptor language in order to translate naturally. The translator will not want to simply translate a pronoun with a pronoun and a pro-verb with a pro-verb. He will want to use the pronouns and pro-verbs of the receptor language naturally. The uses will not match the uses of pronouns and pro-verbs in the source language. We will discuss this matter more when we discuss the analysis of texts and reconstruction in the receptor language. It is simply mentioned here as one kind of generic vocabulary of which it is important for the translator to be aware.

Some languages have a great deal of redundancy while other languages do not repeat the same word over and over but use **substitute words**. For example, the following Waorani text (Adapted from Pike and Saint 1988:116) shows the repetition of the phrases *lots of corn, corn to eat* and other phrases about *corn*. A modified literal translation into English is given below followed by another version using various substitute words.

This is a story about *corn*. Others had a whole *lot of corn*. Since they had *lots of corn*, when others asked "Can we have some of your *corn to eat*?" they refused. One fellow chopped a *corn field*; he chopped a whole great big *field for corn*. He chopped it and had *lots of corn growing,* so much it *grew* like cane in a cane-patch. They said "When your *corn is grown* and we see it is ripe and you are *eating it,* let us *eat it* too." But he replied, "Since you refused to share with me and *ate* all your *corn,* I refuse too. When the *corn* is ripe I alone will *eat it* up.".....

This is a story about corn. Some people had an *abundance.* Because of *that,* when others asked, "Can we have some of your corn to eat?" they refused. So one of these others chopped a cornfield. He prepared a great big field. He planted *his seed* and *it* grew like cane in a cane-patch. The people said, "When *it* is grown and we see that *it* is ripe and that you are eating *it,* let us have *some* too." But he replied, "Since you refused to share with me and ate all of *yours,* I refuse too. When *mine* is ripe I will *devour it* all by myself."

Substitute words are used when the receptor language natural patterns prefer a variety of words to refer to the same thing or event. On the other hand, the reverse may be true. The source text may use **substitute words** which would be more natural in the receptor language if the original noun or verb were used. **Substitute words** should not be translated literally. Rather, the natural patterns for using **substitute words** in the receptor language should be used.

Synonyms

In any language, there are words which are very similar in meaning. However, there are very few exact **synonyms**. Even words which are very similar in meaning will probably not have exactly the same usage in sentence and paragraph structures. The words *often* and *frequently* are close **synonyms**. There will be sets of words which are **synonymous** in their nuclear meaning which, however, contain certain additional positive or negative overtones. One may be more formal and another less formal. One word may be appropriate in one situation and the other appropriate in a different situation. The words *fat, plump,* and *chubby* all have a common meaning. However, there are only certain contexts in which they are interchangeable. *Yell, shriek,* and *scream* are also **synonymous** but with a slight difference of usage. *Police officer, policeman,* and *cop* all refer to the same thing, but *cop* is much less formal than *police officer.* A second language may not have a specific word for each of the **synonyms** of the source language. Sometimes the receptor language may have more words to choose from than the source language. It is very important that the translator be aware of the very minute differences in meaning between words and near **synonyms** so as to choose the word that has the right connotation. (Connotation will be discussed in chapter 13.) For example, when translating into English from some other language which has only one word for *police*, which word should be chosen in English, *police officer, policeman*, or *cop*? The translator would need to know the difference between the near **synonyms**. The reference is to the same person, but the words are used differently.

Antonyms

The **antonym** of a word is the exact opposite, or contrasts in some particular part of its meaning. All languages will have pairs of words which are **antonyms**, but different languages will have different sets. For example, in English, we distinguish *short* and *tall* vertically, and *short* and *long* horizontally. In Aguaruna, there are only two words *sutajuch* and *esajam* which are used for both the vertical and horizontal distinction of length. In English, we have the words *good* and *bad* which are **antonyms**. In Aguaruna, the distinction is made by the word *good, pegkeg*, contrasting with the same word *good* linked to a negative suffix, *not-good, pegkegchau*. That is, there are not two separate words; there is simply *good* and *not-good*. Some languages will have words for *slave* and *free*. Others will simply have a word for *free* while the meaning for "slave" will be *not-free*.

It can sometimes be very helpful to a translator who is looking for a particular word to realize that if he thinks about the **antonym**, the word opposite in meaning, he may be able to find the desired word by constructing a negative form of that **antonym**.

"In some instances, a receptor language may already use a construction with negatives as a normal way of handling certain positive concepts. In Bila'an of the Philippines, the expression *it is not possible we will not* is how *we must* is expressed" (Beekman and Callow 1974:183).

Opposites are a kind of **antonym**—*much* and *little, many* and *few, open* and *shut*, etc. Some languages have a word for only one of the pair and the other is a negative. In Aguaruna, the most complimentary way to say *you are beautiful* is to say *you are not ugly*, and *not many* is a more emphatic way to say *few* than the word *few*.

Reciprocal words

Most languages will also have sets of words which are the **reciprocal** of one another. For example, the words *give* and *receive* have a **reciprocal** relationship to one another. One can say, *"John gave Mary a book,"* or one can say, *"Mary received a book from John."* The meaning is the same since the two actions are **reciprocal** actions. One can say, *"John taught Bill,"* or *"Bill learned from John."* Teach and *learn* are **reciprocal** actions. This may sometimes be very helpful in translation where the receptor language does not have a specific word used in the same way as the source language. It may be that the same meaning can be communicated by using a **reciprocal word.** For example, *the government gave a large grant to the miners*, might in some translation need to be translated conversely, *the miners received a large grant from the government*. Style in some language may make one phrasing more correct than the other. In Muyuw, there is no word for *be born*. Instead of *I was born in 1930*, a translation into Muyuw would need to say *my mother gave-birth to me in 1930*. Also in Muyuw, *he declared all food clean* was translated *no foods were forbidden by him*.

Conclusion

It is very important that the translator be aware of the fact that the vocabulary of the source language will not match the vocabulary of the receptor language. Awareness of the way that vocabularies are structured should help the translator to find equivalents through looking for more **generic** or **specific** vocabulary, by looking for words that are **synonymous** or near **synonymous**, and by looking for **antonyms** and for **reciprocal words.**

EXERCISES – Some Relationships between Lexical Items

A. In front of the word given, write a more **generic word** which includes the given word. In the space after the word given in the example below, write a more **specific word** which is covered by the more generic ones which precede it.

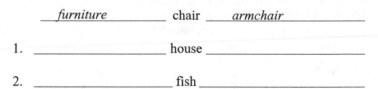

furniture	chair	*armchair*

1. _____ house _____

2. _____ fish _____

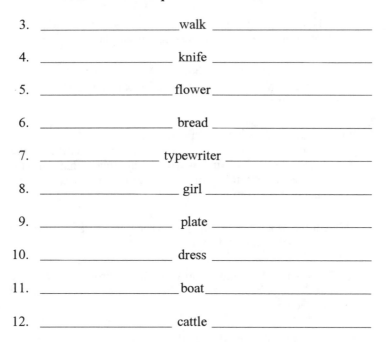

3. _____ walk _____

4. _____ knife _____

5. _____ flower _____

6. _____ bread _____

7. _____ typewriter _____

8. _____ girl _____

9. _____ plate _____

10. _____ dress _____

11. _____ boat _____

12. _____ cattle _____

B. List up to ten members of the class "kinds of game" in any language other than English and arrange them in a tree diagram to show which are the most **generic** and which are more **specific**.

C. Study the translation made for the italicized word in each of the following. Was the change made from **specific** to **generic** or **generic** to **specific**?

1. The *wolf* snatched them and scattered them.
   The savage-animal grabbing at them caused them to scatter.

2. He looked around to see who *had done* it.
   He looked around to see who had thrown the stone.

3. Consider the *lilies* of the field.
   Think about the wild flowers.

4. His *tomb* is with us to this day.
   Even now one is able to see his burial place.

5. Everyone was talking about the *happenings*.
   Everyone was talking about the Independence Day
   celebration.

D. In each of the following, a specific THING or EVENT is referred
   to first by a specific referent and then by **substitute words.**
   Underline the **substitute words.** Remember that **substitute
   words** refer to something already mentioned in the text but use a
   more generic word to do so.

   1. Abidjan is a large city in West Africa. It is located on the coast
      and is a thriving metropolis.

   2. John rescued a young man who almost drowned. When what
      he had done became known, he was given a special award for
      his deed.

   3. Peter ate a big breakfast, and having done that, he went outside
      to watch the sunrise.

   4. The typewriter broke again. I should have thrown the thing
      away long ago. I bought it on discount and it's never been a
      good machine.

E. Give a **synonym** for each of the following:

   1. amusing   6. sage (person)

   2. manage   7. piece

   3. fib   8. badness

   4. durable   9. goodness

   5. connect   10. generous

F. Give an **antonym** for each of the following:

    1. inside   6. to tie

    2. to swell   7. to scatter

    3. to admit   8. to harm

    4. to believe   9. to release

    5. to resist   10. to forgive

G. In a language where there is no literal counterpart of the lexical item italicized, it may be necessary to use a **reciprocal** lexical item as a substitute. Rewrite the following in English using the **reciprocal** action rather than the action italicized here. Then translate the meaning into another language you speak using either one equivalent of the form given here or the **reciprocal**, whichever seems more natural.

    1. John *gave* the book to Bill.

    2. The people *followed* the king into the palace.

    3. When he *heard* that they were coming, he made preparations to receive them.

    4. Mary had *recieved* the flowers from a friend.

    5. Someone *told* her that the incident was not true.

    6. John *loaned* the book to Bill.

    7. Mary *borrowed* a pen from Jane.

    8. I want to *buy* a book from you.

    9. The drummer *led* the parade.

    10. Please *sell* me a book.

11. The French army *conquered* their enemies.

12. The police *pursued* the criminals.

H. The following contain **negative** statements. Restate as **affirmative** statements. Would the **negative** statement or the **affirmative** statement be more natural in a translation into your other language? Experiment with both and choose the most natural.

   1. He may *not* be *rich*, but he is a gentleman.

   2. We *could not deny* that this was the truth.

   3. He was *never unkind*.

   4. This is *not* a *small* mistake.

   5. Parking is *not forbidden* here.

I. In the following translations into English, the italicized words have been translated literally and may or may not be idiomatic or correct. As an exercise, change the italicized words in such a manner that **affirmative** sentences are made **negative** and **negative** sentences are made **affirmative**. Do not change the meaning of the sentences, but, if necessary, substitute words and change grammatical structures. In each case, compare and evaluate the two possible translations.

    Example: Drinking *is not* forbidden.
              Drinking *is allowed*.

   1. Smoking *is forbidden*.

   2. *Not taking* these factors *into account* in determining our economic policy would be utterly absurd.

   3. Supplements to this agreement *are only valid when* they are communicated in writing.

   4. He's *not* a *bad* mechanic.

5. "China is perhaps a vast country," Nehru declared, "but India is *not small* either."

6. He was already beginning to believe that *he would stay alive/he would survive*, but he refused to write an address to his men; he would not engage in propaganda in favor of the army.

7. That is all very well, but it's *little*.

8. He still *hasn't paid off* his car.

9. Applications received after the above date *will be disregarded*.

10. *Hardly* can *any* past generation compare in strength, talent, daring, and readiness for the sacrifice with the forward-looking man of today.

Chapter 8
Discovering Meaning
by Grouping and Contrast

The meaning of a lexical item can only be discovered by studying that particular item in contrast to other items which are closely related. There is no meaning apart from significant differences or contrasts. By grouping together words which are related to one another and then systematically looking at the contrast between these words, one is able to determine the meaning. The shared meaning components and the contrastive meaning components can thus be described more precisely. Lexical items are related in various ways and occur in various kinds of semantic sets.

Part-whole relations

One way in which languages group words is by the relationship known as **part-whole**. For example, in English *chin, cheek, forehead, nose,* and *ear* are all parts of the *head. Head, hand, neck, trunk, arms, legs,* and *feet* are **part** of the *body*. There are many sets made up of words in a **part-whole** relationship in any language. There will be sets of words describing parts of a house, parts of a machine, parts of a village, the structural organization of a country, political organizations, and many others. When a translator is studying the **part-whole** groupings of two languages, it will often become clear that there is no exact equivalent for some of the words. Some will be missing in one language or another. The reason for this is that various languages classify and subdivide broad areas of knowledge in different ways. Slavic languages, for example, do not have separate words for *arm* and *hand*. The Russian word *ruka* includes both the *arm* and the *hand*. In the same way, the word *noga* includes both *leg* and *foot*. One word in Russian covers the part of the body which in English is represented by two lexical items.

Contrastive pairs

Contrastive pairs may be very helpful in determining the meaning of particular words. For example, a person who is translating Russian terminology will need to discover the difference between a *party congress* and a *party conference,* a *worker* and an *employee,* a *technical school* and a *trade school,* and a *territory* and a *national area.* When the source language has closely related pairs like these, it will be very important for the translator to find the components of meaning which distinguish the one from the other if he is to translate accurately.

In English, the words *meat* and *flesh* represent distinctions which are not shared by many languages of the world where only one word is used to cover both areas of meaning. The word *meat* has an added component of meaning, i.e., *food.* The Aguaruna word *neje* must be used to translate both *flesh* and *meat.* The context will make it clear if food is meant.

The principle of **contrast** in identifying meaning is very important. However, before any two lexical items are to be compared, they must belong to a system of some kind. There would be no advantage to comparing the word *leg* with the word *house.* They do not make a pair for comparison. On the other hand, a great deal can be learned about the meaning of words by comparing *leg* with other body parts and comparing *house* with other kinds of buildings. Therefore, in order to study meaning, it is necessary to have words in sets which share some features of meaning and have some **contrastive** features as well.

There are pairs of words in all languages which differ from one another only by a single component of meaning. For example, *show* and *see* contrast only in that *show* has the additional meaning of *cause to.* That is, *show* means *to cause to see.* Other words with this same relationship would be *drop* and *fall* and *make* and *be.* *To drop* is *to cause to fall,* and *to make* is *to cause to be.* There is a common component of meaning, *causative,* in *show, drop,* and *make.* It is not uncommon that a language will have no exact equivalent, no word, for *show, drop,* and *make.* Rather, there will be some form which will indicate *causative* which will be used with *see, fall,* and *be.*

Componential analysis

The **meaning components** of words may also be more easily isolated by looking at lexical matrices. The pronominal systems of the source and receptor languages should be compared to see where there are differences between the two systems which might cause problems in translation. Once the systems are understood, there is the additional need to study the function of pronominal forms in the discourse of the language. (This will be dealt with further in chapter 12.) When displaying a lexical set in a chart, the words go into the boxes, and the columns are labeled by the **meaning components** which are the basis of contrast between the words. Notice, for example, Displays 8.1, 8.2, 8.3, and 8.4 of the subject pronoun systems of a number of languages (Strange and Deibler 1974:18-19):

English

	singular			plural
1ˢᵗ person	*I*			*we*
2ⁿᵈ person	*you*			
3ʳᵈ person	masculine	feminine	neuter	
	he	*she*	*it*	*they*

Display 8.1

Greek

	singular			plural		
1st person	εγώ			ἡμεῖς		
2nd person	σύ			ὑμεῖς		
3rd person	masculine	feminine	neuter	masculine	feminine	neuter
	αὐτός	αὐτή	αὐτό	αὐτοί	αὐταί	αὐτά

Display 8.2

Pidgin

	singular	dual	plural	
			inclusive	exclusive
1ˢᵗ person	*mi*	*mitupela*	*yumi*	*mipela*
2ⁿᵈ person	*yu*	*yutupela*	*yupela*	
3ʳᵈ person	*em*	*tupela*	*ol*	

Display 8.3

Upper Asaro

	singular	plural
1st person	*naza*	*laza*
2nd person	*gaza*	*lingine*
3rd person	*aza*	*ingine*

Display 8.4

Note that English and Greek distinguish gender. Pidgin of Papua New Guinea does not indicate gender but does have an additional member contrast, dual, and also differentiates *inclusive* and *exclusive* in *first person.* In Upper Asaro (Papua New Guinea), free pronouns distinguish neither *gender, dual member,* nor *inclusive* and *exclusive.*

It may be helpful to the translator to make displays which show the contrastive features of meaning for certain areas of vocabulary. Such mapping is arrived at by **componential analysis.** (For a more complete discussion, see Nida 1975a.) **Componential analysis** has often been used to analyze kinship systems (see Lounsbury 1956).

Certain areas of a language lend themselves to **componential analysis** better than other areas. It can be very helpful for those areas where it does apply. It is essential that the words have a relationship one to another which is based on shared and contrasting features. In order to do **componential analysis** of this kind, there needs to be some nonlinguistic behavior that shows the contrast between the symbols. For example, the contrast between generation in kinship can be observed, like the contrast between older and younger, and male and female.

Displays 8.5 and 8.6 show the mapping of English kinship terms and Aguaruna kinship terms. The lexical items are in the boxes of the

English	lineal		colineal		ablineal
	masculine	feminine	masculine	feminine	
second generation previous	*grandfather*	*grandmother*	*uncle*	*aunt*	*cousin*
previous generation	*father*	*mother*			
same generation	*ego*		*brother*	*sister*	
next generation	*son*	*daughter*	*nephew*	*niece*	
second generation following	*grandson*	*granddaughter*			

Display 8.5

chart and the labels show the contrast in meaning of these lexical items. Because we can correlate each lexical item with people in the nonlinguistic world and what they call one another or how they refer to one another, it is possible to analyze these terms.

Aguaruna

			Own lineage		Other lineage	
			masculine	feminine	feminine	masculine
second generation previous			*apach*	*dukuch*		*diich*
previous generation			*apag*	*dukug*		
same generation	ego	male	*yatsug*	*ubag*	*antsug*	*saig*
		female	*ubag*	*kaig*	*yuag*	*antsug*
next generation			*uchi*	*nawantu*	*nuwasa*	*ajika*
second generation following			*tijagki*			

Display 8.6

Notice that English has two words, *brother* and *sister*, which in Aguaruna are three words–*yatsug, ubag,* and *kaig.* Which of the three words is used depends on who is talking. A male calls his sister *ubag* and his brother *yatsug*; whereas, a female calls her sister *kaig* and her brother *ubag.* There are languages in which one cannot simply say *brother* because there may be two or more words to choose from.

Javanese divides this same area of meaning into three terms, but with different components. The forms are *mas* for "older brother," *embag* for "older sister," and *adig* for "younger sibling." A translator must carefully study and compare the kinship terminology of the source language and the receptor language. Each time a kinship term needs to be translated, the translator should consider carefully the referent in the nonlinguistic world, and how that person would be referred to, rather than simply translating literally the word that looks like the closest equivalent.

The kind of analysis we have been talking about points to the fact that each word is a bundle of **meaning components**, and that we can discover these by contrasting one word with another when these words are part of a system; that is, when they are related in some way. There would be no point in comparing words if there were not some **shared components.** In order to form a set, all of the words must contain a **generic component** in common. For example, all of the above have the **shared component** of KINSHIP. In the display which compared the set relating *sheep, horse,* etc., in chapter 7, the **generic component** that made it possible to compare all these was DOMESTICATED ANIMALS.

Kinds of meaning components

We can make a display for the English words *man, woman, boy,* and *girl,* because they are all human beings. They have a **generic component** which they share as the **central component**, HUMAN BEING (see Display 8.7).

	MALE	FEMALE
ADULT	*man*	*woman*
YOUNG	*boy*	*girl*

Display 8.7

In addition to the **central component**, each word will have **contrastive components** which distinguish it from all other words of the set. *Man* has the **contrastive components** ADULT and MALE, *woman* has the contrastive components ADULT and FEMALE, *boy* has the contrastive components YOUNG and MALE, and *girl* has the contrastive components YOUNG and FEMALE. Each word contrasts with every other word by at least one contrastive component.

The **meaning component** which unites any semantic set of this kind is called the **generic component** or the **central component.** The **meaning components** which distinguish them one from the other, and have been used as labels for the displays, are **contrastive components**. These are the components which help in distinguishing one word from another in the set.

Very often two languages will have the same set as far as the **generic component** is concerned, but the **contrastive components** will be different. There may be more lexical items or less lexical items in the set, and the **contrastive components** may not match. For example, the set for HUMAN in English is given in Display 8.7 and the set for Aguaruna is given in Display 8.8.

		MALE	FEMALE
ADULT	married	*aishmang*	*nuwa*
	unmarried	*datsa*	
YOUNG		*uchi*	*nuwauch* (female-little)

Display 8.8

Notice that there is an added contrast in Aguaruna for ADULT MALE in that there are two words, one having the added contrastive component of MARRIED and the other of UNMARRIED. Also notice that the contrast between ADULT FEMALE and YOUNG FEMALE can only be indicated by adding a suffix *-uch* to the word for ADULT FEMALE. This suffix means *little* so that the word for FEMALE CHILD is *little woman*. (However, the suffix is clearly related in form to the word for YOUNG MALE.)

In the previous chapter, we discussed hierarchical relationships between words; that is, taxonomies. Here, also, the taxonomy is based on the shared **generic components** and **contrastive components** which distinguish one lexical item from another. For example, notice Display 8.9 (Beckman and Callow 1974:70).

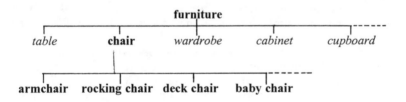

Display 8.9

Notice that all of the words in this set belong to the generic class of *furniture*. The **contrastive components** which separate *table, chair, wardrobe, cabinet,* and *cupboard* will have to do with the shape and the use of these particular pieces of furniture. *Chair* is then the **generic component** for *armchair, rocking chair, deck chair,* and *baby chair.* The meaning of these phrases again depends upon **contrastive components** which have to do with shape and use. If a translator is working on a text which includes terminology relating to the generic class of *furniture,* he will need to think very carefully through the **contrastive**

components in the source language vocabulary and in the receptor language vocabulary in order to choose the best equivalent. If there is no exact equivalent, he may need to include the right components by restating, as indicated previously, when the contrast is focal to the meaning of the sentence or paragraph. If not, he will simply choose the nearest equivalent without further detail.

In looking at the meaning of the lexical items which belong to the same semantic set, one needs to first identify the class to which it belongs (the generic term). Then the individual lexical items belonging to that class can be studied in contrast, the one with the other. For example, *command, promise, rebuke, ask, reply,* and *announce* are ways of speaking; that is, they all belong to the generic class termed *speak.* Because they belong to a common set, the meaning of each can be identified by contrast. Another language may also have a set of lexical items which are part of the semantic domain *speak,* but they may be very different from this set in English. For example, the Waiwai language of Guyana (data from Hawkins 1962) does not have verbs meaning *promise, praise,* and *deny.* The meaning is simply included in the content of the quotation which goes with the verb *say.*

The **generic**, or **central, meaning component** can be said to be more prominent than the other components. Within the word *boy*, the meaning component HUMAN BEING is more prominent than MALE or YOUNG which simply delimits HUMAN. In the sentence *"The boy is here,"* the component of HUMAN is used with natural prominence. However, in certain contexts, one of the contrastive components may come into focus and, therefore, carry marked prominence. For example, in the sentence *"The boy, not the girl, lost the race,"* marked prominence is on MALE which is a noncentral component; that is, it is a contrastive component. In the sentences *"A boy cannot accomplish this task. It will take a man to do it,"* marked prominence is on YOUNG (immaturity), the other noncentral component.

The components of meaning found in the word *boy* can be diagrammed as shown in Display 8.10:

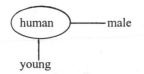

Display 8.10

The relationship between the two **contrastive components** and the **central component**, HUMAN, is one of delimitation, that is, HUMAN is delimited to refer only to a HUMAN that is YOUNG and MALE. The relationship between the **central component** and the **contrastive components** is always one of delimitation; the **contrastive components** delimit (narrow down the meaning of) the **central component.**

In addition to the **central component** and the **contrastive components,** there are often **incidental** (or supplementary) **components.** Their presence or absence is **incidental** for the contrast needed to differentiate a certain set of terms. At another level of study (more specific), these same components may be **contrastive components.** What is **generic, contrastive,** or **incidental** depends on the level of focus of the analysis. It depends on what level of the taxonomic hierarchy at which one is looking.

For example, in contrasting *kinds of furniture,* it is not relevant if the object has *arms* or not. *Chair* is *something to sit on* in contrast to *table, bed,* etc. However, if one is describing the semantic set *kinds of chairs,* then having *arms* is no longer incidental but is contrastive. Also, in moving up from *kinds of furniture* to a more generic class of *human artifacts,* the component *to sit on* which was contrastive for *furniture* is no longer contrastive but only incidental. Since the translator is concerned with the meaning of words, he will often need to investigate minute differences between words in a semantic set. It is the contrastive components that he will want to focus on.

EXERCISES – Discovering Meaning by Grouping and Contrast

A. Compare the words for *parts of a house* in two languages which you speak. If possible, get someone else to list all the parts they can think of in one language, and a different person to list all the parts they can think of in a second language. Then compare the two lists.

B. Diagram the system of contrasts for the kinship terms of another language which you speak. Compare this system with English and Aguaruna presented in this chapter. What differences do you find?

C. In English, the words *view, gaze, stare, glare, peek, peer,* and *glance* are all *ways of looking at things.* What are the **contrastive components** (differences of meaning) which separate them in meaning?

D. List the words which describe *ways of looking at things* in the other language which you know. Do not translate from English, just list all the words from your mind. What are the **contrastive components** which separate them one from another?

E. List the words that describe *ways of speaking* in a language other than English. What are the **contrastive components** (differences of meaning) which separate them from one another?

Chapter 9
Mismatching of Lexical Systems between Languages

Throughout the previous chapters, the mismatching between the lexical items of two languages has been mentioned repeatedly. The purpose of this chapter is to emphasize this mismatch with more examples and discussion. It is this very mismatch which is the challenge for the translator who must find the best way to communicate the meaning of the source language in a receptor language which is often very different in its lexical inventory and different in how that inventory is grouped and divided.

Mismatching of reference

One important aspect of the meaning of a word is its reference–the THING, EVENT, or ATTRIBUTE to which the word refers. Speakers of the language "know the meaning" of a word because of their interaction with the THING, EVENT, or ATTRIBUTE to which it refers. Contrast between members of a semantic set cannot be studied without some means of discovering the contrast that exists in the referential world (the world which the members of the speech community are experiencing, doing things in, etc., and about which they are talking). We have already noted that componential analysis depends on nonlinguistic reference, knowing what is being referred to. Even though the same THINGS, EVENTS, and ATTRIBUTES may exist in the referential world, the systems of reference do not match one-to-one across languages. Languages arbitrarily divide the meaning differently. Notice in Display 9.1 (on the next page) the contrast between English, Mbembe of Nigeria, Hausa, and Greek (Barnwell 1980:24-25). In some cases English uses more than one word to refer to certain items and the other languages use only one word; but in other instances the opposite is true in that English has more than one word for items requiring only one word in the other languages.

97

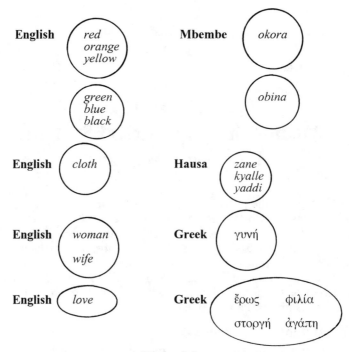

Display 9.1

The following example shows that for the one English word *carry* the Tzeltal language of Mexico has many specific terms. However, there is no general word for *carry*.

jelup'in	to carry across the shoulders
nol	to carry in the palm of the hand
chup	to carry in a pocket or pouch
chuy	to carry in a bag
lats'	to carry under the arm
pach	to carry on the head
toy	to carry aloft
yom	to carry different items together
lut'	to carry with tongs
pet	to carry in the arms
cats'	to carry between one's teeth
lup	to carry on a spoon
lat'	to carry in a container
cuch	to carry on the back

In translating from English into Tzeltal, the translator will have to choose from all the words for *carry* each time he is translating the one English word. The text will need to be studied carefully in order to choose the correct word. However, when translating from Tzeltal into English there is only one word to choose from, the word *carry*. This will be used unless the manner in which the object is being carried is crucial to the focus or theme of the context. Then a descriptive phrase will need to be added in English to make clear the **contrastive meaning components** found in the Tzeltal words. For example, if *pach* occurs in the Tzeltal text, but how the object is carried is not focal, then *carry* would be sufficient in the English translation. However, if the manner in which the object is carried is important to the passage, the translator would add the **contrastive meaning component**, *on the head.*

The Tlingit of Alaska have no general word for *swim*, but instead they have many specific words, depending on the kind of swimming involved, the participants involved, and their singularity or plurality. Note the following (data from Constance Naish):

di-taach (sing.) *ka-doo-ya-taach* (plu.)	(of human being)
ya-x'aak (sing.) *ka-doo-ya-x'aak* (plu.)	(of large fish or sea mammal swimming under water)
ya-heen	(of shoal of fish swimming under water)
ya-hoo (sing.) *ya-kwaan* (plu.)	(of animal or human swimming on the surface)
ji-di-hoo (sing.) *ji-dzi-kwaan* (plu.)	(of animal or human swimming on the surface aimlessly, in circles)
si-hoo (sing.) *si-kwaan* (plu.)	(of bird on the surface)
ya-dzi-aa (sing.) *ya-si-xoon* (plu.)	(of bird or fish swimming under water with head emerging)
dli-tsees (sing.) *ka-doo-ya-tsees* (plu.)	(of something swimming fast and powerfully, especially sea mammal)
ya-ya-goo (sing.) *ya-si-goo* (plu.)	(of porpoises swimming as a school)

In translating from English into Tlingit, the translator would need to be very careful to choose the lexical items which have the **meaning**

components which match the information in the text being translated. A person translating into his own language would know instinctively which would be correct, but he would need to study the source language English text and situation to find the correct word to use in the translation. He cannot ignore these distinctions even though English has only one word for *swim*.

Mismatching of semantic sets

The lexical items of a language represent a great network of interrelated meanings often called a *cognitive network*. Different approaches to the analysis of this network will highlight different aspects of the semantic structure of the language. We have already looked at some of the ways in which one can look at part of the lexicon. Basic to all study of the lexicon is the principle that meaning can be discovered only in terms of semantic contrast. As translators study the meaning of words in either the source language or the receptor language, they are dealing with a system.

Lexical items may be related to one another in various ways. They may have no meaning components in common, being related to one another simply in that they occur together when people are talking about a certain topic. The words are grouped together in the minds of the members of the community using them, because the THINGS and EVENTS referred to are often associated with one another. For example, each language has a vocabulary which will be used when talking about the topic *agriculture*. The English words *plow, plant, harvest, wheat, corn, hoe, binder, thrashing machine*, etc., all belong to this **topic**. There will be subgroups when talking about specific kinds of agriculture. No two languages will have completely matching vocabularies which are used to talk about *agriculture*. There will be many more lexical items in one language than in another. The relationship between lexical items which are related in this way is rather loose. Nevertheless, this loose relationship is one of the elements of cohesion within a text as we shall discuss later in chapter 31.

In addition to this rather loose relationship, there will be subgroups of vocabulary which are very closely related to one another and tied together by some overlap of meaning components. For example, a set of words which would occur when talking about *machinery used in agriculture* would include *plow, harrow, tractor, combine*, etc., in English. These words make up a subset under the broad topic, *agriculture*. When discussing *agriculture*, another subset would be words such as *branch, trunk, root, seed,* and *fruit* which all have a very close relationship to one another in that they are all part of a *tree*. There is a **part-whole** relationship (see page 87 above) between each of these words and the word *tree*.

But even a simple set of words referring to *parts of a tree* will not match exactly from one language to another. In Isnag (Philippines, data from Rudy Barlaan), the *trunk* of a tree is thought of as two parts, rather than only one as in English. The lower part is called *pungut* and the upper part *arutang*. In the Pangasinan language (Philippines), a bamboo plant is divided into three main parts — *lamut* 'roots', *siŋig* 'trunk', and *bwik* 'hair'. The "hair" consists of *bulawit* 'branches' and *boluŋ* 'leaves'.

Some languages do not have as many specific words for *ways of speaking* as others have. Often direct quotations are used, and the form of the quotation carries the meaning rather than a more specific "speaking" word. In some Amerindian languages, there are no words for *command, beg, beseech, ask, tell, proclaim, publish, question, discuss, marvel, deny, permit, desire,* etc. Rather these are expressed by direct quotations. For example, in Waiwai (Guiana), as noted in chapter 2, *"You promised to come,"* would need to be translated *" 'I will certainly come,' you said." "He praised the canoe,"* would be translated *" 'It's a wonderful canoe,' he said"* (Hawkins 1962:164).

The translator needs to match the system of one language, against the system of the second language. Even when there seems to be a word which is equivalent, there may be some components of the word which are different from the components of equivalent words in the source language. For example, Nida (1975a:58-60) uses as an illustration the set *whisper, babble, murmur, sing,* and *hum.* He says that for *whisper* "there may be very low, scarcely audible whispers, in contrast with very loud whispers, but all the various degrees of loudness are subsumed under the designation of *whisper.*" Hwang (1979:1) says:

> ...the most closely corresponding Korean term for *whisper, soksakita,* has as its most important component "minus loudness," in addition to other components given by Nida, "verbal," "nonmusical pitch," and "voiceless." Thus, *soksakita* implies that the speaker says something very softly, close to the hearer's ear, so that a third person would not hear what is being said. Likewise, the semantic components of *babble* and *murmur* in English are not equivalent to those of the Korean terms. *Ongalkølita* 'babble' and *jungølkølita* 'murmur' may both be verbal and pseudoverbal, combinations of consonants and vowels, but without meaning, while in English the former is pseudoverbal and the latter verbal.

In Bora (Peru, data from Wesley Thiesen), there are a number of verb roots which are all used to talk about *coming* and *going;* that is, "movement from one place to another." However, these words do not match the English usage of *come* and *go*. They must be understood in relationship to one another in order to discover the meaning.

peé	go
-te-	go to
uujéte	going arrive at
tsaa-	come
-ua-	come to
wajtsɨ	coming arrive at
-je-	come back to

In Bora, verbs and verb suffixes of direction must be used in relation to the speaker's location. *Come* is used only to refer to the place from where you are speaking. *Go* is used in every other situation. So you can only say *come to my house* if you are speaking from your house. If you are somewhere else you must say *go to my house*. When you say that someone *came* to a given place, it implies that you were there. This means that in many places where *come* is used in English, it must be translated *go* in order to make sense in Bora. However, when the speaker (or writer) is reporting what happened, it depends on the location of the reporter as to which form is used. The translator will not translate *come* from English with *tsaa-* each time, but will study the context to be sure which of the words in the set should be used. The word which a Bora speaker finds most accurate and natural is the correct one.

Mundurukú (Brazil, data from Marjorie Crofts) has two verbs for *come*. *Xe* is used when the speaker is at home and *ajẽm* is used when the speaker is not at home. Maxacalí (also Brazil) has three spatial settings which determine the use of motion verbs. These settings are home area, place-in-passing, and the area of travel between these (see Popovich 1967 for details).

Almost any semantic set which we might compare between two languages will have some mismatch. Kinship terms will not only mismatch, as seen in the previous chapter, but kinship terms also often have extended meanings which cause additional problems in translation. In some languages, kinship terms refer only to blood relatives and are never used in extended ways. However, in English it is not uncommon for someone to call a boy *son* if he does not know his name. But the Piro of Peru do not speak in this manner to those not specifically their own children, and to do so would imply a blood relationship. In a similar circumstance, where one wants to address a younger person in a loving manner, the Piro would use their word for *young man.* Some languages would use the word *cousin*, and others would simply use the word *friend.* One needs to know how kinship terms are used as vocatives; that is, in what extended ways they may be used to address people.

Hwang (1979:2) notes the following for Korean:

> Kinship terms in Korean often have an extended usage outside the kinship system. Thus a male friend of the family (or the parent) may be called an uncle, *ajøssi,* and a female friend an aunt, *ajumøni.* Koreans do not normally distinguish sex for younger siblings, *tongsäng,* but sex distinction for older siblings is obligatory since there is no cover term for them. In fact, there are four terms for older siblings depending on the sex of the ego: *oppa* 'older brother (when the ego is female),' *ønni* 'older sister (female ego),' *nuna* 'older sister (male ego),' and hyøng 'older brother (male ego).'

Cultural mismatch of lexical items

We have already stressed the fact that different languages have different concentrations of vocabulary depending on the culture, geographical location, and the worldview of the people. Because of the different geographical situation, in one language there may be a great concentration of vocabulary that has to do with agriculture, in another a great concentration of vocabulary that has to do with fishing. How these sets of vocabulary relate to one another and can be analyzed has already been discussed. There is, however, an additional aspect to this which is very important to the translator.

At first glance words in one language may look like they correspond to words in another and may even have the same central and contrastive components of meaning, and yet not be equivalent. Notice, for example, the three words which are roughly equivalent in meaning pictured in Display 9.2 (Strange and Deibler 1974:11).

house   oikos   numuno

Display 9.2

The three words *house, oikos,* and *numuno* all refer to more or less the same THING. In all three cases, the generic meaning would be BUILDING, and the contrastive component would be THAT WHICH PEOPLE LIVE IN. However, these words conjure up completely different pictures in the mind of the speakers of the language because of the difference in the cultural objects to which are being referred. A word often does not mean *exactly* the same thing as its equivalent in another language. The **central component** may be the same, and even the **contrastive components** which distinguish it from other words in the language may be the same. However, there may be some other components which were not contrastive when comparing words in a single language which will be very important when comparing words between two languages.

For example, the Greek word *oikos* is used in the sentence *Peter went up on the housetop to pray.* A translation into languages of Papua New Guinea may result in a very distorted understanding if simply translated with the word *numuno.* The round thatched roof would be an inappropriate place to climb up on in order to pray. The component of the meaning of *oikos* which has to do with the fact that the building has a *flat roof* is not contrastive in Greek culture but is contrastive when comparing buildings in Greece with buildings in Papua New Guinea. What may be considered only **incidental components** in the analysis of lexical items in a single language may be **contrastive components** when comparing lexical items across languages.

A translator is not simply dealing with concepts in a system in one language, but rather concepts in systems in two languages. Each language will fence off and label a particular area of reality or experience differently. The translator wants to be as accurate as possible, and so must consider each word carefully in the system until he finds the word or phrase which most accurately equates with the lexical item used in the source language text.

For example, a translator who is wanting to translate the concept which is represented by the Russian word *gidroplan* may find that the English dictionary has many words such as *water plane, sea plane, flying boat, hydro plane, speed boat,* and so forth. He will need to use his knowledge about boats and airplanes, as well as his knowledge of how to compare words in order to discover the components of meaning which are relevant. Such comparison will be very helpful in identifying the word which is wanted. However, it is important to remember that the equivalence desired between the two languages is to be found, not in the language itself, but in identifying the item in the real world and in finding the proper word or words to use to refer to it.

Further difficulties for the translator arise from the fact that concepts in a system frequently occur in clusters, and sometimes also combine or co-occur with other groups of semantically related words. A car owner's manual will inevitably refer to all the interrelated parts of a car which concern the owner, and a study of weaponry will inevitably refer to many kinds of missiles and guns. No special analysis is needed to distinguish between *sticks* and *stones* in any one language since the differences are clear enough. But differentiating words of closely associated meanings is another matter.

Translating words which belong to a set representing a certain area of meaning in the source language may be very difficult when the receptor language system does not match. For example, in certain Slavic languages, *lieutenant general* is the second lowest of the generals. This would be equivalent to a *major general* in the United States. In these same languages, a *major general* is the lowest ranking of the generals or equal to a *brigadier general* in the United States. No matter how these are translated into English, with the use of either the literal equivalence or the U.S. equivalent, the translation will suggest parallel systems of military rank when, as a matter of fact, the systems are not parallel. It is important, however, that the translator be aware of the mismatch between systems.

Differentiating words of closely associated meanings is possible only by contrast. Meanings exist only in terms of a **systematic contrast** with other words which share certain features in common with them and contrast in what they refer to or in what situation they are used.

EXERCISES – Mismatching of Lexical Systems between Languages

A. List all the color words you know in a language other than English. Compare them with English colors.

B. List all the words for the set *ways to carry* in a language other than English. What components of meaning distinguish them from one another?

C. List all the words for the set *manner in which liquids move* in a language other than English. After you have your list complete, compare the words one with another to identify the meaning differences. Then compare them with the English set *drip, leak, spray, splash, pour, flow, gush,* and *squirt.* How do the meanings differ between the two languages?

D. In the following, the Hindi data is given first, then a translation into English using at literal translation of "come" and "go" in English is given, and finally a freer English equivalent is given. What components of meaning other than movement are carried in the morphemic representation "come" and "go" in Hindi? (Data on Hindi taken from "On the Deictic Use of 'Coming' and 'Going' in Hindi" by Anjani Kumar Sinha, University of Chicago in *Papers From the Eighth Regional Meeting*, Chicago Linguistic Society, April 14-16, 1972.)

1. Uskā laṛkā widwān nikal *āyā*. His son a scholar *came out*. (His son *turned out* to be a scholar.)

2. Uskā laṛkā nidar nikal *āyā*. His son fearless *came out*. (His son *turned out* to be fearless.)

3. Uskā laṛkā bewkūf nikal *gayā*. His son a fool *went out*. (His son *turned out* to be a fool.)

4. Uskā laṛkā badmaš nikal *gayā*. His son a rascal *went out*. (His son *turned out* to be a rascal.)

5. Musībat mẽ uskī buddhi nikal *āyī*. In crisis, his wisdom *came out*. (In the crisis *he was* very wise.)

6. Musībat mẽ uskī buddhi nikal *gayī*. In crisis, his wisdom *went out*. (In the crisis *he was* very unwise.)

7. Cījõ ke dām upar caṛh *gaye*. The price of things *went up*. (The price of things *went up*.)

8. Cījõ ke dām nīce utar *āye*. The price of things *came down*. (The price of things *went down*.)

9. Bahut dinõ ke bād mandi ke ant mẽ cījõ ke dām upar caṛh *āye*. At the end of the depression, after a long time, the prices *came up*. (At the end of the depression, after a long time, the prices *went up*.)

10. Bahut dinõ ke bād mahagī ke ant mẽ cījõ ke dām nīce utar *āye*. At the end of the inflation, after a long time, the prices *came down*. (At the end of the inflation, after a long time, the prices *went down*.)

11. Uskā buxār caṛh *gayā.* His temperature *went up.* (His tempera-
     ture *went up.*)

12. Uskā baxār utar *āyā.* His temperature *came down.* (His tem-
     perature *went down.*)

13. Wo brāhman nikal *āyā.* A Brahmin he *came out.* (He *turned
     out* to be a Brahmin.)

14. Wo harijan nikal *gayā.* An untouchable he *went out.* (He
     turned out to be an untouchable.)

E. List the key words for persons of political authority in your
   country. Compare these with the following used during the Roman
   empire for the semantic set *ruler.*

   emperor - over several countries
   king - over one country
   governor - over a region of a country
   tetrarch - over a fourth part of a region of a country

Chapter 10
Multiple Senses of Lexical Items

Defining "secondary sense"

In the previous chapters, lexical items have been looked at from the point of view of the meaning components of which a given word is composed. For the most part, this meaning is discovered by contrasting one lexical item with another in a system. Pairs of words which have some meaning in common may be contrasted; whole semantic sets may be contrasted. Taxonomic studies, componential analyses, the study of antonyms and synonyms, and the "unpacking" of the concepts or meaning components contained in a word all deal with the fact that the same meaning may occur as part of the meaning of various words. So far, we have been talking only about one sense of a given word, the primary meaning. However, most words have more than one **sense**.

As was noted in chapter 1, it is characteristic of words that a single lexical item may have several meanings other than that which most readily comes to mind. These meanings are often called **secondary meanings** or **secondary senses**. The **primary sense** is the meaning suggested by the word when it is used alone. It is the first meaning or usage which a word will suggest to most people when the word is said in isolation. It is the meaning learned early in life and is likely to have reference to a physical situation. But the same word may have a different meaning when used in context with other words. For example, the word *run* in isolation will mean something like *move rapidly by moving the legs rapidly.* But if the same word is used in the context of *river* as in *the river runs, run* has nothing to do with legs or rapidity, although the idea of motion is still there. *Run* in the context of *river* means *to flow.* **Secondary senses** are dependent on the context in which a word is used. A speaker of Mbembe (Nigeria) will tell you that *chi* means *eat*. This is the **primary meaning**. But a speaker of Mbembe will also use this same word in phrases like (from Barnwell 1980:32):

109

MBEMBE	LITERAL ENGLISH	IDIOMATIC ENGLISH
chi akpuka	eat money	(embezzle)
chi eden	eat path	(go first)
chi ngwo	eat bribe	(take a bribe)
chi akpen	eat life	(live it up)
chi onong	eat person	(cheat someone)

When the word *chi* occurs with the word *akpuka*, it means *to embezzle*; when it occurs with the word *eden*, it means *to go first*; when it occurs with the word *ngwo*, it means *to marry*, etc. The meaning changes depending on the words with which *chi* occurs. The words *akpuka, eden, ngwo, akpen,* and *onong* are all *collocates* of the word *chi*. A word which occurs along side of another word is called a *collocate*, i.e., they co-occur.

A person who knows a language very well usually knows immediately by the other words which occur in the phrase or sentence which **sense** of the word is being signaled. Persons who are learning a second language often have a great deal of trouble learning to use a word in its many **secondary senses**. It is usually much easier to translate the **primary sense** of a lexical item than a **secondary sense**. This is because the receptor language will often have a lexical equivalent for the **primary meaning** which very nearly matches the meaning of the lexical item in the source language. However, the **secondary senses** of those same two words will probably not match at all. We noted an example in chapter one of *run*, where the English uses of *run* each had to be translated with a different word in Spanish:

ENGLISH	SPANISH
boy *runs*	boy runs
motor *runs*	motor functions
nose *runs*	nose drips

Any word used in a nonprimary sense will probably not be translated by the word in the receptor language which is equivalent to its primary sense, but by a different word. For example, the **primary**

sense of *key* would be translated into Spanish with *llave*. But notice the following list which shows how they differ in translating **secondary senses**:

ENGLISH TO SPANISH

key	llave (of a lock)
key	clave (of a code)
key	tecla (of a typewriter)

SPANISH TO ENGLISH

llave	key
llave	faucet
llave	wrench

Analyzing senses of words

The process for discovering the various **senses** of words is rather complicated but can be very crucial for making dictionaries, learning a second language, and may also be helpful to the translator when no dictionaries are available which give an adequate description of the **senses** of words in the language. (See Beekman and Callow 1974, chapters 4 and 5 for more detail.) A translator who is truly bilingual in the source and receptor languages will usually recognize a **nonprimary sense**. Nevertheless, there is always the possibility that a literal translation of a word may be used in a **secondary sense**. This literal translation sets up a strange collocation and wrong meaning.

Step 1. Collecting data. One must first collect as many examples of the use of the word as possible. If a person knows the language, he can simply think of all the possible combinations with other words. If not, he will need to find the word in as many texts as possible. A concordance done on the computer will greatly speed up the search. A person who is learning a language, or hoping to make a dictionary, will want to begin early in his research to collect data on each word of the language, building up more words and more examples of their co-occurrence with other words. The goal is to list as many collocates as possible. For our purposes, we shall now assume that we have found the following (the examples are those used by Beekman and Callow 1974, chapter 6):

The bird runs.	The paint runs.
The boy runs.	The solder runs.
The car runs.	The sore runs.
The eye runs.	The stocking runs.
The dog runs.	The stream runs.
The faucet (tap) runs.	The ivy runs.
The jelly runs.	The watch runs.
The nose runs.	The woman runs.

Step 2. Sort the collocates into generic classes. Each grammatical form should by analyzed separately. In this example, we have used only intransitive verb forms. If the noun *run* occurred, this noun form would need to be separated and analyzed separately. One begins by making best guesses, refining the analysis as he goes.

1. Animals (bird, dog, horse)
2. Humans (boy, woman)
3. Parts of the body (eye, nose, sore)
4. Solids (jelly, solder)
5. Liquids (faucet, paint, stream)
6. Vines (ivy, bean plant)
7. Knitted clothing (stocking)
8. Mechanical objects (car, watch)

Notice that, although **animals** and **humans** are given as two different generic classes, the sense of *run* is the same for both. Therefore, a more generic class may be given – **animate beings with legs.** Also *eye, nose,* and *sore* are classified as **parts of the body.** But in connection with *run,* it is not the **part of the body** but the **liquid** that comes from the *eye, nose,* or *sore* which *runs.* Therefore, they can be grouped together with **liquids.** *Jelly* and *solder* are **liquids** also in that they *run* even though they become solids later. Therefore, they are also grouped with **liquids.** This new classification would be as follows:

1. Animate beings with legs, e.g., *bird, dog, horse, boy, woman*

2. Liquids, e.g., *stream, paint, faucet, eye, nose, sore, jelly, solder*

3. Vines, e.g., *ivy, bean plant*

4. Knitted clothing, e.g., *stocking*

5. Self-powered mechanical objects, e.g., *car, watch*

Step 3. Regroup the contexts according to the collocates which belong to the same generic classes as follows:

Animate beings with legs:
The bird runs.
The boys runs.
The dog runs.
The horse runs.
The woman runs.

Vines:
The ivy runs.
The bean plant runs.

Knitted clothing:
The stocking runs.

Liquids:
The nose runs.
The faucet runs.
The stream runs.
The sore runs.
The eye runs.
The paint runs.
The solder runs.
The jelly runs.

Self-powered mechanical objects:
The watch runs.
The car runs.

Step 4. List and label the senses of the word. Once the data is reorganized by the generic classes of the collocates, it is much easier to see the senses of the word. For *animate beings with legs,* the meaning seems to be *to move oneself from one place to another rapidly;* for *liquids,* simply *to flow;* for *vines,* the meaning is *to grow,* etc.

Sense 1. to move oneself from one place to another rapidly
(or to move rapidly using feet) (of animate beings with legs)

Sense 2. to flow (of liquids)

Sense 3. to grow in a spreading way (of vines)

Sense 4. to develop a defect involving movement of threads
(of knit clothing)

Sense 5. to function effectively (of mechanical objects or motors)

This general method can be helpful in looking for translation equivalents in that the primary meaning will probably be translated by the literal correspondence, the second sense listed above may need to be translated with the corresponding word for *flow*, the third sense with a word for *grow*, etc. By analyzing the senses of the source language in this way, the translators will gain ideas for possible translations.

Translating the various senses

If the above analysis were of the receptor language word, that is, if one were translating into English, the analysis would point up the necessity of including, in the context of *run,* a collocate from the generic class mentioned in order to insure the correct meaning. When the meaning is signaled by the context in which the word occurs, it is very important that the context be built into the translation.

The word *dress* occurs in the following contexts, each signaling a different sense of the English word. It is possible to restate the meaning in English.

1. I *dressed* myself.	I *put* my *clothes on.*
2. I *dressed* a chicken.	I *defeathered a chicken and took its innards out.*
3. I *dressed* timber.	I *made* the logs *smooth.*
4. The soldiers *dressed* rank.	The soldiers *lined up in straight* rows.
5. I *dressed* the wound.	I *put medicine on and bandaged* the wound.

The idea of "making or preparing something in a presentable form" is common to all the senses. The common thread of meaning shows that we are dealing with a single word rather than with two or more separate words (Beekman and Callow 1974:97), but each sense will result in a different form for the translation. Note the following equivalents in Pidgin of Papua New Guinea to the preceding sentences:

PIDGIN	LITERAL ENGLISH
1. Mi *putim* klos.	I *put* clothes.
2. Mi *redim* kokoruk bilong kukim.	I *readied* a chicken for cooking.
3. Mi *plenim* plang.	I *planed* a plank.
4. Ol ami oli *stretim* lain bilong ol.	The army *straightened* the line of them.
5. Mi *putim marasin* long sua.	I *put medicine* on the sore.

The Spanish equivalent, i.e., the translation into Spanish, is given below. Notice that only the primary meaning of *dress* can be translated with the word *vestirse*.

SPANISH	LITERAL ENGLISH
1. Yo me *vestí*.	I myself *dressed*.
2. Yo *labraba* madera.	I *worked* lumber.
3. Yo *pelaba* y *destripaba* la gallina.	I *plucked* and *cleaned* the hen.
4. Los soldados se *alinearon*.	The soldiers *lined up*.
5. Yo *vendaba* la herida.	I *bandaged* the wound.

A secondary sense will almost always need to be translated by a different word than the word which denotes the primary sense.

In the Aguaruna language of Peru there are many words which refer to entities in the spirit world. They include *iwanch, wakan, tsugki, pasun, pasuk, nugkui, pagki, iwaji, ajutam,* and others. All belong to a common semantic set and can be contrasted, and components of meaning analyzed as presented in the previous chapter. The nuclear component of each would be SPIRIT BEING. *Iwanch* has the contrastive component *evil, wakan* has the contrastive component of being a *human, soul,* etc. That is, each of these contrasts with the others in the semantic set. But in addition, each of these words has a **primary sense** and a number of **secondary senses**. Some of them are being used in a **secondary sense** when they are included as part of the semantic set, SPIRIT BEING. For example, *pagki* has the **primary meaning** of *boa constrictor*. However, it also has a **secondary meaning** of *spirit being which lives in water and is evil* in contrast to *tsugki*, which is a *spirit being which lives in the water but is good*. A word may be a member of various semantic sets. In some, it will be used in its **primary sense** and in others in one of its **secondary senses**. This, of course, adds to the complications of translation. (See Displays 10.1 and 10.2.)

In the display which diagrams the **senses** of the word *wakan*, notice that nine **senses** have been identified. (The kind of analysis which leads to this type of charting is described in Nida 1964:99-113. Nida's analysis of the English word *spirit* is included to show the contrast with *wakan*.) In the display, the senses are numbered at the bottom with the primary sense as number one. In the discussion of secondary senses above, we showed how the sense is

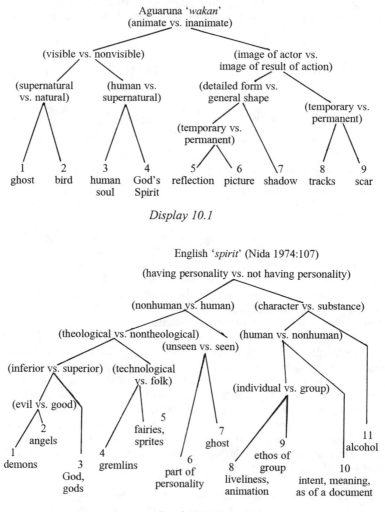

Display 10.1

Display 10.2

signaled by the collocates that go with the word. However, it may not always be a specific word that signals the meaning but the presence of some signal of the components of meaning within the word when used in that **sense**. For example, to signal the sense of *bird*, rather than *ghost*, for *wakan*, something in the context must signal *natural* rather than *supernatural* since *supernatural (ghost)* is the primary meaning of *wakan*.

Wakan has at least nine **senses**. But the meaning will be signaled only if the translation into Aguaruna has built into the context the semantic components that will trigger the meaning. If not, the wrong meaning may result even when the right word is used. For example, if we use the collocate *tiger* for the context, the meaning would still be ambiguous. It could refer to his ghost, his reflection, his shadow, a scar made by him, his tracks, or a picture of him. If an Aguaruna said, *"I saw a tiger's wakan."* it would immediately be understood that it was a ghost, i.e., a supernatural being in the form of a tiger. The meaning *supernatural* is signaled by the verb *see* which indicates a *ghost*. If someone said, *"There is a tiger's wakan in our new book,"* it would immediately signal a picture, since it must be inanimate, an image of detailed form, and permanent. The collocate *book* signaled this. The choice of meaning is signaled by including in the context some other lexical item which will activate the semantic components indicated at the nodes of the chart. *John had a tiger's wakan on his leg* is understood to be a *scar* because the location *leg* indicates this sense. *John saw a tiger's wakan in the sand* would mean *tracks* because of the collocate *sand*.

The two main rules about **secondary senses** are (1) the **secondary senses** of the source language can probably not be translated literally but will need to be understood in order to find a good equivalent, and (2) the **secondary sense** of words in the receptor language will only mean what they are intended to mean if the context includes collocates which will signal the sense desired.

Ambiguity caused by senses not clearly signaled

It should also be noted that lack of context will lead to **ambiguity** in many cases. For example, the phrase *this suit is lighter* is **ambiguous**. It could mean that *the suit does not weigh as much as another* or that *the color of the suit is not as dark as another*. The **ambiguity** comes because of the two senses and lack of context to make it unambiguous. It would be possible to simply say *this suit is lighter in weight* or *this suit is lighter in shade*. However, it is more likely that something else in the context will signal the right meaning. There is no confusion of sense between *this suit is lighter, since it is made of vicuna cloth* and *this suit is lighter than even those spring pastels*. It is often a wider context that signals the secondary sense. But there must be something that causes the reader (audience) to know which sense is meant.

It is important to know the meaning components of the primary sense. For example, in the Chuj language of Guatemala, the word *say* turned out to be a problem for the translator. The word *say* was used in the sentence, *"The people said, 'This man is God.' "* In the story where this was used, the man was not God. The people said it, but it was not true. However, what the translator did not know was that the word *say* in its primary sense includes the component of *the truth*. The word *say* in Chuj means *to say the truth*; that is, the unmarked meaning. In order to indicate that what they said was not true, *say* must be marked. So it had to be translated *"The people said falsely, 'He is a God,' "* to avoid wrong meaning.

No equivalent lexical items will have the same senses from language to language. Even primary meanings that look the same at first may have additional components that can distort the meaning if used without care. One of the most important things in translation is to be sure that the context is sufficient to mark the meaning desired. **Ambiguities** often arise when the translator knows only one or two senses of a word and does not know the context needed to signal the correct meaning.

Notice the three Aguaruna sentences below:

1. *pagki tepawai* (boa lies)
2. *pagki wajawai* (boa stands)
3. *pagki ayawai* (boa they-are)

The first means that *there is a boa snake*, the second that *there is a rainbow*, and the third that *there are water spirits*. All of them use the word *pagki* which has the primary sense of *boa*. This is the unmarked meaning which all native speakers would give as the meaning of *pagki*. But as soon as the word is used in other contexts, the collocates give the other senses. A translator working on the Biblical account of Noah was trying to translate the statement made by God, "I will set my bow (rainbow) in the cloud." The only lexical item in the language for rainbow is the word *pagki*. In order for it to mean rainbow, the word *wajawai* (stand) must be in the context. The first suggestion for translation was "I will cause a boa to stand in the clouds," but the addition of a causative made it refer to an animate object, namely a snake. Also, rainbows cannot be possessed in Aguaruna. The final solution came in using the sentence, "I will cause you to see it, the standing boa." The context *standing* had to be present and other possible misunderstandings eliminated.

EXERCISES – Multiple Senses of Lexical Items

A. In each of the following, the word which is in italics is being used in a **secondary sense**. What is the meaning, and what is the thread of meaning that links it to the **primary sense**?

   1. He *carries* many happy memories with him.

   2. The government has once again *jacked up* the price of oil.

   3. "I've got to *catch* a plane," he said, looking at his watch.

   4. Children *adopt* values and attitudes of their parents.

   5. He had to *carry* the humiliation with him the rest of his life.

   6. They are supposed to *drill* the soldiers regularly.

   7. The work stoppage by municipal employees virtually *crippled* this city.

   8. The working conditions of Granit *fall behind* those of the more modern El Reno.

   9. An *island* for newborn care should be provided in the delivery room.

  10. They aren't *stirred-up* enough about inflation.

B. In the following sentences, the meaning is **ambiguous** because the word which is in italics has at least two senses. Rewrite with two sentences, one adding enough context to signal one meaning, and a second adding enough context to signal a second meaning. Do not change the words given below, only add context.

   1. I bought a book *on* Broadway. (location, subject matter)

   2. I *saw* what he was talking about. (object, idea)

   3. I *ran* into Mr. Jones yesterday.

   4. John *stood up* for Mary.

   5. John *rose* rapidly.

C. Show how the sentences in B would best be translated into another language you speak so as to communicate the two meanings.

D. Choose a word from your mother-tongue (*run, eat,* or *see*), and list as many contexts as you can easily think of, then analyze by the steps given above.

E. Using the following data as in step 1 (collecting the data), follow the above procedures (steps 2, 3, and 4) to discover the senses of *foot* in English. How would each sense be said in another language you speak?

foot of the man	foot of the list
foot of the rabbit	foot of the bed
foot of the table	foot of the mountain
foot of the page	foot of the hill
foot of the stairs	foot of the tree

F. Using the following data as step 1 (collecting the data), follow the above procedures (steps 2, 3, and 4) to discover the **senses** of *hot* in English. How would each **sense** be said in another language you speak? (Selected from Barnwell 1980:36.)

a hot iron	the child is hot
a hot curry	the patient is hot
hot tea	hot pepper
hot soup	a hot argument
hot water	a hot day
a hot rhythm	

Chapter 11
Figurative Senses of Lexical Items

We have already seen that a single word may have various senses and that these senses are signaled by the context; that is, the other words with which it occurs. We noted that the **primary sense** is the sense which will come to the minds of most speakers of the language when the word is cited in isolation, and the **secondary senses** are those which are dependent upon context for an indication of the sense intended. We also noted that **secondary senses** are related to one another and to the **primary meaning** by some thread of meaning.

In addition to the **primary** and **secondary senses**, words also may have **figurative senses**. **Figurative senses** are based on associative relations with the **primary sense** (Beekman and Callow 1974:94). Some types of figures of speech will be discussed below.

Metonymy

The use of words in a **figurative sense** involving association is called **metonymy**. For example, in English it is correct to say, *"The kettle is boiling."* However, a *kettle* cannot *boil*. In the special collocation with *boil*, *kettle* does not mean the *kitchen utensil used for boiling water*, but rather refers to the *water* which is in the *kettle*. It is the *water* which is *boiling*. But the *water* is associated with the *kettle*, it is inside the *kettle*. *Kettle* is being used in a **figurative sense** to mean *water*. A literal translation of *the kettle is boiling* would probably be nonsense in most languages. **Figurative senses** cannot usually be translated with a literal form of the word.

In English, we also say, *"He has a good head."* *Head* is the place where the *brain* is located. It is being used in a figurative way to refer to the *brain*. Also, we say, *"The response from the floor was positive,"* using *floor* in a figurative way to represent the *people* who are in the audience which is seated on the *floor* (probably in chairs). There is an associative relationship which makes the **figurative sense** possible.

The examples given above are all based on a spatial relationship: the *water* in the *kettle*, the *brains* in the *head*, the *people* in chairs on the *floor*. The words *kettle, head,* and *floor* all have a figurative meaning – *water, brains,* and *people* respectively. One word was "substituting" for another. But they are not synonyms. *Kettle* is not a synonym for *water*, nor *head* for *brains*. *Kettle* has a **figurative sense** which occurs in collocation with the word *boil*. The **figurative sense** is also based on collocation. It has the **figurative sense** only when used with certain other words.

Association may have to do with temporal relationship as well as spatial. We say in reference to a holiday, *"We've waited for this day with anticipation."* *Day* referring to Independence Day, is used for the *holiday* which they will have on that *day*. A student may say to his friend, *"Your hour has come,"* meaning *"The time to take your exam has arrived."*

There are also **figurative senses** which are based on a logical contiguity rather than spatial or temporal. For example, one might say, *"Moses is read every day in the Jewish synagogues."* But one cannot read *Moses*. *Moses* is used in a figurative way to stand for *what Moses wrote* – the *law*. There is a logical relationship since Moses is the writer of the *law*. A translation might need to say *the laws written by Moses*. It is not uncommon to hear people say sentences in English like, *"I listened to Bach,"* or, *"I read Shakespeare."* *Bach* is used to mean *the music he composed,* and *Shakespeare* is used to mean *the plays he wrote.*

Sometimes an object is used in a figurative way to stand for that for which it is used. For example, *Martin Beni lives by his gloves* really means, *he makes his living by boxing.*

A statement like the following may be completely misunderstood if translated literally into some languages: *The Provincial Commissioner jailed all the fighters.* The Commissioner probably did not jail them, he simply ordered the police to do it. Although he did not do the action directly, he was responsible for it. The phrase may need to be translated differently so as not to leave the impression that the Commissioner himself did it. It might need to be translated *The Provincial Commissioner had the police jail all the fighters.*

The sentence, *The Prime Minister barred unskilled laborers from entering Papua New Guinea,* might also be misunderstood because the Prime Minister simply initiated the action, but the immigration officials carried it out. An adjustment might need to be made in translation.

An attribute may be used for the object which has the attribute. For example, *Don't substitute the good for the best. Good* means *good work* and *best* means the *best work*. The meaning is *Don't substitute good work for the best work*. Or an object may be used for the attribute it symbolizes as in *The arm of the law reached out to all corners of the country*, where *arm* is used to symbolize *authority*. A literal translation using the word *arm* would give a wrong meaning in some receptor languages.

In each example mentioned above, the relationship was one of association. Therefore, they are examples of **metonymy. Metonymy** occurs in most languages but will not match the specific examples of the **metonymy** of another language. Where the source language uses the name of a city to refer to the inhabitants, many languages in Papua New Guinea will eliminate the **metonymy** by translating the full meaning. For example, *London had elections last week* is translated *the people of London had elections last week*. Translators translating the Bible from English into Motu and Pidgin (Papua New Guinea) adjusted the **metonymy** in the sentence *I am innocent of this man's blood* by using *this man's death* since *blood* is not used in this figurative way in those languages (Deibler and Taylor 1977:1077).

Synecdoche

Figurative senses based on part-whole relationships are also quite common in some languages and are called **synecdoche**. This figure of speech is very common in Greek, so there are many occurrences of it in the New Testament. For example, in the Lord's Prayer it says, "Give us this day our daily *bread*." One specific member, *bread*, of the class *food*, is substituted for *food*. The prayer is really talking about *food*, not just *bread* which is one part of the whole class of *food*. Sometimes a part of an object is used for the whole object. A person may say, "I am not going to let him come under my *roof*." *Roof*, which is a part of the *house*, is substituted for *house*. *Roof* is being used in a **figurative sense**. *Word* is used figuratively in the sentence "His *word* can be trusted," which means "*What he says* can be trusted." Notice the following additional examples of a **part** being substituted for the **whole**:

1. *Only 8 hardy* **souls** *showed up for work.*   persons
2. *There are a lot of lonely* **hearts** *out there.*   persons
3. *She said it to* **my face.**   me

Translating metonymy and synecdoche

In discussing the translation of secondary senses, it was suggested that each sense will probably be translated with a different word in the receptor language since there is usually no match of secondary senses between languages (except perhaps between dialects or languages of the same family). The same is true of figurative senses. The

figurative sense of a word almost invariably will need to be translated
with a word or phrase which is not the literal translation of the word
in the source language. "A single word in one language is likely to be
translated into another language using almost as many different
renditions as there are senses" (Beekman and Callow 1974:104).

There are three general ways in which **metonymy** and **synecdoche** are to be translated. First, the sense of the word may be
translated nonfiguratively; that is, the intended meaning may be
made plain so that there is no longer a **figurative sense** in the
receptor language translation. *The kettle is boiling* would then be
translated *the water is boiling*. *The response from the floor* would
be translated with something like *the people in the audience re-
sponded....* He has a good head* would be translated *he has a good
brain* or *he is very intelligent*. *Moses is read in the synagogue*
would be translated *the law is read in the synagogue*. *The arm of
the law* would be *the authority of the law; he went to the gallows*
would be *he was hanged*; and *Martin Beni lives by his gloves* would
be *Martin Beni makes his living by boxing*.

A second possibility, which may be better in some situations, is
to retain the word in the original, but to add the **sense** of the word.
This should be used if there seems to be a component of emotions or
impact which might otherwise be lost, as in poetry. For example,
Moses is read in the synagogue might be translated *the law (book)
written by Moses is read in the synagogue*. *He just gave the weather*
might be translated *he just gave a weather report (or forecast)*. *The
world is mad* might be translated by *the people of the world* for *world;
your hour has come* by *the hour for your exam has come*. *He drank
three cups* might be translated *he drank three cups of tea;* and *the
government wanted to reintroduce the electric chair* could be translated *the government wanted to reintroduce execution by using the
electric chair*.

The third possibility is to substitute a figurative expression of the
receptor language for the figurative expression of the source language.
It is important that the same meaning is retained. In Aguaruna of Peru,
pan, meaning "bread," would not carry the figurative sense of "food,"
but *yujumak*, which means "manioc," would. In one language, *tongue*
may be used with a figurative meaning of "speech," in another
language *lips* may have this figurative sense. In Aguaruna, *mouth* has
a figurative sense of "speech."

There will also be times in the translation when there is no
figurative expression in the source language, but the best translation
will be the use of a figurative expression in the receptor language. For
example, *he gave them strict orders* might well be translated in
Mbembe (Nigeria) with the figurative expression *he pulled their ears*.

The goal of translation is **not** to eliminate all secondary and figurative senses. It is to use only secondary and figurative senses which are peculiar to the receptor language and eliminate any strange collocations or wrong meaning caused by a literal translation of source language secondary and figurative senses.

Idioms

One class of figurative expressions which occurs in all languages, but which is very language specific, is **idioms.** **Idioms** are expressions of "at least two words which cannot be understood literally and which function as a unit semantically" (Beekman and Callow 1974:121). In English, we say, *he has a hard heart*, meaning "he is indifferent to the needs of others." But the same expression, *to have a hard heart*, in Shipibo of Peru means "he is brave." Shipibo does, however, have an **idiom** which means "he has a hard heart," but translates as *his ears have no holes*. In English, we say, *horse of a different color*, but in Spanish the corresponding **idiom** would be *harina de un costal muy diferente* (flour from a very different bag); English uses *hands of a clock*, but Mbembe uses *the tongue of a clock*.

The Apinayé language of Brazil has numerous **idioms** based on body parts–*eye, eyelid, head, ear,* etc. Examples are given below by giving a very literal translation in the first column and an idiomatic English equivalent in the second column (Ham 1965:2).

LITERAL ENGLISH	IDIOMATIC ENGLISH
I don't have my eye on you.	*I don't remember you.*
I've already buried my eye.	*I'm already ready to go.*
I'll pull your eyelid.	*I'll ask a favor of you.*
My eye is hard on you.	*I remember you.*
My head is strong.	*I'm stubborn, insistent.*
I'll do it with my head.	*I'll do it the way I think it should be done.*
His ear is rotten.	*He is spoiled.*
I ate in your tooth cavity.	*I ate in your absence.*

In English, there are many figurative usages of *heart* which will best be translated using *liver* in some African languages. Notice the following example (Nida 1955:59):

To identify psychological states the Nilotic languages make considerable use of words meaning either "heart" or "liver" (the latter is more common). In Anuak there are scores of such expressions employing *cwing*, 'liver', of which the following are typical: he has a *cwiny* (he is good), his *cwiny* is good (he is generous), his *cwiny* is bad (he is unsociable), his *cwiny* is shallow (he gets angry quickly), his *cwiny* is heavy (he is sad), his *cwiny* is stubborn (he is brave), his *cwiny* is white (he is kind), his *cwiny* is cold (he will not be impolite in eating ahead of others), his *cwiny* is burned (he is irritable), and his *cwiny* is sweet (he is happy).

The same translation principles apply for **idioms** as for other figures of speech. Sometimes it will be necessary to translate with a nonfigurative expression, but sometimes a good receptor language **idiom** may be used. The translator needs to learn to recognize the **idioms** and other figures of speech of the source text. The real danger comes in translating an **idiom** literally, since the result will usually be nonsense in the receptor language.

The translator also needs to develop a sensitivity to the use of **idioms** in the receptor language, and use them naturally to make the translation lively and keep the style of the source language. There will often be words in the source language which are not **idioms**, but are best translated with an **idiom**. For example, the word *peace* is often translated with the **idiom** *to sit down in the heart* in Africa (see Nida and Taber 1969:106).

Euphemism

A **euphemism** is a figurative expression which is in some ways like a metonymy. There is the substitution of one word for another or one expression for another. But a **euphemism** is used to avoid an offensive expression, or one that is socially unacceptable, or one that is unpleasant (see Beekman and Callow 1974:119). All languages have **euphemistic expressions** which substitute for certain words, especially in the area of sex, death, and the supernatural. The Jews avoided mention of the name of *God* by using the word *heaven*. Most languages have ways of saying *die* without using the word which has the primary meaning *die*. English uses *pass away* and many other terms. Hebrew used *gone to the fathers*. *Gone to sleep* and *is sleeping* may also be used for *die*. In Mangga Buang of Papua New Guinea, the **euphemism** *your daughter's eyes are closed* is preferable to *your daughter is dead*. In the Twi language (Africa), *he has gone to his village* means *he died*.

Sex in many languages is referred to **euphemistically.** Such expressions as *to know, to touch, to come together*, and *to sleep with* are used. Other things are referred to **euphemistically** as well. In the United States, old people are now called *senior citizens*. Among the Chol of Mexico, a new baby is always talked of in negative terms such as *ugly* in order to deceive the spirits so they won't want the baby. In Chontal, the devil is **euphemistically** called *older brother* because using his name might make him think he was being called. In Finnish, *he is sitting in his hotel* means "he is in prison."

Euphemisms will often need to be translated by a comparable **euphemism** in the receptor language. The important thing is for the translator to recognize the **euphemistic** nature of the source language expression, and then translate with an appropriate and acceptable expression of the receptor language whether euphemistic or direct. For example, the Greek expression *he is sleeping with his fathers* might be translated *he went to his village* in Twi. However, some languages might simply say *he died*, and to them it would be inoffensive.

Hyperbole

"A **hyperbole** is a metonymy or synecdoche with more said than the writer intended the reader to understand. The exaggeration is deliberately used for effect, and is not to be understood as if it were a literal description" (Beekman and Callow 1974:118). For example, the expression *they turned the world upside down* is an exaggeration. *World* is used to stand for *people*, in this case *many people* but probably not *all the people in the world*. It is a deliberate exaggeration. In English, we say things like *I'm starving* meaning *I'm very hungry; I'm frozen to death* meaning *I'm very cold*; and *he's mad* meaning *he's doing something very foolish*. Such deliberate exaggerations in the source language text may be understood as untruths if they are translated literally. Much care must be taken to be sure that the desired effect is retained in the receptor language but that the correct meaning is also retained.

Notice the following additional examples of **hyperboles** (from Simons and Young 1979):

Pijin: *Desfala kofi nao, ating evri suga nomoa i go insald.*
I think someone has put all the sugar in the world in this coffee.

Maori: *Ehara i te puu, kia pakuu, kia rongohia ai.*
It's not a gun that goes off so you can hear it. (Literal translation which actually means, "It is very quiet."

EXERCISES – Figurative Senses of Lexical Items

A. In the following, one word or phrase is italicized. Is that word or phrase used in its **primary sense**, a **secondary sense**, or a **figurative sense**?

1. I've got to *catch* a plane.

2. The OPEC ministers had once again *jacked up* the world price of oil.

3. Children *adopt* values and attitudes of their parents.

4. I'm *starved*. Let's grab a *bite* to eat.

5. They have the custom of *lighting* windows at Christmas.

6. He was obviously taking *heavy* betting action.

7. They were supposed to *ring* the office regularly.

8. *California* seems to have solved the problem of *gas closings*.

9. Who knows the secret memories he and many of his contemporaries *carry*?

10. Gazing across the green, rolling landscape his smile *faded*.

11. Carter *spent* the Fourth of July with his family at the Camp David retreat.

12. They aren't *stirred-up* enough about inflation.

13. She was born in the *heart* of one of the worst slums in Argentina.

14. The *eyes* of the world are on those two, not on Collins.

15. We did not know a *soul* in the class.

16. I'm *boiling* mad.

B. Identify the figurative usage in the following. Restate nonfiguratively.

1. My tan is peeling.

2. I enjoy listening to Beethoven.

3. Two hundred souls perished in the crash.

4. The arm of the law reaches the whole country.

5. He drank three cups.

6. He went to the gallows.

7. Don't hurt his good name.

8. It takes forever to cook this meat.

9. The world is mad.

10. He was lost in action in Vietnam.

C. Study the Apinayé **idioms** listed above (page 115). How would these be said in a language you speak (other than English)? Is there an appropriate **idiom** with the same meaning?

D. The following **idioms** are from Supyire of Mali, West Africa. (Data from Robert Carlson.) Is there an **idiom** in another language which you speak which has the same meaning?

SUPYIRE IDIOM	MEANING
My stomach got black.	*I forgot.*
My stomach fell on it.	*I remembered it.*
My stomach is sweet.	*I'm happy/content.*
My stomach is hot.	*I'm in a hurry.*
My stomach is cold.	*I'm tranquil.*

E. Multiple senses project

1. Find three examples of each of the following in a magazine or newspaper.

   a. secondary sense
   b. figurative sense

2. Give the following information for each example:

   a. the primary sense of the word
   b. classification as to whether it is secondary or figurative
   c. a translation of the citation using only primary senses of words.

Examples:

1. hold

M. Whitcomb Hess is a writer and former teacher who lives in Athens, Ohio. She *holds* the A.M. from Ohio University (*Christianity Today*, January 31, 1975. Vol. 19, No. 9, p. 4).

The primary sense of *hold* is *to have in one's hands.*

The secondary sense used here is *to possess.* The shared component meaning is *to have.*

The meaning is, "She possesses an A.M. degree which was awarded her by Ohio University."

2. hoof

An entire economy on the *hoof,* Ice Age animals supplied man with food, garments, and tools (*National Geographic*, January 1975, p. 73).

The primary meaning of *hoof* is the *foot of certain animals.*

The figurative sense used here is that of part-whole: constituent for whole, e.g., *hoof* for animals.

The meaning is "An entire economy depended on Ice Age animals for food, garments, and tools."

Chapter 12
Person Reference

In the previous two chapters, secondary senses and figurative senses have been discussed and illustrated. The examples used were referring to the nouns and verbs of a language. As mentioned briefly in chapter 7 above, all languages also have systems of *substitute words*. Pronouns substitute for nouns, and there may be some verbal forms which are pro-verbs; that is, they substitute for verbs. In this chapter, pronominal systems will be discussed from two points of view: (1) the fact that each language has a unique pronominal system, and (2) the secondary and figurative senses of pronouns. Both the mismatching of systems and the fact of multiple senses present a real challenge to the translator.

Pronominal systems

The pronouns of a language form a special semantic set which can usually be analyzed by componential analysis. As indicated in chapter 8 above, pronouns can usually be charted in a matrix which shows the components of meaning found in each lexical item. In Displays 12.1, 12.2, and 12.3, compare the following matrices which have the form of the subject pronouns in the boxes and the contrastive meaning components as labels.

English

	singular			plural
1st person	*I*			*we*
2nd person	*you*			
3rd person	masculine	feminine	neuter	*they*
	he	*she*	*it*	

Display 12.1

Spanish

		singular	plural	
1st person		yo	masculine	feminine
			nosotros	nosotras
2nd person	familiar	tu	vosotros	vosotras
	formal	usted	ustedes	
3rd person	masculine	feminine	ellos	ellas
	el	ella		

Display 12.2

Aguaruna

		singular		plural
1st person		wi		ii
2nd person		ame		atum
3rd person	in sight	near	nu	dita
		far	au	
	out of signt	nii		

Display 12.3

You will notice from Displays 12.1, 12.2, and 12.3 that English, Spanish, and Aguaruna all distinguish between SINGULAR and PLURAL, and also all distinguish FIRST, SECOND, and THIRD PERSON (except for English SECOND PERSON). FIRST PERSON refers to the speaker, SECOND PERSON to the one being talked to, and THIRD PERSON to someone other than the speaker and hearer. Even though there is considerable similarity in the distinctions made, there are some additional distinctions which are different. In English THIRD PERSON SINGULAR, there is a further division based on gender (MASCULINE, FEMININE, and NEUTER). Spanish, however, makes a gender distinction in both SINGULAR and PLURAL THIRD PERSON, but only distinguishes MASCULINE and FEMININE. Notice that in the SECOND PERSON, Spanish distinguishes FAMILIAR from FORMAL. In Aguaruna, THIRD PERSON SINGULAR is further divided by NEAR, FAR, and OUT OF SIGHT.

For each language, there will be a system, and this system sets up obligatory categories that must be used in translation even if they do not occur in the source language system. Basic to all pronominal systems is PERSON; that is, the speaker, the one spoken to, and other persons. Additional features will vary, but it is very common to distinguish NUMBER. NUMBER may include SINGU-LAR, DUAL, PLURAL, and COLLECTIVE. Pame of Mexico has a pronoun which is always used if the person or thing referred to is DUAL. This is not uncommon. However, the Sursurunga language (PNG) is reported to have singular, dual, trial, quadrual, and plural distinctions.

Other categories which are often found in pronominal systems are the distinction between ANIMATE and INANIMATE, GENDER, IN-CLUSIVE versus EXCLUSIVE, and HONORIFICS. Honorifics refer to inclusion within the components of meaning of distinctions which relate to social standings within the society.

Before a translator begins his work, he should study carefully the pronominal system of the source language and the receptor language and make a careful comparison of the two. There may be meaning components in the source language pronominal system which are not found in the pronominal system of the receptor language and vice versa. The meaning components found in the receptor language system will have to be used even though they are not indicated in the source language system. For example, there is no component of meaning in English which distinguishes FA-MILIAR from FORMAL in the second person. However, if one is to translate into Spanish every time the English pronoun *you* occurs, the translator will have to decide which Spanish form he should use, *tu* or *usted*. He will have to make this decision on the basis of the use in the receptor language and not on the basis of the form in the source language.

On the other hand, if a translator is translating from a language which has a semantic distinction in the pronouns related to the social classes, and he is translating into a receptor language which does not make these distinctions, he will not try to artificially introduce these components of meaning, but will simply use the normal pronoun that would be used in the receptor language. It is inevitable that some components of meaning will be lost or added in the translation of pronouns.

The whole matter of the use of pronouns in the receptor language is also dependent on the discourse structure of the language and these matters will be discussed in chapter 30. Although it may seem like some meaning is being lost or added, as a matter of fact, in the total text this is not true since pronouns are simply substituting for nouns and the nouns themselves contain the full range of meaning components. For example, the English word *she* can be used to refer to *the girl next door*. In translating into a language which does not distinguish gender in the pronouns, as for example in Aguaruna, the component of meaning, FEMININE, would be lost when using the Aguaruna pronoun *nii*. However, since *nii* is referring to *girl*, and girl includes the feminine component, no meaning component is lost, if one looks at the total text.

Inclusion and exclusion

Many languages distinguish between **inclusive** and **exclusive**. This is very common in Austronesian languages and in American Indian languages. English has simply one subject pronoun for FIRST PERSON PLURAL, *we*. *We* may at times be talking only about the *speaker and someone else other than the hearer*, and at other times about the *speaker* and the *hearer*. However, in Nahuat of Mexico there are two words. *Temamen* means *we* and *you*; that is, it is **inclusive** *of the hearer. Nehamen* means *we*, but *not you*; that is, the HEARER is not included, and this form is, therefore, called **exclusive. Inclusive** means that the HEARER is included in the FIRST PERSON PLURAL form, and **exclusive** means that the HEARER is not included.

Display 12.4 of the Isnag (Philippines) pronoun system shows the presence of **inclusive** and **exclusive** along with other distinctions (data from Rudy Barlaan).

In translating into a language with an **inclusive-exclusive** distinction, the translator has to decide each time a FIRST PERSON PLURAL pronoun occurs in the source text whether the **inclusive** or **exclusive** form is to be used in the receptor text. For example, in a phrase like *God our Father*, the **inclusive** form would need to be used since he is *Father* of people in general. However, in the Lord's prayer where it says "forgive us *our* sins," the form would have to be **exclusive** since the prayer is to God, and he should not be included as one who has sinned.

Most languages also have a set of pronouns which are usually called possessive pronouns. These pronouns may have an additional component of meaning of being intrinsically **exclusive**. For example, in Chuj of Guatemala, whenever a person speaks of an item as being possessed by another person, it implies that it does not belong to

	Emphatic	Subject	Object	Possessive
1st per. sing.	*iya'*	*ya'/Ca'*	*kiya'*	*ku, -k*
1st per. dual	*da'ta*	*ta*	*kada'ta*	*ta*
1st per. pl. **incl.**	*da'tada*	*tada*	*kada'tada*	*tada*
1st per. pl. **excl.**	*dakami*	*kami*	*kadakami*	*mi*
2nd per. sing.	*ikaw*	*ka*	*kikaw*	*mu, -m*
2nd per. pl.	*dakayu*	*kayu*	*kadakayu*	*nu*
3rd per. sing.	*aggína*	*O*	*kaggína*	*na*
3rd per. pl.	*aggída*	*da*	*kaggída*	*da*

Display 12.4

someone else at the same time. That is, you would not use *my teacher* in talking to any other member of the class because it would exclude them, thus giving a wrong meaning. *My teacher* would be appropriate only when talking to persons not in the class.

In Aguaruna of Peru, the first person singular pronoun *wi* is also intrinsically **exclusive**. If a person says, *"I'm going,"* this clearly implies that *you are not going.* In English, if we say, *"I'm an American,"* it does not imply anything about the person to whom is being spoken. Or if a person says, *"You are a Canadian,"* that says nothing about the speaker. The pronouns in English are neutral as to any reference to anyone other than the person mentioned. However, many American Indian languages have a pronoun system which includes an additional component of **exclusion**. For example, in Huasteco (Mexico), if one says, *"I am an American,"* it also means, *"You are not an American."* The use of first person automatically excludes SECOND PERSON. Implicit **exclusion** is not found in Indo-European languages, but is very common in other languages.

The following shows the importance of **inclusion-exclusion** in Muyuw of Papua New Guinea (Lithgow 1967:14).

> In English pronouns the focus of meaning is on persons who are *included*, and the speaker or hearer may or may not be included. There are also idiomatic usages in which the form used does not include the person in focus.

For example, the second person singular or plural form used in the sentence, *You can do it like this*, besides its literal meaning can also mean, *People can do it like this*, or *One can do it like this* (third person), or *We all can do it like this* (first person).

To exclude other persons, extra words have to be used, such as *You can do it; I won't*, or *You can do it yourself*.

In Muyuw the exclusive aspect of the lexical meaning of the pronouns is in focus. Thus:

1st **inclusive** dual	*yakid*	refers to the speaker and one hearer, and excludes all others
1st **exclusive** plural	*yakamey*	refers to the speakers, and excludes the hearers
2nd plural	*yakamiy*	refers to the hearers, and excludes the speakers
3rd plural	*tasiyas*	excludes the speakers and the hearers

In English, the pronoun which comes to mind in association with *all people* is *they're* (3rd pl.); but in Muyuw the pronoun which is always given is *yakids* (1st **incl.** pl.) *all of us*.

The translation of pronouns into languages such as Muyuw can only be done accurately if one determines which persons are **excluded,** and then chooses the appropriate pronoun.

American Indian languages of South America also often have a form used when reporting something which the speaker has experienced. This form is different from the form used when reporting something which he simply heard. The difference is basically between **first-hand information** and **second-hand information**. When translating into these languages, it is sometimes hard to know from the source text whether the writer is reporting something he actually saw, or something he simply heard from someone else, but this information must be indicated in the translation since it is obligatory to the system.

It is always more difficult to translate from a pronominal system with fewer semantic distinctions into a pronominal system with additional semantic distinctions because the information is not always readily available. For example, when one is translating into a language which has an obligatory category of HONORIFICS, as in some languages in India, and the source text is English where no such distinctions are made, it will be necessary for the translator to understand a good deal about the culture of the source language in order to make good judgments in choosing pronominal forms with HONORIFIC categories.

Secondary senses of pronouns

The problems of translation are not simply matters of different pronominal systems, although this in itself is important. In addition to different systems, each language will have certain secondary or extended uses of pronouns. Each language will have its own system of secondary senses for pronouns in the same way that each language has its own secondary senses for nouns and verbs. In English, it is not uncommon to hear a speaker begin a talk by saying, "Today *we* are going to talk about such and such." The speaker then begins to do all of the talking. This form is called **editorial "we"** in English. The **editorial "we"** is a secondary sense of the pronoun *we* in which the plural form is being used with a singular meaning. English also uses the pronoun *we* when the object being referred to is really *you*; that is, SECOND PERSON. Notice the following examples (data from Eunice Pike):

1. Nurse: It's time for *us* to take *our* medicine now.

2. Nurse: Shall *we* take *our* bath now?

3. Mother: Let*'s* be quiet, shall *we*?

4. Teacher: *We*'re not going to shout, *we*'ll walk quietly to our places.

5. If a child is lost, the one who finds him will say to his mother: "*We* couldn't find mother. *We* couldn't find Daddy and *we* were so frightened."

If *we* was being used in its primary sense, then the nurse would be taking the medicine, the mother would be quiet, the teacher would not shout, and the person who found the child would be frightened. We know that this is not the case. In each of these examples, *we* is being used in a secondary or extended usage. The component of SYMPATHY is being added by using the FIRST PERSON pronoun rather than the SECOND PERSON.

In Aguaruna, it is not uncommon for a person to come to the clinic for medicine saying, *"I'm sick,"* and after the nurse has gotten all of the symptoms and is ready to prescribe, the patient will say, *"It is my wife who is sick."* FIRST PERSON SINGULAR includes not only *myself* but *my family*. The person simply says that someone in his family is sick, and the nurse needs to question further concerning to which family member is being referred.

An American politician will often use *I*, FIRST PERSON SINGULAR, when addressing an audience even though *you*, SECOND PERSON, would seem more correct. For example, he might say "If *I* don't pay my taxes...." It takes the audience out of focus and is a way of being *stern* without being too direct. "If *you* don't pay your taxes," would be too direct and impolite.

There are numerous examples in Shakespeare of extended uses of pronouns. In King Richard (I.I.140–4) the king uses *we* to talk about himself:

> *K. Rich.* "We were not born to sue, but to command;
> Which since we cannot do to make you friends,
> Be ready, as your lives shall answer it..."

There are also examples in Shakespeare of THIRD PERSON being used for FIRST PERSON as in Henry VI (II.III.24) where King Henry says, "Henry will to himself protector be..." when referring to himself. Some translations would require a FIRST PERSON indication in a phrase like "I, Henry, will to myself protector be..." Not all languages have the same secondary usage of nouns and pronouns.

Translating pronouns

There are two matters to consider when translating pronouns. First, the source language and receptor language systems will be different. The translator needs to know the meaning components of the two systems in order to translate using the right receptor language forms. It is important that he not let the source language forms distort his use of the correct receptor language form.

Second, the translator must remember that there are extended usages (secondary senses) of pronouns as well as of nouns and verbs. Whenever a pronoun in the source language is being used in a secondary sense, there is a potential translation adjustment which will have to be considered by the translator. Thus, in the five examples above, the FIRST PERSON PLURAL pronoun of English would probably be translated with a SECOND PERSON pronoun. For example, "It's time for *us* to take *our* medicine," would be, "It's time for *you* to take *your* medicine."

Indefinite pronouns are also often used in different ways in different languages. English normally uses the singular *each, everyone, whoever*, and *any*, but many languages of Africa would use the plural form for general kinds of statements. For example, in English one says *Love your neighbor as yourself;* whereas, in Shilluk one would use a form *Love your neighbors as yourselves* using the plural. English *Be kind to one another* would be *Be kind to all people* in Shilluk (Nida 1955:58). The translator must be careful not to translate general statements literally but to use the proper receptor language form for such statements. This will often involve a change of pronoun.

Figurative uses of person

There are a couple of figures of speech, which, although they do not always involve pronouns, involve a special figurative use of PERSON. The first of these is **personification** in which intelligence or life is attributed to inanimate objects or abstract ideas. For example, in English one says *the sea was angry, the ground was thirsty,* or *the sun smiled.* In each of these cases, an inanimate object, *sea, ground,* and *sun,* is **personified**. Many languages have **personification** as a figure of speech in the language, but in some languages, this particular figure of speech can only be used in legends and would need to be adjusted in all other discourse types. Here the component of ANIMATENESS is being added to the meaning of the object, resulting in a figurative usage. A nonfigurative form may be needed in the receptor language – *the sea was very stormy, the ground was very dry,* and *the sun shown brightly.*

There is also a second figure of speech, **apostrophe**, in which inanimate or abstract things are treated as persons, but in the SECOND PERSON and with direct address. This figure is often used by Shakespeare, as for example in the following from Anthony and Cleopatra (V.I.45-6):

> *Where art thou, death?*
> *Come hither, come! Come, come, and take a queen...*

Notice that *death* is addressed in SECOND PERSON. Not all languages have this figurative use of SECOND PERSON, and it may be necessary to change to FIRST or THIRD PERSON in the translation and say something like *Why do I not die? Oh that I might die, I who am the queen long for to die...*

Referring to persons by their role

It is not uncommon for languages to use **role** rather than FIRST PERSON pronouns. For example, at a business meeting the chairman of the meeting may say, "The *chairman* rules that..." rather than saying, "*I* rule that..." Or a man may say to his wife, "Your *husband* is hungry." He is really saying, "*I* am hungry." The component of FOCUS is being added here by adding the role rather than the pronoun. In the Gospels, Jesus often referred to himself in the THIRD PERSON as *the Son of Man* rather than in FIRST PERSON, *I.* This was again to focus on his role. If role designation is not used in the receptor language in this way, the first person pronoun may need to be used in the translation and focus marked in another way.

The Pame in Mexico avoid the use of proper names by the use of **role** designation. A woman will refer to her husband as the *elder* or *head of the house*, or may refer to the **temporary role**; that is, what he is doing at the moment, for example, *cutter of wood* (Gibson 1965:3). Here again, **role** reference is preferred to pronominal reference.

In some languages, it is not uncommon to continue using a **temporary role** in referring to an individual, even though the **role** is no longer true. For example, the Biblical record talks of *Simon the leper* after Simon had been healed of leprosy. It also talks about the *blind man* after he had received his sight. In Greek, a **temporary role** can be used for designation of a participant even after it is no longer true. However, when translating into another language, one should be very careful that the receptor language also uses **temporary role** in this way. In Aguaruna, to say *Simon the leper* would mean that he still had leprosy, and it is necessary to translate with the phrase *Simon who had been a leper*. *Blind man* would have to be translated *the man who had been blind*, and so forth. In some languages, once a person is introduced into a narrative, he is referred to, not by name, nor by pronoun, but by his **role** relationship to the one in focus. This is true in the Amuesha language (Peru). If the main participant of the story is the *father*, then the *son* would always be referred to as *his son*. If the main participant of the story is the *son*, then the *father* will be referred to as *his father*.

In Shakespeare's play, King Richard the Second, King Richard refers to himself by his name or even his change of role (IV.I.218-221):

> *K. Rich...*
> Long mayst thou live in Richard's seat to sit,
> And soon lie Richard in an earthly pit!
> God save King Henry, unking'd Richard says,
> And send him many years of sunshine days!

Role designation may need to be adjusted in translation to fit the natural uses in the receptor language. The whole matter of when a noun is used versus when a pronoun is used versus when **role designation** is used is different for each language. The translator will need to be familiar with these matters. He should not automatically translate nouns, pronouns, and **role designation** literally, but use them according to the natural patterns of the receptor language. It is always important to have in mind who the referent is and how that referent would be talked about in the receptor language. (For additional discussion of extended uses of pronouns see Beekman and Callow 1974, chapter 7.)

EXERCISES – Person Reference

A. Compare the pronominal systems of two languages which you speak. What meaning components are signaled in one which do not occur in the other?

B. In each of the following, the first version is the source text and the second indicates the receptor language form. What adjustment was made in the translation and why?

> Example: SL: The professor said, "We are going to talk about astrology today."
>
> RL: The professor said, "I am going to talk about astrology today."
>
> The first plural pronoun is changed to singular since only one person is speaking.

1. SL: *We* have a lot which *we* want to tell you.
   RL: *I* have a lot which *I* want to tell you.

2. SL: Why should *my* liberty be determined by other people?
   RL: Why should *our* liberty be determined by other people?

3. SL: Teacher: *We* are going to listen to a story now.
   RL: *You* are going to listen to a story now.
   RL: (What additional adjustment was made in the following?):
   I'm going to *read you* a story now.

4. SL: School principal to teachers: The *administration* has decided to cancel classes on Friday.
   RL: *I* have decided to cancel classes on Friday.

5. SL: *I*'m going now (implying that the addressee is going to want to go also).
   RL: Let*'s* go now.

C. How would the five sentences in B above best be translated into another language which you speak?

D. Rewrite the following, changing the generic word or words to PLURAL, and adjusting other words affected by the changes.

1. Be kind to *one another*.

2. *Whoever* is ready may come with us.

3. Give to *everyone* as much as *he* needs.

4. *Everyone* who comes will hear a great speech.

5. If a *person* loves me, *he* will do what I ask.

E. Would the singular or plural forms be the best way to translate the sentences in D into a second language which you speak? Translate these sentences. What other adjustments did you need to make?

Chapter 13
Lexical Items and Situational Context

In chapter 4, three kinds of meaning were discussed — REFER-ENTIAL MEANING, ORGANIZATIONAL MEANING, and SITU-ATIONAL MEANING. We have now discussed referential meaning in some detail. The **situation** in which words are used is also crucial to the full meaning of words. The particular word that is chosen will depend on various factors of the **situation** in which the communication is made. The translator must be aware of the meanings of words which are conditioned by the **situation**.

Connotation of lexical items

In addition to conveying factual information by reference to THINGS, EVENTS, ATTRIBUTES, and RELATIONS, words also reflect attitudes and emotions. For example, the word *mother* has a positive and emotional response for most people. The word *woman*, on the other hand, is more neutral. But the word *witch* would be negative for the majority of English speakers. Words bring forth an emotional response in people and this response has sometimes been referred to as *emotive meaning*. In the example above, the words *mother, woman,* and *witch* might or might not be referring to the same person. However, even when a word does refer to the same referent, there may be various lexical choices based on connotative or emotive meaning. For example, the words *father, daddy, dad, pop*, and *the old man* are all lexical items which refer to "the kin who is of the previous generation, male, and lineal." The word *father* has a **connotation** of respect; whereas, *daddy* has a **connotation** of intimacy. *The old man* shows some lack of respect for most speakers of English or might be used in jesting. People do not think of words according to their REFERENTIAL MEANING only but also react to them emotionally.

Connotative meanings are often culturally conditioned. A word which has a **positive connotation** in one culture may actually have a **negative connotation** in another, as for example, the English word *tribe*. In some parts of the world, ethnic groups react very **positively**

to being called a *tribe*. In other parts of the world, this same word has **negative connotations**, and people do not want to be called members of a *tribe*. Referentially, the word *tribe* would be referring to an ethnic group, but the positive and negative overtones must also be taken into consideration if the word is chosen to be used in translation, or a wrong meaning may be conveyed.

The word *fox* has **negative connotations** in English when it is associated with the qualities of *cunning* and *deceitfulness*. In some other languages, the equivalent word which refers to the animal *fox* may have no **emotive meanings** at all or may have a **positive connotation**. Words which may be completely neutral in the source language, if translated literally, may have strong emotional overtones in the receptor language. Words also change in their **connotative meaning**. For example, the word *tribe*, mentioned above, may be quite neutral in a given country and later develop a **negative connotation** or a more **positive connotation**. The word *boi* in Pidgin (Papua New Guinea) has **negative connotations**.

Words often occur in sets which range from negative to positive. For example, the English words *skinny, thin,* and *slender* probably have the following connotation for most people: negative for *skinny*, neutral for *thin*, and positive for *slender*. As far as the referential meaning, they are synonyms, but they are used very differently because of **connotation**. In the same way, *fat* is probably negative; whereas, *overweight* is more neutral and *plump* more positive in **connotation.** A translator must be aware of the positive and negative **connotation** of words in the source language so as to translate with an appropriate **connotation** in the receptor language.

Attributes which are near synonyms may not appropriately be interchangeable. For example, the English set *beautiful, handsome, pretty,* and *lovely* are all referring to more or less the same quality. However, *handsome* has additional **connotation** of usually referring to a male person and certain other things such as a horse or a piece of furniture. *Pretty*, on the other hand, would not be used in the same contexts, but rather to refer to a female person, to flowers, etc. *Beautiful* is probably the most neutral and can be used in more contexts than the other words of the set.

Words may also vary in connotation depending on whether they are old or new. Generally speaking, there are words that are *archaic, old-fashioned, neutral,* or *modern*. Each language will have words which would not be appropriate because they are considered *archaic* or *old-fashioned*. In some situations, a translation using words which are *modern* might be inappropriate because, to some speakers of the language, they would not be accepted vocabulary. On the other hand, *archaic* words may be rejected by other members of the society. For example, in English the use of *thee* and *thou* shows that the people who are using the old language are religious and belong to a certain group that still uses that language. Because of this **connotation**, it would be inappropriate to use these words in most translations into English today.

In studying the lexicon of a language, it is important not only to know the referential meaning of the word, but to know which words are considered old or new and, therefore, in a certain sense, are not a part of the neutral present day vocabulary. There may be places in the translation where an old or a new word would be appropriate, but the important thing is to be aware of this possible difference. If archaic words are used, the translation will probably not be used after the older people are gone. Words understood by all speakers of the language are the ones which will be the best choice in the translation.

Words have different **connotative meanings** in one language than in another because of the negative or positive taboos which have developed in the cultures. We have mentioned that words with heavy negative taboos often result in euphemisms. The presence of euphemistic expressions for certain words would be an indication that the word probably has a strong **negative connotation**. In some cultures, there is a negative taboo about saying the name of a person who is dead. In other cultures, there may be a very positive attitude, and children will be named after their recently departed ancestors.

There may also be positive taboos which result in certain **connotations** of meaning. For example, among the Hebrew people, the high respect or positive **connotation** for the word *God* has resulted in euphemistic ways of referring to *God*. Because of great respect, the name is not used in normal conversation, but words like *heaven* or *the most high* are used as substitutes. The substitute words should not be translated literally into a language that does not normally make this kind of substitution. The meaning *God* should be translated overtly.

Speaker-addressee relationship

The choice of lexical items may also depend upon who is talking to whom. The **speaker-addressee relationship** will often determine choices of vocabulary that result in sub-dialects of the language. A person does not talk the same way to a small child as he does to an educated audience at a university. Factors such as age, social class, educational level, and technical expertise of the audience will affect the choice of vocabulary used.

Most languages have some speech variation which is considered "baby talk." In English, if we hear someone say sentences like *Baby want milk* or *Daddy loves you*, we immediately know that the speaker is addressing a very small child. Oral communication with young children may involve special grammatical constructions such as the examples cited above, or it may involve the use of sound changes or the choice of special words. Among the Aguaruna, it is common to hear a woman who is talking to a baby change all of the voiceless sounds to voiced. For example, *tsamau*, which means "banana drink," would be pronounced *chamau* when talking to a small child. When one hears an adult making this sound change, one knows immediately that a small child is addressed. In talking to a small child, the word *daddy* would probably be chosen rather than the other lexical choices mentioned above *(father, dad, the old man)*. *Mommy* would be used in English rather than *mother*. In addition, vocabulary would be rather limited to suit the understanding of the child.

In many societies, teenagers develop a special vocabulary which they use when talking to one another. Although understood by the adults around them, this special vocabulary would not be used by the adults. Also, in any group, there will be vocabulary which is still understood by most of the population but only used by older people, since the words are no longer part of the vocabulary used by the majority. It is, of course, obvious that the translator will want to avoid vocabulary which is age-specific and use the vocabulary which is understood by the majority of the people without any **age connotation**, unless the source text author intends to show age by the choices in the original.

In some languages, there will be differences between **men's speech** and **women's speech**. There will be a difference simply because men talk about different things than women do. Men will have specialized vocabulary to talk about the work that they are involved in, such as house construction, business, shamanism, religious rites, and so forth. The women will have specialized vocabulary for talking about the work that they do in the garden, sewing, cooking, and so forth. There are certain words which have the connotation of being associated with women and others which will have the connotation of being associated with men. Cocama (Peru) has different pronominal sets depending on whether a man or a woman is speaking. Dixon (1971:436-37) reports a difference between everyday speech and **mother-in-law language** in north Queensland, Australia. Every speaker of Dyirbal knows both languages, the regular language and the special language used in the presence of relatives who are considered taboo. (The term "mother-in-law" is used to refer to all taboo relatives.) Completely different vocabulary is used. For example, in Display 13.1 there are three words which express ways to *cut* (Dixon 1971:437).

EVERYDAY LANGUAGE	"MOTHER-IN-LAW" LANGUAGE
nudin (sever)	*dyalngan*
gunban (cut a piece out)	*dyalngan*
banyin (split a log)	*bubaman*

Display 13.1

This language presents an extreme example, but it is not uncommon to have vocabulary which is used in special situations or when talking to certain people. The translator must be aware of these restrictions in choosing lexical equivalents to avoid wrong connotations or misunderstanding.

Levels of politeness are very important in the Japanese culture. "Japanese has a complex inter-connected system of lexical selection and verbal constructions which vary depending on who is speaking, to whom one is speaking, and about whom one is speaking" (Hinds 1973:155).

In his article, Hinds gives lexical items which have the same referential meaning but differ by the added meaning components of *humble, honorific,* and *neutral* (see Display 13.2).

ENGLISH	HUMBLE	HONORIFIC	NEUTRAL
wife	*kanai*	*okusan*	*tuma*
house	*uti*	*otaku*	*ie*
aunt	*oba*	*obasan*	

Display 13.2

The *humble* word is used to refer to oneself and to someone or something immediately connected with oneself. The *honorific* form refers to another person whose status is meant to be elevated.

Levels of politeness are also used in selecting verbs. Note the following examples (Hinds 1973:156):

sasiageru	to give to an equal of high status or to a superior of high status
ageru	to give to an equal or superior
yaru	to give to an intimate or an inferior
kudasaru	to give to the speaker (deferential)
kureru	to give to the speaker (nondeferential)

When translating into Japanese, **levels of politeness** become very important in choosing the correct word. When translating from Japanese, it will probably not be possible in most languages to keep these distinctions, but the translator should be aware of this loss of meaning.

One of the main concerns of the translator who is translating for indigenous minority cultures is the **educational level** of the audience for whom he is translating. If the translation is to be read by people with the level of primary education, the vocabulary chosen must be vocabulary which would be understood by those people. If, however, the translation will be used primarily by people who have a secondary education there will be a great deal of additional vocabulary which might be used. For example, more educated persons tend to have borrowed more words from other languages and use these as part of their own language. Persons with less education would probably not understand many of these borrowed words. A more educated person will have an extensive vocabulary in the areas in which he has studied; whereas, he may lack some in the vocabulary of other people in his culture because he will not have been involved in many of their experiences, due to the fact that he was in school.

Communication situation

In addition to the age, sex, and educational level of the speaker (writer) and the audience, there are also many factors in the **communication situation** which will affect the particular choice of vocabulary. Different vocabulary will be used in giving a **formal** speech from that which would be used in **casual** conversation in one's home or with friends. There will be special pronunciation, words, and grammar for formal speech, informal speech, and casual speech. For example, the word *inebriated* would be used in formal speech, *drunk* in informal speech, and *stoned* in casual speech. A person might be addressed as *Dr. Jones* in a formal speech, *John* in informal speech, and *Buddy* in casual speech. In English, *younger generation* is more formal than *children*, and *kids* is less formal. One would expect to find formal speech used in the classroom, in parliament, when the elders of the village speak to the people, and in radio broadcasts. Informal speaking would be used outside the classroom, around the fires in the village, when eating together, and in most conversations. Casual speaking would occur in the home and with close friends.

The matter of **formal** versus **informal** is often closely related to the location where the speech is made. In writing, there will also be degrees of formality, and one would not write using the same kind of vocabulary when writing a letter to some government official as one would when writing to one's friend. Part of this, of course, would be the difference in subject matter, but even the way of greeting and the way of expressing the content will be different. In writing an official letter, words *residence* or *incision* might be used; whereas, in writing about the same subject to a friend, one would use *house* and *cut.*

Technical terminology may also have special connotative value for those who use them. Sometimes people will use more technical or more formal vocabulary in order to impress the audience with their own level of education or status in the community. The use of technical terms can be a way of speaking which will eliminate some people from understanding because they are not acquainted with the technical terminology. The translator must carefully keep in mind who the audience is for whom he is translating and not use vocabulary which is so technical that it will not be understood. A medical bulletin translated for doctors might use words like *incision, lesion, tonsillectomy,* and *optometrist.* The same information translated for rural people with less education might use *cut, wound, have tonsils out,* and *eye doctor,* respectively.

Within the same language, certain vocabulary items may be used in one **region** or country, and a different vocabulary in another **region** or country, to mean the same thing. For example, the word *cookie* is used in the United States to refer to the same thing which is called *biscuit* in Australia. The American word *trunk* (of a car) is equivalent to the word *boot* in Australia and the word *gas* is equivalent to *petrol.* In New Guinea, the Pidgin speakers in one area use the word *buscat*, and those of another area use the word *puse* meaning *cat.* In West African English, the word *dash* is used for *tip* (money left for a waiter) and *bush* means an *uncultivated* (or *nontown) area.*

It is important that the translator be aware of the **regional differences** and make every attempt to use words which will be understood as widely as possible. If one is translating for the speakers of a local area, then, of course, the particular form used in that area will be chosen.

Cultural meaning of words

One of the most difficult problems in translating is found in the differences between **cultures**. The people of a given **culture** look at things from their own perspective. Many words which look like they are equivalent are not. They have special connotations. For example, the word *pig* has a very negative connotation in the Jewish culture, but in the cultures of Papua New Guinea *pig* has very positive connotations because *pigs* are a very important part of the culture. In the American culture, this word is neutral in most of its uses. This difference is based upon **cultural** variations and the part that *pigs* play in the society.

Different **cultures** have different focuses. For example, the cultures of New Guinea focus on gardening, fishing, foods, trees, plants, and ceremonies; whereas, the culture of America focuses on working, earning money, sports, schooling, and marriage. Some societies are more technical and others less technical. This difference is reflected in the amount of vocabulary which is available to talk about a particular topic. There may, however, also be both technical and nontechnical vocabulary to talk about the same thing within a given society. If the source language text originates from a highly technical society, it may be much more difficult to translate it into the language of a nontechnical society. For example, to translate the Hebrew Scriptures into the languages of Papua New Guinea or the languages of the Amazon of South America, there will be many problems in vocabulary having to do with such things as *priest, temple, sacrifice*, and *synagogue*. If one were translating a book on social science, dealing with African cultures, it might be very difficult to find equivalent words for items of these cattle cultures when translating for Papua New Guinea languages or for Amazon jungle groups. The same would be true in translating documents about the Eskimos and about *snow* for the Arabs who live in the desert. When the cultures are similar, there is less difficulty in translating. This is because both languages will probably have terms that are more or less equivalent for the various aspects of the culture. When the cultures are very different, it is often very difficult to find equivalent lexical items.

The **culture** is often reflected in the figurative usages of words. For example, in America we use *sheep* in a figurative sense as "one who follows without thinking." In Papua New Guinea, people use *cassowary* in figurative speech, but this would never be used figuratively in America because there are no cassowaries. The matter of the figurative uses of objects of the culture will be discussed more in the chapter on metaphors. The important thing to note here is that the object is the same; that is, if we are talking about a *pig* in Papua New Guinea or a *pig* in the Jewish culture, the object is the same. However, the meaning is quite different since in Papua New Guinea *pig* signifies *food* and *wealth*, but among Jewish people, it has a connotation of *unclean* and is a *nonfood* item.

Symbolic actions

In every culture, there will be certain actions which will be **symbolic**. These will occur in the source language text, usually without any indication of what is the significance of the action. If the action is simply translated literally, it may result in zero or wrong meaning. For example, various movements of the head are **symbolic** in most languages. If the text simply says *he nodded his head*, without any indication of why, this might be misunderstood; if in the source language culture, nodding the head meant *yes*, and in the receptor language culture, nodding of the head had no particular **symbolic meaning**. It might also be that in some other culture, nodding of the head would indicate negative rather than positive response. For example, among the Chol of Mexico, wagging one's head from side to side indicates an emphatic *no*, and wagging it up and down signifies *joy*. In some cultures, wagging the head is used as a symbol of *derision*, but to show this same kind of *derision* among the Witoto of Peru, a person would stick out his chin. In most English speaking countries, a person points to himself with his finger towards his chest when saying *I*, first person, but this is not true for the Chinese. The word for *I* or *me* in old Chinese was *tseu* which means *nose*. In China, one still puts his finger on the side of his nose when saying *I (Encyclopedia Americana*, Vol. 12).

If the form of an action is already associated with a different function in the receptor language, it is difficult sometimes to know how to translate **symbolic actions**. If the intended meaning is simply made explicit and the word expressing the action is kept in the translation, it still may not make a lot of sense although in some situations this would help. For example, if the source language text says *shake one's fist,* the translator could add *in anger* in order to clarify the meaning of the gesture. However, if *shake one's fist* is used in the receptor language for some other **symbolic meaning**, this could be very confusing to the readers of the translation. In such cases, it might be better to drop the specific reference to the **symbolic action** completely and simply make explicit the meaning of the action. It might be possible in some instances to use something more generic. For example, instead of saying *he shook his fist at him* one could say *he showed that he was very angry*. The important thing is that the translator be aware of the fact that **symbolic actions** often have different meanings in the receptor language and in the source language. An adjustment may need to be made in order to avoid a wrong meaning or no meaning at all.

EXERCISES – Lexical Items and Situational Context

A. State the **emotive contrast** between the following lists of lexical items which have the same underlying meaning. In what **social context** might each be used?

 1. father, daddy, dad, pop, the old man

 2. die, kick-the-bucket, pass away, leave us, expire

 3. speak, preach, lecture, share, talk

B. List all of the words which are used for *father, die,* and *speak* in a language other than English which you speak. What are the differences in **connotation** between members within each set which you have listed?

C. How would you react to the following words? Rate them 1-5 on a scale with 1 being good and 5 being very bad.

child	death	father	blood
God	school	prostitute	potatoes
bread	colonialism	tribe	vomit
mother	murder	car	traitor

D. Find five different sets of words in a language other than English in which the members of the sets have essentially the same referential meaning but one has a **good connotation**, one a **bad connotation**, and one has a **neutral connotation**.

E. Write a sentence you might say in English with each of these **symbolic actions**. You may change the tense of the verbs. Use natural English:

 1. wrinkling up nose

 2. raised eyebrow

 3. shrug of shoulders

 4. nod of head

 5. clenched teeth

 6. hands on hips, feet apart

    7. chest out, shoulder back

    8. wave of hand towards oneself

    9. wave of hand, no direction

    10. man tipping his hat

    11. chin protruding

    12. smiling

    13. talking out of the side of the mouth

    14. stomp of the foot

F. Which of the above symbolic actions are used in your culture? For each of these, write a sentence you might say with each of these **symbolic actions**.

G. Explain why there are three different ways in which John Smith is addressed in the following:

    1. His neighbor passed him with a quick, "Good morning, John."

    2. The chairman said, "If Mr. Smith will please come forward we will proceed."

    3. The president of the college added, "Professor Smith will be presenting the lecture."

H. In what **communication situation** might "Good morning" in English be accompanied by each of the following:

    1. a salute

    2. a hand shake

    3. a smile

    4. a scowl

    5. a bow

    6. a wink

    7. a wave of the hand

I. Would these same actions (H above) accompany the greeting in the other language which you speak? In what situation?

Chapter 14
Collocation and Concordance of Lexical Items

In the discussion above concerning secondary and figurative senses (chapters 10 and 11), it was noted that it is the **collocates** that determine which sense is indicated in a given phrase or sentence. The word *dress* does not have the same meaning in the phrases *dress the chicken* and *dress the child*. To *dress a chicken* involves "taking the feathers off" but *dressing a child* is "putting clothes on." Because of the **collocates** *chicken* and *child* we know the meaning of *dress*. The matter of **collocation** was only mentioned briefly above. More detail will now be given concerning what is meant by **collocation** and the implications of **collocation** for translation.

Collocation is concerned with how words go together, i.e., which words may occur in constructions with which other words. Some words occur together often, other words may occur together occasionally, and some combinations of words are not likely to occur. Knowing which words go together is an important part of understanding the meaning of a text and translating it well. Some words do not occur together because the combination would be nonsense; that is, it would not make sense because it is outside of reality. In English, we do not say the *cat's wings*, but we often say the *bird's wings*. Only in a fantasy with a flying cat might *cat's wings* be considered good English.

The word **collocate** means to put side by side. Combinations of words will differ from language to language. For example, in English, the verb *have* **collocates** with the word *dream*. We say *I had a dream*. However, in Russian this combination would not be used. Rather, one would say *I saw (in) a dream*. Persons learning a second language often make mistakes because they **collocate** words together which go together in their first language but do not go together in the language they are learning. In English, we say *he has trouble* or *he suffers trouble*, but other languages may say *he sees trouble* or *he drinks*

trouble. The meaning is the same, but different words are combined
to indicate the meaning.

Special collocations

There are certain combinations of words in any language which
are **fixed combinations**. They always occur in a certain order, or they
always occur together. This is especially true of expressions like *spick
and span, hale and hearty, to and fro, now and then*, and *neat and tidy*
in English. Other languages will have completely different combinations which are fixed expressions.

Notice the following expressions from Gahuku of Papua New
Guinea (data from Ellis Deibler) in which no specific meaning can be
assigned to some of the words but the collocation as a whole carries
the meaning. These special collocations are idioms in Gahuku:

ne-helele my-?	*vizekave*	I am afraid.
no-goka my-nose	*vizekave*	He fooled me.
napa big	*vizekave*	It got big.
goive sweet-potato	*vizekave*	He has measles.
a-puta' his-grasp	*vizekave*	He embraced him.
peletani ?	*vizekave*	He juggled it.

In such **fixed** collocations, it is sometimes difficult to identify the
meaning of the parts of the idiomatic expression.

Certain combinations which commonly occur together often occur
in a **fixed order**. If the order is changed, the result will sound unnatural
to the native speaker of the language. In English, some examples are
bread and butter, day and night (other languages prefer *night and day*),
knife and fork, black and white, black and blue, ladies and gentlemen,
and *rant and rave*. It sounds strange to a speaker of English to hear
someone say *gentlemen and ladies* unless *ladies* is an after thought.
Rave and rant would probably never occur. In many languages of Papua
New Guinea, one says *mother and father* and never *father and mother*.

The matter of idioms has already been mentioned. **Idioms** are special **collocations** or fixed combinations of words which have a meaning as a whole, but the meaning of combination is not the same as the meaning of the individual words. They often have the same meaning as other lexical items in the language but carry certain emotive connotations not expressed in the other. For example, in English, the idiom *kick-the-bucket* has the same meaning as *die*, but it shows a certain lack of respect. *Hit the sack* means *to go to bed* but is more informal. Notice the following other English idioms and their meanings:

kick over the traces	to cast off restraint
kick up the ladder	to promote to high position
hit it off	to get along well
read the riot act	to order or warn to stop something
read between the lines	to understand more than is directly stated
pass the hat	to take a collection of money
pass the buck	to shift a responsibility to someone else

Notice, also, the following example from English and three African languages (from Barnwell 1980:56) in which the same meaning is expressed in the two languages but different verbs are used. The form is natural to the language in which it occurs but would not sound natural if translated literally into the other language.

English:	to *keep* the law	**Mbembe:**	to *obey* the law
	to *break* the law		to *spoil* the law
	mending the nets	**Jukun:**	*tying* their nets
	ate wild honey		*drink* honey
	he was *given* wisdom	**Ezaa:**	he was *taught* wisdom

Great care must be taken when translating **idioms**. A literal translation will usually result in nonsense. The translator must first be sure of the meaning of the **idiom**, and then look for the natural equivalent way to express the meaning of the **idiom** as a whole. There are also **special collocations** which may be looked at in sets since the meaning is basically the same. Note the following sets in English (Barnwell 1980:57):

> The king *abdicated.*
>
> The maid *gave notice.*
>
> The principal *resigned.*

In all three cases, the persons *gave up their jobs*, but *abdicated* collocates with *king* and *resigned* with *principal*. One would not say *the maid abdicated* or *the maid resigned*. Note these sets also:

a teacher's *salary*	a *herd* of elephants
a minister's *stipend*	a *flock* of geese
a worker's *wage*	a *school* of fish
	a *pack* of wolves
	a *gang* of thieves
	a *crowd* of people

Sometimes it is possible to analyze the **collocations** on the basis of certain generic meaning components which occur in the words. For example, in the list of sentences below, the **collocations** are correct. If the verbs were exchanged, the result would be a wrong meaning or a metaphorical meaning. The first list **collocates** with nonhumans and the second with humans.

I *washed* the car.	I *bathed* the baby.
I *rented* a typewriter.	He *hired* a secretary.
The puppy *yelps.*	The baby *screams.*
He *sheared* the sheep.	He *cut* the boy's hair.

Notice the difference between English and Shilluk in Display 14.1 (Nida 1964:51).

English:	*break* a stick	**Shilluk:**	*break* a stick
	break a string		*pull* a string *in two*
	break an egg		*kill* an egg

Display 14.1

A literal translation of the Shilluk *kill an egg* would be nonsense in English and *break an egg* would not be good Shilluk.

Translations into English from a Slavic language included these literal translations of Slavic idioms: *speaking point, the idea came to expression,* and *it's Chinese to me.* The correct idiomatic English would have been *point for discussion, the idea found expression,* and *it's Greek to me.* **Collocations** are words joined together in phrases or sentences to form semantically unified expressions. The combination which forms a semantically correct meaning in one language may not do so in another. A translator must constantly be on the lookout for idioms in the source language and translate with care so as to give the correct meaning in the receptor language.

Collocational range

Every word in a language has its **collocational range** or restrictions which limit its meaningful usage. The **collocational range** of every word will be different. No two words have exactly the same **collocational possibilities.** For example, one might expect that *horse, dog, chicken, man,* and *child* might have the same **collocations.** There is some overlap. All of them occur with *eat, drink, walk,* and *run.* However, notice that although *horse, dog, chicken, man,* and *child* all occur with *run,* only *horse* and *dog* **collocate** with the noun *race. Horse race* and *dog race* are acceptable, but *chicken race, man race,* and *child race* do not occur in English. A list of the other words with which a word may occur is called its **collocational range.** Some words will have a very limited range and others a very large list of possible **collocates.**

The **collocational range** of equivalent words between languages will not be identical. It will overlap but not match completely. It is most likely to match in primary usage but not in secondary or figurative usages. *Run,* in its usual sense of *people* or *animals running,* has, for example, a corresponding term in Aguaruna, *tupikau.* But the English **collocations** of *run* with *nose, motor, stockings,* and *plants,* do not occur, nor do such idioms as *run into debt, run into trouble, run out of money,* and *run out of patience* occur as possible **collocations** with *tupikau* in Aguaruna. The **collocational range** of *tupikau* is very limited. On the other hand, in Kasem of Ghana (Beekman and Callow 1974:163), *run* collocates with *pity*. *He ran his pity* means *he took pity on him.*

Every word in a language has its **collocational range** with limitations which do not allow for other combinations. *Bright,* for example, in English, collocates with objects in which intensity of light is involved, such as *sun* and *color. Shiny* collocates with objects in which the surface is significant to the meaning and, therefore, *shiny coin* and *shiny floor* are correct, but not *shiny sun* and *shiny color.* The number of eligible collocations for a word often depends on its place in the generic-specific scale. *Animal,* for example, will have a larger range than *sheep* or *dog.*

Only a native speaker of the language can judge whether or not a collocation is acceptable, especially if one is trying a new collocation. Languages do change and there is constant extension and reduction of the **collocational range** of a word, but a native speaker is the one who must make the final decision on new and acceptable collocations. For example, a translator was trying to translate *white as snow* into a language that did not have *snow* as a vocabulary item. So *white as hail* was tried. The problem was that *white* did not collocate with *hail*, nor did the combination carry the same meaning. The language did have a collocation *clear as hail*, but with a different meaning. Finally, the translator simply translated the meaning directly with a phrase meaning *very white.* This is sometimes the best solution.

The Amuzgo language of Mexico has two words which are equivalent to the English word *love.* The one collocates only with higher status to lower status (God to man, husband to wife, mother to child) and the other only with lower status to higher status (man to God, wife to husband, child to mother). The translator will want to use the natural collocations of the receptor language.

Collocational clashes

People speaking a language which is not their mother-tongue often make **collocational errors**. These errors may be either grammatical or lexical, but, in either case, words are put together which do not naturally go together. Sometimes verbs and nouns are confused. A letter received from a publisher, written by a nonnative speaker of English said, "We have sent the book...we are sorry for the overlook." *Overlook* is a verb in English and the noun *oversight* should have been used. Lexical **collocational** errors are usually called **collocational clashes**. Everyone who has learned a second language has made these kinds of errors. There are also errors which are simply bad grammar, such as saying *they are gone home* rather than *they have gone home.* These errors are not usually made by persons translating into their mother-tongue. **Collocational clashes**, however, are a bit more subtle and sometimes overlooked by the translator.

In most languages, such **collocations** as *black noise, noisy silence, the water walked, he ate water, the bird said,* and *the kettle boiled* would be **collocational clashes**. But notice that some languages, for example, Chuave, do say *ate water*; the *bird said* might be all right in certain stories or poetry or if the bird is a parrot; and *the kettle boiled* is an acceptable **collocation** in English, since it is a metonymy. The problem is that what is a perfectly acceptable **collocation** in one language may be unacceptable or even nonsense in another.

Sometimes there is a **cultural clash** between what is said in the source text and the patterns of the receptor culture. These are not **collocational clashes** of lexical items. They are **cultural clashes**. For example, in the Anggor culture of Papua New Guinea, the women go first on the trail, and the men come last. But in India the men go first and the women follow. If one were translating a story about India into Anggor which said *the men went first,* he would have to leave this fact as it is. It is true that the cultural customs clash, but the meaning of the words do not. The fact of the *men going first* must be kept and not distorted. **Cultural clashes** are not changed; that is, the story would not be changed to make the culture of India into Anggor culture. It might, however, be helpful in such instances to add a phrase in the receptor language such as *following their customs.*

Each language will have lexical **collocational restrictions**. For example, in some languages, *hear* collocates only with *sounds* and not with *people*. One could not translate *I heard John* literally, since *heard John* would be a **collocational clash**. The translation might need to say *I heard John's speech.* In the same way, there are languages where *believe* does not collocate with *people*, but with words or ideas. *I believed him* would need to be translated *I believed what he said.*

In English, we do not say *the animal's fingernail* nor do we talk about *a person's claw*. Some languages would have only one word for both *claw* and *fingernail*. In English, a person has a *hand*, but an animal has a *paw*. Attributive words will also have **collocational restrictions**. It is all right to say *fat dog* in English, but not *fat rope*. The correct **collocation** would be *thick rope*, but one does not usually talk about a *thick dog*. But it is not incorrect to say *thin dog* and *thin rope*, although a *skinny dog* would probably be more correct.

The translator must constantly be alert to the potential pitfall of **collocational clashes** in the translation. To avoid this he will consider as suspect any word not used in its primary sense. If translated literally, it will probably cause a clash. The translator will not expect to be able to translate idioms literally and he will constantly be checking with mother-tongue speakers, if he is not a mother-tongue speaker of the receptor language. Only mother-tongue speakers can best judge whether certain words may go together or not and what the resultant meaning would be. For example, a translator translating into English will always want to check with a mother-tongue speaker of English, if English is not his own mother-tongue.

Concordance

We have already seen that a word will probably be translated in as many ways as the senses in which it is used. Each sense will need a different word for the translation. If a given word was translated the same way every time it occurred in the source language text, the translation would be full of collocational clashes and wrong meanings. There cannot be complete **concordance** between the words of the source language text and the words of the receptor language translation. **Concordance** means consistent matching of lexical items. Because of all the mismatch between language structures, there will never be complete concordance between a text and its translation.

In order to understand this clearly, it is important to focus on the two kinds of **concordance**. There is **real concordance** and there is **pseudo concordance. Real concordance** occurs when within a document the same word or expression is used repeatedly to refer to the same concept; that is, it has the same meaning each time it occurs. There is **real concordance** in this paragraph:

> The boy *ran* to the store, *ran* up to the storekeeper, and asked for a can of milk. Then he *ran* out into the street and, holding the milk tightly, *ran* home as fast as he could *run*.

Each occurrence of *run* has more or less the same meaning. It is used over and over to give the feeling of urgency. It is likely that the translation of each occurrence of *run (ran)* will be with the same lexical item (with changes for tense, etc.) in the receptor language. However, it is possible that some languages would not use *run* for all five occurrences.

Now notice the following paragraph where the word *run* is also used, but the **concordance** is not **real concordance**. *Run* has a different meaning each time:

> The motor of his car stopped *running*. The man didn't know what to do. He was near a brook which was *running* under the road through a culvert. He thought about using some of the water to cool the engine. But he decided he would *run* back to town and see if he might *run* into someone who could help him.

In this paragraph, the **concordance** between the forms of *run* is not **real concordance**. Each sense is different. In translating the four occurrences, each would be translated with a different word. In Aguaruna, the words *make noise, go, run,* and *encounter* would be used in the translation.

The following paragraph is translated from the Chol language of Mexico. One word, *juc'*, has been left in the Chol form to show the **concordance** which occurred in the original Chol text (from Beekman and Callow 1974:153).

> The Lopez family is always working. When we visited them, the father was *juc'* a board, the mother was *juc'* clothes, the oldest boy was *juc'* his machete, and the oldest daughter was *juc'* soap on her dog.

Although the same word is used four times, it will need to be translated four ways in English. When collocated with *board* it means *to plane*, when collocated with *clothes* it means *to iron*, when collocated with *machete* it means *to file (sharpen)*, and when collocated with *soap* it means *to rub*. It is not possible, nor desirable, to keep the **pseudo concordance** of this text when translating it into English. The English should read:

> ...the father was *planing* a board, the mother was *ironing* clothes, the oldest boy was *sharpening* his machete, and the oldest daughter was *rubbing* soap on her dog.

The meaning of the English is the same as the Chol and sounds natural. If the translator attempted to keep the **concordance** by using *plane* in all four places, the English would be misunderstood. No attempt should be made to keep **pseudo concordance** in translation. The very nature of secondary sense and collocational range make this impossible.

However, **real concordance**, which is the deliberate reoccurrence of the same word with the same sense, should be kept. The author may have used it to show the topic, theme, some discourse feature, or for style. If a word is part of the theme in the source language and various words are used to translate it in the receptor language it may be hard to follow the theme of the text. **Real concordance** should be kept when possible. However, the structure of languages is such, and mismatching is such, that it may not always be possible. Some languages do not repeat the same word within a single paragraph or episode but use synonyms and substitute words instead.

For example, we mentioned above that Amuzgo has two words for *love*, one for higher status to lower status and one for lower status to upper status. If the source text has one word *love* and the receptor language has two, the two words will need to be used correctly in the context to convey the right meaning even if there is less **concordance** as a result. Greek has several words to refer to the meaning included in the English word for *love*. The translation from Greek to English will be more **concordant** than the source text because one word will be used to translate several.

There will always be some loss of **concordance** in translation. However, the important matter is that the meaning of the translation be equivalent as nearly as possible to the meaning of the source language and that words which are thematic and intended by the author to be **concordant** be kept **concordant**, if doing so does not distort the meaning. There will be some gain of concordance in cases where alternate words used in the source text have more or less the same meaning and are translated by a single word in the receptor language.

EXERCISES – Collocation and Concordance of Lexical Items

A. In each of the following, there is a single form in italics, but with different meanings, signaled by the linguistic context (the whole sentence). What is the meaning of each usage? Which meaning is primary?

1. The *bill* dropped from his wallet.
    The *bill* was very small for such a large bird.
    He received a *bill* for the rent.
    The *bill* passed by a small margin.

2. The *house* passed the motion.
    His *house* is on the edge of town.
    I belong to the *house* of Israel.

3. A book was on the *table*.
    There is a good *table* in the book.
    They want to *table* the motion.

    4. I stop *by* the bookstand in the evening.
        I was stopped *by* the policeman.
        I sat *by* the fireplace.

B. In each of the following, the word *fired* has a different meaning depending on the words it collocates with. If translated literally into another language, it is probable that a collocational clash would result in the receptor language. Think about how each of these sentences could best be translated into the second language which you speak.

    1. The man *fired* his stove/furnace.

    2. The boss *fired* his secretary.

    3. The manager *fired* up his team.
        (preparation)

    4. The book *fired* his imagination.

    5. The hunter *fired* his gun.

    6. A. J. Foyt *fired* up his car.

    7. The student *fired* off a letter to the editor.

    8. The catcher *fired* the ball to second base.

C. For each of the above in A and B, tell what **collocate** in the linguistic context helps identify the meaning. What is the relationship between the word and the **collocate**?

      ex. The *bill* dropped from his wallet.

          Bill refers to money because it occurs with wallet which is used to carry money (is in the same semantic domain).

D. Translate the sentences in A into a language other than English.

E. The following translation into English has many **collocational clashes**. The wrong English word was chosen in the translation into English. First, rewrite the paragraph changing each word that has a number by it, using a word which would collocate better and be more natural English. After you finish, read the notes below the text to see if you found all the changes needed. (Data from David Strange.)

Today[1] morning as I was walking down the way[2] I saw my first[3] friend a small[4] way ahead of me. I accelerated and caught above[5] with him. When I arrived[6] up with him I tumbled[7] into stair[8] adjacent[9] to him but he was in such a haste[10] that I could not keep up with him. Therefore[11] I said, "Stroll[12] more slowly you are strolling[12] also[13] fast."

[1]We say *this morning* not *today morning*.

[2]The usual word is *road* not *way*.

[3]*First* would mean *first* in time, not importance; *best* is the right word.

[4] The phrase we use is *a little way* not *a small way*.

[5]*Caught up* with him is the right phrase; *above* does not collocate with caught.

[6]*Arrive* does not collocate with *people. Arrive* is used only for places. The correct word would be *caught up with*.

[7]The idiom is *fell into step; tumble* will not fit here.

[8]*Stair* and *step* mean the same in some contexts but only *step* fits here.

[9]*Adjacent* is generally only used about things and usually in a more technical type of context. *Next* is the proper word when collocating with *him* (people).

[10]*Haste* and *hurry* mean the same but English uses *a hurry* but never *a haste*.

[11]*Therefore* might be used in speeches or books but not in ordinary conversation. Most people would say *so*.

[12]*Stroll* means to *walk slowly* so it does not collocate with *slowly. Walk* is the word that should be used.

[13]*Also* and *too* can mean the same. However, in this context the meaning is "comparative" rather than "in addition." *Also* lacks the meaning of "comparison" which *too* has. The word here has to be *too* not *also*.

F. Make a list of objects which collocate with each of the following verbs in English: *get, reach, pull, drive,* and *take.* Then, without looking at the English list, make a list of objects which collocate with the equivalent word in another language. Do the lists match?

G. Is the **concordance** (the italicized word) in each of the following **real concordance** or **pseudo concordance**?

   1. A good scholar is full of *ideas.* New *ideas* come to him daily. He is always open to the *ideas* of other people as well.

   2. As I was *running* the water in the sink, I could tell by the sound that the refrigerator wasn't *running* very well.

   3. I *saw* the teacher frown as he *saw* through what was going on.

   4. The mother *dressed* her baby, put her on her back, and went out to *dress* a chicken for dinner.

   5. John *ate* all the meat he could, and then gave some to his son to *eat.* After they had *eaten,* they gave some to the dog to *eat* also.

   6. John *took* a trip to Europe. He wanted to *take* a look at the beautiful cathedrals. As he was going up the stairs of one of them, he *took* a tumble and ended up in the hospital. He *took* a chance and got up before he was well because he was tired of *taking* naps all day long.

Chapter 15
Lexical Equivalents
when Concepts are Shared

In chapter 1, translation was described as the process of studying the lexicon, the grammatical structure, and the communication situation of the source language text, analyzing it in order to determine the meaning, and then reconstructing this same meaning using the natural forms of the receptor language. The translator is constantly looking for **lexical equivalents** between the source language and the receptor language. However, as discussed in the previous chapters, this is sometimes a very complicated process.

The fact that the receptor language is spoken by people of a culture which is often very different from the culture of those who speak (spoke) the source language will automatically make it difficult to find **lexical equivalents.** The lexicon of the two languages will not match. This mismatch will make it necessary for the translator to make many adjustments in the process of translation. Languages will group semantic components together in a great variety of ways. This makes a literal, one-for-one equivalence of lexical items impossible. Also, the translator is looking for the most natural and accurate way to express the meaning. Therefore, the form of the translation may be quite different from the form of the source text, even when the concepts are shared between the two languages.

The next three chapters bring together the various discussions concerning the lexicon which have been presented in chapters 6 through 14, and suggest how a translator may find an appropriate **lexical equivalent**. There are three matters which must be looked at in choosing adequate **lexical equivalents**. First, there will be concepts in the source text which are **known** (shared) in the receptor language, but which will be translated by a nonliteral equivalent; second, there will be concepts in the source language which are **unknown** in the receptor language; and third, there are lexical items in the text which are **key terms**; that is, they are important to the theme and development of the text and need special treatment. In this chapter, the first will be discussed, i.e., **lexical equivalents** when the concepts are shared by the two languages. In chapters 16 and 17 the other two matters will be discussed.

Nonliteral lexical equivalents

As pointed out in the previous chapters, even though most of the concepts which occur in a particular text are also found in the receptor language, they are expressed in different ways. There is an extensive core of meaning components which are shared between languages. However, total matching cannot be assumed. There will be some concepts which occur in one language which will be unknown in the second language. But, even when the same concepts do occur, the way in which they are expressed in the two languages is often very different.

As already discussed, languages combine meaning components differently, and meaning components are divided and grouped differently in one language from another. There is usually complete mismatch between the secondary senses and figurative senses of lexical items between languages. An idea may be expressed from a different perspective; that is, figuratively in one language and nonfiguratively in another, or positively in one and negatively in another. In light of the tremendous diversity in the lexicon of various languages, how is it possible for a translator to choose the best **lexical equivalent** for the translation?

First of all, it is essential that the translator accept the fact that a single source language word may be translated by one word or by a number of words in the receptor language, and that what is several words in the source text will sometimes be translated by a single word. Often the source language words will be translated by a completely different set of words. That is, the translator must not expect that there will be a **literal equivalence.** There will be times when words will match between the two languages. This is most often true when a source language word is being used in its primary sense and the receptor language is likely to have an equivalent word with that same primary sense. Even when dealing with primary senses there is not always complete matching, but there is likely to be more matching.

The translator should remember that "how many ideas and what combination of ideas may be combined into one word is a language-specific feature that only occasionally corresponds between unrelated languages" (Beekman and Callow 1974:176). It should be remembered that languages differ (1) as to the number and selection of meaning components combined in a word, and (2) as to the semantic interrelationships that may exist between words. The translator should not expect concepts to be represented the same way in the receptor language as they are in the source language text being translated. Since the lexical structures of the two languages are different, the way the concepts are expressed will be different.

Descriptive phrases

In chapter 6, the semantic complexity of words was presented and the necessity of "unpacking" the meaning components of a word in order to translate into another language using a phrase or clause was discussed. Because many of the words in any text are semantically complex, it will be expected that many times a single word will be translated by several words, that is, a **descriptive phrase,** in the receptor language. The meaning is still equivalent. The single Greek word πατροπαράδοτος was translated into English as *received by tradition from your fathers.* The word *glutton* in English might need to be translated *one who eats too much.* Or *praise* might need to be restated to read, *says, "It is good."* The second example shows that words which imply speech may sometimes need to be restated by expressing them with direct speech in the receptor language.

The translator needs to remember also that the process of "un-packing" (restating) semantically complex words sometimes works in reverse. Several words or phrases in the original may become a single word in the translation, i.e., they are "bundled" into one lexical item. We have already given examples of this in the previous chapters.

Finding equivalent translations for money terms is often difficult. For example, *nickel* is a *coin worth five cents.* It is not hard to restate the meaning using words of the same system. The complication comes when these need to be equated to words from another money system. Sometimes it is possible to give the equivalent in an amount in the other system. For example, *five dollars* could be translated as *one hundred pesos,* if those amounts were equivalent. The problem is, of course, that the value of monetary units changes over the years, and it is very difficult to be sure of an exact equivalence. The alternative is to borrow the lexical form from the source language, but this would mean almost nothing to the reader of the receptor language in many cases. In some cases, even though a specific coin is named, the value is not in focus. The name in the source language could be kept, for example, *a type of money called peso.* When the value of the money is in focus and it is important to include this, it is sometimes possible to equate the value in the receptor culture by talking in terms of "so many days' wages" or some other reference that will make the value relatively clear. In this case, a **descriptive phrase** clarifies the amount.

The matter of money is simply used as an example of the kinds of problems the translator finds, and demonstrates the impossibility of literal equivalence. No one-word-for-one-word translation is possible. Such a literal translation would not carry the meaning. The meaning must be kept the same while the form will change – one word for many, many words for one, a nonfigurative expression for a figurative one, a figurative expression for a nonfigurative one, a reciprocal form for a direct form, etc.

Using related words as equivalents

In chapter 7, equivalents involving synonyms, antonyms, and reciprocal lexical items were discussed. Two languages often do not have a matching of **synonyms** related to a given concept. For example, English has a number of terms such as *goodness, holiness, righteousness,* and *virtue*, but Aguaruna has only one word, *pegkeg*, which would be the best equivalent for any one of these synonyms. On the other hand, if one were translating Aguaruna into English, one would need to evaluate each context of *pegkeg* to decide which of the synonyms would be the best choice in English. The choice will depend on the collocational range of each of the synonyms. Although there is overlap in the meaning of the **synonyms**, there may well be restrictions of collocation which will need to be considered in choosing among the **synonyms**. Also, as mentioned in chapter 13, the connotations of **synonyms** are distinct and need to be taken into consideration. The words *policeman* and *cop* are **synonyms** but cannot be used interchangeably in most contexts.

It is also very common to find synonymous words or expressions used together as **doublets**. A **doublet** consists of two near synonymous words or phrases which occur as a unit, for example, *spots and blemishes, holy and righteous,* and *strangers and foreigners.* The source language needs to be studied to discover the reason for the use of **doublets**. It may be simply to emphasize the idea or to modify the area of meaning slightly. It may be that the use of **doublets** is simply for stylistic reasons. It will not always be possible or stylistically appropriate to keep both.

Some languages also have doublets which are based on **generic-specific** relationship. For example, some languages, like Greek, will use two speaking words together such as *answering said*, where *answering* is more **specific** and *said* is more **generic**. If this is characteristic of the source language but not of the receptor language, the translator should not retain the **doublet** but use the natural quotation openers and closers of the receptor language. It may be that, for some receptor languages, doublets will need to be used when the source language does not use them, in order to follow the natural style of the receptor language. The meaning of the **doublet** is to be translated faithfully, using whatever form is most natural in the receptor language.

Lexical Equivalents when Concepts are Shared

Lexical equivalents may also sometimes be found throug
of **negating antonyms**. There may be no direct equivalent in the
receptor language, but there may be a lexical item with an exact
opposite meaning, and by negating this, the desired meaning may be
obtained. We have already used the example of *bad* being translatable
into Aguaruna only by *pegkegchau* 'not good.' When using a **negated
antonym** as a lexical equivalent, it is important to check out the
collocation to be sure that it will be appropriate in the context in which
it will be used. For example, in the Colorado language of Ecuador, the
word *good* is a highly generic word and collocates with *health*.
However, when *good* was negated it could no longer be used with
health; that is, it was not natural to say *not good health* in Colorado.
In English, we say *good health* and *poor health*. The collocational
range of a word and its **antonym** (and thus its negated antonym) are
seldom identical. Nevertheless, being aware of **antonyms** (and thus
negated antonyms) in both languages may help the translator find a
needed equivalent.

The use of a **reciprocal lexical item** as an equivalent is another
possibility which is discussed in chapter 7. For example, *John gave me
the hat* and *I received the hat from John* would be **reciprocal equivalents**. The translator needs to be open to the possibility that this will be
the best lexical equivalent in some situations. However, the **reciprocal**
may have a different connotative meaning, a different collocational
range, or a change of focus. For example, in changing to the **reciprocal**,
the grammatical form is often changed from active to passive. However,
passive may have a special function not intended in the source text.

Generic-specific words

Lexical equivalents involving **generic** or **specific terms** is another
possibility which we have mentioned several times and which can be
extremely useful. A lot has already been said about the **generic-specific**
relationship of words. There are three problems in translation related to
generic-specific words (Beekman and Callow 1974:185–86):

1. The source language text may use a **generic term**, but the
   receptor language may only have a more **specific term** in that
   semantic area;

2. The source language uses a **specific term**, but the receptor
   language only has a **generic word** available in that semantic
   area; or

3. The receptor language word used in the translation is intended
   to be understood in a **generic sense**, but is interpreted by the
   receptor language speakers in a **specific sense**.

As has been pointed out repeatedly above, concepts are grouped together under a **generic** label in different ways in different languages. In English, we have only one word for *banana* which is used for all varieties. In some Amerindian languages, there are a dozen of more **specific names** and there may or may not be a **generic term**. Because of the mismatch in **generic terminology** between languages, there may be times in translation when a lexical equivalent which is more **generic** can be used and times when a lexical equivalent which is more **specific** can be used.

Since languages vary greatly in **generic** vocabulary but are more alike in **specific** vocabulary, it will be easier to find a **specific** equivalent. There may be no **generic** equivalent for the source language **generic** word. For example, the word *miracle* is a generic term in the sense that it refers to a variety of miraculous actions–healing, calming a storm, exorcism, and so forth. In the Trique language of Mexico, there is no word for *miracle*. A text calling for an equivalent for *miracle* had to be translated *heal the sick and do other such deeds*. In the sentence *There was a light on the table*, the word *light* might have to be translated with a more **specific** equivalent. The more **generic** word *light* might not be appropriate for this context. It would be important to find out the form of the *light* referred to in the source language text. Then a more **specific** name for it such as *candle* or *lamp* could be used as an equivalent.

Sometimes the source language will have a **specific term** for which the receptor language has only a more **generic term**. Particularly, if the contrastive components of the **specific term** are not in focus, the **generic term** may serve very well as a translation equivalent. If necessary, the **generic word** may be modified with a descriptive phrase to add any contrastive components which are needed for a clear understanding of the source language lexical item. The word *bread* in the English phrase *daily bread* is a **specific** word representing a **generic** idea. It is referring to *food* and it would be quite proper in a translation to use the more **generic** word *food*.

Sometimes when a person is referred to in the source language text by occupation, as for example, *farmer, sower, tanner*, it may be necessary to use the **generic** term and use a verb phrase to complete the lexical equivalent; for example, *a man who farms, a man who sows, a man who tans hides*. Sometimes in the source language, the name of the **specific** plant or animal will be used in the text, and there may be no exact equivalent in the receptor language. If the characteristics of the **specific** plant or animal are not in focus, the more **generic** classification could be used. For example, *lilies* might be translated *flowers*, or *wolf* might be translated *wild, dog-like animal*. Whether or not this would be the best translation will depend, of course, on the context in which the word occurs.

In the discussion of taxonomies, it was mentioned that the same word may occur at several levels of the taxonomic hierarchy. For example, in English, *man* means not only *mankind* in general but *man* as in contrast to *woman, man* as in contrast to *boy*, and so forth. In Vietnam, the phrase *rice* refers to any grain whether it includes *rice* or not. In some contexts, *rice* refers to the **specific** grain, in others it might be referring to *wheat*. The word *rice* can be used to refer to other types of grain as well as to *rice*. In Muyuw of Papua New Guinea the word *canoe* refers to *boats* of any size or description, all *land vehicles*, and any type of *airplane*. Also, in Papua New Guinea, some languages use the word *pig* in a **generic sense** to refer to other *large four-legged animals*.

When words which have both a **generic usage** and a **specific usage** are being used, it is important that the translator build into the context sufficient clues to indicate which usage is the correct one for the translation. One needs to be aware of the ambiguity which can arise because of the characteristic of **generic words** which may be used in a more **specific sense** as well as a **generic sense**. The translation will need to include the collocate which will cause the reader to know if the meaning is **generic** or **specific.**

Secondary and figurative senses

Chapters 10 and 11 dealt with **secondary** and **figurative senses** of lexical items. The principles guiding the translation of the **secondary** and **figurative senses** were given there. The important rule for the translator to keep in mind is that **secondary** and **figurative** senses will almost never be translated with the equivalent lexical item of the source language. We cannot over-emphasize the fact that equivalent lexical items will almost never have the same **secondary** senses from language to language. Even **primary meanings** that seem to be the same may have additional components that are different. In addition to finding an adequate lexical equivalent, the translator must build into the context sufficient collocates to indicate the desired meaning.

Figurative senses and figures of speech will almost always need adjustment in translation. Sometimes a nonfigurative equivalent will be needed in the receptor language; sometimes a different figure of speech with the same meaning may be found.

All **figurative usage** should not be eliminated from the translation. Sometimes it will be possible to translate a nonfigurative word of the source language with a **figurative equivalent** in the receptor language. For example, the word *hypocrite* was translated with the following idiomatic figurative phrases in four Nigerian languages (Nida, lecture notes):

> *man with two hearts*
>
> *man with swollen lips*
>
> *man with sweet mouth*
>
> *man who talks with two mouths*

In the Totonac language of Mexico, a word meaning *a two-worded person* is used for a *hypocrite* (Nida 1947:132).

When concepts are shared between the source and receptor languages, the important rule for the translator is to find the most natural and accurate way to communicate the same meaning in the receptor language as was intended by the author in the source language. This may mean that a very different form will be used in order to insure correct meaning and natural expression.

EXERCISES – Lexical Equivalents when Concepts are Shared

A. Below are two versions, the source language (SL) and the receptor language (RL). Describe the adjustment that was made in the translation.

　1.　SL: The *wealthy* live here.
　　　RL: *People who have lots of money* live here.

　2.　SL: The *wolf* snatched them and scattered them.
　　　RL: The *savage animal* snatched them and scattered them.

　3.　SL: *No fewer than* ten people came last night.
　　　RL: *At least* ten people came last night.

　4.　SL: Mary *borrowed* the book from James.
　　　RL: James *loaned* the book to Mary.

　5.　SL: Everybody is talking about *what is happening*.
　　　RL: Everybody is talking about *the high enrollment at the college*.
　　　(Understood from the context)

6. SL: She *glanced* at the teacher.
   RL: She *looked quickly* at the teacher.

7. SL: Someone in the department *embezzled* the money.
   RL: Someone in the department *ate* the money.

8. SL: The baby's nose was *running*.
   RL: The baby's nose was *dripping*.

9. SL: The boy was sitting at the *foot of the stairs*.
   RL: The boy was sitting at the *bottom of the stairs*.

10. SL: They were supposed to *ring* the office after nine.
    RL: They were supposed to *telephone* the office after nine.

B. In each of the following pairs, the SL is given literally and the RL is an idiomatic English translation. Describe the adjustment made in the translation. Hyphens in the SL indicate a single word. (These are not consecutive sentences from one text.)

1. SL: One person fish-hook throwing-in sun going-down he-went.
   RL: There was a man who went down to the river one evening to fish.

2. SL: Toad brushing-off after-throwing-him-into-water he-left-him.
   RL: He brushed the toad off into the water and left him.

3. SL: He forgotten-about-it house going-up that frog after-eating one-who-desired-to-go-to-sleep toad-also becoming-person arriving he-went-up-to-him.
   RL: He forgot about it and went up to his house. After eating the frog, he tried to sleep. The toad turned into a person and came up where the man was trying to sleep.

4. SL: Fox quickly fish grabbing-lots coming-out he-laid-them-down.
   RL: Fox came up quickly with a great many fish which he laid on the ground.

C. Translate the four examples in B above into a language other than English.

D. In each of the following pairs, the SL is literal Denya (Cameroon) and the RL is an idiomatic English translation. Describe the **lexical equivalent** used for all nonliteral equivalents in the translation. Hyphens in the SL indicate a single word in Denya. (These are not consecutive sentences from one text. Data adapted from Abangma: 1987:73–77).

1. SL: Poverty, thing which they-call that poverty, thing it-bad.
   RL: Poverty, that is, what is called poverty, is bad.

2. SL: You-are-if poor, you are people eyes open. In gathering your speech person he-put-not head there.
   RL: If you are poor you are worthless in people's eyes. In a gathering nobody pays attention to what you say.

3. SL: You-are-if poor you-know not put children in school. Schooling it-requires money.
   RL: If you are poor, you will not be able to send your children to school. Schooling requires money.

4. SL: It-has laws which they-make town it-walk well.
   RL: The village has laws which make it go well.

5. SL: Even-if you-are there, even-if you-are not there, and you-fell law, they-ate you.
   RL: Whether you are a member or whether you are not a member, but happen to break the law, you are fined.

E. Translate the examples in D above into a language other than English. Is the form of your translation more like Denya or more like English? Is it natural receptor language style?

Chapter 16
Lexical Equivalents
when Concepts are Unknown

Perhaps one of the most difficult problems facing a translator is how to find **lexical equivalents** for objects and events which are not known in the receptor culture and, therefore, there is no word or phrase in the receptor language which is easily available for the translation. As has been pointed out before, a translator has to consider not only the two languages but also the two cultures. Because of the difference in culture there will be some concepts in the source language which do not have **lexical equivalents** in the receptor language. This may be because of difference of geography, of customs, of beliefs, of world view, and of various other factors.

When the concept to be translated refers to something which is not known in the receptor culture, then the translator's task becomes more difficult. The translator will not just be looking for an appropriate way to refer to something which is already part of the experience of the receptor language audience, but he will be looking for a way to express a concept which is new to the speakers of that language.

There are three basic alternative ways in which a translator can find an **equivalent expression** in the receptor language. These are (1) a generic word with a descriptive phrase, (2) a loan word, and (3) a cultural substitute (Beekman and Callow 1974:191-211). The translator needs to be aware that each alternative has certain potential problems. In each particular context, it will be important to consider all three possibilities in order to decide which will be most appropriate for the particular context. There are certain words in any text which are **key words.** When the **key words** of the source language text are unknown in the receptor language, the problem is even more critical. The matter of **key words** will be discussed in chapter 17.

Form and function

As the translator is confronted with words in the source language which have no equivalent in the receptor language vocabulary, his first responsibility will be to understand clearly the meaning of the word and the use of that word or phrase in the context in which it occurs. He will ask himself, "What are the most important meaning components of the word or phrase being translated? What is the original author trying to communicate in that particular context?" Sometimes the author is concerned with the **form** of the THING or EVENT, but sometimes the **function** is more important. There will also be times when the meaning of the word itself is not as important as the effect which the author is trying to create. The translator will want to find a way to express the important meaning components of the word and phrase; that is, the ones which are in focus in the context.

THINGS and EVENTS can be looked at from the perspective of the **form** of the THING or EVENT, or from the perspective of its **function**. This distinction is very important in looking for **lexical equivalents**. For example, *pencil* has the **form** of being long, pointed at one end, made of wood with graphite in the middle, and usually having an eraser at one end. But the **function** of a *pencil* is to write. A *quill* which is used for writing would have the **same function** but a very **different form**. In describing the **form** of a *dog*, we would talk about its size, shape, color, location of eyes, ears, etc. The **functions** of a dog in some cultures would be hunting and guarding property. In other cultures, the **function** might be simply a pet to keep one company. **Form** has to do with the physical aspects of a particular THING or EVENT, but the **function** has to do with the significance, the reason for, or the purpose of the THING or EVENT.

In previous chapters, we have shown how an equivalent may be found by stating the meaning components of a word in a **descriptive phrase**. For example, *island* might be translated *land surrounded by water*. In the Inibaloi of the Philippines, the natural expression for *island* is *small place in the sea*. One possible way of finding equivalents for unknown concepts is by stating the meaning components of the source language word. When this is done, a generic word plus a descriptive modification is used. For example, the word *anchor* does not occur in the vocabulary of many languages. The phrase *they weighed anchor* might be translated into one of these languages with a phrase such as *they lifted the heavy iron weights they used to keep the boat still*. Or, if some animal such as *wolf* was not known in the culture, the generic term *animal* and the descriptive modifiers *fierce* or *wild and dog-like* might be used. This kind of equivalent has already been discussed in previous chapters. However, in deciding to use this particular kind of equivalent, it is very important that the translator study the context to see whether the **form** or the **function** of the lexical item is the focus in the passage. A descriptive modification of a generic term may include a description of the **form**, a description of the **function**, or a description of both.

Sometimes a **comparison** will adequately carry the meaning. As already mentioned, the **form** has to do with any feature or characteristic of a thing such as its size, shape, quantity, color, taste, temperature, substance, and material, or the visible movements of an event. The **function** refers to the significance of the THING or EVENT, that is, the reason for it or its purpose, or in some cases, the usage of the THING. Not every component of the source language concept will be significant in the context. The descriptive modification will not make explicit all of the components but simply those that are significant to the passage.

Understanding correspondence of **form** and **function** is crucial to finding good lexical equivalents. (We are not talking about linguistic form as discussed in chapter 1, but physical form.) There are four possibilities. First, a THING or EVENT in one language and culture may have the same **form** and the same **function** in another language. For example, *ear* with the **function** of *hearing* is the same in all cultures and languages. Second, the **form** may be the same but the **function** may be different. *Bread* may be found in two cultures and a word for *bread* in both. However, in one culture it may be the main food, the staple that is eaten at every meal; whereas, in another culture it may be a special treat and served only as dessert or as a food for parties. The **form** is the same but the **function** is different. In a context like the Lord's Prayer "Give us this day our daily *bread*," the word *bread* with the **function** of "party food" would not be appropriate. It would be better to translate with the more generic word *food* to avoid a wrong significance.

A third possibility is that the same **form** does not occur, but another THING or EVENT with the same **function** does occur. For example, in one culture, *bread* may be the "staff of life," that is, the main food. In another, as among many language groups of the tropical forest area, the "staff of life" is *manioc*. *Bread* and *manioc* have **different forms**, but they have the **same function** in the two cultures.

A fourth possibility is that there may be no correspondence of **form** and **function** at all. The term in the source text may refer to something which does not exist in the receptor culture, and there is no other item which has the same **function** as this term had in the source culture. For example, *sheep* are referred to in texts from the Middle East. In some instances, *sheep* has the **function** of being a *sacrifice for sin*. However, among the tropical forest groups of the Amazon, the animal *sheep* does not occur nor is there a comparable *animal sacrifice for sin*. There is no correspondence of either **form** or **function**. The translation will need to use a descriptive phrase for both the **form** and the **function**.

So far, all of the examples have been of THINGS in the source language. The correspondence of **form** and **function** also applies to EVENTS. For example, *run* in its primary sense has the same form and meaning in all languages. The **form** is *moving oneself from one place to another by rapid movement of the legs*. The **function** is *to get from one place to another in a hurry*. **Form** and **function** are the same in all languages. The action of *beating one's chest* has the **function** of showing *remorse* or *repentance* in Jewish culture. In another, as among the Otomí of Mexico, this same **form** has the **function** of showing *anger*. The **form** is the same, the **function** different. The Korku of India have a word meaning to *carefully plant grain in rows*; whereas, some other language may have a word which means to *scatter grain over the field*. In both cases, the **function** is the same, *to plant the grain so that it will germinate*. But the **form** is different. The two ways of planting are not the same.

There are, however, some actions which do not occur in other cultures nor is there any other action with the same **function**. For example, in some cultures, there is the EVENT of *tattooing* a person's face at a certain age, and the **function** is to show that the person is now an adult. But there may be other cultures where *tattooing* does not occur and there is no word for it. Also, there is no special event which occurs to indicate that a person has become of age. There is no correspondence of either **form** or **function** of the action *tattoo*.

The **function** of a THING or EVENT is often culturally unique and unknown to other peoples. If the **form** is retained without clarifying the **function**, wrong meaning may result. Whenever there is no correspondence of **form** or **function**, some adjustment will be needed in the translation. The translator must keep in mind the following two principles: (1) the **form** that a word makes reference to may be substituted, omitted, described, or otherwise adjusted to avoid wrong, zero, or obscure meaning, and (2) the **function** that a word makes reference to may be made explicit to avoid wrong, zero, or obscure meaning. The implications of these principles are now discussed in detail and illustrated below.

Equivalence by modifying a generic word

We have already seen in previous chapters how it may be necessary to translate by using a generic term and stating the other meaning components clearly; that is, by paraphrasing. When words found in the source language do not occur in the receptor language, it may be especially helpful to analyze the source language word to discover its generic component, the contrastive components, and the function of the word in its context. Then from this analysis, an adequate equivalent may be found in the receptor language.

When a generic word is to be used as the equivalent lexical item, and modified so as to carry the correct meaning, there are four possible modifications which may be made. These are:

1. by making explicit the **form** of the item,

2. by making explicit the **function** of the item,

3. by making explicit **both** the **form** and the **function**, or

4. by modifying with a **comparison** to some THING or EVENT which does occur in the receptor language.

The use of a generic word as a base for constructing an adequate equivalent is extremely useful. Sometimes the generic term by itself will be sufficient if the focus is not on other meaning components or on **function**. But many times, more needs to be added in order to make clear the **form** or **function**, or both. Notice the following examples which have been used by translators to translate words which do not have equivalents in the second language (selected from Beekman and Callow 1974:194–98):

MODIFIED WITH FEATURES OF FORM
(the generic word is in italics):

treasure	lots of valuable *things* (Mazahua, Mexico)
sea	flat *water* (Wantoat, New Guinea)
wine	fermented grape *juice* (Hopi, USA)
wine	strong *drink* (Trique, Mexico)
flour	ground dry *grain* (Sierra Otomí, Mexico)
incense	*that* which smokes and is fragrant (Ifugao, Philippines)

MODIFIED WITH A STATEMENT OF FUNCTION
(the generic word is in italics):

centurion	*man* that commands 100 soldiers (Mazahua,Mexico)
synagogue	*house* where they study the doctrines of God (Wantoat, New Guinea)
ship	*that* with which we can walk on water (Chichimeca Pame, Mexico)
anchors	*those things* that make the boat stay (Chol, Mexico)
rudder	*board* to steer with (Tetelcingo Aztec, Mexico)

There will be some times when the only way to convey the correct meaning of the source text word or phrase is by modifying the generic word with both the **form** and the **function**. A description of the appearance or action, as well as its purpose, may be needed. Whether or not both are needed will depend on the context of the word in the source text. The following are examples in which both **form** and **function** are made explicit as modification of the generic term. Again the generic term is in italics.

MODIFIED WITH BOTH FORM AND FUNCTION:

mainsail	*cloth* on the pole that was in the front of the boat in order that the wind might push the boat (Tetelcingo Aztec, Mexico)
mainsail	big *cloth* that is stuck to the head of the boat... the *cloth* which takes the wind so that the boat enters the trail (Lalana Chinantec, Mexico)
winepress	*hole* in a rock where they could take out the juice of the grapes (Huixteco Tsotsil, Mexico)
cast lots	there were little round *things* which they *played* with which make it evident who would be favored (Lalana Chinantec, Mexico)
anchors	*irons* to which they attached ropes in order that they would get stuck in the dirt so the boat would not move (Tetelcingo Aztec, Mexico)

The fourth possible way to modify a generic term in order to discover a good lexical equivalent is by using a comparison. The **form** and **function** are not made explicit, but rather, a comparison is made to something which is already well known in the receptor language and for which there is a lexical item. The following are examples of this type of adjustment.

MODIFIED BY A COMPARISON:

rudder	*thing* like an oar (Sierra Otomí, Mexico)
wolf	*animal* like a fierce dog (Aguaruna, Peru)

Which of the four options discussed above might be chosen at a given point in the translation will depend on how the source language word is being used in the text. Questions will need to be asked about the prominence of the word in the source language document. A lexical item which is focal to the understanding of the paragraph or section of a text will need to be modified in more detail than a lexical item which is incidental to the main theme. If the **form** of the item is important to the text, then the **form** must be included, but if the **function** is really the key to the text, then the translator must be sure that the **function** is included in the modification.

It takes careful study of how the word in the source language is used in order to decide which kind of adjustment should be made. A couple of good rules to remember are (1) focus on the most important meaning components the word or phrase has in the context and be sure those are communicated, and (2) be sure that no meaning components are lost which are important to the context.

Another warning needs to be given in using modifications of this nature. The translator needs to be careful that the modification does not become so long and complicated that the sentence becomes hard to understand, and the reader's attention is taken away from the main theme of the passage. The first question to ask is, "Is **form** or **function** in focus in the passage, or both?" Only what is needed, should be included. For example, in one context, *anchor* may be rather insignificant and only the fact that it detained the ship may be important. There would be no point in complicating the translation with a long description of the **form** of the *anchor*. But in another text, the *anchors* and their **form** might be important because they play a major role in what is happening. A translator must use good judgment in choosing how much to include. Complicated modifications can make the receptor language text very difficult to read. The purpose of the modification should be to help the receptor language reader understand, not make it difficult to understand.

Equivalence by modifying a loan word

A **loan word** refers to a word which is from another language and is unknown to most of the speakers of the receptor language. **Loan words** are commonly used for the names of people, places, geographical areas, etc. These words will often need to have a classifier added so that it is clear whether the word is the name of a person, town, country, river, or what. *John* could be translated *a man named John*. Once this was included, the name could be used without the classifier later if the language structure indicated this as the best way to handle reference to participants. There are other ways in which **loan words** can be used in translation, besides being modified with a classifier. They may be modified in the same ways mentioned above for generic terms–by modification which specifies the form or function, or both. Notice the following examples where the word in italics is the **loan word**:

MODIFIED BY A CLASSIFIER:

dove	a bird called *dove* (Wantoat, Papua New Guinea)
passover	celebration called *passover* (Sierra Zapotec, Mexico)
Amazon	river called *Amazon* (Aguaruna, Peru)
lion	animal called *lion* (Aguaruna, Peru)
Levite	Jew of the group called *Levite* (Aguaruna, Peru)

MODIFIED WITH A DESCRIPTION OF FORM,
FUNCTION, OR BOTH:

priest	*priest*, the person who deals with that given to God (Kalinga, Philippines)
anchors	irons called *anchors* tied with ropes so the boat could not go any further (Teutila Cuicatec, Mexico)
Satan	*Satan*, ruler of the demons (Sambal, Philippines)
myrrh	expensive, sweet-smelling oil called *myrrh* (Aguaruna, Peru)

Although the use of a **loan word** may sometimes be the best solution to finding a lexical equivalent, there are also some dangers of which the translator needs to be aware. A **loan word** is a word from another language. There are two kinds of foreign words; **borrowed words** which have been assimilated into the receptor language prior to the translation process, and those **loan words** which are completely new to the receptor language speakers.

Languages are constantly borrowing words from other languages. Many of these become so much a part of the language that the speakers do not think of them as foreign. They are part of the language. English has words borrowed from French, German, and other languages. *Chauffeur* is borrowed from French, and *kindergarten* is borrowed from German. These words were borrowed years ago and are now part of the English language. A **borrowed word** is known to most of the speakers of the language, even those who speak no other language. These can be used in translation just like any other lexical item in the language.

Loan words as used here, however, are not part of the receptor language lexicon. They are words of another language which have no meaning to speakers of the receptor language unless they have learned the language from which the **loan word** comes. A **loan word** will have no meaning unless it is modified in some way to build the meaning into the context and so into the word. The word *Chiriaco* is meaningless to speakers of any language except Aguaruna. But all Aguarunas know its meaning. It can be used as a **loan word** in another language if a classifier is added; that is, if we say *the river called Chiriaco*. The **loan word** now has some meaning; it has a generic component of *river*. A person translating Aguaruna legends into English will soon find that there is a word *ajutap* which has no equivalent in English. But the translator may want to retain the word as a **loan word** using a phrase like *ajutap, that power received through visions*. After the **loan word** has been introduced with a modifying phrase, it may be possible to use just the **loan word** in later references to *ajutap* in the translation. If a **loan word** is used, it is important that in each occurrence the context contains enough information so that the meaning of the source language word is not lost or distorted.

Equivalence by cultural substitute

There will be some lexical items where neither a generic term nor a loan word with modification will be possible as a translation equivalent. There may be times when the source language lexical items can best be translated by using the word for some THING or EVENT which is not exactly the same but occurs in the receptor language. A real-world referent from the receptor culture is substituted for the unknown referent of the source culture. When form is not in focus, this works well if the function of the two referents is the same. For example, the substitution of *coyotes* for *wolves* works well, if one is translating stories from Canada into an Amerindian language of Mexico. Or the EVENT *bury* might be translated with a word meaning *place in a tomb*, if the form were not in focus, since the function is the same–*to dispose of the dead body*.

Although a **cultural substitute** may sometimes be the best alternative for a given translation situation, there are some serious cautions which the translator must keep in mind. When a historical EVENT is being translated, or a narrative of an actual happening, the reference to specific THINGS and EVENTS is important to a faithful translation. To introduce different THINGS and EVENTS would violate a fundamental principle of translation, that of being faithful to historical and present-day facts. A translator does not want to change facts which are being reported. If the story is about someone who was eating a *banana*, it would be inappropriate to say that he was eating an *orange*. It would be much better to say that he was eating a fruit called *banana* with a loan word and add other modification if that is crucial to the story.

When a historical document is being translated, the use of **cultural substitutes** may be anachronistic; that is, something is introduced which did not even exist at the time or in the place referred to in the source text. To translate a document written several hundred years ago with words like *radio* and *airplane* would be very **anachronistic**. The translator must be true to the facts of a narrative. Therefore, some of the other solutions mentioned above would be better for equivalents for lexical items of this kind. Some **anachronistic** equivalences may need to be used, but some are more problematic than others. The use of measure equivalents such as *kilometer, dollar,* and *kilo* is not as serious as using names of objects, such as *car* for *chariot*.

There are, however, some texts which are not of this nature and are more didactic or written to create a certain effect rather than to relate facts. In these texts, it is more likely that **cultural substitutes** would work well. For example, in translating a didactic text into Aguaruna, there was a section which talked about how a person's life could be assessed by his actions. An illustration was used in the source text which said "can a fig tree bear olives, or a vine figs?" Neither *figs* nor *olives* are known to the Aguarunas. At first the translator used the loan words and added modification. The readers got so involved in figuring out what a *fig* tree and an *olive* were like that they missed the teaching of the text. The focus of the paragraph is not what *figs* and *olives* are like. In a subsequent translation, **cultural substitutes** were used–can an *avocado* tree bear *palm fruit*, or a *vine* bear *avocados*. The text was easily understood, and the main focus of the passage was not distorted.

In Muyuw (Papua New Guinea), the *watering of gardens* is unknown. A source text was teaching about evangelism. It said, *Paul planted, Apollos watered, and God gave the increase*. In Muyuw, men have two gardening tasks, so the translator used a **cultural substitute** and translated *Paul planted, Apollos put in the stakes* (up which the plants grow), *and God made the plants grow*.

Some **cultural substitutes** which have been used in translation are listed below:

lamp	bamboo torch (Papua New Guinea)
corner stone	main pole (of house) (Papua New Guinea)
recline at table	sit down to eat (English)
lion	jaguar (South America)
foxes	bush rats (Africa)
fox	hyena (Africa)

The translator needs to ask a number of questions before considering the use of a **cultural substitute**. How similar are the two THINGS or EVENTS? If they are quite similar (*coyote* and *wolf*), then there is less likely to be a problem. Could a descriptive equivalent be used without greatly distorting the text? If so, then the descriptive equivalent is preferred to the cultural substitute. How culturally isolated are the receptor language speakers? If they are very isolated and have seen little of cultural items from other areas, it may be necessary to use more **cultural substitutes** in the translation.

There is another caution which needs to be noted. If the translator decides not to use a **cultural substitute** for a specific word in a historical passage, then there would probably be no reason to use it in a didactic passage. That is, he will want to use the same solution in both places in the same document. The usage will reinforce and help in the teaching of the new concept in the historical part of the text if he also uses it in the didactic part. If there is a historical part of the document which refers to *fig trees*, and so they are going to be introduced by a descriptive phrase of some kind, then the same may as well be used in the didactic portion of the same document. There should be concordance of lexical equivalents (for the same sense of a word) throughout the document.

Cultural substitutes always result in some distortion of meaning and should not be used unless the other possible solutions have proven insufficient. On the other hand, a **cultural substitute** does establish dynamic equivalence, without which part of the original message (the didactic or emotive part) might not be understood.

EXERCISES – Lexical Equivalence
when Concepts are Unknown

A. In the sentences below, the first line represents a source language text and the second line the receptor language translation. The italicized word was unknown in the receptor language. Study the equivalent to see if the generic term is modified by a description of (1) form only, (2) function only, (3) both form and function, or (4) a classifier.

1. The *queen* of the Ethiopians came to visit.
   The woman who ruled the people of Ethiopia came to visit.

2. They ate the roots of *sago lilies*.
   They ate the roots of a local wild flower.

3. She was invited to a *baby shower*.
   She was invited to a party where women friends give gifts to an expectant mother.

4. The *heathen* were invited to attend.
   People who do not know God were invited to attend.

5. They came to a *village* by the river.
   They came to a small town by the river.

6. He went to *Abidjan*.
   He went to a city called Abidjan.

7. He saw an *angel*.
   He saw a messenger from heaven.

8. The *president* spoke first.
   The man who has most authority in the country spoke first.

9. They put *bits* in horses' mouths to guide them.
   They put a metal bar with strings in the horses' mouths and pull the strings to guide them.

10. They used a *sickle* to cut the harvest.
    They used a long curved knife to cut the harvest.

B. Identify the following lexical equivalents as a (1) generic word plus modification, (2) loan word plus modification, or (3) cultural substitute.

   1. They crossed the *Amazon* the next morning.
      They crossed the Amazon river the next morning.

   2. *Foxes* have holes in which they live.
      Bush rats have holes in which they live.

   3. He was lost for six days in the *wilderness*.
      He was lost for six days where no people live.

   4. They were going down the road in a *chariot*.
      They were going down the road in a cart pulled by horses.

   5. The *harmattan* was very bad last week.
      There was a great deal of dust in the air last week because of the winds from the north.

   6. The men put the corn in a *wagon* and went to town.
      The men put the corn in a conveyance pulled by oxen and went to town.

   7. They were playing *volleyball*.
      They were playing a game called volleyball.

   8. They fastened him with *chains*.
      They fastened him with ropes made of metal.

   9. *Peter* was sitting up begging.
      The dog, Peter, was sitting up and begging.

  10. The *king* stood in front of the people.
      The chief stood in front of the people.

  11. They have *manioc* every day.
      They eat a root called manioc every day.

  12. There was plenty of *bread* for everyone to eat.
      There were plenty of corn cakes for everyone to eat.

C. Go through all of the sentences in sections A and B thinking about how the italicized word might need to be translated into your mother-tongue or some language other than English which you know. You might find that a different type of adjustment would be better for that language than the one for the translation quoted here. Write out a suggested translation in your language.

D. The two paragraphs, below the following list (a-o), represent a "source language text" and a supposed "translation" of that text into some receptor language. Certain words and phrases are italicized in both paragraphs, and in the receptor language paragraph, there is a blank after each italicized word or phrase. Referring to the list below, put a letter in each blank to show what kind of transfer has taken place between the source language and the receptor language at that point. For example, if the particular italicized word or phrase is an example of a loan word plus a generic term, modified to show form, then put *j* in the blank. Each of the letters will be used at least once.

a. a generic term, modified by comparison

b. a nonliteral equivalent rendering of a concept already known in the receptor language

c. a loan word with no modification

d. a cultural substitute

e. a loan word along with a generic term, modified as to both form and function

f. a generic term, modified as to function

g. a generic term used for a specific term, without modification

h. a literal equivalent rendering of a concept already known in the receptor language

i. a generic term, modified as to form

j. a loan word, along with a generic term, modified as to form

k. a loan word, modified as to function

l. a loan word, along with a generic term, modified by comparison

m. a generic term, modified as to both form and function

n. a specific term used for a generic term, without modification

o. a loan word with a classifier

SOURCE LANGUAGE:

Oalin, a respected, grey-haired munag, arose and spoke: "*Brothers and sisters*, our *ancestors* came here from *Kolanga*, guided by the munags. They planted *wheat* and vineyards, and also brought in *mabos* and *geelas* and made *pastures* for them. With their *sickles* they harvested the *crops*, and the *wine vats* were full. But, as you know, the *Duricharchs* have always opposed the munags, and now that opposition has developed into open rebellion. They have refused to wear the *tunics*, and they have broken into the *vaults* and removed the *totem poles*, which none but properly consecrated munags dare touch. So," Oalin continued, "my judgment is that all Duricharchs be fined twenty *boshges*, and that their leaders be put in *jail* for six months."

RECEPTOR LANGUAGE:

Oalin __·c__, a respected, grey-haired munag, arose and spoke: "*Brothers and sisters* _____, our *ancient grandfathers* _____ came here from *the country of Kolanga* _____, guided by the munags. They planted *grain* _____ and grapes, and also brought in *mabos to ride on* _____ and *those cow-like animals called geelas* _____, and made *pastures* _____ for them. With their *machetes* _____ they harvested the *grain and grapes* _____, and the *holes in the ground which were used to store wine in* _____ were full. But, as you know, the *Duricharch political party, composed of peasants and dedicated to the overthrow of order* _____, have always opposed the munags, and now that opposition has developed into an open rebellion. They have refused to wear the *long garments* _____, and they have broken into the *places where valuables are kept* _____ and removed the *ornately-carved images called 'totem poles'* _____, which none but properly consecrated munags dare touch. So," Oalin continued, "my judgment is that all Duricharchs be fined twenty *silver-dollar-like coins* _____, and that their leaders be confined for six months in the *building where criminals are put* _____."

Chapter 17

Special Problems
in Finding Lexical Equivalents

For each particular translation project, there will be some unique problems of lexical equivalence. However, there are also some matters which are likely to present special problems in any translation. Every translator is faced with finding adequate equivalents for the *key words* in the source text. There will be some words which at first seem to be adequate equivalents which will turn out to be *false friends*. There will be the problem of loss of some meaning components and the gain of others – the problem of keeping a balance between which components become implicit and which are made explicit. Matters such as these will be discussed in this chapter.

Key words

Almost any text which one might wish to translate will have some **key words**. **Key words** are words which are used over and over in the text and are crucial to the theme or topic under discussion. A text may have several **key words**. The translator must identify the **key words** and as much as possible use a single receptor language lexical item on each occurrence of the **key word**. **Key words** are most often words which represent an essential or basic concept of the text. They are often thematic. As the translator studies the source text, he should note the **key words** and give special attention to finding adequate lexical equivalents before beginning the actual drafting process.

For example, if one is translating an agricultural bulletin about irrigation for a language in which irrigation has never been employed as a way of doing agriculture, the lexical equivalents for the words of the source language related to the process of irrigation will need to be worked on carefully. There will be a number of terms used repeatedly in the source text for which lexical equivalents should be determined before beginning the translation of the whole. The procedures are those described in the previous chapters. The reason for drawing special attention to this matter here is not that any different procedures are used, but that an adequate equivalent for a **key word** will be more crucial to communication than an adequate equivalent for other words in the text. If the **key words** are not translated in such a way as to communicate the meaning clearly, the point of the whole text may be lost. If a **key word** is translated by a variety of equivalents when the SAME MEANING is intended, the text will be less cohesive and the theme less obvious. On the other hand, the translator should not use the same word in different contexts if the result is pseudo-concordance. (See chapter 14.) The translator will want to standardize the form to be used when the SAME MEANING is intended.

Often there will be sets of words which contrast with one another and yet, because of overlap in components of meaning, could be confused if not clearly distinguished from one another in the selection of lexical equivalents. For example, if one were to translate material about the Middle East, it would be necessary to decide on a good lexical equivalent for the three **key words** *church, mosque,* and *synagogue.* If translating into a language in which there is no cultural equivalent, that is, no building which is designated for religious activity, it would be necessary, not only to come up with an equivalent for designating such a building, but also a way to further distinguish the three kinds of buildings. The principles discussed previously for finding lexical equivalents would apply. The central or generic components would need to be identified for each word, and then the contrastive components of all three should be focused on. Notice the following analysis of *church, mosque,* and *synagogue*:

> **Generic components** – shelter, used for religious purposes
>
> **Generic class** – kinds of shelters used for religious purposes
>
> **Specifying components:**
>
> > *church* – used by Christians
> >
> > *mosque* – used by Muslims
> >
> > *synagogue* – used by Jews

More specifying components would need to be considered if comparing the three words used in the Bible – *tabernacle, temple,* and *synagogue.* Notice the following analysis (Larson 1975:44):

Generic components – shelter, used for religious purposes by Jews

Generic class – kinds of shelters used for religious purposes by Jews

Specifying components:

tabernacle	*temple*	*synagogue*
(a) Place where God met the people	(a) Place where God met the people	(a) Place where Jewish people met for religious teaching
(b) Temporary (portable)	(b) Permanent	(b) Permanent
(c) Only one	(c) Only one	(c) Many in different places
(d) People went to make sacrifices	(d) People went to make sacrifices, pray, teach, learn, burn incense	(d) People went for reading of the law, teaching, prayer

In choosing a term to translate any one of this set, the term to be used to translate the others of the set will need to be considered also. This is true of any semantic set. Display 17.1 shows examples of lexical equivalents used in several languages; that is, a literal back-translation into English of the receptor language equivalent. Not all the contrastive components listed in the analysis above are included in the lexical equivalents given in Display 17.1. Enough is included to make clear the distinction between the three **key terms.**

	tabernacle	*temple*	*synagogue*
Aguaruna (Peru)	big house built of skins and cloth	place-to-worship God	Jews' gathering place
Kahgel (New Guinea):	cloth gathering house	house where they sacrificed	Jew people's gathering house for hearing God's talk
Gahuku (New Guinea):	cloth house of religion	large house of religion	Jews' house of religion
Nark (Philippines):	cloth religion house	large religion house	Jews' religion house

Display 17.1

Key words which refer to parts of the material culture are usually not too difficult to translate. Social and political relationships may be more complicated. However, terms which deal with the religious aspects of a culture are usually the most difficult, both in analysis of the source vocabulary and in finding the best receptor language equivalents. The reason is that these words are intangible, and many of the practices are so automatic that the speakers of the language are not as conscious of the various aspects of meaning involved. Here again, it is often helpful to consider words in sets rather than individually.

In looking for the best equivalent for *priest*, the translator would consider the whole system of religious activity and try to match up the functions of each person who has a religious role in order to find the one that would most closely equate with *priest*. It might be necessary to make a modification of some kind to the word chosen in order to be more accurate and convey the same meaning as the source text word. What at first might look like a good equivalent, may actually represent a person with a very different role in the two cultures. For example, the functions of a Jewish *priest* in Israel are not the same as those of a Brahma *priest* in India. This would probably not be too important in translating the word *priest* in some texts. However, if *priest* is a **key word** in the source text of a translation being made from Hebrew into a language of India, careful attention would need to be given to the term used.

In the previous chapter, the possibility of using a loan word (a word from another language) was discussed. This may sometimes need to be done for **key words.** Loan words may be necessary when there is a great deal of difference between the two cultures. This can be especially applicable for such words as the names of religious and political groups and for religious offices. It is sometimes better to use a loan word, and modify it so as to communicate the right meaning, than to try to use a receptor language term which, although partially overlapping in meaning, has components which will give a very wrong meaning. For example, if the word for *priest* had implications of sorcery or idolatry in the receptor language, it might be better to use the source language word and indicate in the context through modification the role of the source culture *priest*. Sometimes it is possible to use the receptor language term and modify it to correct lack of acceptable equivalence. "Languages can combine terms in new ways to express new concepts or to avoid negative denotations and connotations" (Beekman 1980:38).

Whenever a loan word is used, or a new combination developed, for a **key term**, even though the term or combination is new, it must be completely natural both semantically and grammatically. That is, even if the concept is new, the manner in which the words are combined should be completely natural. Occasionally, it will be necessary to use a receptor language term which is missing some desirable components or which has some components of meaning which are not desirable. When this is true, the difference in total meaning will need to be cared for by the corrective influence of the context. This is preferred to loan words for most **key terms.**

In some texts, there will be "**token words**" which are best kept as loan words. These would include such things as "the characteristic words of a time period that denote a fact of civilization, such as the name of a fashionable dress, a new product or invention, or a current fad" (Newmark 1974:71). "**Token words**" are often transliterated in order to retain a sense of time in history. This is often done in novels and short stories. For example, in translating Spanish novels into English, words like *plaza* and *patio* are often used as "**token words**" to give a Spanish flavor to the translation. However, words should not usually be transliterated in religious, political, or historical documents.

Newmark makes the following suggestion concerning **key words** (Newmark 1981:15):

> ...The appropriate equivalents for keywords should be scrupulously repeated throughout a text in a philosophical text; theme words are the writer's main concepts and terms of art; in literary works, the stylistic markers are likely to be an author's characteristic words...in an advertisement... they may be token-words... In a non-literary text, there is a case for transcribing as well as translating any key-word for linguistic significance.

Symbolic words

In many texts, there will be some **key words** which will acquire **symbolic** value. They come to carry figurative or metaphorical meaning as well as the basic meaning of the word. When this occurs, it may be necessary to adjust it in the translation.

Newmark (1981:153) states that:

> In imaginative writing all key-words acquire symbolical value, and become potential metaphors grounded in the culture. Like key-words in a technology, they are suddenly forced to bear figurative meaning. When such words are translated they may have to be supported with an attribute unless there is a strong cultural overlap between source and target language countries.

Special attention needs to be given to **key words** which are also **symbolic words** so that the metaphorical intent of the source text author is not obscured. "These symbols may be retained in the translation without sacrificing meaningfulness by giving a slight clue to the sense intended or by accompanying the imagery with its nonfigurative sense" (Beekman and Callow 1974:136). Religious and political documents are very likely to have **key terms** which have **symbolic meaning** as well as literal meaning. This may occur in other literary documents as well, and the translator needs to be conscious of this **symbolic meaning** as he translates so as not to eliminate the symbol by translating only with the direct meaning.

Word combinations and false literal translation

In most languages, there are groups of words which function in the same way as a single word. For example, the French phrase *livre de classe* (literally, "book of class") is equivalent to English *textbook.* The Russian expression for *desk* is *pis 'mennyj stol* (literally, "writing table"). In languages with a literary history, many of these combinations come to be entries in the dictionary of the language. A glance down a page of an English dictionary will reveal such entries as *minor premise, mint julep, minus sign,* and *house of representatives.* Each phrase consists of two or more words and may involve various parts of speech. Hence, there are combinations such as *miracle play, home loan office, pale blue,* and *lock up.*

Words also combine to form compounds in many languages. A compound is a new word which is created by stringing together simple words, which are the constituent parts. There is almost no limit to the kinds of combinations which can be formed. Some examples in English are *armchair, driveway, horsepower, pickpocket, outlook, kindhearted, babysitter, undertaker,* and *overtake.* German and Hungarian have an unusual propensity for compounding and pursue its possibilities a good deal further than English.

The above mentioned types of word combinations deserve the closest attention by the translator. The meaning of a combination as a whole cannot always be determined by the meaning of the individual constituent parts. For example, a translation from the French *pomme de terre* would be *potato* in English and not the literal *apple of earth* suggested by the French. The meaning of many word combinations must be learned, as if they were individual simple words. For example, a translation into English stated that "Bulgaria is now a synonym of our industrial might, a major center of *black metallurgy.*" This combination is meaningless in English. *Iron and steel industry* would be better.

Sometimes a translator may settle for the literal translation of a word combination because he does not know that there is another, more idiomatic form. If the literal translation sounds plausible, the translator may miss a better rendering. For example, the literal translations *naval infantry* and *war fleet* might seem all right for English, but the more correct translation would be *marines* and *navy*, respectively. In translating technical terminology, where many word combinations of this kind occur, the translator must always be on the alert so that he does not fall into the error of a false literal translation.

False friends

One of the major causes of translation error on the lexical level, when translating into related languages, is that of **false friends**. **False friends** may be defined as words in the source language which look very much like words in the receptor language because they are cognate with them, but in fact mean something different. For example, the Spanish word *asistir* is a **false friend** to the Spanish-English translator because its real meaning is *to attend* and not *to assist*. But *to assist* is the word which immediately comes to the mind of the translator when he first hears or reads *asistir*. But it is the wrong meaning. The Russian word *vizit* is a **false friend** to a Russian-English translator because it really means *official call* (as by a doctor or clergyman) rather than any ordinary *visit*. The translator must be careful not to assume that because the words in two languages look alike they have the same meaning. In the development of languages, the meanings will change. Some or all of the semantic features of the source language word may be lost. They may retain one special feature or may change meaning completely.

False friends are most often thought of in terms of languages which are historically related. But in addition, there may be **false friends** as a result of borrowing. For example, many of the Amerindian languages of Mexico have borrowed Spanish words but often the loan word then shifts in meaning from the original Spanish word. The Spanish word *plaza* refers to the *town square*. But among the Mixes it has been borrowed and refers to any *group of people selling things*. This is because most of the selling of goods takes place in the town square on market days. In the same way, the Chols have borrowed the word *patio*, which in Spanish refers to an *open courtyard*. In Chol, it refers to *a place for drying coffee*. This is because the wealthier Mexican homes often used the *patio* for drying coffee. "The translator must be careful not to assume that a loan word has the same meaning as the same word in the language from which it was borrowed" (Beekman and Callow 1974:198).

There may also be some concepts in the source text which seem to be similar to the concepts which are known in the receptor culture, but which, on closer examination, may be found to have very different functions or significance. The speakers of the receptor language will interpret these in light of their own culture, and the meaning may become distorted. Here, again, the importance of form and function comes into play. The form may be the same, but if the function is different, the meaning may be lost in the translation process. For example, a text which talked about *cutting branches from trees and spreading them on the road* to honor an approaching person was easily translated into a certain African language. *Cutting branches and spreading them on the road* was a familiar concept. But in the African culture, it was associated with *blocking the road to prevent an unwanted person from approaching*. However, in the source text the significance had been *to honor and welcome someone coming down the road*. In the African language translation, the misunderstanding was finally corrected by saying *palm branches* and indicating the function.

Implicit and explicit components of meaning

Throughout these chapters on lexical equivalents, it has become clear that the lexical items of the source language seldom match exactly the lexical items of the receptor language. It would seem that there is more mismatch than match. How, then, is it possible to translate at all? The answer comes in the fact that it is not the **word** that is being translated, but the **total meaning of the words in combination**. That is why, after having discussed lexical equivalents, we have only begun to discuss translation. The next part of this text will deal with larger units—combinations of words into clauses, sentences, paragraphs, and texts.

In discussing clauses and sentences, the matter of **implicit** and **explicit information** will come into focus again and again. But it is also important to mention, before leaving our emphasis on lexical items, that in the translation process, some components of meaning of the source text will no longer be **explicit** and some components which are not **explicit** in the source text will be made **explicit** in the translation. This is because of the very nature of languages. Categories included in various semantic sets will be different. Some will be obligatory in one language and different ones obligatory in another. In order to find an equivalent lexical item, the translator may need to make components of meaning **explicit** which are **implicit** in the source document. There will always be some loss and some gain of meaning. No two language systems match exactly.

However, a translator, who desires to communicate the same information as found in the source text, will come close to reaching his goal by a constant awareness of the differences between languages by a careful analysis of the source text meaning, both referential and situational, and by choosing only natural and clear forms in the receptor language translation.

EXERCISES – Special Problems in Finding Lexical Equivalents

A. Find three short articles, one in a magazine, one which is a chapter in a book, and one in a newspaper. Identify the **key words** of the article. How might these **key words** be translated in a language which you speak, other than English?

B. In each of the following translations into English, the italicized words have been translated literally and may or may not be idiomatic or correct. Evaluate the italicized words as translations. Improve them if you can, substituting words and, if necessary, changing grammatical structures.

   1. The agrarian reform called for a *second distribution* of the land.

   2. This was *unfit for drinking* water.

   3. Let us take a look into the future. The year is 1980. Vitosha, the immortal beautiful adornment of Sofia, Bulgaria, has been made into a national park with numerous *hoists, tour bases,* hotels, and restaurants...

   4. In 1961 Galati started building a number of completely new *micro-districts*. We went to see one of them, Tiglina, noted for the wide use of industrial building methods....Two years after construction began, some 18,000 families were already living here. And another such *micro-district*, Tiglina 2, is going up nearby.

C. In each of the following translations from French into English, the italicized words have been translated literally and may or may not be idiomatic or correct. Evaluate the italicized words as translations, in each case, comparing them with various alternative translations which are given in parentheses. Choose the best translation. Improve them if you can, substituting words, and, if necessary, changing grammatical structures.

1. His words *accuse* (show up, bring out, betray) a great ignorance.

2. There's no sense wasting one's time *discoursing* (talking, making speeches).

3. His *engagements* (commitments, involvements, obligations) do not permit him to join the organization at this time.

4. The attendant tied an *etiquette* (label, tag, ticket) on my luggage.

5. Anyone who owns a car ought to be insured against *eventual* (possible, potential) accidents.

6. What are your *projects* (plans, affairs, works) for next year?

7. Last year the textile industry made great progress in *rationalization* (efficiency, streamlining its production processes, introducing labor-saving methods).

8. We always managed to get tickets for interesting *spectacles* (events, exhibitions, happenings).

D. In each of the following translations from Spanish into English, the italicized words have been translated literally and may or may not be idiomatic or correct. Evaluate the italicized words as translations, in each case, comparing them with various alternative translations which are given in parentheses. Improve upon them if you can, substituting words and, if necessary, changing grammatical structures.

1. The ambassador did not hesitate to express the *disgust* (displeasure, annoyance) of his government.

2. There was a *discrepancy* (disagreement, divergence, difference) between the two delegations on the subject of disarmament.

3. *In actuality* (at the present time, right now), there is a serious housing problem.

4. In the statistics of world armament, it appears as the most heavily armed country of the world *in appreciation of* (considering, in relation to) its *dimensions* (size, territory, measurements).

5. Eleven million children are unable to *assist in* (come to, be present at, attend) school.

PROPOSITIONAL STRUCTURE

Chapter 18
Propositions

In Part II above, ways of identifying the meaning components of the lexical items of a language were presented. Words from various languages were compared showing how very differently languages organize the lexicon. Ways of finding adequate lexical equivalents were discussed. However, translation is much more than finding word equivalences. The source text structures must be abandoned for the natural receptor language structures without significant loss or change of meaning. Therefore, we turn now to grammatical structure. The emphasis will be on identifying the semantic structure, i.e., the meaning of the grammatical structures, and comparing how that meaning is expressed in different languages. In chapter 3, an overview of semantic structure was given. The students would benefit from rereading chapter 3 before beginning the study of this third part of the book.

In this section, Part III, **propositions** will be the focus of discussion, and in Part IV the combination of **propositions** within texts is discussed. (The word **proposition** is used here in a broad sense to include a single event or state and the concepts which are immediately related to that event or state. *John ran* is a **proposition**. *The flower is beautiful* is a **proposition**.) A **proposition** most often takes the form of a clause or simple sentences in the grammatical structure, but not always. It may be encoded in a variety of forms. However, whatever the grammatical form, it is encoding a semantic **proposition**. The skewing between grammatical forms and the **propositions** will be discussed below.

Defining propositions

Concepts, as discussed in the previous chapters, consist of meaning components. Or, said another way, meaning components combine into concepts. We look now at how concepts unite to form the next level of groupings called **propositions**. A **proposition** is a grouping of concepts into a unit which communicates. It is a semantic unit consisting of concepts, one of which is central and the others directly related to the central concept. For example, the concepts JOHN, PETER, and HIT may be combined to form **propositions**. The action HIT is the central EVENT concept. What the **proposition** communicates will depend on the relationship of the other two concepts to HIT. If JOHN does the hitting and PETER is the one who was HIT, then the **proposition** would be *John hit Peter*. If JOHN was the one who was HIT, the **proposition** would be *Peter hit John*.

Even though the difference in English is signaled by order, in the semantic structure, the order is unimportant. The important thing is that we know which concepts combine to form the **proposition** and the relations between the concepts. There are many ways in which the semantic structure of a **proposition** can be symbolized. For example, a formula like the following might be used to show the difference between the two **propositions** above.

agent: John....**activity:**HIT....**affected:**Peter

agent: Peter....**activity:**HIT....**affected:**John

In the first example, JOHN has an **agent** relation to HIT; whereas, in the second, JOHN is the **affected** and PETER is the **agent**. The order in the semantic structure is not important but the relations (**agent, affected**) are. Some languages will tend to encode the **agent** first, others will tend to put it at the end, after the **activity**. In the grammar, the semantic **agent** is most often expressed as the subject of the sentence. One knows who hit whom in English by the word order in the grammar. Other languages will have the opposite order, and perhaps additional markers to indicate the **agent** and the **affected.** For example, a number of languages would use the order *John Peter hit* when JOHN is the **agent**.

In order to talk about semantic structure, it is necessary to choose a form for writing **propositions**. Since this text book is in English, we will arbitrarily choose the normal English form to indicate the **propositions**. In more technical material, formulas could be used. The English forms are simply a way of displaying the information. The translator must choose the natural forms of the receptor language in the translation and not translate **propositions** literally.

Any one **proposition** may be encoded in various ways in a given language. The translator will look for the best way; the most natural way. For example, the **proposition** *John hit Peter* might be translated into English with any of the following forms, depending on the context in which it occurs:

> *John hit Peter.*
>
> *Peter was hit by John.*
>
> *The hitting of Peter by John...*
>
> *Peter, who was hit by John,...*
>
> *Peter, the one John hit,...*

Which grammatical form is used in the translation will depend on the relation that the **proposition** has to other **propositions** and how the receptor language (in this case English) will most naturally express the **propositions** and the relations between them.

A **proposition,** then, may be described as a semantic unit consisting of concepts (THINGS, EVENTS, ATTRIBUTES) in which one concept is central and the other(s) related to it through a system of RELATIONS. If the central concept is an EVENT concept, then the **proposition** is an **Event Proposition**; if the central concept is a THING or ATTRIBUTE, then the **proposition** is a **State Proposition** (Beekman, Callow, and Kopesec 1981:52). This difference will be discussed after the method for identifying **propositions** within a text is discussed.

Identifying event propositions

Identifying **event propositions** begins by classifying the concepts that are represented by the lexical items in the text. For example, the following sentence is first analyzed by determining which words represent EVENT concepts, which represent THING concepts, and which represent ATTRIBUTE and RELATION concepts.

E   T   E   A

The destruction of the city was planned well.

Then, the grammatical sentence can be re-expressed in **propositions** with the EVENTS as the center of the **propositions**. There are two EVENTS, *destroy* and *plan*. The two **propositions** are:

(Someone) destroyed the city.

(Someone) planned well.

However, the **propositions** cannot be expressed without including the PARTICIPANTS. Notice that *someone* has been used in the **proposition** to indicate the AGENT; that is, the one who did the ACTION. Because the text does not indicate who did the action, a generic term has been used in the **proposition**. If the rest of the text were available, it might be possible to be more explicit.

The steps for rewriting as **event propositions** are:

1. Look for the forms which express EVENT concepts in the text. Express each of these concepts with a finite verb.

2. Identify the PARTICIPANTS (persons or objects that do the action or to which the action is done).

3. Rewrite as a **proposition** with the EVENT expressed as a finite verb and the PARTICIPANTS made explicit, using the form in which there is no mismatch of grammar and semantics in English. That is, the form used for the **proposition** should indicate by the English structure who the agent is by putting the agent as the subject, who or what the affected is by putting it as the object, etc. The relations between the concepts are shown by the normal English signals used when there is no mismatching.

4. The relations between the **propositions** then need to be studied and a rewrite made expressing these relations, reordering the **propositions**, etc. This fourth step is not included here. It will be discussed in Part V.

Notice the following application of these steps:

TEXT: *John rejected Peter's offer.*

Step 1: The EVENTS are *reject* and *offer.*

Step 2: The PARTICIPANTS are *John* and *Peter.*

Step 3: *John rejected. Peter offered* (to do something).

Step 4: The order would be changed; that is, *Peter offered* before *John rejected.* The relationship between the two **propositions** is sequential, one happened and then the other.

TEXT: *His graduation depended on her help.* (Referring to a past event.)

Step 1: The EVENTS are *graduate* and *help* (*Depend* is encoding a **conditional** relation.)

Step 2: The PARTICIPANTS are *male-person* and *female-person.*

Step 3: *He could graduate.*
If she helped (him).

Step 4: The order of the events is *helped* and then *graduate.* The relation between **propositions** is condition-CONSEQUENCE. *(If she helped him, then he could graduate.)*

Using these four steps, one is able to analyze any text, recasting it in such a way that the underlying semantic structure is made clear. The whole text is written in **propositions** with all the EVENTS, PARTICIPANTS (THINGS), ATTRIBUTES, and RELATIONS made explicit. Even though a translator may not find it necessary to rewrite every passage he is translating, there will be many times when it will be necessary to do this kind of an analysis before an adequate equivalent can be found. Even when a translator thinks he knows the meaning, making it explicit in **propositions** may help him to find a more accurate way to translate the text.

A **proposition** is the smallest unit of communication. Concepts have meaning only in that they refer to THINGS, EVENTS, ATTRIBUTES, or RELATIONS. However, it is only when a concept occurs with other concepts that there is meaningful communication. The combination must not result in nonsense except perhaps in fantasy, poetry, apocalyptic materials, etc. The combination is a **proposition** only when the combination makes sense. A single **proposition** is understood by the speakers of the language to be a single event (that is, a single action, experience, process, or state). If there is more than one EVENT, there is more than one **proposition**. For example, the sentence *John, jumping over the fence, ran, and dove into the lake* would be three propositions: (1) *John jumped over the fence,* (2) *John ran,* and (3) *John dove into the lake.* Notice that a **proposition** has the form of a simple sentence; that is, a sentence which has only one predicate (verb), only one clause. A **proposition** is a single predication.

In the following examples, the source text has been rewritten as **propositions** (without indicating relations since these have not yet been studied).

Source language: *Disobedience brings much suffering.*

Propositions: (Someone) disobeys.
                         (Someone) suffers.

Source language: *The compliment was received well by Mary.*

Propositions: (Someone) complimented Mary.
                         Mary responded well.

Source language: *The men who are now thinking about running for president will begin their campaigns soon.*

Propositions: Some men are now thinking (about something).
                         They want to be president.
                         They will campaign soon.

Notice that *running for president* is an idiom. The meaning is indicated in the **proposition** *they want to be president*. In these examples, we have only done the first three steps of the analysis. One could not do a good translation of these **propositions** without the fourth step; that is, determining the relations between the various **propositions**. The order would need to be changed and the relations made clear. Step four will be discussed later.

Classifying propositions

There are two main kinds of **propositions – Event Propositions** and **State Propositions**. If the **proposition** has an EVENT as the central concept, it is an **Event Proposition**; if not, it is a **State Proposition**. A **State Proposition** will have a THING or ATTRIBUTE as the central concept.

All **Event Propositions** consist of at least a central EVENT concept and an additional THING concept. The central EVENT concept may refer to an **action**, an **experience**, or a **process**. **Actions** would be such concepts as RUN, HIT, EAT, and SWIM. **Experiences** are concepts which refer to the activities of the five senses or to cognitive or psychological activities, as for example, SMELL, SEE, HEAR, THINK, and COVET. **Processes** always represent a change of state (from one condition or state of being to another). For example, DIE, BECOME SOUR, and FREEZE are processes (Beekman, Callow, and Kopesec 1981:56).

The following are examples of **Event Propositions**; the EVENT has been italicized:

Actions: The boys *ran*.
                John *ate* the food.
                Mary *gave* the book to Peter.

Experiences: Mary *knew* little.
                  The boys *heard* the whistle.
                  John *saw* the cow.

Processes: The milk *soured*.
                The dog *died*.
                The ice *melted*.

    State Propositions do not have an EVENT concept central to the **proposition**. They consist of THINGS and ATTRIBUTIVES which are related the one to the other by state relations. A **State Proposition** has two main parts; the topic and the comment. The topic is the CONCEPT being talked about, and the comment consists of the THING or ATTRIBUTE being used to describe or identify the topic plus the state relation. For example, in the English sentence *The book is Peter's*, the topic is BOOK, and it is related to the central concept PETER by the relation of **ownership**. So the meaning is *The book is owned by (belongs to) Peter*. The various kinds of relations which occur in **State Propositions** will be discussed in chapter 20. The central concept in a **State Proposition** is the THING or ATTRIBUTE which occurs as part of the comment. This is central because it is the important (often new) information that is being presented about the topic (often old information). Notice the following examples in which the three parts of **State Propositions** are given first, and then the English equivalent is given. The central CONCEPT is in bold.

CAR...ownership...**ME**	The car is **mine**.
DOG...naming...**FIDO**	The dog's name is **Fido**.
DIRECTOR...identification...**MR. JONES**	The Director is **Mr. Jones**.
JOHN...location...**HOUSE**	John is in the **house**.
JOHN...description...**BIG**	John is **big**.

    English uses the verb *be (is)* to express many **State Propositions**. Aguaruna, however, would translate the above as follows (literal backtranslation):

1. car-possessed-first-person
2. dog Fido name-owner
3. director that-one-Mr. Jones his-name
4. John house-in stays
5. John big-is

These same **propositions** would be expressed with the following structures in Otomí of Mexico, and Gahuku of Papua New Guinea (data from Richard Blight and Ellis Deibler):

OTOMÍ	GAHUKU
1. This is my car.	1. My-car exists.
2. Dog he-is-named the Fido.	2. Dog name-(phrase-closure-marker) Fido-is.
3. Director he-is-named the Mr. Jones.	3. Overseer-man-(phrase-closure-marker) Mr. Jones is-he.
4. John lives there in the house.	4. John-(phrase-closure-marker) house-in is-he.
5. Is big the John.	5. John-(phrase-closure-marker) man big is-he.

The semantic structure, that is, the **proposition**, remains the same, but each language will express the **proposition** with different grammatical forms.

Situational meanings of propositions

So far, we have been discussing the **referential meaning** of the **proposition**. But propositions also must be looked at from the point of view of the **situation** in which they are used. What is the author (speaker) trying to do with the proposition? What is the author's purpose? The author may be asking a *question* or making a *statement*, or giving a *command*. The proposition which is diagrammed below is the same for each of these three usages:

Referential meaning:	JOHN....**agent**....HIT....**affected**....BALL
Statement:	John hit the ball.
Question:	Did John hit the ball?
Command:	John, hit the ball!

The referential meaning is the same, but the usage is different for each proposition. Both Event and State Propositions may occur with any of these three situational meanings. These are often called the **illocutionary forces** of the proposition. In writing propositions, simple English sentences and English word order, and punctuation may be used to indicate the **illocutionary force** of the propositions as was done above. Intonation often indicates **illocutionary force** in oral English. Note the following examples:

State proposition which **commands**: You be nearby!

State proposition which **questions**: Is Mary your sister?

State proposition which **states**: The dog is in the barn.

Event (action) proposition which **commands:** (You) run fast!

Event (process) proposition which **questions**: Did the milk sour?

Event (experience) proposition which **states**: We heard the sound.

In the grammar of some languages, the **illocutionary force** is shown by word order, in others by special particles, affixes, or words. The **illocutionary force** is often encoded by **mood.** Each proposition is either a STATEMENT, a QUESTION, or a COMMAND. This will be represented in the translation by the natural forms of the receptor language. A proposition has only referential meaning until the **illocutionary force** is added. No real communication can be carried on without this situational meaning being included as well. It is possible to know the concepts which make up a proposition and their relation to one another and still not know what the speaker means. For example, we might have the EVENT *eat*, the AGENT *tiger*, and the AFFECTED *traveler* but still not know what the speaker means, unless we know whether he is asserting a fact *(The tiger ate the traveler)* or asking a question *(Did the tiger eat the traveler?)*. The intent of the speaker in saying something is, therefore, part of the communication.

Sometimes the **illocutionary force** is stated by the speaker. Instead of simply saying, *"Go!"* as a command, a person might say, *"I command you to go!"* In this sentence, the **illocutionary force** is actually stated by *I command*. Notice the following:

1. Go!	*I command* you to go!	**Command**
2. He went.	*I say* that he went.	**Statement**
3. Why did he go?	*I am asking* why he went.	**Question**

In the first column, the **illocutionary force** is indicated by the **mood** of the sentence. In the second column, it is made explicit. In the third column, the **illocutionary force** is classified. Normally, a proposition or a propositional cluster is either a COMMAND, a STATEMENT, or a QUESTION.

Another way of looking at the three distinctions in **illocutionary force** is to think of a **statement** as intended to give information to the hearer, a **question** as intended to gain information from the hearer, and a **command** as intended to encourage or solicit the action of the hearer. The intent of the speaker is in focus as it relates to what he wants of the hearer.

Technically, the implied propositions *I command, I say,* and *I ask* are called **performatives**. The purpose of the speaker is not always stated explicitly as in column two above. It is more often indicated by the mood of the sentence as in column one. However, the **performative** is an important part of the semantic structure, i.e., the meaning of the proposition. Without knowing if the **author's purpose** is to STATE, QUESTION, or COMMAND, it is impossible to understand the communication.

EXERCISES — Propositions

A. Look again at some of the examples on the preceding pages (and listed below). How would you express the meaning in a language other than English? Look back at the propositions if necessary. Give at least two grammatical forms for each. For example, *John saw the cow* would have at least two other forms in English: *The cow was seen by John* and *The cow which John saw...*

1. The destruction of the city was well planned.

2. John rejected Peter's offer.

3. His graduation depended on her help.

4. Disobedience brings much suffering.

5. The compliment was well received by Mary.

6. The men who are now thinking about running for president will begin their campaign soon.

7. The car is mine.

8. The dog's name is Fido.

9. John is in the house.

10. The milk soured.

B. First underline the EVENT words in the following sentences. Then identify the PARTICIPANTS which are related to the EVENT and rewrite with propositions. If the participants are implicit, you will need to make them explicit.

1. Peter is my witness.

2. Peter has some knowledge of these happenings.

3. The car was sold by John.

4. There was not much investment left.

5. Visitors are always impressed by the beauty of the Islands.

6. Those to whom judgment was committed answered.

7. We obeyed his command.

8. Work continues on the new building.

C. Using the propositions you wrote for B above, how would you express the eight sentences in a language other than English?

D. Each of the following is a proposition with the function of STATEMENT. Rewrite the proposition to indicate a QUESTION. Then rewrite it to indicate a COMMAND. Then translate into a language other than English first as a statement, then as a question, and finally as a command.

1. John is happy.

2. Mary ran to the house.

3. The boy ate the meat.

4. John saw the river.

5. Mary gave the flowers to Jane.

Chapter 19
Case Roles within Event Propositions

Propositions are combinations of concepts, as we have noted in the preceding chapter. The combination is significant because the concepts are united by special relations. They are a unit. A group of concepts makes up a proposition. In Event Propositions, the THING and ATTRIBUTE concepts are related to the central EVENT concept by relations which are often called **case roles**. In State Propositions there are **state relations** which relate a THING to another THING or a THING to an ATTRIBUTE. Relations found within Event Propositions will be discussed first, and then those found within State Propositions.

Case roles defined

1. The **agent** is the THING which does the action; that is, the person or the object which is the doer of the EVENT. The **agent** is in italics in the following propositions:

> *John* ran fast.
>
> *John* read the book.
>
> The *deer* jumped over the fence.
>
> The *water* flowed swiftly.
>
> The *dog* ate the meat.

As can be seen in the above examples (when there is no mismatch of semantics and grammar), the **agent** is encoded as the subject of the sentence. The **agent** case occurs when the EVENT is an action. *Ran, read, jumped over, flow,* and *eat* are actions.

2. The **causer** may seem very much like **agent** at first. The difference is that the **causer** is the THING which instigates the EVENT rather than actually doing it. A person or object causes an action or process to happen. The **causer** is also encoded as subject of the

sentence when there is no skewing between grammar and semantics. Note the following in which the **causer** is in italics:

> *Peter* made Mary cry. (Peter caused Mary to cry.)
>
> *The pole* strengthened the building. (The pole caused the building to become stronger.)
>
> *John* made Peter leave. (John caused Peter to leave.)
>
> *Malaria* killed her. (Malaria caused her to die.)

Notice also the following examples of **causer** from Kiangan Ifugao (Philippines, data from Richard Hohulin). (The gloss "MK" stands for *marker*. The form marks nouns for certain syntactic information not crucial in these examples.):

> a. *Impabain   mu Pedro nah em kinali.*
>   Cause-shame you Peter   MK you said-it.
>
>   You caused Peter to be shamed by what you said.
>
>   *You* is the **causer** and *Peter*, in this case, is the **affected**, i.e., he became ashamed.
>
> b. *Pangaasim ta   painnilam   ke Juan an*
>   Please-you so-that you-cause-to-know MK John that
>
>   *mundogo hi   ina   na.*
>   is-sick   MK mother his.
>
>   Please inform (lit. you-cause-him-to-know) John that his mother is sick.
>
>   Here again, *you* is the **causer** and *John* is the **affected**.

3. The **affected** is the THING that undergoes the EVENT or is affected by the EVENT. The **affected** refers to the one who experiences an EVENT or the person or object which undergoes the EVENT, that is, "feels the **effect** of" it. The **affected** is in italics in the following examples:

> The dog ate the *meat.*
>
> The tree fell on the *house.*
>
> The *butter* melted.
>
> The *water* evaporated.
>
> *Mary* smelled the smoke.
>
> *Jane* became sad.
>
> *Tom* saw the snake.

When there is no skewing between semantics and grammar, the **affected** is encoded as the *object* of the verb when the EVENT is an **action**. When the EVENT is an **experience** or **process**, it is encoded as the *subject* of the grammatical sentence in English.

4. The **beneficiary** is the THING that is advantaged or disadvantaged by the EVENT. The **beneficiary** is not affected as directly as the **affected**. For example, in the proposition *Mary gave the book to her mother*, *the book* is the **affected** and *her mother* is the **beneficiary**. Note the following examples in which the **beneficiary** is in italics:

> John sold the car for a *friend.*
>
> Mary bought a present for *Tom.*
>
> Jane gave the flowers to *Elizabeth.*

5. The **accompaniment** is the THING which participates in close association with the **agent, causer,** or **affected** in an EVENT. It is like a **secondary agent, causer,** or **affected**. Note the following examples in which **accompaniment** is in italics:

> John went to the park with *his dog.*
>
> The ice cream melted along with the *butter* (the ice cream and also the butter melted).
>
> I ate dinner with *my wife.*
>
> The fork was on the table with the *knife* and *spoon.*

With is a common grammatical marker for accompaniment in English grammar.

6. The **resultant** is that which is produced by the EVENT. There is always a close relationship between the EVENT and the **resultant**. For example, some languages have similar forms for the action and the **resultant** as in *sang a song, house-made a house, fenced a fence,* etc. Note the following propositions in which the **resultant** is in italics and is the result of the EVENT:

> Mary sang a *song.*
>
> The boys ran a *race.*
>
> The soldiers fought a *battle.*
>
> They played a *game.*

When there is no skewing between grammar and semantics, the **resultant** is encoded as the *object* of the verb.

7. The **instrument** is the THING used to carry out an EVENT. It is usually an inanimate object. Note the following examples in which the **instrument** is in italics:

> Mary wrote with a *pencil.*
>
> John cut the string with a *knife.*
>
> Mary covered the child with a *blanket.*
>
> The workmen widened the road with a *bulldozer.*
>
> Jane pointed at the picture with her *finger.*

With is a common grammatical marker for **instrument** in English grammar. Notice in number 5 above that it is also the form used to indicate **accompaniment**. The one form, *with*, has two semantic functions.

8. The **location** is the THING which identifies the spatial placement of an EVENT, that is, the source, the place of, or the destination of an EVENT. Notice the following examples in which the **location** is in italics:

> Jane ran away from *home.*
>
> John flew in from *Chicago.*
>
> Peter walked through the *park.*
>
> Mary stayed in the *house.*
>
> Jane went to the *store.*

It is also possible to divide **location** and be more specific as to whether it is the source location, the destination location, or the location at which an event is occurring. However, for our purposes in this text, we have put them together as **location.**

9. The **goal** is the THING towards which an action is directed. For example, in the proposition *he shot the arrows at the target, the arrows* would be the **affected** and *the target* the **goal**. Notice these additional examples in which the **goal** is in italics:

John prayed to *God.*

I hit the stick against the *fence.*

Peter threw the rock at the *fence post.*

John laughed at *Peter.*

10. The **time** identifies the temporal placement of the EVENT. It tells when the EVENT took place. Or it may indicate the duration of the EVENT. Note the following examples in which **time** is in italics:

John went to college *three weeks* ago.

Her mother stayed for *three weeks.*

They will come at *three o'clock sharp.*

Tomorrow the sun will shine.

Soon someone will come for us.

11. The **manner** is the qualification of the EVENT. It is the manner in which the ACTION, EXPERIENCE, or PROCESS was carried out. Note the following examples in which the **manner** is in italics:

The man ran *quickly.*

The butter melted *slowly.*

John wrote the letter *perfectly.*

The baby became sleepy *gradually.*

The plant grew *rapidly.*

12. The **measure** is the quantification of the EVENT. Notice the following examples in which **measure** is in italics:

Jane prays *frequently.*

They widened the road by *twenty feet.*

The corn had grown *three inches.*

Skewing between event propositions and grammatical forms

In all of the examples given above, English sentences in which the sentence is equal to the semantic proposition are used. That is, the

agent is the subject of the sentence, the **accompaniment** occurs as the object of the preposition *with,* and the **location** occurs as the object of the preposition *from, in,* and *through.* But as we have pointed out before, there is a great deal of skewing between form and meaning in any language. In addition, the forms which encode the same meaning are different for different languages, so there is a double problem for the translator – the skewing between form and meaning in the source language and the different skewing between the form and meaning of the receptor language. In analyzing the source language, the translator is straightening out the skewing in that language. But once he has done this and has a semantic analysis, he is faced with the job of reconstructing in the receptor language, and that involves again incorporating skewing between the meaning and form by using the skewing which is characteristic of the receptor language, which will probably not be the same as that of the source language.

We look now at some examples of the kinds of skewing that occur. For example, one **case role** may be encoded in several ways in the source language, depending on the context, and in several ways in the receptor language. The forms may or may not match. For example, the **agent** in the proposition *Peter ate the banana* is *Peter.* Notice the different ways in which the **agent** is encoded in the following:

Subject:	*Peter* ate the banana.
Object of Preposition *by:*	The banana was eaten by *Peter.* The eating of the banana by *Peter...*
Modifier:	*Peter's* eating of the banana...
Subject in relative clause:	The banana which *Peter* ate...

The above examples show that the proposition may be encoded in different forms and, therefore, the **agent** will be encoded by occurring in different grammatical positions. This is true of all of the **case roles** presented above. Notice that *banana,* which is the **affected** in the proposition, also is encoded in a variety of ways:

Object:	Peter ate the *banana.*
Subject:	The *banana* was eaten by Peter. The *banana* which Peter ate...
Object of the preposition:	The eating of the *banana* by Peter... Peter's eating of the *banana...*

Which form is chosen for English, illustrated above, will depend on the context in which the proposition is being encoded. The point that is important here is to understand that there are several forms which encode the same proposition.

Now looking at it from another point of view, languages will also sometimes have one form which is used to encode several **case roles.** Notice, for example, the following (examples from Frantz 1968:22) in which the preposition *with* is used:

1. I ate ice cream *with* my spoon.

2. I ate ice cream *with* my wife.

3. I ate ice cream *with* my pie.

In this example, the word *with* is used to signal three different RELATIONS. In the first, *with* signals that *my spoon* is the **instrument.** It tells what was used to do the eating. In the second, *with* signals **accompaniment** of the **agent.** It indicates that *my wife* ate ice cream also, at the same time and place as I did, i.e., I was accompanied by my wife, and we both ate ice cream. In the third, *with* signals that *pie* is an **affected** and that the *pie* was **accompanied** by *ice cream.* That is, I ate pie, and with it I also ate ice cream.

And so we see that one **case role** may be encoded by several forms, and that one form may be used to encode several **case roles.** It is this complexity in languages that makes translation a complicated task. The skewing of the source language will be different from the skewing of the receptor language. This causes double complication as mentioned before.

It is impossible in this book to give examples of all the possibilities or even mention them. But an awareness of this skewing should alert the translator to be ready for multiple encoding of the semantic structure and, the reverse, multiple meanings of grammatical forms. One of the reasons why literal translations do not communicate is that they keep the source language skewing. The skewing in the source language will not match the skewing of the receptor language. This is why it is helpful to think of the semantic structure (the meaning) rather than the grammar (forms) as one translates.

For example, the three sentences above, which contain *with* encoding different meanings, would be translated by three different forms in most other languages. In Aguaruna (Peru), the forms would be:

1. I ice cream-(object marker) my-spoon-(instrument marker) I-ate.

2. My-woman-(accompaniment marker) ice cream-(object marker) I-ate.

3. Pie ice cream-(object marker)-also I-ate.

In Aguaruna, the *with* of English is translated in three different forms. Aguaruna has **case role** markers. The first sentence uses the instrument marker *-i;* the second sentence uses the accompaniment marker *-jai;* and the third uses the suffix *-shakam* which means *also.*

Complex concepts within the proposition

In the example given above, most of the propositions included only simple concepts. However, **complex concepts** often occur. Just as meaning components group together to form concepts, so concepts may group together to form complex concepts. For example, the proposition *the dog bit the boy* has only simple concepts – DOG, BIT, and BOY. These are related to one another by DOG being the **agent** of BIT and BOY being the **affected**. But in the proposition *the big dog bit the little boy who lives on the corner* the **agent** and **affected** are both complex concepts. The **agent** is the BIG DOG. BIG is an ATTRIBUTE which identifies or describes DOG. DOG is the central concept and BIG delimits (or restricts) this concept by adding the information that the DOG is a BIG one.

The **affected** in the above proposition is BOY. But here again, BOY is delimited by adding the ATTRIBUTE, LITTLE, and by adding a whole proposition which further delimits BOY by indicating that it is a specific *boy, the one who lives on the corner.* A concept may be delimited by another concept or by a proposition. When this occurs, there is a **complex concept.**

little   ⟶   (boy) ⟵— lives on the corner

The relationship between the central concept and the modifying concepts is one of **delimitation.** That is, the noncentral concepts (or propositions) which modify the central concept, **delimit** it in some way. In analyzing the meaning of a text, this must be taken into consideration. A proposition which modifies a concept is not a part of the chain of EVENTS of the text. It is not functioning in the same way as other propositions in which the EVENT is on the main line of the story or argument.

It is possible to have quite a number of concepts within a **complex concept**. For example, if we begin with the concept HOUSE, it could be further delimited in some of the following ways:

> *that house*
> *that white house*
> *that big white house*
> *that big white colonial house*
> *that big white colonial house which is down the street*

In the last expansion above, a proposition is modifying HOUSE, delimiting it even further. This is what is often called an embedded proposition, that is, a proposition which occurs within a concept. This embedded proposition modifies HOUSE in the same way that BIG, WHITE, and COLONIAL modify HOUSE. The concepts or propositions which modify (and thus delimit) a concept sometimes are descriptive, sometimes help identify, and sometimes are simply a comment about the central concept.

In analyzing propositions, a single concept or a complex concept may occur as the **agent, affected, location,** or other **case roles.** The word **role** is also a useful word in talking about concepts as well as in talking about propositions. The relation between a THING and an EVENT may be **agent...EVENT,** for example. We can then say that a certain concept has the **role of agent** or the **role of goal,** or any one of the **case roles.** In the proposition *the little boy ran to the house quickly,* LITTLE BOY is a complex concept with the **role of agent,** *ran* is the EVENT which is central to the proposition and has the **role of activity,** HOUSE has a **location role,** and QUICKLY has the **role of manner**. The **role** name indicates how the CONCEPT relates to the EVENT.

English allows for long complicated grammatical encoding of **complex concepts.** In some languages, the proposition will need to be translated by more than one sentence so that concepts can be added one by one. The Tunebo language of Colombia has a characteristic stylistic redundancy in which some new information is added with each repetition; that is, the proposition is expanded gradually. Notice, for example, the following (Headland 1975:5):

> *Wicárara yaújacro.*
> Wicara   killed.
> He killed it in the Wicara area.
>
> *Ritab cuítara yaújacro.*
> Ritab by,   killed.
> He killed it by Ritab Stream.

In English, a single sentence would be used: *He killed it in Wicara by the Ritab Stream.* Notice the following from Tunebo (Headland 1975:5) with four repetitions:

> *Erara bowar icara bijacro.*
> There forest in   went.
> There I went out in the forest.

> *Ruwa   yacay   bijacro.*
> Animal hunting went.
> I went hunting.

> *Ri   Sarari cajc bijacro.*
> River Sarari land went.
> I went to the area of the Sarari River.

> *Cutuji bijacro.*
> Cutuji went.
> I went to Cutuji.

The English might well be a single sentence: *I went hunting in the forest of the Cutuji area near the Sarari River.*

However, many sentences are needed to encode the meaning of the preceding examples in a clear way in a given language. There are always just two basic propositions:

> I went into the forest.

> I hunted animals.

However, *forest* is further delimited as being that forest *which is in the Cutuji area,* and the part of that area *where the Sarari River is.* Each of these is an embedded proposition. *Forest, which is in the Cutuji area, where the Sarari River is* is a **complex concept.** This concept might be diagrammed as shown in Display 19.1.

Display 19.1

The above two propositions would be translated into Aguaruna with the following sentences:

> *Sarari, Cutuji nunui*   *webiajai,*
>   that-(location marker)   went-I

> *"Wi kuntin maatajai,"*   *tusan.*
> I   animal will-kill-I   I-saying

If the audience did not know that *Sarari* is a river and that *Cutuji* is an area through which the Sarari runs, then the form would be:

> *Namak*   *Sarari*   *tutai*   *Cutujinum...*
> River   Sarari   that-called   Cutuji-in

The matter of how a **complex concept** is to be translated must be considered carefully so as not to distort the meaning of the proposition in which it occurs. It would not be natural Aguaruna to translate with four sentences as in Tunebo, nor to combine *went* and *hunting* as a single verb phrase as in English. Since the proposition about *hunting* is the reason for the one about *going,* Aguaruna uses a quotation for the *hunting* proposition. Relations between propositions will be discussed in part IV. However, it is important to note that there is not a one-to-one correspondence between the number of propositions and the number of sentences in the grammatical form of the source text. The grammatical form of the receptor text will also not have a perfect match between the number of propositions and the number of sentences. Nor will sentences in the source text match sentences in the translation.

Illustrative text

All of the examples given above have been rather simple, looking at one or two propositions at a time. We look now at a text consisting mostly of Event Propositions. We will take the following Aguaruna text as the source language, analyze the semantic structure of the text, and then suggest possible English translations. The sentences are numbered in the source text to make it easier to talk about them. It is not expected that there will be the same number of propositions in the semantic structure as sentences in the source language. Nor would one expect the translation into the receptor language to correspond in number of sentences to either the source language or the semantic structure. The text is called *Trip to Tuntugkus* and was written in Aguaruna (Peru) by Silas Cuñachí.

1. *Wi*   *wegabiajai*   *ijakun*   *Tuntugkus*   2. *Nunikan*
   I   I-went   I-visiting   Tuntugkus   I-doing-so

wakabiajai   *kampatuma*   *kanajan.*   3. *Wawaim juakin,*   *duwi*
I-went-up   three-times   I-sleeping.   Wawaim I-leaving   there

wakan   *ashi*   *wainakiajai*   *aents*   *wainchataijun.*
I-going-up   all   I-saw   people   those-I-had-never-seen-obj.

    4. *Dutika*   *ai*   *minak,*
      After-doing-so   being-(different-subject-marker)   to-me

"Pataajuitme,"   *tujutuinakui,*   *shig*   *aneeyajai,*
you-are-my-relative   when-they-said-to-me   very   I-was-happy

ditajai   *ijunjan.*   5. *Dita*   *sujuyanume*   *yuutan,*   *tuja*
with-them   I-uniting.   They   they-gave-to-me   food-obj   and

senchi   *kuitabianume*   *mina*   *huwajun.*   6. *Kuashat*
very-much   they-took-care-of   mine   my-woman-obj.   Lots

umuyanume   *nijamchin,*   *tujash*   *wika*   *umutsiajai*   *mina*
they-drank   manioc-beer-obj   but   I-topic   I-did-not-drink   mine

duwagjai.
and-my-wife.

    7. *Ijatan*   *umikan*   *wakitkiabiajai mina pujutaijui.*
      Visit-obj I-completing I-returned   mine to-me-staying-place.

    8. *Waketkun*   *mawabiajai*   *makichik japan.*   9. *Nunikan*
      I-returning   I-killed   one   deer-obj.   I-doing-thus

shig   *aneasan*   *tajabiajai.*
very   I-being-happy   I-arrived-back.

The first sentence has two EVENTS, GO and VISIT. Therefore, there are two propositions: *I went to Tuntugkus. I visited (people).* Sentence 2 has three verbs in the Aguaruna. *Doing so* is a pro-verb which serves as a connective in the grammar. It does not add any new information. *I went* is also a repetition of information from sentence 1. The new information is the proposition *I slept three times.* Sentence 3 includes the EVENTS *leave, go up (river), see,* and *see.* The propositions are: *I left Wawaim. I went up (river). I saw many people. I had not seen these people before.*

It soon becomes evident that the EVENTS are not in order. That is, for example, *I slept three times* occurred in the actual trip after leaving Wawaim and before visiting in Tuntugkus. Sentence 1 is an introductory general statement. Sentence 2 fills in the information of how long it took to get there. Then sentence 3 goes back to the beginning, but also adds the new information about where the trip started and about seeing the people. The information might need to be rearranged when translating into another language.

The following is a suggested listing of the propositions represented by the Aguaruna text. Implicit propositions and concepts are given in parentheses:

1. I went to Tuntugkus.
   (Tuntugkus is a village.)
   I visited (people).

2. I slept three times.

3. I left Wawaim.
   (Wawaim is the village where I live.)
   I went up (river).
   I saw many people.
   I had not seen these people before.

4. The people said to me
   You are my relative.
   I was very happy.
   I united with (the people).

5. (The people) gave me food.
   (The people) took care of my woman well.

6. (The people) drank lots of beer.
   The beer was made of manioc.
   My woman and I did not drink the beer.

7. I visited.
   I finished.

8. I returned to the place where I live.
   I killed one deer.

9. I was very happy.
   I arrived back (at Wawaim).

Actually, it would not be possible to rewrite these into a good story without knowing the relations between the propositions. The relations which occur between propositions will be discussed in Part IV below. However, for the sake of seeing that propositions are encoded by very different structures in different languages, the following possible translations into English are suggested. Compare the form of the English with the grammatical structures of the source text and with the semantic analysis.

A. *I went to Tuntugkus to visit. The trip took three days. I left Wawaim and went up river to Tuntugkus. There I saw lots of people whom I had never seen before.*

The people there said that I was their relative. I was very happy staying there with them. They gave us lots of food and took good care of my wife. They drank lots of manioc beer, but my wife and I didn't drink it.

When we had finished visiting, we returned home, killing a deer on the way. I was happy to be home.

B. *My wife and I went to visit in the town of Tuntugkus. We left our town which is called Wawaim, went up river, sleeping three times on the way, and arrived in Tuntugkus. We saw many people whom we had not seen previously.*

We were very happy staying there with the people of Tuntugkus. They said that we are relatives. They took good care of my wife and gave us both lots of food. They themselves drank a lot of manioc beer, but my wife and I didn't join in the drinking.

After visiting, we returned home. On the way home I killed a deer. I arrived back in Wawaim very happy.

EXERCISES – Relations within Event Propositions

A. What is the **case role** of the word which is italicized in the following?

1. *Mary* likes fried bananas.

2. John opened the door with a *key*.

3. Peter washed the car in the *garage*.

4. Jane sang a song for *her mother*.

5. Jane exercises *twice a day*.

6. Jane sang a *song* for her mother.

7. The *candy* melted.

8. *Peter* went with John.

9. *Later* he will come back.

10. John opened the door *quickly*.

B. Rewrite the following propositions with as many grammatical structures as you can think of in English. Then write them in another language which you speak in as many forms as you can in that language.

   1. John ate the apple.

   2. The little boy ran away.

   3. John saw the big black horse.

   4. The butter melted.

   5. Jane sang a song.

C. What propositions are included in the meaning of each of the following?

   1. My watch is from Switzerland.

   2. My watch is from Sears.

   3. My watch is from my Dad.

D. How would you translate each of the sentences in C, above, into a language which you speak, other than English?

E. In each of the following sentences, identify the semantic role of the italicized words as **agent, affected,** or **beneficiary.**

   1. *She* beat *the carpet.*

   2. *The dish* broke.

   3. *Mary* sang for *Tom.*

   4. *Peter* washed hurriedly.

   5. *The carpet* has been beaten.

   6. *I* received *a letter.*

   7. *Jane* made *herself a dress.*

   8. *Paul* bought *a Datsun.*

F. Translate the Aguaruna text called *Trip to Tuntugkus* given at the end of this chapter, into a language other than English. Use the natural grammatical forms of that language. Choose those forms which will most clearly communicate the content of the story.

Chapter 20
Relations within State Propositions

In chapter 18, we defined and illustrated State Propositions. State Propositions do not have an EVENT concept as the central concept. Rather, they consist of THINGS and ATTRIBUTES which are related the one to the other by various **state relations**. English uses forms of the verbs *be* and *have* to express many **state relations**. Other languages use affixes or special lexical items. In analyzing the source text, it is helpful to the translator to identify the **state relations** carefully since they are not likely to be translated into another language with a literal form of the verb *be* or *have*. For example, in English, one says *John is in the house* when the relation between *John* and *house* is location. But in Aguaruna, the verb *is* could not be used, rather the verb which means *live/stay* would be used, and the form would be *John house-in stays. Be* in Aguaruna would be used only to refer to inanimate objects. The purpose of this chapter is to acquaint the student with the various **state relations** and point out some of the skewing between State Propositions and the grammatical forms which encode them. (Many of the examples in this chapter are from Fleming 1977.)

State relations defined

A State Proposition consists of two **main parts** and the relations between them. These two parts are the **topic** and the **comment**. The **topic** is the THING or ATTRIBUTE being talked about. The **comment** is what is being said about the topic. A number of examples are given in Display 20.1. Notice that the *topic concept* is given in the first column, the *relation concept* in the second, and the *comment concept* in the third. An English surface form representing the proposition is given in the fourth column.

For the translator, the important thing to remember is that a rewording of forms representing State Propositions will be very helpful in finding the best translation equivalent because it will make explicit the **relation** between the **topic** and the **comment**. For example, the following all have the same grammatical form in English; that is,

TOPIC	RELATION (STATE ROLE)	COMMENT	ENGLISH FORM
dog	**naming**	Fido	*The dog's name is Fido.* *The dog is called Fido.*
that car	**ownership**	I	*That car is mine.* *That car belongs to me.*
car	**location**	garage	*The car is in the garage.*
red	**classification**	color	*Red is a color.*
dog	**classification**	animal	*A dog is an animal.*
that table	**substance**	wood	*That wooden table...* *That table is made of wood.*
branch	**partitive**	tree	*A branch is part of a tree.* *A branch of a tree...*
story	**depiction**	Bill	*The story is about Bill.*
picture	**depiction**	Mary	*The picture is of Mary.* *Mary's picture.* *It is a picture of Mary.*
director	**identification**	Mr. Jones	*The director is Mr. Jones.* *Mr. Jones, the director...*
book	**description**	small	*The book is small.*
Mary	**kinship role**	my sister	*Mary is my sister.* *My sister Mary.*
Bill	**social role**	doctor	*Bill is a doctor.* *Bill works as a doctor.*
this bag	**containership**	rice	*This bag has rice in it.* *This bag contains rice.*
evidence	**existence**		*There is evidence.*
God	**existence**		*There is a God. God exists.*
weather	**ambience**	hot	*It is hot.*
(varies in context	**ambience**	dark	*It is dark.*
(time)	**time**	noon	*It is noon.*
(time)	**time**	8 o'clock	*It is 8 o'clock.*

Display 20.1

the form is a possessive noun phrase. However, each of them is encoding a different relation and so will probably not be encoded with a possessive noun phrase in other languages.

my dog	the dog which belongs to me	**ownership**
my picture	the picture which depicts me (a picture of me)	**depiction**
my doctor	the doctor treats me	**social role**

Notice also the following English noun phrases which re-express some of the illustrative sentences above and which actually contain a State Proposition:

the wooden table	the table is made of wood	**substance**
Bill's doctor	the doctor who treats Bill	**social role**
bag of rice	bag contains rice	**containership**
the knife on the table	the knife is located on the table	**location**

By making explicit the relation that is expressed by the source language, one is then more able to find an idiomatic equivalent in the receptor language.

Multiple encoding of state propositions

With State Propositions, as with Event Propositions, any given proposition may be encoded several ways in the same language. For example, notice the variety of ways ownership is encoded in the following:

1. *John's house*

2. *John has a house*

3. *John owns a house*

4. *The house John owns*

The same proposition, *John owns a house*, also is encoded in a variety of ways in other languages, but these do not match the English forms. Note the following:

AGUARUNA

1. *jega*	*Juandau*	*nunu*
house	John-(ownership suffix)	that-one

2. *Juanka*	*jee*
John	house-his

3. *jega*	*Juandau*	*awaii*
house	John-(ownership suffix)	it-is

Aguaruna has a suffix *-dau* which encodes the relation **ownership.** But the proposition can also be encoded by a possessive noun phrase as in the second example above.

GAHUKU

1. *Zoni*   *nene*   *numuni*   *molo-noive*
   John   phrase-marker   house   put-has-he

2. *Zoni-ni*   *numuni*
   John-'s   house

3. *numuni*   *nene*   *Zoni-ni*   *neve*
   house   phrase-marker   John-'s   is

The translator's responsibility is first to identify the **topic, relation,** and **comment** in the source text so as to understand the meaning clearly, and, secondly, to find the best way to express that meaning with natural receptor language forms which fit the context. Literal translations of forms which encode State Propositions will distort the meaning of the translation. The following are ways of encoding the containership relation in English exemplified by the proposition *the jug contains water.* The **topic** is JUG, the **relation** is CONTAINERSHIP, and the **comment** is WATER.

> *The water jug*
> *The jug containing water*
> *The jug of water*
> *The jug with water in it*
> *The jug which contains water*
> *The jug contains water.*
> *The jug has water in it.*

Which of these is chosen will depend on the context in which the proposition is being used in relation to other propositions, that is, the text as a whole. These matters will be discussed more later. For now, the important thing is to see the great variety. There will be a similar (but different) variety in other receptor languages.

Multiple functions of grammatical relation markers

As can be noted by looking at the examples in the section above, the state relations are sometimes encoded by verbs, sometimes by prepositions, and sometimes by the position of the words next to one another in English. Languages will have words, suffixes, enclitics, verbs, and various other ways to mark relations. To illustrate the multiple functions of relation markers, let us look at some English prepositions which encode state relations.

The preposition *at* has the primary function of **location** as in the sentence *She is at the store.* But it has a secondary function of encoding the relation **time** in the sentence *She came at 10 o'clock.* In the first, it is marking **location** in a State Proposition, and in the second, it is marking **time** in an Event Proposition. In the sentence *John shot the arrows at the target,* the preposition *at* is marking the relation **goal.** Just as other lexical items may have secondary senses, so words which have a relational meaning may also have secondary senses or functions.

Although the location marker *at* has this secondary function of indicating **time**, in Spanish it is the location marker *en* which has this secondary function. Notice the following contrasts:

English: *She is typing* **at** *this moment.*

Spanish: *Está escribiendo a   máquina* **en** *este   momento.*
        Is   writing   by   machine   in   this   moment

The preposition *in* may also have a secondary function of **time** in English in such sentences as *I bought this milk* **in** *the morning.* The form is the same as that used in *There are two cows* **in** *the field*, but, in this second sentence, the primary meaning of **location** is indicated rather than **time**.

Grammatical relation markers may also be used in figurative ways. For example, in English, *over* has a primary meaning of **location** as in *The airplane flew* **over** *the house*, meaning "directly above." However, *over* also has a figurative meaning of "superior authority" in a sentence like *He has two people* **over** *him in the office.*

So, we see that, not only are the **relations** encoded in a variety of ways in a given language, but also forms which indicate these **relations** may be used with several different meanings and in figurative ways. Once again, we see that there is no literal correspondence between semantic structure and grammatical structure. The skewing is different for each language so that a literal translation will not communicate adequately the meaning of the source language.

Complex concepts in state propositions

Just as concepts may be simple or complex in Event Propositions, so also in State Propositions. The topic may be a simple concept like DOG or a complex one like THE BIG DOG WHICH IS INSIDE THE FENCE in the sentence *The big dog inside the fence is named Fido.* In this example, BIG modifies DOG; that is, it describes DOG. DOG is further delimited by the embedded State Proposition *the dog is inside the fence.*

Just as the topic may be complex, so also the comment may be complex. For example, in the sentence *The jug contains dirty water which is from the river*, the topic is the JUG which is a simple concept, the relation is **containership,** and the **comment** is a complex concept, DIRTY WATER WHICH IS FROM THE RIVER. The central concept is WATER, a THING. The delimiting concept DIRTY is an ATTRIBUTE which describes the WATER. And WATER is further delimited by a State Proposition WHICH IS FROM THE RIVER. Notice that when a proposition is embedded, that is, it is part of a complex concept, we have used the relative pronouns of English, *who, which,* etc., rather than repeating the central concept to which it refers. Therefore, the form *which is from the river* stands for the proposition WATER IS FROM THE RIVER. The use of *which* indicates an embedded proposition whose topic is the central concept of the complex concept to which it belongs.

The following sentence includes three State Propositions, number 1 is the main proposition, number 2 is embedded in the topic, and number 3 is embedded in the comment:

> *The man who owns the car is in the house made of brick.*

The three propositions are:

1. The man is in the house. **location**
2. The man owns the car. **ownership**
3. The house is made of brick. **substance**

Propositions 2 and 3 are embedded, that is, they delimit the **topic** and **comment,** respectively. So the complex concept which is the topic is THE MAN WHO OWNS THE CAR. The complex concept which is the comment is THE HOUSE WHICH IS MADE OF BRICK. The relationship between the topic and comment is **location**. The basic proposition is THE MAN IS IN THE HOUSE.

One might like to think of ATTRIBUTIVE modifiers as also being embedded State Propositions. For example, THE BIG MAN can be taken as BIG modifying MAN, or it can be taken as THE MAN WHO IS BIG. Either way, BIG is delimiting MAN. If the second way of looking at it is chosen, then all complex concepts have embedded propositions.

Illustrative text

All of the examples given above have been rather simple, looking at one proposition at a time. We look now at a text which is made up mostly of State Propositions. We will take the following Aguaruna text as the source language, analyze the semantic structure of the text, and then suggest possible English translations. The sentences are numbered in the source text to make it easier to talk about them. It is not expected that there will be the same number of propositions in the semantic structure as sentences in the source language. Nor would one expect the translation into the receptor language to correspond in number of sentences to either the source language or the semantic structure. The text is a description of *owls*.

1. *Pumpukuk*   *makichik*   *pishak*   *muuntai.*
   Owl-topic   one   bird   it-is-big.

2. *Wainchataiyai*   *tsawai*   *wekaguk,*   *tujakush*
   It-is-not-that-seen   while-day-time   walking   however

kashi   *waintayai,*   *shinaush*   *antugtayai.*
at-night   it-is-that-seen   noise-also   it-is-that-heard.

3. *Pumpukuk*   *makichik*   *pishak*   *shiigchawai,*
   Owl-topic   one   bird   it-is-not-beautiful

iwaajaamuchui.   4. *Pujuuwai*   *tampetnum,*
it-is-not-decorated.   It-is-one-who-lives   in-cave

apijanmashkam.   5. *Yuuwai*   *katipin,*
also-in-dense-woods.   It-is-one-who-eats   rat-obj

tukagmachin,   *shuutan*   *aatus.*   6. *Jii*
insect-obj.   cockroach-obj.   all-those   Its-eyes

apui.   7. *Nujishkam*   *punuakui.*   8. *Ujeg*
are-big.   Its-beak-also   it-is-curved   Its-feathers

washuwai.
are-speckled.

The text includes both State Propositions and Event Propositions. However, in sentence 1, there is no word which stands for an EVENT. OWL is a THING, ONE an ATTRIBUTE, BIRD a THING, and BIG an ATTRIBUTE, also. Since THINGS are being related to THINGS or ATTRIBUTES, we know we have State Propositions. The first proposition classifies OWL as being a BIRD. The second proposition indicates that not just any bird is meant but only a BIRD which is BIG; that is, it identifies which kind of BIRD. The use of ONE in Aguaruna is like an article in English and does not indicate the number ONE. The semantic structure of sentence 1, then, consists of two propositions; one embedded within the other. The topic is OWL(S), the relation **classification,** the comment BIRD. *The owl is a bird.* BIRD is delimited by the further proposition WHICH IS BIG.

Sentence 2 begins with the EVENT SEE but does not indicate in the Aguaruna who does the seeing. The EVENTS WALK, MAKE NOISE, and HEAR all lack **agents** as well. Display 20.2 presents a suggested list of the propositions occurring in the text grouped by the sentence in which they occur. If the proposition is a State Proposition, then the relation is indicated on the right.

State Proposition	Relation
1. The owl is a bird	**classification**
which is big	**description**
2. (People) do not see owls	— —
when (people) walk	— —
while (it) is day time	**time**
(People) do see owls	— —
when (people) walk	— —
while (it) is night time	**time**
(People) hear noise	— —
when (owl) makes moise	— —
3. The owl is a bird	**classification**
which is ugly (not-beautiful)	**description**
which is plain (not decorated)	**description**
4. Owls live in caves	— —
Owls also live in woods	— —
which are dense	**description**
5. Owls eat rats, insects, and cockroaches	— —
6. Eyes are big	**description**
eyes are part of owl	**partitive**
Beak is curved	**description**
Beak is part of owl	**partitive**
Feathers are speckled	**description**
feathers are part of owl	**partitive**

Display 20.2

The Aguaruna text could be translated into English in a number of ways. If it was to be read by children, one form might be used; if it were for a scientific magazine, a different style would be used. The information would be the same, but the forms would be different because of the audience. Notice the following two translations from Aguaruna into English. The first might occur in a book for new readers and the second in a more advanced book.

1. The owl is a bird. It is a big bird. People do not see owls when they are walking around in the day time. They see them at night. They also hear them when they hoot.

   The owl is an ugly bird and very plain. It lives in a cave or a dense wood. It eats rats, insects, and cockroaches. It has big eyes. It has a curved beak. And its feathers are speckled.

2. The owl is a large bird which is seen only at night. People hear them hoot but seldom see them.

   They are ugly and plain in appearance with big eyes, a curved beak, and speckled feathers. They live in caves or in dense woods and eat rats, insects, and cockroaches.

EXERCISES – Relations within State Propositions

A. Returning to the text just presented about the owl, first translate each proposition into a language you speak other than English. Then, using these propositions, rewrite into the natural grammatical forms of the language. First write in a style that would be enjoyed by children. Then rewrite the same information in a style suitable for adults. Do not translate from the English translations but rather from the semantic structure (propositions).

B. What is the state relation which associates the two words in italics in each of the following:

> Example: a *branch* of a *tree*
>   a branch is part of a tree (partitive)

1. A *dog* is an *animal*.

2. A *palm* is a kind of *tree*.

3. *John* is my *brother*.

4. *John* is *tall*.

5. The *man* is *Jackson*.

6. The *car* is *white*.

7. a *house* of *brick*

8. a *glass* of *milk*

9. the *teacher's student*

10. the *village school*

C. In each of the following, the **topic, relation,** and **comment** are given. How would you express the proposition in English? How would you express it in a language other than English?

> Example: boy...**location**...school
> The boy is at school.

1. beetle...**classification**...insect

2. John...**kinship**...brother

3. weather...**ambience**...nice

4. jug...**location**...table

5. president...**identification**...Mr. Njock

6. Samuel...**social role**...professor

7. glass...**containership**...water

8. picture...**depiction**...Mary

9. picture...**ownership**...Cristina

10. boy...**description**...naughty

D. Rewrite the following text as propositions. Then translate it into another language which you speak.

> *The white house in the forest is small. A tall tree grows in front of it, and a stone fence encircles the barrel which catches the rain water from the roof of the house. A very elderly woman lives there with her three big white cats.*

Chapter 21
Skewing between Propositional Structure and Clause Structure

In the previous three chapters, propositional structure has been defined and illustrated. In most of the examples given, the proposition equaled the grammatical clause or simple sentence. However, in text material, the kind of material a translator will be working on, there is always a lot of skewing. In this chapter, we will look at some of the common skewing between propositions and the clauses which encode them.

Passive constructions

The distinction between **passive** and **active** verbs is common to many languages. In the semantic structure, all event propositions are active and the **agent** expressed. But in the surface structure grammar of languages, the passive form often occurs. The function of the passive construction is very different from language to language. In a passive construction, the verb of the clause is in the passive voice, and rather than having the **agent** as the subject, the **affected** is often the subject of the clause or sentence. Notice the following:
In English, we would probably use the **passive** more than the **active**

> **Active**: *Someone stole my car last night.*
>
> **Passive**: *My car was stolen last night.*

to report this incident. Because the focus is on *my car*, the **passive** form is used. Also, the thief is unknown, and so the **agent** cannot be specified. However, either sentence is natural English.

The proposition *John painted the house* could be said in English using either the **active** or **passive**:

> **Active**: *John painted the house.*
>
> **Passive**: *The house was painted by John.*

Both sentences mean the same thing. Grammatically, the first is **active** and the second is **passive**. When the form is **active**, the person who does the action, that is, the **agent**, is the subject of the sentence. When the sentence is **passive**, the **affected**, *house*, is the subject.

English uses the **passive** to focus on the **affected, resultant, benefactive**, etc. **Passive** is also used in English in order to maintain the **topic** with a third person pronoun throughout the paragraph. Notice the following paragraph in which the third sentence is in the **passive** in order to keep the paragraph structure based on the **topic**, *John*.

> ***John*** *went to town.* ***He*** *did some shopping and started to return home. Then suddenly* ***he*** *was struck by a car.*

It would be possible to use an active verb and say *then suddenly a car struck him*. However, the **topic**, JOHN, is maintained throughout the paragraph by using HE as the subject of the second and third sentences. To do this, the **passive** is used in the third sentence.

Other languages will have other functions for **passive** constructions. In East Africa, and some parts of Asia, the **passive** is used only when the speaker has negative feelings about what he is saying or when he wants to cast an undesirable value on what he is saying (Filbeck 1972:332). For example, in Thai, the **passive** is often used to communicate a sense of unpleasantness. The Thai sentence *The boy was sent to school* would indicate that the boy was being forced to go against his will or that school is a very unpleasant experience. Unpleasant experiences like *kill, hit, blame, accuse*, etc., are almost always used in the **passive** form.

In Hebrew writings, the **passive** is often used to avoid the name *God*. Here the reason is great respect and awe. The name of *God* was considered too holy to say lightly. So if *GOD* was the **agent** in the proposition, the Hebrew form would be **passive** in the grammar. For example, the proposition *God will forgive them* would be *they will be forgiven*.

Many non-Indo-European languages have no **passive** construction. This is true of many languages in Papua New Guinea, for example. This means that in translating from English into these languages, each time a **passive** construction occurs in English, the translator may need to discover who performed the action in order to supply the correct subject in the receptor language translation. To translate the sentence *John was taken to prison*, the translator would need to know who took John to prison. It might be possible to say *they took John to prison*, but it may be necessary to be more explicit. Perhaps the context will show if it was the *police*, some *soldier*, or someone else. The translator may need to supply the implicit information from somewhere else in the text or from the real life situation if it needs to be made explicit. Some languages may have ways, other than **passive**, for leaving the **agent** unexpressed.

There are also languages which use the **passive** more often than the **active**. This is true of Tojolabal of Mexico. If all the **active** verbs of a source text were translated with **active** verbs in Tojolabal, the result would be a very unnatural sounding translation with possible meaning distortions as a result of the many **active** forms. In English, we say *I killed my chicken*, but in Tojolabal the better form would be *My chicken died because of me*.

In Aguaruna (Peru), the **passive** is used almost exclusively in introductions, and conclusions, but not in the body of the text. A shift to **passive** would indicate that the author is now giving a summary statement. In Nomatsiguenga (Peru, data from Wise 1968:5), the use of the **passive** indicates that the speaker is an uninvolved observer of the action; that is, he is reporting the story as he heard it.

What does this mean for the translator? It means that he must recognize the difference between **passive** and **active** constructions, be aware of the usages in the source language and in the receptor languages, and not expect to be able to translate literally **passive** for **passive** and **active** for **active**. Some adjustments will no doubt need to be made. The aim of the translator is to use the natural receptor language form.

Abstract nouns

The primary functions of the grammatical class called nouns is to represent what is semantically classified as a THING. However, not all nouns represent THINGS. As we noted previously (see page 63–4), some nouns represent what is semantically an EVENT or an ATTRIBUTE. When a noun represents an EVENT or an ATTRIBUTE rather than a THING, it is called an **abstract noun**. For example, *obedience is important* means *that (people) obey is important*. The agent is left implicit when the abstract noun *obedience* is used. **Abstract nouns** always represent a skewing of the grammatical structure and the semantic structure. In analyzing the source text, the translator will often need to restate the **abstract nouns** as verbs, adjectives, or adverbs. Notice the following examples in which the **abstract noun** is used in the first column and the restatement as a verb, adjective, or adverb is given in the second:

1. *Love* is patient.	1. People who love are patient.
2. *Salvation* is near.	2. Someone will soon save (someone).
3. *knowledge* of the law	3. Someone knows the law.
4. He persuaded him by *kindness*.	4. He persuaded him by being a kind person. (Or...by being kind to him.)
5. The *chosen* came forward.	5. Those whom (someone) chose came forward.
6. *Quickness* is necessary.	6. It is necessary that (people) act quickly.

The translator needs to recognize **abstract nouns** and be able to analyze them. In the receptor language translation, he will want to use those **abstract nouns** which are already in use in the language in the ways which are natural to the speakers of the language. If there is no **abstract noun** in the receptor language used in the same way as the **abstract noun** of the source language, the translator will not attempt to create new **abstract nouns** but will use the natural patterns, translating with verbs, adjectives, or adverbs. By restating in such a way that the grammar and semantic structures match each other more closely, the message is often understood more easily. West African languages will very often use a verb in the translation where an **abstract noun** occurs in English. This is also true in other parts of the world. For example, in many languages, the statement *love is not jealous* will need to be translated with something like *when we love others, we are not jealous of them.*

The translator needs to remember that if he translates **abstract nouns** literally into the receptor language, the translation may be completely misunderstood because the use of a noun may make the reader think of an object. This is because nouns usually indicate a THING. So when a translator translated *fear* with an equivalent noun in the sentence *fear fell on the people*, it sounded to the readers like *fear* was the name of a person or some object which *fell* just like *the book fell on the floor*. When a verb is nominalized, it often sounds like it is referring to an object or person. This may lead to wrong meaning.

A literal translation of *death no longer has power over him* would mean in some languages that *death* is a person's name. This would give a wrong meaning. The sentence might need to be translated *he will never die again*. The correct translation will be the natural form used in the receptor language.

When translating from English into the Zoque language of Mexico, the **abstract nouns** usually had to be adjusted as in the following (Wonderly 1953:14):

Source: We have *boldness* and *access...*
Translation: We do not fear to enter...

Source: In my *prayers...*
Translation: When I speak to God...

A translator translating into Cuicateco of Mexico found the same problem. The verb form had to be used when translating an **abstract noun** which represented a semantic EVENT. This will be true in many languages and needs to be carefully considered by the translator. As has been mentioned before, it may mean that a verb will need to be used and the implicit agents and persons affected made explicit. For example, the sentence *"Judgment has come"* can be rewritten using a verb only after the information is supplied as to who is judging whom. Without knowing the broader context in which it is used, one might think of many possibilities: *the time has come when the king will judge the people, the chief is judging (punishing) the captured enemies,* etc. We could think up many possibilities. It is impossible to translate **abstract nouns** with equivalent clauses without knowing who the participants are. This must be found in the preceding or following parts of the text, or sometimes in the real life situation.

Genitive constructions

Some European languages have a grammatical form known as the **genitive construction**. This one form is used in the grammar to encode a great variety of semantic structures. In English, the **genitive construction** is most easily recognized by the word *of* occurring between two nouns. For example, the following are some **genitive constructions**: *the house of John, the wing of the bird, the destruction of the city,* and *the branches of the tree.* The possessive phrase is often used in the same way as the **genitive construction**. For example, the following are some possessive phrases of this kind: *John's house, the bird's wing, the city's destruction, the tree's branches.*

The reason the **genitive constructions** of English, and other languages, cause problems for the translator is because the one surface form is used to represent so many different meanings. The translator must discover the meaning behind the construction before being able to translate it adequately into another language. Some **genitive constructions** stand for a State Proposition, some for an Event Proposition, and some for two propositions. Whenever a **genitive construction** occurs in an English source text, the translator must ask himself what meaning is indicated.

First, let us look at some examples of **genitive constructions** which stand for State Propositions. In the first column, the **genitive construction** or possessive phrase is given, and in the second, it is reworded as a State Proposition.

1. *the house of John* *(John's house)*	1. The house belongs to John.
2. *the wing of the bird*	2. The wing is part of the bird.
3. *the man's brother*	3. The man has a brother.
4. *the man's picture*	4. The picture belongs to the man. The picture depicts the man.
5. *the goodness of the queen*	5. The queen is good.
6. *a city of Africa*	6. The city is in Africa.
7. *a cup of cold water*	7. The cup contains water.
8. *the book of the law*	8. The book is about the law.
9. *a crown of gold*	9. The crown is made of gold.
10. *the ability of Mary*	10. Mary is able/capable.

Many **genitive constructions** are used to encode Event Propositions. Below, the **genitive construction** is given in the first column, and the Event Proposition for which it stands is given in the second column.

1. *the error of Jonathan*	1. Jonathan erred.
2. *the obedience of the children*	2. The children obeyed someone.
3. *the death of John*	3. John died.
4. *the fear of the soldiers*	4. (people) feared the soldiers, the soldiers feared (someone)
5. *day of vengeance*	5. day when (someone) will avenge
6. *the growling of the lion*	6. The lion growled.

Sometimes the event is only implicit. Note the following:

1. *the law of Moses*	1. the law which Moses wrote
2. *the days of Churchill*	2. the days when Churchill lived
3. *the God of peace*	3. the God who causes (people) to be peaceful
4. *the song of Peter*	4. the song which Peter wrote; the song which Peter *sang*
5. *the violence of the crowd*	5. The crowd was acting violently.

When two abstract nouns occur in the **genitive construction**, the semantic structure will often contain two propositions. Notice the following:

1. *the labor of love*	1. (someone) labors because (they) love (someone)
2. *the forgiveness of sins*	2. (someone) will forgive that; (someone) has sinned
3. *fear of death*	3. (someone) fears that he will die
4. *the knowledge of his will*	4. (someone) knows what (someone) wills
5. *the teaching of judgment*	5. (someone) teaches about how (someone) will judge

When possessive noun phrases are used in English, there is often an implied event which may need to be made explicit in the translation. Note the following:

1. *Jacob's well*	1. the well which Jacob dug
2. *their temples*	2. the temples which they built
	the temples which are in their land
	the temples where they worship
3. *the doctor's patient*	3. the patient whom the doctor treats

Sometimes the **genitive construction** can be ambiguous and hard to interpret. As mentioned before, *the shooting of the hunters* can mean either *(someone) shot the hunters* or *the hunters shot at (something)*. The ambiguity arises because, when a **genitive construction** is used to encode an EVENT, some part of the Event Proposition must be left implicit in order to use the **genitive construction**. Sometimes the agent is left implicit, sometimes the affected, and sometimes the activity. Compare the following:

1. *the judgment of Peter*	1. Peter judges (someone)
2. *the servant of Peter*	2. (someone) serves Peter
3. *the gardener of Peter*	3. the person who (takes care of) the garden for Peter

Notice that in the first, the AFFECTED is left implicit; in the second, the AGENT is left implicit; and in the third, the ACTIVITY is left implicit and, therefore, it is ambiguous. One of the problems for the translator is determining what the implicit information is and knowing when it is necessary to include it in the translation.

Because of the very wide range of different meanings which can be represented by a **genitive construction**, special care must be taken by the translator to identify the meaning of the source text. Some of the implicit information may be needed to adequately translate into the receptor language. Once the meaning is identified, then natural forms of the receptor language should be used in the translation. Notice the following sentence in which a **passive construction**, a **genitive construction**, a **possessive construction**, and **abstract nouns** all occur within one sentence.

> *The concern of the leader was revealed by his gifts to his people.*

Was revealed is passive. The AGENT of *revealed* is *the leader*. Restated actively, the sentence would read *the leader revealed his concern*. *The concern of the leader* is a **genitive construction** meaning *the leader was concerned for (the people)*. The possessive phrase *his people* stands for *the people whom he leads*. The word *concern* is an abstract noun. It stands for an EVENT. The word *leader* stands for a PERSON and EVENT, i.e., *the one who leads*, and *gifts* stands for an EVENT and some THINGS, i.e., *gave (something)*. The sentence is rewritten as propositions below. Notice that in writing the propositions, the passive construction, the **genitive construction**, the possessive phrase, and the abstract nouns are all eliminated. They are grammatical devices of the source text but not part of the semantic structure.

> (Someone) leads the people.
>
> He was concerned for the people.
>
> He revealed this to the people.
>
> He gave (things) to the people.

Notice that all of the participants and events are made explicit in the semantic rewrite. However, when the translator puts this information into the receptor language, some information will again be made implicit. It may not be the same as that which is implicit in the source language sentence. For example, a natural translation into Aguaruna would be as follows:

> *The big his-followers-to many things-object he-gave, "Them I-am concerned-about," one-who-says he-being.*

The word *big* is used for any leader. Notice that the reciprocal of *leader* is used for the *people*, i.e., *followers*. The sentence is active. And the reason, i.e., *to show his concern*, is translated by a direct quotation in Aguaruna. Each language will have its own special grammatical forms which will best communicate the meaning of the source text.

EXERCISES – Skewing between Propositional Structure and Clause Structure

A. Each of the following is a **passive construction**. Rewrite the sentences using an **active form** in English. Then translate the sentences into a second language which you know. Did you use an active or a passive construction for the translation? Are both acceptable?

1. Peter was arrested.

2. The letter was written quickly by John.

3. It was reported that he was at home.

4. The lion was killed.

5. Two names were suggested by the committee.

6. The president will be loved for his generosity.

B. Each of the following is an **active construction**. Rewrite the sentences using a **passive form** in English. Then translate the sentences into a second language which you know. Did you use an active or a passive construction for the translation? If both are possible, which seems more natural?

1. The judge summoned Mark.

2. Everyone will hate you if you do that.

3. We do not restrict you.

4. The hunters killed a deer.

5. The police took John to the jail.

6. Jonathan wrote the letter to the mayor.

C. Underline the **abstract nouns** which occur in the following sentences. Then rewrite each sentence without abstract nouns; that is, change the form using verbs to represent EVENTS and using adjectives and adverbs to represent ATTRIBUTES. In addition, change any **passive** constructions to **active** ones. After you have rewritten the sentences in English without abstract nouns, translate them into another language which you speak. Think about whether it is more natural to use a noun form or a verb form to represent the words you underlined in the sentences. Make your translation sound as natural as possible.

1. Her beauty was noticed by everyone.

2. They are afraid of death.

3. Do you have faith?

4. I have life.

5. Stealing is a strong temptation.

6. The purification of the temple was done by the priests.

7. The destruction of the city was terrifying.

8. We were witnesses to the destruction of the city.

9. The rapidity with which he fled surprised everyone.

10. His resurrection from death was discussed by many.

D. Restate each of the following as a proposition or as propositions. Add any implied concepts expressing an EVENT or STATE.

1. jar of water

2. garment of camel's hair

3. the hour of incense

4. people of Hong Kong

5. assurance of failure

6. promise of his return

7. the sufferings of Peter

8. the city of Abidjan

9. a city of Africa

10. the kindness of the leader

E. The following paragraph contains some **abstract nouns** and some **genitive constructions**. First, underline every word which stands for an EVENT. Then rewrite the information in propositions. Using this rewrite, translate the paragraph into a language other than English.

The suffering in the refugee camp ended with the arrival of donations of food from overseas. The supervisory committee organized the inhabitants of the camp into smaller groups so as to insure fair distribution of food and clothing to each family.

F. Imagine you are preparing to translate into a language which has the following characteristics:

    a. no preposition "with"

    b. no passive form

    c. agent role must always coincide with grammatical subject

Recast the following into a form which can be readily transferred into such a language, and which expresses the underlying relations clearly. There may be more than one proposition involved (from Barnwell 1980:176).

1. They built a house with a red roof.

2. The dish ran away with the spoon.

3. She made a dress with the cloth.

4. He climbed the hill with the rucksack on his back.

5. He climbed the hill with the sun in his eyes.

6. He climbed the hill with a line of children behind him.

7. He climbed the hill with no hope of reaching the top.

8. He climbed the hill with a rope and a pickaxe.

Chapter 22

Skewing of Illocutionary Force
and Grammatical Form

At the end of chapter 18, the importance of the illocutionary force of a proposition was discussed. Each proposition and each propositional cluster expresses either a **command**, a **question**, or a **statement**. When there is no skewing between the semantic structure and the grammatical form, the illocutionary force will be the same as the grammatical mood of the sentence. A semantic **question** will be encoded by an *interrogative sentence*, a semantic **statement** will be encoded by a *declarative sentence*, and a **command** will be encoded by an *imperative sentence*. However, languages are complicated by the extensive skewing between the illocutionary force and the grammatical form.

Secondary functions of interrogative sentences

The label, **rhetorical questions**, has often been used to indicate interrogative grammatical forms which are used with a nonquestion meaning. The speaker uses a grammatical form which in its primary usage would indicate a question, but the speaker's purpose is to command or to make a statement. When this kind of skewing occurs, the question form is called a **rhetorical question**.

The purpose of a **real question** is to ask for information. For example, we ask *"Where is your house?"* or *"What time are you coming home?"* The question form is used, and the speaker's purpose is to ask for information. There is no skewing. **Real questions** do not usually cause problems for translators. The translator finds the appropriate form for asking for the same information in the receptor language. In teaching situations, **real questions** are also used to find out if the students remember the information which they have been taught.

Rhetorical questions, on the other hand, are not **real questions**. They are question forms used with a purpose other than to ask for information. They may look like **real questions**, since the form is the same, but the meaning is not that of a question. For example, the question *Mary, why don't you wash the dishes?* has the form of a question and might in some contexts be asking for information; that is, it might be used in its primary function. But this question in English is often used as a way of making a friendly suggestion. It is not as strong as an imperative form, *Mary, wash the dishes,* but neither is it a question. It is a suggestion. The proper answer is, *Okay, I will.* If it were a real *why* question asking for information, the answer would give a reason, something like, *Because I'm just too tired.*

In many languages, the secondary usage of this type of question, that of making a suggestion, would need to be translated by an imperative sentence or some other special form. If translated literally with *why* in many Amerindian languages, it would indicate either a real question, or if interpreted as a rhetorical question, would indicate *rebuke.*

Rhetorical questions are also used in English to show *rebuke,* but the form is different. To show *rebuke,* the *when* question is often used. A mother who is angry with her son for not doing his part of the family chores may desire to tell him to *empty the garbage.* She has told him to do it before, he knows it is his duty. She wants to convey all of this meaning–the command and the emotion she feels about it. To do so she will not use a command form but rather a question–a *when* question–*When are you going to empty the garbage?* Because of the emotive meaning being communicated, there is a skewing of semantic illocutionary force and grammatical form. The semantic illocutionary force is one of *command,* but the grammatical form is that of a *question* which would normally be used to ask about *time.* If translated literally with a *when* question, in many languages, it would be understood as a real question, and the speaker's purpose of *command* would be lost (Larson 1979:14–18).

Not all languages use question forms with a secondary function of command. The translator must first analyze the source question. Is it a **real question** or is it a **rhetorical question**? If it is a **real question**, the translation will not be difficult. If it is **rhetorical**, he must discover the meaning, the illocutionary force of the speaker, and then decide how that same purpose can best be communicated. For example, the sentence given above, *When are you going to empty the garbage?* would not be translated with a *when* question in Aguaruna. The more appropriate form would be: *Quickly, quickly, why are-you-like-that? Quickly garbage you-throw-out!* The form is completely different from English, but the information and emotive meaning communicated are the same.

Yaweyuha of Papua New Guinea would use neither an interrogative form nor an imperative form but a negative statement (a declarative form) to communicate the same speaker's purpose. *You didn't empty the garbage* would be the best form. Although the grammatical form is that of a negative declarative sentence, the meaning is that of a command, *You empty the garbage!* If *you didn't empty the garbage* was translated literally into another language other than Yaweyuha, it would probably be understood as a statement rather than a command. An adjustment will need to be made in the translation so as to communicate both the illocutionary force of command and the emotional frustration of the speaker.

In preparing for translation, it may be very helpful for the translator to first study the functions of **rhetorical questions** in the source language and then in the receptor language. The functions need to be identified, but it is also important to focus on the form, since different forms may have different secondary functions. For example, there are three different questions in English which can be used with the illocutionary force of command. One shows impatience, another is noncritical (polite), and the third is critical. Note the following contrast of form and meaning:

1. *When* are you coming?	1. You come right now!
2. *Why don't* you come?	2. You come with me (if you like)!
3. *Why did* you come?	3. You should not have come!

Notice that the *when* shows impatience, the *why* plus a *negative* is a noncritical suggestion, and *why* without the *negative* is critical. (For more examples from English, see Larson 1979:14–18.)

There are many functions of **rhetorical questions**. Each language will have its own list of functions and specific question forms which may be used rhetorically. Some functions in English are: to emphasize a known fact in order to communicate a suggestion or command, to indicate doubt or uncertainty, to introduce a new topic or new aspect of a topic, to show surprise, to admonish or exhort, and, most common of all, to express the speakers evaluation.

For example, a teacher might say to a student, *"How can I pass you, if you don't turn in your assignments?"* The interrogative form is used to **emphasize a known fact**, *"I can't pass you, if you don't turn in your assignments."* The form is interrogative but the meaning is a statement of fact. Someone might say, *"What are we going to eat?"* as a way of expressing concern or uncertainty about the high cost of food. The meaning is *"I am concerned about how I will have enough money to buy the things we need."*

In some languages, such as English, the **introduction of a new topic** or the beginning of a speech is often cast in an interrogative form. The speaker may say, *"Why is there so much unemployment these days?"* and then, not waiting for an answer, he begins to tell the audience about the reasons for unemployment. The interrogative form is simply a way of beginning the topic and really means *"I am going to tell you why there is so much unemployment these days."*

In Vagla of West Africa, there are certain types of stories which are always introduced by *"Do you know how it happened that...?"* The topic is introduced by a question. If the receptor language does not use questions as topic introducers, a different and appropriate form will need to be used in the translation from English or Vagla into another language.

English also uses **rhetorical questions to show surprise**. For example, some guests may arrive a bit early for dinner and the housewife who is preparing the dinner sees them coming up the path and says *"Are they here so soon? I haven't even gotten dressed yet."* She is not asking a real question. She knows they are there. She is showing her surprise and really saying, *"I'm surprised they are here so soon."* **Rhetorical questions** are also used to admonish or exhort in English. For example, a mother may say to a child, *"Why are you always bothering grandfather?"* The real meaning is *"You shouldn't bother your grandfather so much."* Notice that the form is a *why* question in the affirmative which is a critical statement in English.

After the translator has determined the meaning of the question form (interrogative) in the source language, he must also consider whether or not the receptor language will use a question form in the context, and if a question is used, whether or not the correct meaning will be conveyed. Sometimes a **rhetorical question** will also be appropriate, but the form of the question will need to be quite different from the source language form. The forms of the source language will not necessarily match the forms of the receptor language. For example, a *why* question in English may have quite a different form in Gahuku (Papua New Guinea, data from Ellis Deibler) even when a question is used. *Why are you putting your muddy hands on my car?* would be translated *This being my car, are you putting your muddy hands on it?* The translator will use the natural forms of the receptor language. Sometimes an interrogative sentence will be translated by a declarative sentence, sometimes by an imperative sentence.

In Korku of India, it is not uncommon to have a series of three or four questions together. They are **rhetorical** and are expressions of indignation or perplexity. **Rhetorical questions** are also used to make a statement, to arouse thought or get attention, or to express attitudes of wonder, admiration, doubt, reproach, indignation, and other emotions (see Kirkpatrick 1972:28–32).

This skewing of form and meaning will often lead to misunderstanding if an adjustment is not made in translation. In Vietnam, a Britisher who had the custom of having a cup of tea in the middle of the morning asked his Vietnamese friend, *"Would you like to drink tea?"* The friend looked perplexed and said, *"No."* The question made the Vietnamese friend think, *"Maybe he doesn't want me to drink tea."* The form in Vietnamese would have been *"Take this tea and drink it!"* an imperative sentence. This would have been understood clearly as a friendly invitation to drink tea together. This would be closer to the semantic structure since the speaker's purpose was to suggest in a positive way that his friend join him in drinking tea. The important thing to note is that if one were translating a story in which an English speaker were quoted as saying *"Would you like to drink tea?"* into the Vietnamese language, he would not use an interrogative form, he would use the appropriate imperative sentence. Only by understanding the function of rhetorical questions in the source language and in the receptor language can translators be free from introducing wrong meaning through literal translations of questions.

Secondary functions of declarative sentences

We just noted that in Yaweyuha of Papua New Guinea a negative statement **(declarative sentence)** is used to communicate a command. *You didn't wash the dishes* is used with the meaning of *You wash the dishes!* which is a command. The grammatical structure is that which is normally used to encode a statement, but the proposition in the semantic structure is a command. A translator must not assume that a **declarative sentence** will be translated by a **declarative sentence**. He must first be sure of the function of the sentence. Does it have the meaning of statement? If so, it will be translated as a statement. But if it is used in a secondary function, such as to command, then an adjustment will need to be made in the translation. A literal translation of *You didn't wash the dishes* from Yaweyuha into most languages would give a wrong meaning since **declarative sentences** are not often used to communicate the meaning of command.

In Pijin (Solomon Islands), a statement may be used as a question. The sentence *Ating plande hos long kandere blong iu* literally says *I think there are lots of horses in your country*, but the meaning is *Are there lots of horses in your country?* A **declarative sentence** is used to communicate a question.

In Denya (Cameroon), the past indicative mode (a **declarative sentence**) is the natural mode for events of a narrative. This would be the normal primary function of past indicative. But the past indicative mode also has a secondary function in that it is also used to indicate a command when the action is to be done occasionally. For example, *person he-sent you place you-went* means *if you are sent on an errand, you should go*. The semantic proposition *you should go* is encoded by a past indicative grammatical form *you-went*. Notice the following example also: *you-received holiday you-came you-saw us* means *when you are on holiday, come and see us*. The Denya form is past indicative (statement), but the function is command (Abangma 1987:80–82). This, again, is an example of the skewing between the grammatical form and the illocutionary force of the proposition in the semantic structure. If a translation into English kept the indicative form *you came and saw us*, the meaning of the Denya source text would be distorted. The imperative *come and see us* is the correct English translation for the Denya past indicative clauses in this context.

Secondary functions of imperative sentences

We have seen that grammatical questions and statements are sometimes used with secondary functions. **Imperative forms** seem to be more limited in secondary functions. However, there are examples of **imperative sentences** which are used with a nonimperative meaning.

For example, if the following two propositions were to be translated into Aguaruna, an **imperative form** would be used for the second.

1. He hung up the shirt.
2. The shirt will dry.

The second proposition is the reason for the first. In English, we would say *He hung up the shirt to dry* or *He hung up the shirt so it would get dry*. Both propositions are statements and would be translated with a **declarative sentence** in English. However, in Aguaruna, and some other Amerindian languages, the second proposition, the reason, would be translated by a direct quotation with an **imperative sentence**. The form would be *He hung up the shirt, "Let it get dry," saying*. The Aguaruna grammatical form is an **imperative**, but the proposition which it is encoding is a statement, the reason.

The purpose of mentioning these examples is to alert the translator to the skewing between the grammatical forms and the illocutionary force of the propositions which are being encoded. As the translator analyzes the source text, he will be looking for possible skewing – **interrogative sentences** which stand for **statements** or **commands, declarative sentences** which stand for **commands** or **questions**, and **imperative forms** which stand for **statements**. Once the meaning is discovered, then the translator will need to decide which grammatical forms of the receptor language will best communicate the intended meaning. It may be quite a different form from the one used in the source text.

The following chart shows the possible skewing of semantic illocutionary force and the grammatical form:

ILLOCUTIONARY FORCE   **GRAMMATICAL FORM**

1. Statement   a. Declarative clause
                               (or sentence)

2. Question   b. Interrogative clause
                               (or sentence)

3. Command   c. Imperative clause
                               (or sentence)

The heavy line indicates the correspondence when there is no skewing. Dotted lines indicate the possible skewing between illocutionary force of the proposition and the grammatical form of the clause or sentence.

The following sentences (examples from Pike and Pike 1977:49–50) illustrate the match and mismatch in English. In each case, the response is given to help make clear the meaning of the sentence.

1. a.   *Abe got into my watermelon patch yesterday...Oh?*
        (Statement force as declarative form; norm)

   b.   *Do you realize that you're trespassing... I'm just leaving!*
        (Statement force as interrogative form)

   c.   *(Go right ahead,) take just as many as you like—so you can go to jail... We won't do it again!*
        (Statement force as imperative form)

2. a.   *You mean to say Abe entered your melon patch?... He certainly did!*
        (Question force with interrogative form; norm)

   b.   *Did Abe get into the melon patch?... No.*
        (Question force with interrogative form; norm)

   c.   *Get out of my own melon patch!... Yes.*
        (Question force as imperative form)

3. a.   *You don't belong in here!* (meaning, *Get out!*)... *I'm leaving.*
        (Command force as declarative form)

   b.   *How come you are in my watermelon patch?* (meaning, *Get out!*)... *I'm leaving.*
        (Command force as interrogative form)

   c.   *Get out of my watermelon patch!... Yes sir, right away.*
        (Command force as imperative form; norm)

Negation

So far, examples of propositions which are affirmations have been used for most of the examples. Any statement, question, or command can be **negated**. That is, any proposition in addition to being either a statement, question, or command, is also either **affirmative** or **negative**. The **affirmative** is unmarked. If the proposition is **negative**, this must be indicated. The **negative** may **negate** the whole proposition, or it may simply **negate** one of the concepts within the proposition. Notice the following:

> *No* women came to the house.
>
> The boy ate *no* meat.
>
> The people did *not* go away.

In simply looking at propositions in the semantic structure, **negatives** seem very simple. However, languages handle **negatives** in many different ways in the grammatical structure. A **negative** in the source text will not always be translated by a **negative** in the receptor language. Some languages use a double **negative** which will be translated into some receptor languages by an **affirmative** statement. For example, the Greek text *without him was not anything made that was made* was translated into Chinanteco of Mexico with the **affirmative** statement *all things came into being because he made all that exists.* The double **negatives** *without* and *not* cancel one another out so that the meaning is **affirmative** rather than **negative**. Another similar example from Greek is the form *he did not speak to them without a parable* meaning *he spoke to them with parables each time he spoke.*

In English, the words *till, until,* and *except* often occur with a **negative** form in the sentence. These sentences may need to be translated by **affirmative** statements in other languages. For example, *you will not see me until next week* might need to be translated *you'll see me again next week but not before then.* In Aguaruna, the correct form would be *next week we'll-see-each-other.*

Where some languages use **negative** words, others will use a word like *only.* For example, where Greek says *It is no longer good for anything except to be thrown out* the natural English form would be *It is now good only to be thrown out.* Care must be taken in the placement of **negatives** lest the exact opposite meaning be communicated. For example, the sentence *He did not buy the car in order to go to work, but so his wife would have a car to use,* if translated literally into some languages would mean that *he did not buy the car.* But he did buy it. So a completely different form may need to be used such as *When he bought the car he did it so that his wife would have a car to use, not so that he could use it to go to work.*

When there are two propositions together, one **negative** and the other **affirmative**, the grammatical structure of some languages will have a preferred order. Some languages will put the **affirmative** first and the **negative** second. For example, a statement in Greek, says *for I came from heaven, not to do my own will, but the will of him that sent me.* In many Amerindian languages, a translation of this sentence would need to change the order of the last two clauses and say *for I came down from heaven to do the will of him who sent me and not to do my own will.* The **negative** must follow the **affirmative** in these languages.

There may also be grammatical structures in some languages in which the **negative** is not placed with the verb which is being **negated**. This is a skewing of grammatical and semantic structures. Notice the following (from Grimes 1975:237):

English: *I didn't think she would be ready.*

Meaning: *I thought that she would not be ready.* The **negative** goes with *be ready* in the semantic structure even though it occurs next to the verb *think* in the grammar.

The important thing for the translator to keep in mind is that the grammatical forms which indicate **negation** will vary from language to language. The source language **negation** should not be translated literally without carefully studying the meaning and the receptor language forms for **negation**. There may be considerable mismatch between the source text and the idiomatic translation.

Irony

Sometimes a speaker will say **exactly the opposite of what he means.** For example, on a very overcast, gray, and gloomy day a person may say to a friend, *"Cheerful day, isn't it?"* (Roy 1981:407). The speaker has said just the opposite of what he means. He has said *cheerful* when he means *gloomy*. This kind of skewing between the meaning and the grammatical forms is called **irony**. In **irony**, an affirmative statement may be made when a negative statement is meant.

For example, a person may say, *"I always wanted to live in Chicago,"* meaning *"I have never wanted to live in Chicago."* Usually, the statement is made with a special intonation indicating **irony**. But in written documents, there may be insufficient signals to let the translator know that the statement is **irony**. However, the total context will usually show the inappropriateness of interpreting the statement directly and show that the opposite is meant.

Some languages like Trique and Otomí of Mexico, add a morpheme at the end of the **ironical statement** which reverses the meaning. Languages will often have special devices to mark this skewing of semantics and grammar. But the translator needs to watch for **irony** in the source text and know the best way to signal **irony** in the receptor language. A direct literal translation usually cannot be made.

Irony is used in Shakespeare in such passages as the following (Antony and Cleopatra III.I.31–34):

> That magical word of war, we have effected;
> How, with his banners and his well-paid ranks,
> The ne'er-yet-beaten horse of Parthia
> We have jaded out o' the field.

Here Ventidius is using irony in the phrases *magical word of war* and *his well-paid ranks*. The real meaning is the opposite, that is, he is referring to the horrors of war and to the ill-paid soldiers. At one point Shakespeare uses *noble* in its normal sense to refer to Antony (Antony and Cleopatra II.II.14–5) in the phrase *Here comes The noble Antony.* But at a later point he uses it ironically in the phrase *'Tis a noble Tepidus...* in a speech by Agrippa. (Antony and Cleopatra III.II.6–8). A straight literal translation could give the wrong meaning. The translator is challenged to find the natural way to indicate irony in the receptor language.

EXERCISES – Skewing of Illocutionary Force and Grammatical Form

A. What is the purpose of the speaker in using a **rhetorical question** in each of the following situations?

1. John tries to tell his college friend what to do. His friend replies, "*Are you the prime minister?*"

2. Some children are playing around with a car that is parked near their house. An adult comes along and says, "*Is that your car?*"

3. Two women friends are chatting as one, Mary, is cooking dinner. Mary says to her friend, "*Why don't you set the table?*"

4. Mother comes into the kitchen and finds her thirteen year old son reaching into the cookie jar. She says, "*What do you think you are doing?*"

5. A teacher has become upset with some boys in the back of the room who keep making noise. She has told them to stop it, or she will have to ask them to leave. They don't. Finally, she says, "*When are you going to stop that noise?*"

6. A woman is trying to fix a broken chair. Her husband walks into the room and is watching her. She says, "*Why don't you help me fix it?*"

B. Each of the following is an **interrogative sentence**. Assume that it is a **rhetorical question** and change the form to a **declarative sentence.**   *statement!*

1. Didn't I give you the book?
2. Isn't it springtime?
3. How can you believe him?
4. Who's afraid of him?
5. Shouldn't you go home soon?

C. Each of the following is an **interrogative sentence**. Assume that it is a **rhetorical question** and change the form to an **imperative sentence**.

    command

1. When are you going to study?

2. Would you like to sit down?

3. Why open the windows?

4. Why not open the windows?

5. Why do you do it that way?

D. Study the sentences in part A above. How would you translate the quotation into a language which you know other than English? Would it be better to use a declarative sentence or an imperative sentence?

E. The following **rhetorical questions** were found in texts in the Tikar language of Cameroon. The context in which they are used is noted. What seems to be the function of the interrogative sentence? Restate either as a **declarative** or **imperative sentence**. How would you translate each of these into a second language which you speak? (Examples from Jackson 1982):

1. A small boy meets a bigger boy dressed in rags but smoking a cigarette. He says, *"Will you succeed by smoking?"*

2. Two people discuss a mysterious suicide and one comments, *"Who knows the real reason?"*

3. A person recounts a dispute of the day before. He turns to a fellow witness and says, *"I'm speaking the truth, aren't I?"*

4. In the introduction to a speech enumerating problems in the village, a chief says, *"Will you listen or won't you?"*

5. One person asks another, "Where is Elizabeth?" The other responds, *"Didn't she go to the dispensary?"* (indicating that the first speaker knows that she did).

6. A person says the opposite of what he intended to say. He then says to himself, *"What am I saying?"*

7. A woman explains how she has run out of money to finish building her house. She says, *"What shall I do?"*

8. A person describes a major decision that he faces. He says, *"What path shall I stand in?"*

9. A bird in a folk tale talks to himself after losing his nest to another. He says to himself, *"Where is Bird going to sleep today?"*

10. One parent comments to the other when their child does something extraordinary, *"What kind of a child is this?"*

F. In each of the following, the form is a **declarative sentence,** but the illocutionary force is that of a command. Rewrite the sentence as an **imperative sentence.**

1. You don't belong in here!

2. The door is open.

3. Your hair is a mess.

4. You are walking on my flowers.

5. That soup is good. (said to a child who isn't eating his soup)

G. Rewrite each of the following **negative statements** with an **affirmative statement.** (Note that you may have to use two sentences.) Then decide whether a **negative** or **affirmative statement** would be the best translation into the second language you speak. Translate the statements into that language.

1. *Not* one of them will go to town *without* my permission.

2. Anyone who does *not* pay his bill will *not* be able to stay in school.

3. He did *not* speak *without* exaggerating.

4. You will *not* see me *until* I finish writing this story.

5. *Unless* he earns more money, he *can't* go to school.

6. John has *no* brother *except* Bill.

7. There is *nothing* hidden *except* to be revealed.

8. He does *not* need to wash, *except* his hands.

9. I will *not* blow the whistle, *until* you finish.

10. We have *no* leader *except* Peter.

Chapter 23

Figurative Propositions/Metaphors
and Similes

Defining metaphor and simile

Metaphors and **similes** are common figures of speech found in many languages. These figures of speech are **comparisons**. For example, the following are **similes**:

> He ran *like* the wind.

> The moon is *like* blood.

> Benjamin is *like* a ravenous wolf.

Notice that in each of the above examples, the word *like* is used. In English, a **simile** always has the word *like* or *as*. **Metaphors** do not have the word *like* or *as*, but they are also **comparisons** that can often be rewritten as **similes**. The **comparison** is always that of some likeness. Notice the following **metaphors**:

> That child is a greedy little pig.

> He's an ox.

> He's a rock.

Notice that these could just as well be said as **similes**:

> That child is *like* a greedy little pig.

> He is *like* an ox.

> He is *like* a rock.

Metaphors and **similes** are grammatical forms which represent two propositions in the semantic structure. As noted before, a

271

proposition consists of a topic and the comment about that topic. For example, *John is tall* consists of the topic *John* and the comment *is tall*. *Bill hit the ball* consists of the topic *Bill* and the comment *hit the ball*. When a **metaphor** or **simile** occurs in the text, it can be very helpful to the translator to analyze it and find the two propositions which are the semantic structure behind the figure of speech. The relationship between the two propositions is one of comparison. The comparison comes in the comment part of the propositions. The comments are identical, or there is some point of similarity.

Analyzing metaphors and similes

The simile in English, *John is as tall as a bean pole* is based on the two propositions:

1. John is tall.
2. A bean pole is tall.

This is very simple and easy to analyze because the **topic** in both cases is given and the **comparison** (the likeness) is also given. The **topic** of the first proposition is being compared to the **topic** of the second. The comments are identical. The **topic** of the second proposition is often called the **image** (or **illustration**), the thing that the first **topic** is like. The **point of similarity** is found in the comments. A metaphor or simile, then, has four parts (see Beekman and Callow 1974 for more discussion):

topic	the topic of the first proposition (nonfigurative), i.e., the thing really being talked about.
image	the topic of the second proposition (figurative), i.e., what it is being compared with.
point of similarity	found in the comments of both of the propositions involved or the comment of the EVENT proposition which has the image as topic.
nonfigurative equivalent	when the proposition containing the topic is an EVENT proposition, the COMMENT is the nonfigurative equivalent.

Below are some examples of these four parts. In most of the examples at the beginning of the chapter, only the **topic** and the **image** of the simile were given. The **point of similarity** is implicit. To analyze the simile, we can state the two propositions explicitly. In the sentence *The moon is like blood*, the two propositions are:

1. The moon is (red).
2. Blood is (red).

Above, the implicit information is in parentheses. The analysis is as follows:

topic   *moon*

image   *blood*

point of   *red*
similarity

In the following, the metaphor consists of a sentence which is encoding an Event Proposition, and so the four parts must be identified. *The righteous judge will give you the crown of life.*

1. (The officials) give (the victorious athlete) a crown.
2. (God), who judges righteously, will give you (eternal life).

topic   God, who judges righteously

image   officials

point of   receive a reward for doing well
similarity

nonfigurative will give you eternal life
meaning

To analyze metaphors and similes, it is very helpful to write out the propositions which are basic to the comparison. The **topic, image, point of similarity** (found in the comments about the **topic** and the **image**), and the **nonfigurative meaning** (when the propositions are Event Propositions) should all be included. Only when these have been identified, can an adequate translation be made into a second language. The meaning in the source text must be discovered first.

The correct understanding of any metaphor or simile depends on the correct identification of the **topic, image,** and **point of similarity**. This is not too difficult in such sentences as *the book is as heavy as an elephant*. It is clear that *an elephant is heavy* and *the book is heavy*. The comparison to *an elephant* is being made to emphasize how heavy the book is. The book is not literally equal in weight to an elephant. There is an exaggeration as well as a simile. However, the sentence *the box is as heavy as my suitcase,* has the same form that a simile has. This is not figurative, however. It is simply a true comparison and is nonfigurative. We should not assume that every comparison is a figure of speech. *John eats like his overweight brother* is a real comparison, but *John eats like a pig* is a simile. The first means that John overeats in the same way that his brother does. The second is based on some characteristic of a *pig* which is also a characteristic of *John*. The **point of similarity** is not given. Maybe the proposition is *the pig eats too much,* or *the pig eats fast,* or *the pig eats sloppily.* Until we can fill in the comment about the *pig,* we do not know the **point of similarity** to *John.*

The sentence *that animal is a tiger* is not metaphorical. But the sentence *John is a tiger* is a metaphor. John is being compared to a *tiger* because of some **point of similarity**, some common characteristic. Here, again, there is a problem in analysis because the comments are missing. The **topic**, *John*, and the **image**, *tiger*, are included. In what way are they alike? This question must be answered in order to correctly interpret the metaphor. Often the context in which a metaphor is used will give clues which will help in the interpretation.

Live and dead metaphors and similes

Just as literal comparisons must not be confused with metaphors and similes, so also a distinction needs to be made between "**live**" and "**dead**" metaphors. "**Dead**" metaphors are those which are a part of the idiomatic constructions of the lexicon of the language. "**Live**" metaphors, on the other hand, are those which are constructed on the spot by the author or speaker to teach or illustrate. When a "**dead**" metaphor is used, the person listening or reading does not think about the primary sense of the words, but only about the idiomatic sense directly. For example, *leg of the table* is an **idiom**. It is easy to see that there is a comparison between the leg of a table and the leg of a person or animal. However, one no longer thinks about a person when using the expression *leg of the table.* An **idiom** is a "**dead**" **metaphor**. That is, the person using it no longer thinks of the comparison on which it was based. A "**live**" **metaphor,** on the other hand, is one which is understood only after paying special attention to the comparison which is being made. A "**dead**" **metaphor** is one which is understood directly without paying attention to the comparison. All languages have **idioms**, that is, "**dead**" **metaphors** which are constantly used without anyone thinking about the comparison.

In English, there are many **idioms** such as *run into debt, foot of the stairs, the head of state,* and *foot of the class.* Although it is obvious that each of these is built on a type of comparison, they are "**dead**" **metaphors** since native speakers who use them do not think about comparison, but think directly of the meaning of the idiom. They are understood directly without giving attention to the primary sense of each of the words.

It is usually easy for a native speaker to recognize the difference between **"live"** and **"dead"** **metaphors** in his language. For one who is translating, it is important to make this distinction since **"dead"** **metaphors** will be translated directly, without any attempt to keep the metaphorical content of the **idiom**. However, **"live"** **metaphors** are treated differently in the translation process (see page 277–78). It is, therefore, important to identify them in the text which is being translated. Then they need to be analyzed carefully to be sure that the correct meaning is being communicated.

It is often easy to identify a metaphor because there will be other things in the context, either in the written text or in the situation, which are related to the **image** being used in the metaphor. In conversation, metaphors may occur in isolation, but it is easily understood from the situation that a comparison is being made.

In written material, metaphors often consist of a number of **images** or a general **image** running through the text. Notice, for example, the following paragraph in which the harvesting of wheat is being compared to the ocean. This is more than a simple metaphor, it is a sequence of metaphors in which the harvest in the countryside is compared to the ocean. The **"live"** **metaphors** in the text have been italicized.

From the distance the tractor appeared to be *floating* over the hills, *riding up* to their *crests* and *down* to their *hollows*; the wheat undulated as the wind passed over it making *waves*. The grain *sprayed* into the harvestor and the platform in a steady *cascade*. It was a plentiful haul. Matthew wouldn't have to be *fishing for compliments* this year. He had proven himself a good *steward* and *brought his ship safely to port*. Now he figured he could afford to *hoist his sail* a little: he wasn't afraid any more of *slipping into a whirlpool* of debt. Seated on the tractor, he watched it *ride smoothly over* the *dips* and *swells*, and figured that he had *weathered out the storm*.

In the text above, *fishing for compliments* and *weathered out the storm* are both italicized because, in this particular text, they are used in order to create the effect of the ocean. However, these are both **idioms**, which in most contexts would not create in the mind of the reader a picture of the ocean.

Problems in interpreting metaphors

Not all **metaphors** and **similes** are easily understood. If they are translated literally, word-for-word, into a second language, they will often be completely misunderstood. There are a number of reasons why **metaphors** are hard to understand and cannot be translated literally.

First of all, the **image** used in the **metaphor** or **simile** may be unknown in the receptor language. For example, a **simile** based on *snow* would be meaningless to people who live in some parts of the South Pacific where snow is unknown. In English, we can say, *"I washed my clothes white as snow."* To make a similar comparison in a language in the South Pacific some other image would probably be used such as *white as seashells* or *white as bone*. The sentence *his clothes were like a chimney sweep's face* might be meaningless in many parts of the world where there are no chimney sweeps. The **simile** would not be understood.

The fact that the **topic** of the **metaphor** is not always clearly stated may also pose a problem for the readers. For example, in the sentence *the tide turned against the government*, the **topic**, *public opinion* is left implicit.

Sometimes it is a **point of similarity** that is implicit and hard to identify. For example, the sentence *he is a pig* does not include the **point of similarity**. In some cultures, a reference to *pigs* would give the idea of *dirty*, but in other cultures it might mean *one who is a glutton*, and in another culture it might mean *someone who doesn't listen to people*. When the **point of similarity** is not stated, it is often hard to interpret the **metaphor**. *He is an ox* could have various meanings. One could think of the characteristics of an ox as *strong, huge,* or *unintelligent*. But which characteristic is in focus in the **metaphor**? It is not indicated. This makes it very difficult to interpret the **metaphor** in order to translate it.

One of the more serious problems is the fact that the **point of similarity** may be understood differently in one culture from another. The same image may be used with different meanings. For example, to say *John is a rock* might mean he is *still*, that is, he *doesn't move*, or it might mean in another culture that he *can't talk*, or in still another culture might mean *he is always there*. In some other culture, it might mean that he is *very strong*. When someone is likened to a *sheep*, this **image** also has very different meanings from one culture to another. It has been found to mean *long-haired man, a drunkard, a person who doesn't answer back, one who just follows without thinking,* and *a young fellow waiting for girls to follow him*. Translating literally *he is a sheep* into a second language could lead to a very wrong meaning if the **point of similarity** is not made clear.

There is also the possibility that the receptor language does not make comparisons of the type which occur in the source text **metaphor**. For example, in the source text there might be a sentence which says *there was a storm in the national parliament yesterday*. But it may be that the receptor language does not use *storm* to talk about a heated debate. The appropriate comparison might be with *fire* as in *heated debate.* The nonmetaphorical meaning is that "there was a debate in the national parliament in which people strongly disagreed with one another." In the source text, the **image** is *a storm at sea.* It may not be possible to keep this **image**, but an appropriate one in the receptor language will need to be found if the **metaphor** is to be kept.

Languages differ in how frequently **metaphors** are used and in how easily new **metaphors** are created in the language. Concerning Pijin of the Solomon Islands, Simons and Young say, "In Pijin, literal statements are taken as such, and a bold statement that something is something else tends to be rejected outright" (1979:168–9). Similes are used, however. For example, the following is used for *pedestrian crossing:*

ples fo kat kros long rod, luk olsem snek long si

literally: a place to cross the road that looks like a sea snake

If a language group is constantly making up **new metaphors**, it may not be a problem to introduce a new one in the translation. However, it should be carefully checked to be sure that it works. There are some languages in which **new metaphors** are seldom created, and to translate the **metaphor** into such languages could cause serious problems of understanding. In languages where **metaphors** are not used a great deal, it may be difficult for the readers to understand a **metaphor** translated directly from the source language.

On the other hand, in languages where **metaphors** are used very frequently, many of the **images** will already have a metaphorical meaning in the language. If the source text is using the **image** in a different way, there can be misunderstanding since the **point of similarity** commonly thought of in the receptor language will be the natural interpretation. For example, to translate *John is a rock* literally, when the source text meant *he is severe* and the receptor language metaphorical meaning for *rock* is to *have hard muscles,* could only lead to a wrong meaning.

Translating metaphors and similes

In light of these various problems – the difficulty in discovering the meaning of **metaphors** in the source language and the misunderstanding that there may be in their interpretation – the translator must give careful consideration whenever a **metaphor** is found in the source text. The first step towards adequate translation of a **metaphor** (or **simile**) is to determine whether the comparison is a **"live"** **metaphor** or **simile**, or whether it is simply a **"dead" figure**. If the words which are figurative are simply an **idiom**, i.e., a **"dead" metaphor**, then the **image** does not need to be kept, but the meaning can be translated directly, i.e., nonfiguratively, as we noted in chapter 11.

However, if the comparison is a **"live" metaphor** (or **simile**), then the first task of the translator is to analyze the **metaphor** carefully. It can be very helpful to write down explicitly the two propositions with the **topic**, the **image**, and the **point of similarity**. If any one of these is unclear, the text needs to be looked at as a whole to see what would be an appropriate interpretation in the particular paragraph where the **metaphor** is used. Once the translator is satisfied with the interpretation of the **metaphor**, he is ready to consider how it might be translated into a second language.

The aim of the translator is to avoid wrong, zero, or ambiguous meaning. A literal translation of a **metaphor** or **simile** often leads to wrong meaning or no meaning at all. Sometimes it is simply ambiguous. Figures which are translated literally need to be checked out carefully with a number of speakers to be sure that the right meaning is being communicated.

In the case of **metaphors**, it is possible sometimes to keep the **metaphorical image.** For example, in the sentence *the road is a snake, snake* means something like *crooked.* If snake has this **metaphorical meaning** in the receptor language there would probably not be a problem in a rather literal translation. In some languages, it would be much clearer if the **metaphor** was changed to a simile and the sentence was *the road is like a snake.* It may be that the comparison is correctly understood in the receptor language in this form. If not, it can be spelled out more carefully in a form such as *the road is as crooked as a snake.* **Similes** are more easily understood than **metaphors** in most languages. Also, when the **topic, image**, and **point of similarity** are all included, there is little possibility of misunderstanding. Notice the three possible steps in the following:

1. He is a pig.
2. He is like a pig.
3. He is dirty like a pig.

1. He is an ox.
2. He is like an ox.
3. He is as strong as an ox.

When a **metaphor**, as in number 1, is used there is more possibility of a misinterpretation. When it is changed to a **simile**, as in number 2, it is more easily understood, but the **point of similarity** is still missing. If the **point of similarity** is also added, as in number

3, there is the least possibility of misunderstanding. On the other hand, the natural form used for **metaphors** and **similes** in the receptor language is the one that should be used. Is the **point of similarity** usually included in a **metaphor** in the receptor language? If it is only occasionally included, when is it included?

It may be that the translator will want to substitute a different **metaphor** in the receptor language, one that carries the same meaning as the **metaphor** in the source language. For example, we mentioned the sentence above, *there was a storm in parliament*. It might be good in some languages to change the **metaphor** from *storm* to *fire*, and the translation would read the *parliament was on fire last night*. If this is the **metaphor** which will be most clearly understood and indicate that there was *fierce debate in parliament*, then it would be the best **metaphor** to use. As long as the nonfigurative meaning of the **metaphor** is not lost, or distorted, a **metaphor** from the receptor language might well be substituted.

There will be times when the translator will want to keep the **metaphor** of the source text, but it will be necessary to include the meaning so as not to lose the intended force of the **metaphor**. For example, *the tongue is a fire* might be kept in the translation and the meaning added: *The tongue is a fire. A fire destroys things, and what we say can ruin people.*

There will be some times when the translator will simply need to ignore the **image** in the source text. That is, he will simply translate the meaning directly without using a **metaphor**. The source text *there was a storm in the national parliament last night* might simply be translated directly *there was a lot of argument and debate in the national parliament last night*. Or the sentence *he was a pig* might simply be translated *he is a messy person*.

In summary, there are five ways that **metaphors** may be translated (a **simile** would follow steps 3, 4, and 5):

1. The **metaphor** may be kept if the receptor language permits (that is, if it sounds natural and is understood correctly by the readers);

2. A **metaphor** may be translated as a **simile** (adding *like* or *as*);

3. A **metaphor** of the receptor language which has the same meaning may be substituted;

4. The **metaphor** may be kept and the meaning explained (that is, the topic and/or point of similarity may be added); and

5. The meaning of the **metaphor** may be translated without keeping the **metaphorical imagery**.

Comparing with the above list, the **metaphor** *no man is an island* may be translated into the receptor language in these five different ways:

1. No man is an island.

2. No man is like an island.

3. No man is a mountain peak.

4. No man is an island. An island is by itself, but no person is isolated from others.

5. No man is isolated from all other people.

EXERCISES – Figurative Propositions/Metaphors and Similes

A. The following are **metaphors** which are found in the Chinantec language of Mexico. The **point of similarity** is not stated in the **metaphor**, but has been put in parentheses at the end of the sentence so that the **metaphor** can be interpreted correctly. Rewrite each **metaphor** in a language other than English in each of the five possibilities mentioned above.

1. Peter is a snail. (slow)

2. John perched up high. (to be mean)

3. He is a turkey. (dumb)

4. This task is women's work. (easy)

5. Giving birth is like producing squash. (very difficult)

B. What problem might be encountered in trying to translate each of the following? Translate them into a language other than English.

1. He is fast just like a greyhound.

2. I am just a machine.

3. Athens is the mother of arts and eloquence.

4. Like a leopard, the mugger stalked his prey.

5. Those pigs ate all the food.

6. He galloped into the room.

C. Think of five sentences in a language other than English which contain **metaphors.** Identify the **topic, image,** and **point of similarity** in each of the **metaphors.**

D. Identify the **topic, image,** and **point of similarity** in each of the following. It may be helpful to write the two propositions first in order to see the **topic, image,** and **point of similarity** more clearly.

1. The king put a yoke upon the necks of his people.

2. John was a shining lamp.

3. You are a mist that appears for a little time and then vanishes.

4. I will come like a thief.

5. He is as tall as a giraffe.

6. His hair was white as snow.

7. People are like grass, here today and gone tomorrow.

8. He is the head of the department.

9. His eyes were like fire.

10. His voice was like a trumpet.

Chapter 24
More on Propositional Analysis

To analyze a text from a semantic standpoint, it is necessary to identify the **propositions** which are represented in the text. The internal structure of the **proposition** needs to be analyzed and also the relations between the **propositions** as they build into larger and larger units. In this section of the book, we have concentrated on the analysis of the **propositions** themselves. In the next section, attention will be given to the relation of one **proposition** to another as they group into larger and larger units. As we deal with **propositions** individually, we must always keep in mind that they are units which have functions in larger and more complicated semantic units.

However, before we turn our attention to these larger units, there are a few more details concerning the **proposition** itself which need to be considered. In chapter 4, the distinction between REFERENTIAL MEANING, SITUATIONAL MEANING, and ORGANIZATIONAL MEANING was discussed. (The student would profit from rereading that material at this time.) So far, we have been discussing the **proposition** from the point of view of REFERENTIAL MEANING and SITUATIONAL MEANING. The REFERENTIAL MEANING has to do with the **concepts** which are referred to in the **proposition** and the **relations** between them. The SITUATIONAL MEANING has to do with the speaker-hearer relationship, especially whether the **purpose** of the **proposition** is to state, question, or command. The purpose of this chapter is to look at the ORGANIZATIONAL MEANING of **propositions** and then to give an example of the **propositional** analysis of one paragraph of a text.

Coherence of a proposition

ORGANIZATIONAL MEANING has to do with unity and with the way that units go together to form other units. In the **proposition** it has to do with the way **concepts** group together to form **propositions.** A **proposition** should not be nonsense. The **proposition** should be a combination of **concepts** which are **related** to one another in such a way that the result makes sense.

The concepts *monkey, climbed,* and *tree* are semantically compatible. As long as the relations are *monkey* as **agent,** *climbed* as central **action** concept, and *tree* as **location,** the **proposition** makes sense. But if the *tree* were the AGENT and *monkey* the **location,** the statement would be incoherent. It would be nonsense. A **proposition** must be structured in such a way that the result is coherent, that it makes sense, i.e., so that it has structural unity.

Prominence within a proposition

As pointed out previously, a proposition consists of a **topic** and a **comment.** What is being talked about is the **topic** and what is being said about the **topic** is called the **comment.** In a text, the same **topic** may occur in a number of propositions and be the theme of the larger unit. Without a **topic** there would be no communication. The **topic,** however, is not necessarily the most prominent part of the structure of a proposition. The **comment** is the naturally prominent part, since it is the new information and is what the author is wanting to communicate about the **topic.**

As we noted in chapter 18, each proposition has a central concept to which the other concepts are related by case relations. This central EVENT, THING, or ATTRIBUTE concept is normally found in the **comment.** The central concept of the proposition, then, which is normally found in the **comment,** would be the naturally prominent concept.

While each proposition may be analyzed as a **topic** and **comment** combination, the **topic** of a text can only be determined after looking at propositions in sequence. In such a sequence of propositions, the **topic** of the text will be more clearly revealed. Nevertheless, it is important to think about the **topic** of a proposition, since there are two kinds of **topics, natural topics** and **marked topics.**

The natural topic

Topics may be **natural,** or they may be **marked.** In Event Propositions, the **natural,** unmarked **topic** will be the THING concept that does the action; that is, the AGENT or CAUSER. In propositions which have both an AGENT and an AFFECTED, the AGENT is the **natural topic.** Notice the following examples in which the **natural topic** is in italics (examples from Beekman, Callow, and Kopesec 1981:61):

> *John* threw the ball.   (AGENT)

> *Jane* made the child eat his dinner.   (CAUSER)

If the EVENT concept is an experience, the **natural topic** is the THING concept with the role of AFFECTED:

> *Peter* saw a snake.   (AFFECTED)

Where the EVENT concept is a process, then the **natural topic** is the THING concept with the role of AFFECTED:

> The *butter* melted.   (AFFECTED)
>
> The *rope* steadily lengthened.   (AFFECTED)
>
> *I* fell over.   (AFFECTED)
>
> *He* died.   (AFFECTED)

Each of the above examples is a statement. If the proposition were a question, the **topic** would be replaced by the appropriate question word. For example, *Who* fell asleep? *Who* made the child eat his dinner? *What* melted?, etc.

Marked topics

The **topic** of a proposition is not always the **natural topic**. When some other concept in the proposition is the **topic**, then the **topic** must be **marked**. Grammatical structures of languages have a great variety of ways of **marking the topic**. A concept is considered to be a **marked topic**, even though it is not a **natural topic**, when it is the **topic of the proposition**. Notice the following examples where there is a **marked topic** in italics and its case role is indicated in parentheses (examples from Beekman, Callow, and Kopesec 1981:61–62):

1. *The ball* shattered the window.   (INSTRUMENT)

2. *A prize* was presented to the student with the best grades.   (AFFECTED)

3. *The President's wife* was presented with a beautiful bouquet of flowers by the little girl.   (BENEFICIARY)

In the above English sentences, the **marked topic** is marked by placing it first in the sentence. This is only one way that languages mark the **topic**. For example, in Aguaruna, there would be no change from normal order to **mark the topic**. However, there is a special suffix *-ka* which occurs on the end of a unit. This suffix marks that particular unit as the **topic** of the sentence (see Larson 1978:183–90).

In the above examples, the **topic** was referring to a THING. However, a **marked topic** may also be referring to an ATTRIBUTE or an EVENT. Notice, for example, the following sentences:

His height is a great advantage.

His diligence in studying is well known.

His piano playing is outstanding.

Notice that in the first example, *his height* is representing the proposition *he is tall.* A whole proposition is the **topic** of the sentence. In the second example, *his diligence in studying* represents the **event proposition** *he studies diligently.* And in the third, *his piano playing* represents the **event proposition** *he plays the piano.* So in the surface structures of languages, the **topic** of a sentence may be a whole proposition. In English, the proposition is represented in the grammar as a nominalized form. The proposition has been **topicalized.** When **topicalization** of this kind occurs in the grammatical structure, it is important for the translator to identify in the semantic structure the proposition which has been **topicalized** in the grammatical structure. Not all languages will mark the **topic** by turning the proposition into a noun phrase. An adjustment may need to be made in the translation.

Some languages **mark the topic** by changing to the passive voice. Passive constructions were discussed in chapter 21. Both Greek and English use the passive voice in this way. For example, in the following, the affected is **marked as the topic** by making it the subject of a passive verb.

The *flowers* were given to Betty by Bill.

He was guarded by six soldiers.

Again, it is important to remember that forefronting and use of passives to **mark the topic** of a sentence is a device which is used in the grammar of specific languages. Many languages use affixes to **mark the topic.** As has already been mentioned briefly, Aguaruna of Peru has a suffix *-ka (-k)* which **marks topic.** For example, in the following two sentences the *-k* on the end of the first word is such a **topic marker.**

Pumpukuk	*makichik*	*pishak*	*shiigchawai.*
owl-topic	one	bird	beautiful-not-it-is

Gracielak	*tikima*	*duwegmachui.*	
Graciela-topic	very	fat-not-she-is	

In the two sentences above, the **natural topic** is marked by *-k*. However, if the **topic** is not the **natural topic** of the proposition, then the **marked topic** would take the *-k* as in the following:

Nii	*nu*	*jegak*	*shiig*	*wainmaitsui.*
he	that	house-topic	well	he-is-not-able-to-see

The **unmarked topic** would be the AGENT *he*, but in this sentence the **topic** is **marked** and is the AFFECTED, *that house*. In Aguaruna, verbs, as well as nouns, may be **marked for topic**. The **topic marker** for both is *-k* or *-ka*.

In some languages, forefronting shows focus; in others, intonation shows focus. There are numerous ways in which some part of the meaning can be made more prominent by special devices in the grammatical structure. For example, in English, prominence can be marked to show a contrast of focus, or an all-inclusive focus, or intensive focus or highlighting. Notice the following examples (from Beekman, Callow, and Kopesec 1981:62):

Contrastive forms: *Bill, not John*, mowed the lawn.

All-inclusive focus: She took *her whole family – parents, grandparents, brothers* and *sisters, cousins, etc.* – to the Amusement Park.

Intensive focus: *Billy himself* was invited.

Highlighting: *It was her Uncle Walt* she forgot to invite.

Notice that in the following, Bill is the **natural topic**: *Bill gave her the flowers*. It is possible to add **marked prominence** to this **natural topic** as in the following: *It was Bill who gave her the flowers*. Or one might say: *Bill was the one who gave her the flowers*. In these two sentences, *Bill* is the natural topic (the agent of the action). However, **marked prominence** is added by the surface structure device of stating *It was...who*, and *...was the one who*.

The translator needs to be aware of the fact that there are special devices used to show special **marked prominence** in the source text. He will not normally translate these forms literally into the receptor language. However, care should be taken so that the **topic** of the receptor translation is the same **topic** as that of the source text. Each language will have its own features for **marking** other kinds of **prominence** as well as the **topic**. The matter of **topic** and of other kinds of **prominence** is a very complicated one. A great deal more study of many languages is needed to compare the various ways in which **topic** is marked and in which other kinds of **prominence** are added to the information. The purpose of mentioning it here is to alert the translator to be aware of the fact that there will be special forms or orderings which have the function of **topicalization** or **marking prominence.** (The entire subject of prominence is treated more fully in chapter 32.)

Rewriting a text as propositions

Throughout the discussions in this section of the book, we have tried to emphasize the correspondence between a single **proposition** and the grammatical clause or simple sentence. When there is a direct correspondence between grammar and semantics, a **proposition** will be equal to a clause or simple sentence. However, in the source text there will be a great deal of skewing between semantics and grammar. In the receptor language, there will also be a great deal of skewing but at different places and/or in different ways. It can be very helpful to a translator if he is able to rewrite a text as **propositions.** We have already done some of this in the examples given throughout the book. In chapter 18 steps for identifying **propositions** were listed. We now want to look at a text and rewrite this text as **propositions.** The steps for identifying **propositions** are spelled out in detail on pages 204–5. To summarize they are:

1. Identify all EVENT concepts and express as verbs.

2. Identify the PARTICIPANTS.

3. Rewrite the sentence with the EVENTS expressed as verbs, and PARTICIPANTS made explicit.

4. Identify the RELATIONS between the propositions.

We will not be able to do step 4 until, we have completed the next section of the book. It would be good for the student here to review chapter 18, the section on identifying propositions.

Step 3 above, to rewrite as propositions, is very general. The following restrictions in rewriting **propositions** are helpful if one wishes to do a detailed analysis of the semantic structure of a text. These are an elaboration of step 3.

3. a. Only the finite form of the verb should be used (if at all possible).

   b. The natural topic should be expressed by the subject of the clause. A marked topic should be underlined. (We have used **bold** type for the marked topic in the example following Propositional rewrite.)

   c. Implicit information such as the topic and point of similarity of a simile or metaphor should be stated.

   d. Only the primary senses of English words should be used in the propositions.

   e. All figurative senses, except similes and metaphors, should be expressed in a nonfigurative way.

   f. All genitive constructions should have the full meaning made explicit.

   g. Embedded propositions should be rewritten as separate propositions in the form of relative clauses.

Embedded propositions should be rewritten as separate propositions in the form of relative clauses.

The following is an excerpt from C. S. Lewis's book *The Horse and His Boy*, pages 52–53. Following the paragraph chosen for semantic analysis, the material is rewritten in **propositions**. This is meant to be an example of how one might rewrite a text in order to see the meaning more clearly. Of course, in order to translate into a receptor language, one would also need to know the relations between the **propositions**. (This matter will be discussed in the following section of the book.) *Shasta* is the name of the boy and *Bree* is the horse.

> Shasta was pretending to lead but it was really Bree, who knew the way and kept guiding him by little nudges with his nose. They soon turned to the left and began going up a steep hill. It was much fresher and pleasanter, for the road was bordered by trees, and there were houses only on the right side; on the other they looked out over the roofs of houses in the lower town and could see some way up the river. Then they went round a hairpin bend to their right and continued rising. They were zigzagging up to the centre of Tashbaan. Soon they came to finer streets. Great statues of the gods and heroes of Calormen – who are mostly impressive rather than agreeable to look at – rose on shining pedestals. Palm trees and pillared arcades cast shadows over the burning pavements. And through the arched gateways of many a palace Shasta caught sight of green branches, cool fountains, and smooth lawns. It must be nice inside, he thought.

Propositional rewrite

There is one number for each proposition. However, when the proposition is embedded, i.e., part of a complex concept, it is not capitalized and is not put on a new line. Information which is implicit in the source text paragraph is made explicit in the proposition in parentheses.

1. Shasta pretended
2. (that he) led.
3. **Bree** really led.
4. (Bree) knew the way.
5. (Bree) guided (Shasta).
6. (Bree) occasionally nudged (Shasta) slightly with his nose.
7. (Bree and Shasta) turned to the left soon.
8–9. (Bree and Shasta) began to go up a hill (which was) steep.
10. (The atmosphere) was much fresher (than the valley).
11–12. (That which surrounded them) was pleasanter (than in the valley).
13. Trees grew along side the **road.**
14. Houses were on the right side only.
15–16. (Shasta and Bree) looked to the left (down at) the roofs, (which were part of) the houses in the town.
17. (Shasta and Bree) could see up the river a long distance.
18. (Shasta and Bree) turned to the right.
19–20. (Shasta and Bree) then turned back toward the direction (where they came from).
21. (Shasta and Bree) zigzagged up some more.
22–23. (Shasta and Bree) arrived at the center (part of) the town which is called Tashbaan.
24–26. (Shasta and Bree) soon arrived (at the place where) the streets (are) finer (than the ones they had seen before).
27–28. **Statues** which were very large (were there).
29–31. Some statues (depicted) the gods (which people who lived in the land called) Calormen (worshiped).
32–34. Some statues (depicted) heroes (which people who lived in the land which is called) Calormen (remembered).
35–36. (The statues were) on high pedestals (which) shone.
37. The statues (were) impressive.
38. The statues (were) ugly.
39. **Palm trees** (were there).

40–41. **Arcades** (which were supported) on pillars (were there).

42–43. (Arcades and palm trees) cast shadows on the pavement (which was) very hot.

44–45. (Shasta) looked through the many gateways (which were) arched.

46. (The gateways) opened to many palaces.

47. Shasta saw the many palaces.

48–51. Inside the gateways Shasta glimpsed branches (which were) green, fountains (which were) cool, and lawns (which were) smooth.

52. Shasta thought

53. (that) it would be nice for him

54. (if) he were inside.

Now let us look at the examples in the above **propositions** which will show the kinds of changes which are made in rewriting as **propositions**. Every change will not be discussed, rather only certain illustrations pointed out. First of all, notice that the source text consists of nine sentences. There are fifty-four **propositions** written here to represent the meaning. The source text, of course, reflects the groupings of the **propositions**, which will be discussed later. But in rewriting a text as **propositions**, there will normally be many more **propositions** than sentences in the source text. Some **propositions** include one or two embedded **propositions** which delimit a concept. This is shown by the numbers which indicate more than one **proposition** and by the words *which, where,* and *who* (numbers 8–9, for example). If a **proposition** begins with *that* and is not capitalized, it is the content of the preceding EVENT as in number 2.

The first step suggested is to identify the EVENTS in the source text. This text, for the most part, uses verbs to encode EVENTS. However, there are a few EVENTS which are encoded in the grammatical form of adjectives. (The numbers used below are from the **propositions**.) The source text for number 36 says *on shining pedestals. Shining* is an adjective which is encoding an EVENT *to shine.* In the **proposition**, a verb is used – *the pedestals shone.* Notice number 43. The source text says *burning pavement. Burn* is an EVENT. However, there is the additional problem that this is a secondary sense of *burn.* The secondary sense of *burn* is *to feel as if burning.* The meaning then is *to be very hot.* So in the **proposition**, the ATTRIBUTIVE *hot* is used and the skewing is eliminated. There is also an example where the source text has what looks like a verbal adjective, but the referent is a THING. Notice 40–41. The source text says *pillared arcades. Pillars* are THINGS.

So in the **proposition**, it is used in that way – *Arcades which were supported on pillars.*

The second step is to make all PARTICIPANTS explicit. In the source text, Shasta and Bree are mentioned by name only the first time they occur. In the **propositions**, they are explicitly named as the AGENT of all the EVENTS for which they are agents, but in parentheses since they are not explicit in the source text. In 10–12, the source text simply says *it was much fresher and pleasanter.* What does the *it* stand for? In the **propositions**, the interpretation has been chosen that the *atmosphere was much fresher* and *that which surrounded them was pleasanter.*

Step 3 is to rewrite the **propositions** eliminating the skewing between the grammar and the semantic structure using English forms. The points listed above, just before the story of Shasta and Bree, as *a* through *g* are ways to do that. We look now at the examples of each of these.

Point *a* says to use only the finite form of the verb. Notice the form of the verbs used in the **propositions**: pretended, led, knew, guided, nudged, turned, began, was, were, grew, etc. All of them are simple finite verbs. No participles, gerunds, etc., are used.

Point *b* says that the **natural topic** should be expressed as the subject of the clause, and a **marked topic** should be underlined. This is done throughout. For the most part, the **topic** is unmarked and simply the **natural topic.** However, there are some places in the source text where **topic** is marked. In 3, the form *it was really Bree* marks *Bree* as the topic. In 13, the *road was bordered by trees* is a passive construction with *road* as the subject showing that *road* is **marked as topic**. As a matter of fact, the next few propositions are all about the *road*. The *road* is important in the text until proposition 27 when the *statues* are **marked as topic.** Here, there is forefronting, but that in itself would not make it a **marked topic**, since as the **topic** of a State Proposition that would be the **natural topic.** But the elaborate attribution brings it into focus as the **topic.**

Point *c* says that the implicit information of a **simile** or **metaphor** should be made explicit. There are no examples of this step in this text.

Point *d* says that only the **primary senses** of English words should be used in the propositions. An example is found in number 35. The source text says *...statues..rose on...pedestals.* The **primary sense** of *rise* is *to move upward.* But the pedestals are not *moving.* A **secondary meaning** of *the state of being up high* is the one intended in the source text. And so the proposition says *the statues were on high pedestals.* A State Proposition is used with no mismatch of English words and meaning. Another example is found in 48–51. In the source text, it says *Shasta caught sight of green branches. Caught* is not used in a **primary sense**. *Sight* is a noun which stands for an EVENT. Actually, the whole phrase *caught sight of* is an **idiom** meaning *glimpsed*, and so this might also illustrate point *e.* The proposition reads *Shasta glimpsed branches.*

Point *e* says that all **figurative senses**, except **similes** and **metaphors**, should be expressed in a nonfigurative way. A good example of this is *hairpin bend* which is an idiom and, in numbers 19–20, is stated nonfiguratively by saying *turned back toward the direction from which they had come.* Many languages will have an idiom to describe this, but it probably won't be about *hairpins.*

Point *f* says that all **genitive constructions** should have the full meaning made explicit. There are a number of **genitive constructions** in the source text. Each has been rewritten explicitly. Notice a few of them. First, *roofs of houses* in 15–16 is interpreted as having the relation of PARTITIVE – that is, *roofs, which were part of the houses.* In 29–34, the source construction *statues of the gods and heroes* contains two **genitive constructions** which have the relation of DEPICTION, and so the proposition says *some statues depicted gods, some statues depicted heroes.* There is another **genitive construction** also – the phrase *heroes of Calormen.* This has been made explicit by giving the full meaning of *Calormen* as *people who live in the land which is called Calormen.*

And finally, point *g* says that **embedded propositions** should be rewritten as relative clauses. The **embedded propositions** occurring in this text delimit a THING or are the content of an EVENT. There are quite a number of them. Anytime there are two or three numbers together rather than a single proposition with only one number, there is **embedding** of this type. Notice 8–9 where *steep* delimited *hill.* In 22–23, the classification of Tashbaan was made explicit by adding *town* and using a relative clause *which is called Tashbaan.* In the last propositions, 52–54, there is a relative clause used to show the content of the EVENT *think.* The source text says *It must be nice inside, he thought,* and the rewording in the proposition says *Shasta thought that it would be nice for him if he were inside.*

We have now illustrated the rewriting of a short text into propositions. It is not expected that the average translator will take the time to propositionalize the text completely. By working through these steps, it can be very helpful for the translator to be able to rewrite paragraphs that are especially difficult. By making all of the meaning explicit, it is then easier to think of the best way to say it naturally in the receptor language.

EXERCISES – More on Propositional Analysis

A. What is the **topic** in each of the following? If there is no **marked topic**, the **natural topic** should be identified. Remember that English uses forefronting and passive constructions especially for **marking topic.** You might want to rewrite the sentence as a proposition first, and see what change was made. For example,

> *The ball was hit by John,* encodes the proposition *John hit the ball.* It is easy to see that *the ball* has been put at the beginning of the English sentence and a passive verb used. This is because *the ball* is the marked topic.

1. The meat is being cut.

2. Jim saw a star.

3. It was Mary who went.

4. The one who healed him was the doctor.

5. The water is evaporating.

6. John gave Mary the flowers.

7. Mary was given the flowers by John.

8. The flowers were given to Mary by John.

B. Rewrite each of the above sentences as a **proposition** or series of propositions (if you didn't do so before), and then translate these **propositions** into a second language which you speak using appropriate receptor language topic marking devices.

C. The following are English surface forms for the **proposition** *John shot the tiger with an arrow.* However, in each there is a special form used to indicate which concept is being made **prominent** in the sentence. Which concept is being made **prominent** in each sentence? How would you translate each sentence into the second language which you speak and keep the **prominence** intended in the source language sentence?

1. It was John who shot the tiger with an arrow.

2. A tiger was shot with an arrow by John.

3. John's arrow shot the tiger.

4. It was a tiger that John shot with an arrow.

5. He shot it with an arrow.

6. John shot the tiger with it.

D. Rewrite the following as **propositions**, following the steps given above (page 288).

There was a man who went down to the river one evening. The sun went down and it got dark. When he was returning to his house he heard a frog croak. So he lit a fire, and when he tried looking for the frog, he saw him and a toad sitting together on a rock singing. He grabbed the frog and took him, but he brushed the toad off into the water and left him.

E. Using the analysis done in D above, translate the same paragraph into a second language which you speak.

F. Using the analysis done in D above, rewrite the paragraph in English in another form; that is, change the **order of the propositions**, the use of nouns and pronouns, or whatever is necessary to come out with a different form which has the same meaning. (See the example on pages 232, 243.)

G. Rewrite the following in **propositions**. Then translate it into a second language which you speak.

One beautiful day when the sun was shining, Alligator went up out of the water onto a sand bar, and sunning and sunning himself he fell into a very deep sleep. As he lay there like that, Buzzard, who was flying by, saw him. He landed by him and began pecking him to see if he was dead.

COMMUNICATION RELATIONS

Chapter 25
Addition and Support Relations

In the preceding section, the analysis of a text into propositions was discussed and illustrated. However, a text does not consist of a long list of propositions only. These propositions group together into larger and larger units. In chapter 3, there was a discussion of semantic hierarchy. It was noted that meaning components unite to form concepts, concepts unite to form concept clusters, and concept clusters unite to form propositions. The materials in sections II and III have illustrated these groupings. The groupings, however, continue. In narrative texts, for example, **propositions** unite to form **propositional clusters**; these clusters unite to form **semantic paragraphs; semantic paragraphs** unite to form **episodes; episodes** unite to form **episode clusters; episode clusters** unite into **parts;** and these unite to form a **discourse.** The number of levels of groupings will depend on the length, type, and complexity of the text. Not all levels occur in each text. The names for groups will vary with the different discourse types. It is the idea of grouping that is important to understand.

Notice that the above is a statement about semantic structure. These groupings are related to the grammatical units, but there will of course be a certain amount of skewing, as we shall see later. If there were no skewing, then, as mentioned previously, the **proposition** would equal the *clause* or *simple sentence,* the **propositional cluster** would match the *complex sentence,* etc. The following chart shows the match between the semantic structure and the grammatical

proposition	*clause/simple sentence*
propositional cluster	*sentence (of more than one clause)*
semantic paragraph	*paragraph*
episode	*section*
episode cluster	*division*
part	*part*
discourse	*text*

structure of narrative discourse when there is no skewing of groupings. A discourse consists of a hierarchy of semantic units of increasingly larger sizes.

These groupings, in the left hand column, are called **communication units**. Just as the concepts within a proposition are related to one another by **case (role) relations** such as AGENT, AFFECTED, and LOCATION, so propositions are related to one another by **communication relations** such as **reason**-RESULT, **means**-PURPOSE, and **grounds**-CONCLUSION. The role in capital letters identifies the HEAD proposition (or HEAD cluster) and the role in lower case letters identifies the proposition (or cluster) which supports the HEAD.

Propositions related by **communication relations** form **propositional clusters**. **Propositional clusters** are related to each other by the same set of **communication relations** to form **semantic paragraphs**. **Semantic paragraphs** are related to one another by **communication relations** also. The **semantic paragraphs** group together to form **episodes**, etc. The nature of these units will be discussed in chapter 29. The units at each level are related to one another by **communication relations.** The purpose of the next few chapters is to study these **communication relations,** giving names to them so that we can talk about them.

It is not expected that the student will easily master the technical names for all of these relations. It is hoped, however, that he will be able to use these chapters as an effective reference guide when trying to decide on the analysis of a particular text. There will certainly be times in the translation process when he will need to do a careful analysis of the relation between two units in order to translate them adequately. These chapters should provide a source to which he can go in order to study the relation. Unless we know how two propositions are related to one another, we do not know what is being communicated. For example, we might have the following two propositions (example from Barnwell 1980:178):

Mary swept the floor.

The floor was dirty.

There are a number of ways in which these two propositions could be related to one another. For example, the first might be the RESULT and the second, the **reason.** That is, the meaning to be communicated could be *Mary swept the floor because it was dirty.* However, the relations between these two propositions might be **concession**-CONTRAEXPECTATION. The meaning then would be *Even though Mary swept the floor, the floor was dirty.* Another possible relation is that of **condition**-CONSEQUENCE. If this were the relation, the meaning would be *If the floor was dirty, Mary swept it.*

Notice that in order to understand what is being communicated, we must know what communication relation is intended. These relations are sometimes called by hyphenated names such as, **reason**-RESULT, **concession**-CONTRAEXPECTATION, and **circumstance**-HEAD. One proposition is the **reason** and the other the RESULT. The hyphenated name for the communication relation is simply indicating the **role** that each of the propositions has in the communication. For example, in the sentence *Mary swept the floor because it was dirty,* the proposition *Mary swept the floor* is the RESULT, and the proposition *the floor was dirty* is the **reason.** Therefore, we can say that the proposition *Mary swept the floor* has the role of RESULT, and the proposition *the floor was dirty* has the role of **reason.** The relation between the two propositions is called **reason**-RESULT.

Larger units related to concepts

Before beginning the systematic presentation of communication relations, it is important to distinguish between the relations which a proposition may have with a concept and the relations which a proposition may have with other propositions. When the concept was defined, a number of examples of complex concepts were given (see chapter 19). In a complex concept, there is an embedded proposition which in some way delimits (restricts) one of the concepts in the proposition. For example, in the following there are two propositions:

> *The man who came to town left quickly.*

The two propositions are: (1) *The man left quickly* and (2) *The man came to town*; however, the relation is not between the two propositions. Rather, the second proposition **delimits** *man.* It **identifies** which *man* is being talked about. It indicates that it is *the man who came to town* and not some other man. The proposition is embedded within the concept.

Propositions may relate to concepts within another proposition by **delimitation relations.** The **delimitation relations** are **identification** and **description.** An example of **description** would be: *John, who was very tall, ran quickly.* The two propositions are: (1) *John ran quickly* and (2) *John was very tall.* The second is simply describing *John.* The second proposition is related to a concept within the first proposition. **Identification** distinguishes one item from other similar items by pointing out a contrastive feature. For example, in the sentence *John, who is the last one in the line over there, will come with us.* **Description** simply gives information about the item. For example, *The apples, which are beginning to spoil, are in the bowl.*

Sometimes a proposition or propositional cluster occurs which is also related to a concept but rather than **delimiting** by **identification** or **description** it is only loosely related to the concept. It may be a **comment** of some kind or a **parenthetical** piece of information. These units have an **associative** relation to the concept which evoked the **comment** or **parenthesis.** For example:

> *John went to the store early in order to buy bread. By the way, Mrs. Jones still works there. He bought six loaves.*

In the above, the proposition *Mrs. Jones still works at the store* is parenthetical and relates to the concept *store* in an **associative relation.** The **associative relations** occur primarily in relating larger communication units. However, sometimes a **comment** or **parenthesis** occurs within a propositional cluster. **Comment** is used to label **associative** units which are more closely tied to the concept to which they relate. There is usually some overlap which gives a weak coherence. **Parenthesis** is used for those **associative** units which are more peripheral to the HEAD proposition. There is no overlap.

The four kinds of relations which occur between concepts and higher level units may be diagrammed as shown in Display 25.1.

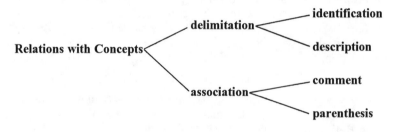

Display 25.1

Compare the following contrastive examples:

1. **Identification**: The man who was standing nearby helped John.

2. **Description**: That man, who is short, fat, and bald, will be arriving at 4 p.m.

3. **Comment**: Pedro Rodriguez, by the way he is my uncle, is President of the University.

4. **Parenthesis**: The thief (someday the police will catch him) robbed the bank on the corner last night.

The relation between a proposition and a concept will be indicated by different forms in other languages. Some examples from Ese Ejja (Bolivia) are given below (Shoemaker, Shoemaker, and Larson 1978:43). Ese Ejja uses a nominalized verb to show **identification**, as in the following:

1. *Ecuea ecue ano,*   *ecue papa mejojji,*   *Ese Ejja poa.*
   Mine my grandmother, my dad conceiver Ese Ejja was

   My grandmother, my paternal grandmother, was Ese Ejja.

2. *Ma ohua radio ejjasajaqui'yo quecua'yojji, ohua ana.*
   That he radio broken fixer he doing

   The one who fixes broken radios is doing it.

The following is an example of a proposition which is descriptive, i.e., it describes the *tiger.*

Maya pea ibia poeje, maya ibia quea-mase neenee.
Then another tiger will-come that-one tiger is-fierce very

Then another tiger will come, one which is very fierce.

Notice that the proposition *the tiger is very fierce* is expressed in a clause beginning with *maya*, glossed as *that one.*

Each language will have special forms to show the relations between propositions and the concepts they delimit or comment on. The translator will want to use the most natural form for the particular context in which the relation is being used.

Addition and support relations

We turn now to propositions which are related to other propositions by communication relations. Two terms which are very important in understanding communication relations are the terms **addition** and **support**. In grammatical structures, the words **coordinate** and **subordinate** would be used for the corresponding relations. **Addition** and **support** are used for the relation between communication units in the semantic structure in order to draw attention to the fact that these are semantic relations and not grammatical ones. It is true that quite often the semantic units in an **addition** relation will be signaled in the grammatical structure by **coordinate** grammatical units. Likewise, semantic units which are related by **support** relations will often be signaled by **subordinate** grammatical constructions. However, in order to make it clear that we are describing semantic communication relations, the words **addition** and **support** will be used.

Two propositions which have the relation of **addition** are of equal natural prominence. One does not support the other. For example, in the sentence *John went home, ate supper, finished his homework, and went to bed,* there are four propositions in sequence: *John went home, John ate supper, John finished his homework,* and *John went to bed.* They are all equal and constitute a series. The relation of **sequence** is one kind of **addition** relation. We will look into various kinds of **addition** relations later.

When one proposition is less prominent, it is called a **support** proposition. It supports the proposition which is more prominent. For example, in the sentence *Mary swept the floor because it was dirty,* the HEAD proposition is the RESULT, *Mary swept the floor* and the **support** proposition is the **reason**; that is, *because it was dirty.* There is a great variety of **support** relations which will be defined and illustrated below.

Chronological and nonchronological

Another classification of communication relations which is important to understand is the difference between **chronological** and **nonchronological** relations. Those relations in which the propositions are related to each other in terms of time are said to be **chronological** relations. Where the time element is not focal in the relationship, the relations are labeled as **nonchronological.** In the examples above, the first one about *John* has four propositions which are related chronologically; that is, first *John went home, then he ate supper, then he did his homework,* and, finally, *he went to bed.* These are in **chronological** sequence, that is, there is an element of time in the relation between them. However, in the second illustration, *Mary swept the floor* is the RESULT of the **reason,** *the floor was dirty.* Causality is the focal relationship. Since time is incidental, and not focal, the relation is classified as **nonchronological.** It is true, however, that the **reason** usually precedes the RESULT in time of occurrence in the happening being recorded in the text. Therefore, the main groupings of communication relations could be diagrammed as shown in Display 25.2 (Beekman, Callow, and Kopesec 1981:80).

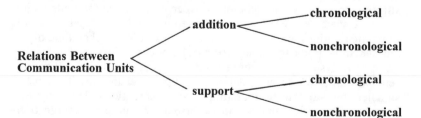

Display 25.2

Chronological addition relations

There are two relations in addition to the subclassification of chronological. They are called **sequential** and **simultaneous.** If two propositions have a **sequential** relation to one another, the one event follows the other event in time, and there is no overlap of time between the events. For example, the sentence *The bus will stop in the market-place and then continue to the bus terminal* consists of two propositions which are in **sequential** relation to one another. The first proposition *The bus will stop in the marketplace* refers to an event which occurs first, and the second proposition *The bus will continue to the bus terminal* is referring to an event which follows the first event. Therefore, the two propositions are in **sequential** relation to one another. One will happen first, and the other will happen afterwards. They are in chronological order. They are also related by addition in that one is not more prominent than the other. They are of equal prominence.

If the events of the two propositions occurred at the same time, the relation is **simultaneous.** Either event may be either a momentary happening or a continuous happening, and the overlap in time may be partial or complete. For example, *He plays the piano for her and she sings for him* is an example of the **simultaneous** relation. The proposition *he plays the piano for her* and the proposition *she sings for him* refer to two events that occurred at the same time. They are also in an addition relation since neither is more prominent than the other. They have equal prominence.

Notice the following two examples. In the first, the events are in **sequential** relation. One event follows the other in sequence. The three events are of equal prominence and, therefore, labeled HEAD 1, 2, and 3. In the second example, the three propositions are in **simultaneous** relation. All three events occurred at the same time. No one is more prominent than the other, so we labeled them HEAD 1, 2, and 3. They are related by happening **simultaneously** as shown in Displays 25.3 and 25.4 (example from Beekman, Callow, and Kopesec 1981:82).

1.

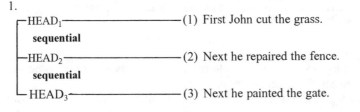

    ┌─HEAD₁───────────────(1) First John cut the grass.
    │ **sequential**
    ├─HEAD₂───────────────(2) Next he repaired the fence.
    │ **sequential**
    └─HEAD₃───────────────(3) Next he painted the gate.

First John cut the grass. After that he repaired the fence and then painted the gate.

Display 25.3

2.

```
┌─HEAD₁───────────────(1) Al cut the grass.
│   simultaneous
├─HEAD₂───────────────(2) Bill repaired the fence.
│   simultaneous
└─HEAD₃───────────────(3) Carl painted the gate.
```

Al cut the grass. Meanwhile Bill repaired the fence. At the same time Carl painted the gate.

Display 25.4

The **sequential** and **simultaneous** relations have been illustrated by single propositions. These same relations will apply to the relation between propositional clusters, between paragraphs and higher level units. Display 25.5 is an example of the **sequential** relationship between three propositional clusters.

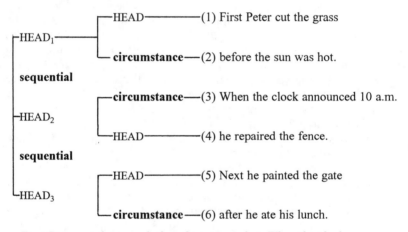

First Peter cut the grass before the sun was hot. When the clock announced 10 a.m. he repaired the fence, and then he painted the gate after he ate his lunch.

Display 25.5

Display 25.6 is an example of **simultaneous** relationship occurring between three propositional clusters.

Notice that in the English grammatical structure, the **sequential** relation is indicated by such words as *first, after that, and then. Next, and,* and other forms are also used. **Simultaneous** relation in English is indicated by such forms as *meanwhile, at the same time, and,* etc.

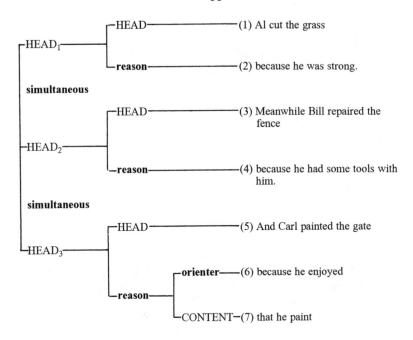

Because he was strong Al cut the grass while Bill repaired the fence because he had some tools with him. Carl painted the gate because he enjoyed painting.

Display 25.6

Other languages will have other forms. Although conjunctions of these kinds are found in many languages, other devices are also common. The **sequence** relation is often indicated by the repetition of the verb of the first clause at the beginning of the second clause in Aguaruna. This repeated verb may also be preceded by a pro-verb which also serves to mark the sequential relation. Notice the following:

Majamjan	*tiwiki*	*ajugka*		*ukuiuwai.*
toad-obj	brushing-off	having-thrown-him-into-he-water		he-left-him

Dutika	**ukuak**	*nigka*	*pachiakas*	*jegaa*	*waka...*
after-doing-so	leaving-him	he	forgetting-about-it	house	going up...

The propositions for the above are seen in Display 25.7

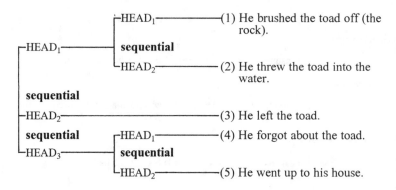

```
                ┌─HEAD₁─────────────(1) He brushed the toad off (the
                │                        rock).
┌─HEAD₁─────────┤  sequential
│               │
│               └─HEAD₂─────────── (2) He threw the toad into the
│                                      water.
│  sequential
├─HEAD₂──────────────────────────────(3) He left the toad.
│  sequential    ┌─HEAD₁───────────(4) He forgot about the toad.
└─HEAD₃──────────┤  sequential
                 └─HEAD₂───────────(5) He went up to his house.
```

Display 25.7

In Wojokeso of Papua New Guinea (adapted from Longacre 1972c:38–39), both the object noun and the verb stem are repeated at the beginning of the following sentence to show sequence. In the example below, the words meaning *fruit* (of a tree called *nalokuso*) and *we picked* are repeated. The propositions are given in Display 25.8. EVENTS and THINGS which occur only once in the semantic structure, occur twice in the grammar of Wojokeso to show the sequential relation between the EVENTS (*pick* and *look-for*).

...nalokuso	*ife'nimalohwefohe.*	**Nalokuso**	*ife'nontae*
fruit	we-picked-indicative	fruit	we-picked

tongo	*uhwonimalohweso*	*posaefo*
game	we-looked-for-and	empty

```
┌─HEAD₁───────────────────────────────(1) We picked fruit.
│
│  simultaneous
│              ┌─ concession ─────────(2) (At the same time) we
│              │                           looked for a game (bird).
└─HEAD₂────────┤
               │                  ┌─RESULT──(3) (But we didn't find a bird.)
               │                  │
               └─ CONTRA-         (4) (because the nest) was
                  EXPECTATION ─reason─   empty.
```

Display 25.8

In the same way, examples could be found of **sequential** relations between paragraphs and episodes, etc. In a story, very often one episode follows another chronologically with one occurring first, the next second, and so on. These episodes would be in a **sequential** relation one to another. However, in a story, there are many times when one episode will be presented, and then the author will present another episode which is occurring at the same time in another location. These two episodes would be in **simultaneous** relation one to the other.

Chronological support relations

The **sequential** and **simultaneous** relations, described above, relate events which are of equal prominence; that is, in an **addition** relation. There are also units related to one another which are not of equal prominence. One of the units **supports** the other. There is a **support**-HEAD relation between the two units. The ones described here are considered **chronological** since they focus on the temporal aspects of the events; however, one is the HEAD and the other(s) support the HEAD. The relation called **progression** is a lot like **sequential** described above. That is, it is a series of events which have a temporal relation the one to the other. However, in the **sequential** relation no one event is more prominent than the other.

When the **progression** relation is present, some of the events are in a support relation to one of the events which is more prominent. That is, there may be a series of events which lead up to a final event which is the prominent one. The propositional cluster often consists of a series of **steps** leading up to a GOAL. Notice the examples in Displays 25.9 and 25.10.

1.

$step_1$ ——————————————(1) Peter arose very early

progression

$step_2$ ——————————————(2) then he left the house

progression

$step_3$ ——————————————(3) then he went to the river

progression

GOAL ——————————————(4) then he began fishing.

Peter rose very early, left the house, went to the river and began fishing.

Display 25.9

2.

```
 ┌─step₁─────────────────── (1) Peel the tomatoes
 │ progression
 │
 ├─step₂─────────────────── (2) then add a little salt
 │ progression
 │
 ├─step₃─────────────────── (3) then add some spices
 │ progression
 │
 └─GOAL──────────────────── (4) then boil the tomatoes six minutes.
```

Peel the tomatoes, add a little salt and some spices and then boil them six minutes.

Display 25.10

In a larger discourse for example, there may be a series of paragraphs, each one describing an event which leads up to a final major event. These paragraphs would then be in a relation of **progression** to the HEAD paragraph which would be the GOAL. The relations, **sequential, simultaneous,** and **progression,** are commonly found in narrative and procedural discourses. The events being described either follow one another in **sequence** or happen **simultaneously** or are grouped in such a way that the **sequence** is more of a **progression** leading to a GOAL.

Other **chronological support** relations are discussed in chapter 28.

Skewing of order

Chronological ordering of EVENTS may also present special problems for the translator. The EVENTS of a discourse refer to happenings in real life situations which occur in a certain order. However, these are often reordered in the grammatical sentence or paragraph in such a way that the order is not the same as real (chronological) order. The sentence *He died without having any children* had to be translated into Wahgi of Papua New Guinea as *Not having any children, he died.* In Duna, the sentence *He bound up his wounds, pouring on medicine* had to be translated *After pouring on medicine he bound up his wounds.* It will help the translator if he consciously thinks about the order of the events referred to before translating them. If some are not in chronological order, what needs to be done in the receptor language? Does the order need to be changed? Or is there a special grammatical form that indicates that the clauses or sentences are out of chronological order? What is the most natural receptor language form?

So far, our examples have been short source language texts of a sentence or two. There may be propositions or propositional clusters within the semantic paragraph which are not presented in chronological order in the source text. Flashbacks are common in some languages. Special forms in the grammar indicate that there is a flashback to an event that took place prior to the other events already mentioned in one story. The following paragraph does not present the main EVENTS in chronological order:

> *John went into the house, leaving the people standing out in the cold. He returned to confront them again, after discussing the whole situation with his wife and telling her the whole story.*

Notice that the order in the paragraph is *went, left, returned, discussed,* and *told.* However, the chronological order of EVENTS is *left, went, told, discussed,* and *returned.* It may be more natural in some languages to change the order to match the chronological order. The resulting paragraph might be something like:

> *John left the people standing out in the cold and went into the house. He told his wife the whole story, discussed it with her and then returned to confront the people again.*

In describing this problem, Deibler and Taylor (1977:1064) say:

> Related to the need for retaining chronological order in most Papua New Guinea languages is the difficulty in handling flashbacks where they cannot be removed by reordering the sequence of events. In these cases one must be careful to introduce the flashback by whatever words are necessary to indicate "previously" or "before that event occurred." In some languages the flashback is further set off by repeating the clause which preceded the flashback.

As discussed above, the grammatical order may not be **chronological.** The translator needs to be aware of this and see if the order will need to be changed in the receptor language. When the EVENTS are in **chronological** order, it is often easier to follow the discourse than when they are out of order. A simple example would be the nursery rhyme: *Jack and Jill went up the hill to fetch a pail of water. Jack fell down and broke his crown, and Jill came tumbling after.* The EVENTS are in chronological order in the nursery rhyme. They could be encoded in English in nonchronological order as follows: *Jill fell*

*down the hill after Jack fell down and broke his crown. They had gone
up the hill to fetch a pail of water.* The second ordering communicates
the same information but the first is much more natural in English and
easier to understand (example from Kopesec). The translator aims not
only to communicate the same meaning but to do it in a natural and
clear form.

Nonchronological addition relations

Most **nonchronological** relations are of a **support**-HEAD variety.
However, there are a couple of relations which are **addition** relations.
The one is called **conjoining** and the other **alternation.**

In the examples given above, addition was illustrated by events
that were chronologically related; that is, **sequential.** In **conjoining,**
the propositions are not chronologically related. However, the two
events are of equal prominence, and there is no choice between one
or the other. Both are true. For example, in the sentence *Mary does
the housework and Jean does the cooking,* there are two propositions
which are completely equal in prominence which are simply conjoined. Conjoining, then, occurs when two propositions are in a
parallel relation to each other in the discourse. First, they are of equal
prominence; second, they are not chronologically related; and third,
both events apply, that is, there is no alternation.

Other examples (Barnwell 1980:192) are the following:

1. *He teaches chemistry and writes science fiction in his spare time.*
   This consists of two propositions, *he teaches chemistry* and *he writes
   science fiction in his spare time.* They are **conjoined** and of equal
   prominence.

2. *The children broke the china, kicked the paint work, and dropped
   sticky sweets on the best carpet.* Here three propositions are
   conjoined–*the children broke the china, the children kicked the
   paint work,* and *the children dropped sticky sweets on the best
   carpet.* No one of the propositions is more prominent than the
   others. There is no chronological relationship, and there is no
   alternation. They are simply **conjoined.**

Keley-i of the Philippines (data from Richard Hohulin) has two
words which are equivalent to the English *and* and have the function
of **conjoining**. However, these two links have a number of functions.
But when used in a list or series, one is used if the ideas are
semantically related, and the other is used if they are not semantically
related. In this way, they function to organize the information.

The relationship **conjoining** occurs not only between propositions
but also between propositional clusters, between semantic paragraphs,
between episodes, and so forth.

Alternation is also nonchronological and of the addition type. In **alternation** either one proposition or the other applies. For example, in the sentence *Is the dog alive or is he dead?* there are two propositions, *Is the dog alive?* and *Is the dog dead?* The relation between these two propositions is one of **alternation**. That is, a choice must be made between the two propositions. There is no time element so they are not chronological. One does not support the other. They are simply **alternatives.** Further examples are as follows:

1. *Go quickly or else shut the door. Go quickly* and *shut the door* are two propositions. The relation between them is that of **alternation.**

2. *John always plays golf or goes to a football game on Saturday afternoon.* Here, again, are two propositions, *John always plays golf on Saturday afternoon* and *John always goes to a football game on Saturday afternoon.* However, the two propositions are related by **alternation** which is signaled by the English grammatical form *either/or.*

Alternation is indicated by many different surface forms. In Aguaruna (Peru), the word *atsa*, which has a primary meaning of *no*, is used. Notice the following:

Wetatmek	**atsa,**	*pujustatmek.*	Will you go or stay?
will-you-go?	no	will-you-leave?	

In Gahuku (Papua New Guinea), the two clauses would be in juxtaposition; the first is interrogative and the second declarative. Notice the following:

Vitape,	*vamitane.*	Will you go or stay?
go-will-you?	go-not-will-you	

Gahuku also uses such combinations as the following: *Are you sick? You are tired,* meaning *Are you sick or are you tired?* and *Leave, if you will not do that, sit down,* meaning *Leave or sit down!*

In Ese Ejja of Bolivia (Shoemaker, Shoemaker, and Larson 1978:8), **alternation** is indicated by the word *pojja'a* meaning *perhaps* in the second clause. Notice the following:

1. *Eye poqui sa-poani cuei   yasijje, bai   yasiffe **pojja'a.***
   I   go   wanting river to   lake to   perhaps

   I want to go to the river or to the lake.

2. *Ache   shono miya poeje'yo   so'o?   E'e **pojja'a***
   Which time   you come-will diminutive? Yes perhaps

   poe   sa   po   ajja.
   come   want do   not

   Will you come back, or do you not want to come back?

The **alternation** relation also applies at various levels of the semantic hierarchy.

EXERCISES – Addition and Support Relations

A. Each of the following sentences contains two propositions. First, identify the two propositions. One of the propositions is **delimiting** a concept in the other proposition. Which concept is being **delimited?**

1. The man who lives across the street goes to work early.

2. Jane lives in the house on the corner.

3. The train which leaves the station at 7 p.m. goes to Huancayo.

4. Mr. Jones, who is a professor at the University, is coming to lunch.

5. I went to the store where my son works.

B. Which of the **delimiting** propositions in A above have the role of **identification**, which have the role of **description?**

C. In each of the following English forms, the part which is encoding a proposition which delimits is italicized. Classify the role of the proposition which it stands for as **identification, description, comment,** or **parenthesis.**

1. The students, *who were a good-tempered crowd,* pulled down the marquee very quickly.

2. The man *who wishes to be leader* must be willing to serve.

3. The exercise *the students are doing today* is not difficult.

4. The exercise, *which is very difficult,* is due today.

5. The exercises *which I hate doing* are due today.

6. The exercises, *I wonder who dreamed those up,* are due today.

7. The sun, *which had been hidden behind a bank of clouds,* suddenly broke through.

8. Do you know *who that is in front of my house?*

9. The baker *on the corner, he makes delicious bread,* is gone today. (two delimiting propositions)

10. The *smiling* guide told us about it.

D. Each of the following contain two or more propositions. Identify the propositions. Rewrite them as propositions. Is the relation between the propositions that of **addition** or **support**-HEAD?

1. He put the cat out before he locked the front door.

2. When the sun went down, John became afraid.

3. He ate rapidly because he was hungry.

4. He ate rapidly, quickly washed the dish, and dashed out the door.

5. Jane met Paul while living in London.

6. If he passes the exam, he will be fully qualified.

7. A flash of lightning was followed by a loud clap of thunder.

8. The farmer plowed the field and planted it with rice.

9. Before she replaced the plates in the cupboard, she washed the shelves carefully.

10. John went to town in order to buy the groceries.

E. Each of the following contain two or more propositions. Identify the propositions. Rewrite the material as propositions. Is the relation between the propositions **sequential, simultaneous,** or **progression (step**-GOAL)?

1. He played the guitar while she danced.

2. The bus will stop in the market place and then continue to the bus terminal.

3. John ate breakfast, left the house, went to the office, and began working.

4. The captain watched as his soldiers drilled.

5. Folding the paper carefully, cutting a piece off the end, putting a pin through the point, he made a small airplane.

6. John scraped, sanded, and varnished the chair.

F. Each of the following contain two or more propositions. Identify the propositions. Rewrite the material as propositions. Is the relation between the propositions **conjoining** or **alternation?**

1. Jack doesn't like dogs and his sister doesn't like cats.

2. Jack either goes fishing or goes hunting every Saturday.

3. Mary does the cooking and Jane washes the dishes.

4. He teaches chemistry and writes science fiction in his spare time.

5. Mary will go to the movie, or she will come by here.

G. Match the five examples below with one of these five relations:

    a. **sequential**
    b. **simultaneous**
    c. **step**-GOAL
    d. **conjoining**
    e. **alternation**

    ____ 1. The painting is finished and the plumbing is installed.

    ____ 2. He went for a walk after watching the film.

    ____ 3. I can either go to town or work in the garden.

    ____ 4. While Mary did the housework, I went for the groceries.

    ____ 5. He took out paper and pencil, adjusted the light, and began writing the exam.

H. Now go back through the above exercises, thinking about the analysis which you did of the propositions and relations. How would you best translate each of the above English sentences into another language you speak? (You may need to use more than one sentence in the receptor language if that is more natural.)

Chapter 26

Orientation and Clarification Relations

The various nonchronological support-HEAD relations are divided into three types: **orientation, clarification**, and **logical.** In these relations, there is a HEAD constituent and a support constituent. The support constituent is one that **orients, clarifies**, or **argues.** The following shows what the supporting unit is doing in relation to the HEAD unit:

1. The **orientation** relations: the supporting unit orients by adding information which has to do with time, location, subject matter, and so forth.

2. The **clarification** relations: the supporting unit clarifies by explaining further or restating.

3. The **logical** relations: the supporting unit argues for the head unit by giving **reasons, grounds**, and so forth.

This chapter will discuss the first two types, and the following chapter will discuss **logical** relations.

Orientation relations

In the group of relations which are called **orientation** relations, there are two main types of relations consisting of a support role and a HEAD. They are **circumstance**-HEAD and **orienter**-CONTENT.

Circumstance-HEAD

Circumstance-HEAD is a relation in which the **circumstance** provides background information about the HEAD unit. **Circumstance** is also sometimes called **setting** when referring to larger units. It presents information concerning the location or time or some other circumstance. Note the following.

Location is expressed in the **circumstance** proposition in the following sentence: *Walking along the cliff top she saw Bill.* There are two propositions: (1) *she was walking along the cliff top* and (2) *she*

319

saw Bill. The first is the **circumstance** because it tells the location where the main event happened. The second proposition is the main proposition and has the role of HEAD of the propositional cluster. The first proposition supports the second by telling what the participant was doing at the time of the main EVENT.

> ┌─**circumstance**————(1) She was walking along the cliff top.
> └─HEAD————————(2) She saw Bill.

Going up river he saw a huge alligator also has two propositions. *He was going up river* tells the location of *he saw a huge alligator* which is the HEAD.

> ┌─**circumstance**————(1) He was going up river.
> └─HEAD————————(2) He saw a huge alligator.

Time is expressed in the **circumstance** proposition also. The **circumstance** proposition indicates the time when the HEAD event happened. For example, in the sentence *As the sun began to rise they left the village*, the first proposition *the sun began to rise* tells the time when the HEAD proposition *they left the village* took place. The relation between the two propositions is that of **circumstance**-HEAD. The first is the **circumstance**, and the second is the HEAD.

> ┌─**circumstance**————(1) The sun began to rise.
> └─HEAD————————(2) They left the village.

Background information is also expressed in the **circumstance proposition**. In the following English forms, the part of the sentence which is representing the **circumstance** proposition is italicized:

1. She ironed the shirt *while the bread was baking.*

2. He came out of the house *wearing ragged clothes.*

3. He left Darwin *not knowing where to go.*

The **circumstance**-HEAD relation is sometimes divided into the three types just described and called **location**-HEAD, **time**-HEAD, and **circumstance**-HEAD (see Barnwell 1980:206). In the examples which follow, this distinction will not be made in the labels.

Orienter-*CONTENT*

In the **orienter**-CONTENT relation, the proposition which is the **orienter** serves to introduce the CONTENT. The **orienter** proposition would be propositions like *John said to Mary..., John heard..., John wanted..., John remembered..., John purposed...*, and so forth. The main EVENT of the **orienter** is a speech EVENT or a perceptual, cognitive, volitional, or evaluative EVENT. Display 26.1 gives some English event words of each type (adapted from Beekman, Callow, and Kopesec 1981:93).

TYPE	SAMPLE EVENT WORDS
speech	said, commanded, warned, promised
perceptual	saw, heard, felt, smelled, tasted
cognitive	knew, remembered, thought, agreed
volitional	decided, willed, wanted, purposed
evaluative	is good, is true, is false *, is important, is unlikely, is impossible, is possible .*

Display 26.1

In the sentence *The boy said that he was hungry*, the proposition *the boy said* is the **orienter** and the proposition *the boy is hungry* is the CONTENT. More appropriately, this proposition should be stated as *I am hungry* since it is the boy who is speaking, and it would, therefore, be in first person. Some languages will allow either direct speech or indirect speech in the grammatical form. Others use only direct speech (see pages 367-8 of chapter 28). English uses both: (1) *The boy said, "I am hungry"* and (2) *The boy said that he was hungry*.

The proposition *the boy said* is a statement. The **orienter** may be a **statement, question,** or **command** proposition. Notice the following in which the propositions are on the left and the English grammatical form on the right:

PROPOSITIONS	ENGLISH FORM
1. ┌**orienter**————Did he ask (someone)?	*Did he ask if John were*
└CONTENT————"Is John going to town?"	*going to town?*
2. ┌**orienter**————You tell him.	*Tell him not to go!*
└CONTENT————"Do not go!"	

Notice the following examples of nonspeech orienters:

1. ┌─**orienter**────Peter thought   *Peter thought that Mary*

   └─CONTENT────that Mary had left.   *had left.*

2. ┌─**orienter**────Mary wanted   *Mary wanted you to come.*

   └─CONTENT────that you come.

3. ┌─**orienter**────The boys saw   *The boys saw the men*

   └─CONTENT────that the men were   *leaving.*
                leaving

All of the above have an Event Proposition as the **orienter**. **Orienters** may also be State Propositions. Statements such as *it is not good that, it is true that,* and *it is important that* also serve as **orienters** to the CONTENT which follows. Notice the following:

1. ┌─**orienter**────It is not good   *It is not good for Mary*

   └─CONTENT────that Mary go to town   *to go to town today.*
                today.

2. ┌─**orienter**────It is true   *It is true that it rained*

   └─CONTENT────that it rained yesterday.   *yesterday.*

3. ┌─**orienter**────It is impossible   *It is impossible for them*

   └─CONTENT────that they finish today.   *to finish today.*

Very often the **orienter** constituent is a single proposition and the CONTENT which goes with it can be a very large and complicated unit, even sometimes being an embedded discourse.

In summary, the **orientation roles** can be diagrammed as shown in Display 26.2. Notice that the far right subclassifications are not used in the displays which follow. They are presented here to show the wide range of orientation relations, but only **circumstance**-HEAD and **orienter**-CONTENT will be used in the examples. **Introduction, setting,** and **preliminary incident** are orientation roles used in narrative discourses and will be discussed in chapter 29.

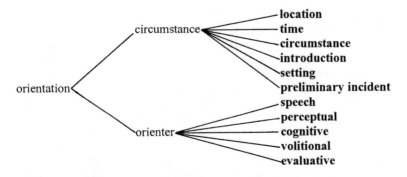

Display 26.2

The following examples of orientation relations are taken from texts in the Ese Ejja language of Bolivia (Shoemaker, Shoemaker, and Larson 1978). Notice especially (1) the Ese Ejja forms, (2) how they are rewritten as propositions, and (3) how they are translated.

1. **Ese Ejja**: *Jjono* *ishi* *majje,* *mique* *bacua* *manoje-yo.*
          Ayahuasca drink after your child will-die

    ⌐time ——————— After I drink ayahuasca.

    └HEAD ——————— Your child will die.

    Translation: After I drink the ayahausca drug, your child will die.

2. **Ese Ejja**: *Ecuana* *mijo* *jjashahuabaquinani* *poe'yani.*
          We you-about thinking are-coming

    ⌐circumstance ——————We are thinking about you.

    └HEAD ———————We are coming.

    Translation: Having been thinking about you, we are coming to see you.

3. **Ese Ejja**: *"Achejje* *quea-nee?"* *huahuiajja* *canaje* *Señora*
          where-at hurts? ask she-did Mrs.

        Cristaniya
        Crystal

    ⌐CONTENT——————Where do you hurt?

    └orienter ——————— Mrs. Crystal asked.

Translation: Mrs. Crystal asked, "Where does it hurt?"

Clarification relations

The **clarification relations** are divided into two subgroups on the basis of whether there is overlap in the information content of the two units which are being related. When there is overlap of the information, the relations are HEAD-**restatement** in type. The **restatement** may be an equivalent statement, an amplification, or a more specific or more generic statement. Therefore, there are four relations: HEAD-**equivalence**, HEAD-**amplification**, GENERIC-**specific**, and SUMMARY-**specific**. When there is no overlap of information, the relations are HEAD-**comparison**, HEAD-**illustration**, HEAD-**manner**, and **contrast**-CONTRAST. The clarification relations are presented in Display 26.3.

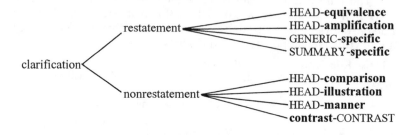

Display 26.3

Clarification by restatement

HEAD-equivalence

HEAD-**equivalence** indicates that the two units convey the same meaning. They are equivalent. The meaning is the same, and the second proposition is just a restatement of the first. Sometimes the restatement is a synonymous expression, sometimes it is the negation of an antonym, and occasionally, a figure of speech is used to restate the same information.

Equivalence often has the function of adding prominence by repetition. The speaker wishes to make a stronger impact upon the hearer. Notice the following English sentences and the propositional analysis following. The two propositions are in an **equivalence** relation (examples below are from Barnwell 1981):

1. *Rejoice and be glad.* (Synonymous) The two propositions *you rejoice* and *you be glad* are two ways of saying the same thing. The two propositions are equivalent.

2. *I was dumbfounded, flabbergasted, and amazed.* This sentence has three propositions which are nearly synonymous. *I was dumbfounded, I was flabbergasted,* and *I was amazed.* The three propositions are in an equivalent relationship one to another.

3. *I am telling you the truth, I am not lying.* The two propositions represented by this sentence are also in an equivalence relation since the second, *not lie* has the same meaning as the first, *speak that which is true.* The information is the same, but restated by using an antonym and a negative modifier. Another example is found in the sentence *Believe and do not doubt.*

```
┌─HEAD──────── Believe!
│
└─equivalence──── Don't doubt!
```

Many examples of **restatement** through the use of different figures of speech are found in Hebrew poetry. For example, Psalm 18:4 says, *The cords of death encompassed me, the torrents of perdition assailed me.* In the first half of the sentence, *cords* is the image used to describe death. In the second half, *torrents* is the figure used to describe *perdition* which is another way to talk about *death.* Here, again, there is **equivalence** by a restatement of the same information.

HEAD-amplification

HEAD-**amplification** is a relation between two communication units in which one of the units communicates some of the information which is in the other plus some further information. The additional information may clarify such matters as participants, time, the location, or the manner. For example, the two propositions which are represented by the sentence *He practices medicine; he practices at the clinic in town,* illustrate this relation. The second half is an **amplification** of *He practices medicine.*

```
┌─HEAD──────────He treats (people who are sick) with medicine.
│
└─amplification──── He treats (the people) at the clinic in town.
```

GENERIC-specific

In the GENERIC-**specific** relation, the **specific** part gives more precise detail. The GENERIC unit includes the information which is in the **specific** unit. The more generic proposition often includes lexical items which are in a GENERIC-**specific** relation to lexical items in the

specific proposition (see pages 69-74). Notice, for example, the following display in which the first proposition includes the word *cut* and the second, the word *chop*, which is a specific kind of *cutting*.

> ┌ GENERIC──────He cut up the meat.
>
> └ **specific** ──────He chopped the meat into small pieces.

A GENERIC proposition may introduce a series of **specific** propositions. Notice, for example, *John worked hard all day. He cut the grass, trimmed the hedge, dug the vegetable patch, and staked the tomatoes.* These two sentences represent five propositions. The first proposition, *John worked hard all day*, is generic. The propositions which follow, *he cut the grass, he trimmed the hedge, he dug the vegetable patch,* and *he staked the tomatoes,* are four **specific** propositions all of which are classified as "kinds of work done in the garden." The structure of these propositions can be diagrammed as shown in Display 26.4.

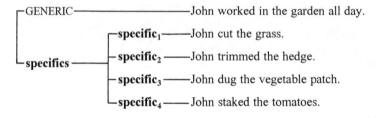

Display 26.4

Sometimes the **specifics** are given first followed by the GENERIC proposition. In English, one could say: *John cut the grass, trimmed the hedge, dug the vegetable patch, and staked the tomatoes. He worked in the garden all day.*

Some examples of clarification by restatement are seen in Displays 26.5 and 26.6. Notice carefully the form of the source text, the propositional display and the English translation.

1. **Ese Ejja**: *E'e   de,   eya queca cojja misi; quea cojja apo.*
         Yes indeed I   am   eye   dim   am   eye   dark

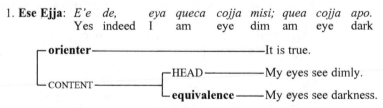

Translation: It's true that I can't see very well. Everything is dark.

Display 26.5

2. **Ese Ejja**: *Majoya   Queba   cuia   canaje,   jaabichaquinaje,   eshe*
                    Then   Deaf One   hit   it-did   knocked-down   life

ma'   cuia mee   a   canaje,   ana-aiya.
without   hit cause   do   it-did   the-cow

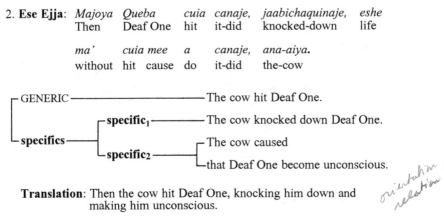

GENERIC ——————————————— The cow hit Deaf One.

specific₁ ——————— The cow knocked down Deaf One.

specifics

The cow caused

specific₂ ——————

that Deaf One become unconscious.

orientation relation?

Translation: Then the cow hit Deaf One, knocking him down and
making him unconscious.

Display 26.6

When analyzing larger texts, it often seems more appropriate to use
the word SUMMARY for the GENERIC unit. In a text, there is often a
generic restatement of several communication units. SUMMARIES of
this kind help to identify the boundaries between larger units of a text.

Clarification with no overlap of information

We will now examine clarification relations in which there is no
overlap of information. The one part is not a restatement of the other
part, and the two parts are not saying the same thing. The second part
is simply clarifying by adding **new information**. This new information
may be a **comparison**, an **illustration**, the **manner**, or a **contrast**. We
will look now at examples of each of these kinds of comparisons.

Comparison-HEAD

The relation of **comparison**-HEAD is based on the point of
similarity between two units. We have already discussed one of the
main kinds of comparisons in the chapter on metaphors and similes
(chapter 23). Except for metaphors, the **comparison** is usually clearly
stated in the grammatical structure with such words as *as, like,* or *than*
in English. For example, *He's as tall as Bill.*

It is typical in English that there will be some information left
implicit in the grammatical form, leaving the impression that there is
only one proposition when actually there are two. Notice the following
example:

His hair is white as snow.

The final *is white* is left implicit. Notice the propositions below.

┌─**comparison**────────Snow is white.

└─HEAD──────────────His hair is white.

In the sentence *I am taller than he*, the second proposition is represented by the word *he*. The full proposition would be *he is tall*. The **comparison** is between *I am tall* and *he is tall*.

┌─ HEAD──────────────I am very tall.

└─ **comparison**───────He is tall.

Illustration-HEAD

The role of **illustration** is used when talking about the **comparison** role which is filled by larger units such as paragraphs. Some prefer to use the word **example.** We will use the word **illustration** here. An **illustration** is simply a large comparison. The following example is from the Bible (Mark 4:30-32) (the illustration is italicized): God will begin to rule over very few people and will eventually rule over very many people just like *the mustard plant starts as a very small seed and grows to be a very large plant.*

Manner-HEAD

In **manner**-HEAD relations, the **manner** clarifies and supports the HEAD by providing information which answers a question, "In what way, how did the event take place?" It often refers to something which happened simultaneously. It describes how a certain event was done. For example, the sentence *He went away walking rapidly* consists of two propositions: *He went away* and *He walked rapidly*. The second proposition has the role of **manner.**

┌─HEAD─────────────He went away.

└─ **manner**───────He walked rapidly.

The following also contains a **manner** proposition: *She swept the floor in the way her mother taught her.*

┌─HEAD─────────────She swept the floor (in a certain manner).

└─**manner**───────────Her mother taught her to sweep the floor in a certain manner.

Contrast-CONTRAST

The relation of **contrast**-CONTRAST occurs when there are at least two points of difference between the two units and one point of similarity. One of the points of difference involves an opposition. When two propositions are related by **contrast**-CONTRAST, there must be:

1. A point of difference or contrast.

2. A difference by opposition (usually a positive-negative).

3. A likeness; that is, at least one point of meaning overlap.

The English sentence *I went to classes today, but Bill didn't,* consists of two propositions *I went to classes today* and *Bill didn't go to classes today.* The first difference is between *I* and *Bill.* The **difference by opposition** is between *went* and *didn't go.* The **likeness** or overlap of meaning is in the phrase *classes today.* Therefore, the relation between the two propositions is one of CONTRAST-**contrast.**

> ┌CONTRAST────I went to classes today.
>
> └**contrast**────Bill didn't go to classes today.

In the grammatical structure, which is encoding **contrast**, some of the information may be left implicit. For example, in the sentence *Everyone went to the party except Bill,* the phrase *except Bill* stands for the proposition *Bill did not go to the party.* English uses the word *except* to express the relation, and only the difference between *everyone* and *Bill* is stated in the sentence. However, the **difference by opposition** is found in *went* and *did not go,* and the **likeness** is in the phrase *to the party.*

> ┌CONTRAST────Everyone else went to the party.
>
> └**contrast**────Bill did not go to the party.

The point of likeness or meaning overlap may not always be expressed identically as in the phrases *classes today* and *the party.* The likeness may be expressed with synonyms or antonyms, but there is still **contrast.** For example, in the sentence *John is very smart, but Bill is not very brainy,* the first difference is between *John* and *Bill.* The **difference by opposition** is found in *is* and *is not.* The **likeness** is found in *very smart* and *very brainy* which have partial overlap of information by being synonymous in this context.

In the sentence *He stayed behind but I departed,* the first **difference** is between *he* and *I.* The **difference by opposition** is found in the usage of the reciprocal concept *departed. Stayed* and *departed* are opposites. The two propositions are *he stayed behind* and *I departed* (which means the same as *I did not stay*). No negative occurs to show the opposition since the antonyms themselves show opposition. The **likeness** comes in that *staying behind* and *departing* share meaning since they are reciprocal concepts. (For more examples of **contrast,** see Barnwell 1980:97.)

Mismatch of relation markers

Different languages will have very different ways to encode a given relation. For example, the relation HEAD-**comparison** is marked quite differently in English than in the languages of Papua New Guinea. English has three degrees of **comparison** – normal, comparative, and superlative. Notice the following examples:

NORMAL	COMPARATIVE	SUPERLATIVE
big	*bigger*	*biggest*
fast	*faster*	*fastest*
bad	*worse*	*worst*
good	*better*	*best*
quickly	*more quickly*	*most quickly*
quick	*quicker*	*quickest*
slow	*slower*	*slowest*

In English, the **comparative** is used when only two things are compared, and the **superlative** when three or more things are compared. For example, *Lae is bigger than Madang, but Port Moresby is the biggest city in Papua New Guinea.* But not all languages have these forms. In a translation, it might be necessary to say *Lae is big, Madang is not as big. Port Moresby surpasses all the cities of Papua New Guinea; it is very big.*

The translation of **comparatives** may involve various kinds of adjustments. Several possibilities are given here to show the variety of grammatical forms which may be used to encode the semantic **comparative** relation.

Sometimes the word *very* occurs to mark **comparative** in the grammar. The following sentence is from Ese Ejja of Bolivia:

Tumi Chucua ecuea quea-boti nee; Gonzalo ecuea boti'ama.
Tumi Chucua mine like   very Gonzalo mine like-not

In English it means *I do not like the town of Gonzalo as much as I like Tumi Chucua*. Notice that the Ese Ejja uses *very* in one clause and *not* in the other.

Sometimes an *antonym* can be used (**contrast** by opposites). The English sentence *Oranges are sweeter than lemons* translated into Ese Ejja would be:

Nanaja	*quea-biquia;*	*nemohue*	*quea-sese.*
Oranges	are-sweet	lemons	are-sour

The Ese Ejja sentence:

Donaldo	*quea-ao*	*nee;*	*Juan*	*quea-ao*	*pishana.*
Donald	is-tall	very	Jack	is-tall	a-bit

is equivalent to the English sentence *Donald is taller than Jack.* The sentence:

Mai	*quea-ca'a;*	*pashiye*	*quea-tona.*
Palm	is-hard	pala-maria (wood)	is-soft

is equivalent to the English sentence *Palm wood is harder than pala-maria wood.*

Spanish uses the following forms meaning *Peter is big, John is bigger, and David is the biggest:*

Pedro es grande.
Peter is big.

Juan es más grande.
John is more big.

David es el más grande.
David is the more big.

The receptor language will have its own special forms for encoding the **comparative degree**, and these may be very different from the source language forms. **Comparisons** in which the **superlative** relation is indicated are more complicated because three things are being compared. English has a suffix *-est* to add onto words like *big*, *little*, etc., to show **superlative** as indicated in the lists above. The following examples show ways that these kinds of **comparison** are handled in some languages of Papua New Guinea:

English:

The Gulf Province is bigger than the East Sepik Province, but the Western Province is the biggest.

Suggested rewording for Papua New Guinea languages:

1. The Western Province is big, and the Gulf Province and the East Sepik Province are not as big.

2. The Gulf Province is big; the East Sepik Province is small; but the Western Province is very big.

Many other examples could be given showing the skewing between the semantic structure and the grammatical structure in *encoding comparisons*. Only a few are given in order to alert the translator to the problem. Comparisons should not be translated literally. The translator must study the source text to find the semantic relation (the meaning) and then translate with the appropriate forms of the receptor language. He will use the patterns of skewing peculiar to the receptor language but not those peculiar to the source language.

EXERCISES – Orientation and Clarification Relations

A. The following examples in English illustrate the **circumstance-**HEAD relation. Some indicate location, some time, and some indicate other background information. Identify the part of the sentence which is encoding the **circumstance** proposition. Then translate the sentence into another language which you speak using appropriate forms to show the **circumstance**-HEAD relation.

1. As she was walking along the street, Mary saw her friend.

2. Just as the sun was going down, they came to the village.

3. He came into the house soaked from head to foot.

4. When the clock struck noon, everyone disappeared.

5. They left the canoe where the path came down to the river.

6. She arrived at the party wearing a beautiful blue dress.

B. In each of the following examples, underline the part of the English sentence which is encoding the **orienter** proposition. Then translate the sentence into the language which you speak other than English.

1. Mary wanted to eat some wild fruit.

2. "I'm tired of studying," said Bill.

3. Fred said that he didn't know the answer.

4. John saw that they would soon have too many people for the small canoe.

5. As they walked through the garden, Mary felt that summer had begun.

6. "Don't go near the water fall," Adam warned the children.

C. In each of the following, there are two propositions which are related by **restatement**. Is the relation between the propositions HEAD-**equivalence**, HEAD-**amplification**, or GENERIC-**specific**? Label the two propositions to show which is the HEAD and to show the type of restatement.

1. ⌐   -Be brave.   Be brave and don't be
        -Don't be afraid.   afraid.

2. ⌐   -He came towards me.   He came walking
        -He was walking.   towards me.

3. ⌐   -He shouted loudly.   He shouted loudly,
        -He announced his wares at   announcing his wares
          the top of his voice.   at the top of his voice.

4. ⌐   -It rained on New Year's Day.   It rained on New
        -It came down in torrents.   Year's, coming down
                                  in torrents.

5. ⌐   -The economy improved.   The economy
        -People and the business were   improved, and people
          making more money.   and the business were
                                  making more money.

6. ⌐   -The people were amazed.   The people were
        -The people wondered.   amazed and wondered.

D. In each of the following, there are two propositions which are related by HEAD-**clarification** relations. Is the relation between the propositions HEAD-**comparison**, HEAD-**illustration**, HEAD-**manner**, or HEAD-**contrast**? Label the two propositions to show which is the HEAD and to show which type of clarification occurs.

1. ⌐   -This dress is beautiful.   The blue dress is more
          -The blue dress is more   beautiful than this one.
          beautiful.

2. ⌐   -He did his work in a certain   He did his work in the
          way.   way in which he had
          -He had been told how to do   been told to do it.
          his work.

3. ⌐   -I ate apples and peaches.   I ate apples and
          -Mary ate only peaches.   peaches, but Mary
              only ate peaches.

4. ⌐   -He went away.   He went happily away.
          -He was happy.

5. ⌐   -John came yesterday.   John came yesterday,
          -Bill didn't arrive.   but Bill didn't arrive.

E. Translate the examples in C and D above into a language other than English. Use natural receptor language forms to indicate the relations.

Chapter 27
Logical Relations

Logical relations are nonchronological **support**-HEAD relations in which there is always the notion of **cause**-EFFECT. Although they are classified as nonchronological, inasmuch as the effect usually follows the cause in temporal sequence, there is usually, but not always, a temporal element (God is good, because he is God). However, the time framework is not the important matter, but rather the **logical relationship** between the two units. The **logical relations** are sometimes called argumentation relations. (See Beekman and Callow 1974:300 and Barnwell 1980:178.)

Each of the **logical relations** will be discussed and exemplified. However, in order to focus on the contrast between them, the following examples are given. In each sentence, there are two propositions which are being encoded. Following the English grammatical form, these propositions are given and the relations labeled.

1. **Reason**-RESULT: John washed the car because it was dirty.

 ┌RESULT ——————— John washed the car

 └**reason** ——————— (because) the car was dirty.

2. **Means**-RESULT: By washing the car, John got it clean.

 ┌**means** ——————— (By) John washing the car,

 └RESULT——————— the car became clean.

3. **Purpose**-MEANS: John washed the car in order to get it clean.

 ┌MEANS——————— John washed the car

 └**purpose** ——————— (in order that) the car be clean

4. **Concession**-CONTRAEXPECTATION: Although John washed the car, it isn't clean.

```
┌─concession————————(Although) John washed the car,
│
└─CONTRA-  —————————the car isn't clean.
  EXPECTATION
```

5. **Grounds**-CONCLUSION: The car is clean, so John must have washed it.

```
┌─grounds ————————The car is clean,
│
└─CONCLUSION——————— (so I conclude that) John washed the car.
```

6. **Grounds**-EXHORTATION: The car is dirty, so you wash it, John.

```
┌─grounds ————————The car is dirty.
│
└─EXHORTATION——————(So I command that) you, John, wash the car!
```

7. **Condition**-CONSEQUENCE: If the car is dirty, John will wash it.

```
┌─condition————————(If) the car is dirty,
│
└─CONSEQUENCE————————John will wash the car.
```

In each of the pairs listed above, one of the relations is given in capital letters. This is the relation which has natural prominence and is the HEAD of the propositional cluster. For example, the RESULT is normally more prominent than the **reason**. However, if the other proposition were more prominent, it could be marked as prominent by the grammatical form of the language. For example, in the sentence *It was because the car was dirty, that John washed it*, the author wished to make the **reason** equally as prominent as the RESULT. This is done in English by forefronting the reason clause and adding *it was*. When the **reason** proposition is more prominent than the RESULT, the relation would be diagrammed:

```
┌─result————————John washed the car.
│
└─REASON———————— (Because) the car was dirty.
```

Reason-RESULT

In the **reason**-RESULT relation the proposition which has the role of **reason** answers the question "*Why* this result?" In English, this relation is often marked with such words as *because, so*, and *therefore*. Notice the following English sentences:

    1. Mary took a vacation *because* she was tired.

    2. *Since Mary* was tired, she took a vacation.

    3. Mary was tired *so* she took a vacation.

    4. Mary was tired, *therefore* she took a vacation.

In each of these, the English grammatical structure matches the propositional structure, but a different form is used to mark the relations.

However, as we will discuss more later, there is often skewing. For example, *Mary was discouraged by the great amount of work.* The sentence represents the RESULT, *Mary was discouraged* and the **reason**, *Mary had a lot of work to do.* The preposition *by* is being used in a secondary function here to mark the **reason**-RESULT relation. *By* usually signals **means**.

In Aguaruna of Peru, the **reason**-RESULT relation is not marked by special particles, as in English, but always consists of a direct quotation. Note the example shown in Display 27.1 (Larson 1978:91):

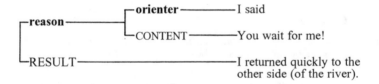

Translation: Because I had asked them to wait for me, I returned quickly to the other side.

Display 27.1

In the following sentences, the part of the sentence which encodes the **reason** proposition is italicized:

    1. *John was so angry* he shouted at the children.

    2. *Because he was exhausted* Bill went to bed early.

    3. *Peter forgot to bring money*; therefore he ate no lunch.

    4. The children couldn't play outside *because it was raining*.

Means-*RESULT*

Means-RESULT is the relationship in which the **means** proposition answers the question "*How* did this result come about?" The **means**-RESULT relation is often expressed in English by words like *by* or *through*. For example, *He won the race by practicing a lot*. The RESULT is *he won the race*, and the **means** by which he did this was *he practiced a lot*. **Means** always carries the idea of intention, whereas, **reason** does not.

In the following sentences, the part of the sentence which encodes the **means** proposition is in italics:

    1. *By working very hard*, he finished early.

    2. They protected the house from the thieves *through constant vigilance*.

    3. The students won the tournament *by playing together well*.

    4. *By putting money in the bank*, he saved enough to buy a house.

Languages will vary in how these relations are shown in the grammar. In Ese Ejja (Bolivia), the verb can take the suffix *-jje* which indicates **by means of.** Notice the following example:

Ese Ejja:

Doctoraa	*yacua*	*cajje*	*se*	*jjaajaquija'yo*
Doctor	inject	he-by	we	will-recover

    ┌─**means** ─────────── By means of the Doctor injecting (us)

    └─RESULT ─────────── we will recover.

Translation: We will get well by having the Doctor give us a shot.

Purpose-*MEANS*

Purpose-MEANS is a relationship in which the MEANS proposition answers the question "*What* was done in order to achieve this purpose?" Here again, there is deliberate intention in that a deliberate MEANS was used to bring about a particular **purpose**. The difference between **means**-RESULT and **purpose**-MEANS is that the RESULT was actually brought about but the **purpose** may or may not have been fulfilled. Notice the difference between the following:

means-RESULT:	By studying hard, he passed his exam.
purpose-MEANS:	In order to pass the exam, he studied hard (but he didn't pass).

Purpose-MEANS relation is often signaled in English by the conjunctions *in order to* and *so that*. Sometimes the infinitive is used. For example, *She went to call him to dinner* consists of two propositions; the MEANS, *she went* and the **purpose**, *(in order that) she call him to dinner*.

In the following sentences the part of the sentence which is encoding a **purpose** proposition is in italics:

1. John went to the store *to buy a book.*
2. *In order to get there on time*, they took a taxi.
3. I came *to wake you up.*
4. He hung it up *to dry (in order that it dry out).*

Notice the following example in which Ese Ejja uses the suffix *-jii* to indicate the role of **purpose**:

Ese Ejja:	*Chaco*	cue	*miya,*	*daquijji*	*epo'yojii.*
	Work	imperative	you	clothes-having	to-be

```
┌MEANS──────You work!
│
└purpose────in order that you have clothes.
```

Translation (English): You must work in order to have clothes.
Translation (Yaweyuha of Papua New Guinea): "Clothes I-will-get," saying, work you-must-do.

Display 27.2 (adapted from Beekman, Callow, and Kopesec 1981:102) may be helpful in showing the contrast between the three relations discussed above.

Cause-Effect	**Intention**	**Effect:**	**Cause answers the question:**
REASON-RESULT	no	actual	*Why* this result?
MEANS-RESULT	yes		*How* did this result come about?
MEANS-PURPOSE		potential	*What* action was undertaken to achieve the intended result?

Display 27.2

Concession-*CONTRAEXPECTATION*

The **concession**-CONTRAEXPECTATION relation has an element of "unexpectedness." There are three parts: (1) a **cause** (the **concession** part), (2) an **expected effect**, and (3) an **unexpected result** (the CONTRAEXPECTATION part). In English, usually only two of the three parts are made explicit in the grammar. Notice, for example, the following sentence: *Although the doctor told Bill to stay home, he went to the ball game.* The three parts are:

1. The **cause**: The doctor told Bill to stay home.

2. The **expected effect**: Bill stayed home.

3. The **unexpected effect**: Bill went to the ball game.

Notice that the second proposition, that is, the **expected effect**, is not included in the English sentence. Only the **cause** and the **unexpected effect** occur. However, the English sentence, *In spite of the doctor's instruction, Bill went to the ball game instead of staying home*, includes all three. The English sentence *The doctor told Bill to stay home, but he didn't* includes the **cause** and the **expected effect** negated. All these forms have the same meaning.

In English, this relation is often signaled by words like *although, even if, in spite of,* and *even though*. In the following sentences, the part of the sentence which is encoding a **concession** proposition is in italics. Implicit information is added in parentheses.

1. *Although the children ate a lot of green apples,* they didn't feel sick. (Implied **expected effect**: They ought to feel sick.)

2. *I waited a long time* but no one came. (Implied **expected effect**: Someone would come.)

3. *In spite of what the man said* they didn't stay. (Implied **expected effect**: They would stay.)

4. *Even if I get up early* I'll have to hurry. (Implied **expected effect**: I shouldn't have to hurry.)

Notice the following example in which Ese Ejja uses the word *jama-tii* to indicate the **concession**-CONTRAEXPECTATION relation. Study the three parts.

Ese Ejja: *Jjeya quea-pame nii, **jama-tii** chacochaco jjima.*
Now nice very nevertheless work not-yet

┌─**concession** ————————— It is a very nice day (or the weather
│ is nice today).
└─CONTRAEXPECTATION ——— He didn't go to work yet.

The **cause**: The weather is very nice today.

The **expected effect**: He would go to work.

The **unexpected effect**: He didn't go to work.

Translation: It's a very nice day; nevertheless, he hasn't gone to work yet.

Grounds-*CONCLUSION*

The **grounds**-CONCLUSION relation answers the question "What fact is this conclusion based on?" The relationship between the **grounds** and the CONCLUSION can be stated with the words *therefore, I conclude that,* or *one concludes that* between the two propositions. For example, *The door is unlocked, so Mary must be home* consists of two propositions. The **grounds**, *The door is unlocked*, and the CONCLUSION, *Mary must be home*. The relationship could be stated: *The door is unlocked, therefore, I conclude that Mary is home.* In English, the **grounds**-CONCLUSION relation typically uses the words *so* and *must be*. In the following sentences, the part of the sentence which is encoding the **grounds** proposition is in italics.

1. *The wind is blowing*, so it must be that it is going to rain soon.

2. It must be late *because it's getting dark.*

3. Mary must have come, *I see her son by the door.*

Notice the following example from Ese Ejja in which the relation of **grounds**-CONCLUSION is indicated by the clauses being next to one another. There is no word or suffix to indicate this relation, only juxtaposition:

Ese Ejja: *Ova Maria pojia'a mano'yonaje   Maria pojja'a manoje.*
She Mary perhaps sicken-permanent Mary perhaps ill-die

┌─**grounds** —————Mary has become very ill.
│
└─CONCLUSION———— Perhaps Mary will die.

Translation: Mary has become very ill and will probably die.

Grounds-*EXHORTATION*

The **grounds**-EXHORTATION relation is most like the **grounds**-CONCLUSION relation, however, in **grounds**-CONCLUSION the CONCLUSION is a statement, and in **grounds**-EXHORTATION the EXHORTATION is always a command. Notice the difference between the two following examples:

Grounds-CONCLUSION: The floor is clean, therefore, someone must have swept it.

Grounds-EXHORTATION: The floor is clean, so keep it that way.

The words which typically are used in English to mark the **grounds**-EXHORTATION relation are *so* and *therefore*.

In the following sentences, the part of the sentence which is encoding the **grounds** proposition is in italics:

1. *Father just painted the table*, so don't touch it.
2. *It's getting late*, let's go to bed.
3. Go home now since *you have to go to school tomorrow*.
4. *Peter likes fish*, so give him plenty.

Notice the following example in which two forms of the Ese Ejja are given to illustrate the **grounds**-EXHORTATION relation. In the first, there is a relation marker, *jamajje*; but in the second, the two clauses are simply next to each other with no form to indicate the relation except the juxtaposition and the information content:

Ese Ejja: 1. *Ena   poeje,   **jamajje**   a'a   poquijji!*
                   Rain   will-come   so   don't   go

              2. *Ena   poeje,   a'a poquijji!*
                   Rain   will-come   don't go

The semantic structure is the same for both:

┌**grounds**: —————— Rain will come.
│
└EXHORTATION: ——— You do not go!

Translation: Don't leave, it's going to rain.

Condition-*CONSEQUENCE*

The **condition**-CONSEQUENCE relation is also of the cause-EFFECT type. However, the cause, that is, the **condition**, is either hypothetical or there is some element of uncertainty. This relation has often been subdivided into **contrary-to-fact** and **potential fact.** This subdivision is pointed out in Barnwell (1980:183–4). Both types are characteristically signaled by the word *if* in English. *If that had happened, then this would have happened.* For example, *If it had rained, I would have stayed home; If John gets home in time, we'll go.*

In a **contrary-to-fact condition**-CONSEQUENCE relation, the **condition** is hypothetical or imagined and did not, will not, or is not expected to actually take place. It is simply describing a condition which might have been but as a matter of fact did not occur or is not expected to. For example, notice the English sentence *If I were younger, I would go to Europe.* The first proposition is the **condition** and is **contrary-to-fact** since *I am not younger. I would go to Europe,* which is the **consequence**, is also simply hypothetical. In the sentence *If he had not missed the bus, he would be there now*, the first proposition is the **condition** and the second is the CONSEQUENCE. Neither is a **fact.** They are only imagined. Notice that the **contrary-to-fact condition**-CONSEQUENCE examples given above are in the past tense. That is, they are things that might have happened but did not. Sometimes **contrary-to-fact** propositions are in the future tense. This is true when they refer to EVENTS which are not expected to happen. For example, *If I were to die tomorrow, who would run the store?*

The second type of **condition**-CONSEQUENCE relation is that of a **potential fact.** The propositions are either in the present or future. It is also unknown whether the **condition** will be met which will result in the CONSEQUENCE or not. For example, *If you get there early, you will get inside.* Since it has not yet happened, this is simply a **potential fact.** The CONSEQUENCE of *getting inside* is dependent on the **condition** of *getting there early.*

In the following sentences, the part of the sentence which encodes the **condition** proposition is in italics. The first four examples illustrate **contrary-to-fact**, and the second four **potential fact.**

1. *If you had asked me*, I would have helped you.
2. *If he had eaten his dinner*, he wouldn't be hungry now.
3. John would have caught the bus, *if he had not stopped to talk.*
4. I would have come earlier, *if you had asked me to.*
5. *If a will is not signed*, it is not valid.
6. *If you get up early*, you will see the sun rise.
7. *If somebody kicks the ball into the net*, it's a goal.
8. Go inside, *if you have a ticket.*

There are a number of grammatical forms which indicate **condition**-CONSEQUENCE in Ese Ejja. In the examples below, only the Ese Ejja gloss and translation are given since the English translation shows which part of the source sentence is **condition** and which is CONSEQUENCE.

1. **Ese Ejja**: *Ba'i*   *esho'ijo*   *quecua,* *so'*   *ma'*   *acue.*
             Moon   new-on   plant   grain   none   indeed

    Translation: If you plant corn at the time of the new moon, it certainly will have no kernels.

2. **Ese Ejja**: *Ecue* *huanase* *dojo'yajo* *eyayo* *miya* *quechuajeaje!*
             My   wife   take-if   I   you   will-kill-emphatic

    Translation: If you take my wife, I will kill you.

3. **Ese Ejja**: *Ena* *chama* ***jojjemo*** *shijje* *tii* *ajja* ***pomee.***
             Rain   none   **if**   corn   grow   not   would

    Translation: If it doesn't rain, the corn won't grow.

4. **Ese Ejja**: *Miya poqui* ***majje*** *ca*   *poquei'yo*   *cue*   *ya!*
             You go   **if**   emphasis go-permanent imperative focus

    Translation: If you go, you had better leave for good.

Mismatch of order

We have already illustrated (see pages 308–9) the fact that there is no fixed **order** between propositions, rather there are relations. In encoding a group of propositions, the order used will simply be the natural **order** of the receptor language. This **order** may be quite different from the **order** of the source language. For example, the English sentence *I will go to town in order to buy some bread* would be translated into Upper Asaro of Papua New Guinea in this **order** (Deibler and Taylor 1977:1062):

Beleti *ma*   *meni*   *hiz-el-ove*   *lo*   *tauni-u'*   *v-ol-ove.*
Bread   some   payment   make-will-I   saying   town-into   go-will-I.

In English, the **purpose** usually follows the main clause. However, in Upper Asaro, and many other languages, the **purpose** comes first in the grammatical structure. In this example, there are two propositions which are related as follows:

```
┌─HEAD───────(1) I will go to town.
│
└─purpose──────(2) I will buy some bread.
```

In English, the clause which realizes the HEAD proposition comes first, but in Asaro, the **purpose** comes first. Notice also that the form of the **purpose** clause in Asaro is a quotation. Translators seldom err in the word order within a clause. But there is a tendency to translate clauses, sentences, and paragraphs in the same order as in the source text.

Sometimes there is a choice of order in the receptor language grammar. Look at the two propositions in English:

```
┌─HEAD───────I went to town.
│
└─reason──────I wanted to buy something.
```

They can be translated either *I went to town because I wanted to buy something,* or *Because I wanted to buy something, I went to town.* In some languages, the **reason** proposition will always precede the HEAD proposition in the sentence as in the Asaro example above. This is especially true of languages which normally end the sentence with a main independent verb. Since this verb is usually encoding the EVENT of the HEAD proposition, all the clauses which encode other propositions of the propositional cluster will precede the clause encoding the HEAD proposition.

Some languages, in Papua New Guinea and in the Amazon area of South America, for example, have a preferred order, that of the subordinate clause (encoding a support proposition) almost always occurring before the clause to which it is subordinate (the HEAD proposition). A tendency in English is just the opposite; that is, the subordinate clause more often follows the main clause. It can be very helpful to the translator to study the order of clauses in the receptor language as preparation for translation. The translator translating into Rennellese of the Solomon Islands found out that the **reason** clause must always be last in the sentence. On the other hand, the **concession** clause must always precede the main clause of the sentence. Each language will have its own correct or preferred order.

Implicit constituents and relations

In the semantic structure, all of the information is included. However, in the grammar, some of the information may be left

implicit; that is, it may not be encoded at all. (This matter is discussed in chapter 4 and again in chapter 34.) We have illustrated how this happens when the PARTICIPANTS or the EVENT of a proposition are left **implicit** in the clause or sentence. For example, when the passive form is used, the AGENT is not always indicated in the clause. Or sometimes it is the EVENT that is left **implicit** (see page 250).

In the same way, at higher levels of the hierarchy, constituents of the semantic structure may be left **implicit** in the grammatical form. Or the relations may be left **implicit**. Constituents and relations which may be left **implicit** in one language may need to be made **explicit** in another language. Languages do not have the same rules concerning when information may be left **implicit**.

Notice the following:

> *The two boys were under the window waiting their chance*
> *to crawl in and seize the treasure. Suddenly John said,*
> *"Not now. Someone is coming."*

In the last sentence, the form *not now* stands for a whole proposition, most of which is left **implicit**. Only the time and the negative are left **explicit**. The whole proposition would be *let's not go into the room now*. The immediate context makes the **implied** information clear in English. However, it may not be best to leave it **implicit** in all languages. For example, in Aguaruna (Peru), it would not be possible to say *not* without a verb. The natural form for this situation in Aguaruna would be *jasta* which simply means *wait*. Each language will have a natural way to express this proposition in this situation. No doubt some information will be left **implicit**.

Notice also that in the above example the two propositions inside the quotations are:

```
┌─ EXHORTATION ──────── Let's not go into the room now.
│
└─ grounds ──────────── Someone is coming.
```

The relation is not indicated in the grammatical form of English. The word *because* could be used in English: "Not now, because someone is coming." However, it is not needed. It is left **implicit** and the meaning is clear from the context. In some other language, however, the relation marker may be needed in the grammatical form for correct meaning.

In Ese Ejja of Bolivia, the relation markers are often left **implicit**, and the juxtaposition of the two clauses in the grammatical sentence is all that signals the relation. The sentence *Moon new-on plant, grain none indeed* is the literal Ese Ejja form for the meaning:

```
┌─condition──────────you plant corn at the time of full moon
│
└─CONSEQUENCE────────corn will not produce kernels
```

In English, it would be necessary to make the relation **explicit** using the marker *if*. *If you plant corn at the time of the full moon, there will be no kernels.*

The reason for leaving some information **implicit** is clear. If every bit of information from the semantic structure were made **explicit** in the grammatical form, many things would need to be repeated over and over. Look again at the propositional display of the paragraph about Shasta and Bree (page 290–91) and compare it with the original paragraph in Chapter 24. The information which has been left **implicit** is old information; that is, it has already been said before. As a discourse develops, the information that has already been introduced may be assumed to be known. Old information is what can be left **implicit**, and languages will have special forms for doing that. They may have pronouns and pro-verbs. These will substitute for nouns and verbs. Grammar books regularly use the term **ellipsis** to refer to information that has been given already and then left implicit.

Each language will have its own grammatical devices for leaving information **implicit**. Old information does not need to be repeated over and over. But how this is done will depend on the language structure. It will not be the same in the receptor language as in the source language. The translator wants to use the natural **ellipsis** rules (or patterns) of the receptor language and not copy the **ellipsis** of the source language.

So far, we have only mentioned examples in which the source language left something **implicit** which was made **explicit** in the receptor language. The opposite may also be true. For example, there may be semantic redundancy which can be reduced. A sentence like *John's mother-in-law was sick with a high fever* might be translated simply *John's mother-in-law had a high fever*. Since *having a high fever* implies *being sick* it may not need to be made **explicit.** Some languages will introduce quotations with phrases like *asking said* and *answered saying*. But this may be unnatural in the receptor language, and one or the other will be left **implicit.** The stylistic requirements of the receptor language will influence the use of explicit information and help determine when it may be left **implicit.** The important matter is to be sure that it is indeed still implied and significant meaning is not lost.

The translator will want to use the natural forms of the receptor language. These forms may make it necessary and desirable to make some **implicit** information of the source text **explicit** in the translation, and it may also make it desirable to make some **explicit** information of the source text **implicit**.

Multiple functions of grammatical relation markers

In the previous chapters, communication relations were presented with some examples. English words which are typical of a particular relation were mentioned. However, it is important that a translator realize that words in the grammar which have a primary meaning such as **sequential, reason,** and **alternation,** etc., may have secondary senses just like other words have secondary senses. They may have other functions than the primary usage which first comes to the mind of the mother-tongue speaker. For example, *if* in English has a primary meaning of **condition** in the **condition**-CONSEQUENCE relation. But in the following context it does not mean **condition**:

> *The door is open. If the door is open, Mary must be home.*

In this example, the fact that *the door is open* is the **grounds** for the CONCLUSION that *Mary must be home. If* is used in a secondary function. The English word which has the primary meaning of **grounds** would be *so. The door is open, so Mary must be home.* It would also be correct in English to say *Since the door is open, Mary must be home.* When *so* is used, there is no skewing between the semantic relation being encoded and the grammatical form.

The conjunction *but* in English has a primary meaning of **contrast**. *Mary baked a cake, but she didn't bake any cookies.* However, *but* is also used with a variety of secondary functions. Unless the translator translating from English is aware of this, he might translate with a receptor language **contrast** marker when **contrast** is not the meaning of the source text. In each of the following, clauses are united into a single sentence by the word *but*. Notice, however, that the semantic relation is not **contrast.**

1. John is short *but* he is good at basketball.   **concession-** CONTRAEXPECTATION

2. John robbed the bank, *but* the police caught him. (see below)

3. John is handsome *but* irresponsible.   **conjoining**

4. It never rains *but* it pours.   **circumstance-** HEAD

The semantic structure of these four sentences is shown in Display 27.3:

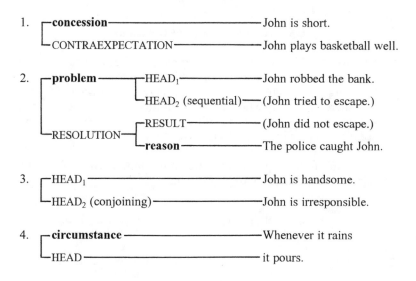

1. concession —————————— John is short.
   CONTRAEXPECTATION —————————— John plays basketball well.

2. problem —— HEAD₁ —————————— John robbed the bank.
   HEAD₂ (sequential) —— (John tried to escape.)
   RESOLUTION —— RESULT —————————— (John did not escape.)
   reason —————————— The police caught John.

3. HEAD₁ —————————— John is handsome.
   HEAD₂ (conjoining) —————————— John is irresponsible.

4. circumstance —————————— Whenever it rains
   HEAD —————————— it pours.

Display 27.3

In number 2, two propositions were left **implicit**. The *but* not only does not indicate **contrast**, but it stands for these two **implicit** propositions. The form *John robbed the bank and then tried to escape; however, he did not escape because the police caught him* would be the form in English if there were no skewing of constituents or relation markers.

In English, *so* frequently marks **grounds**-CONCLUSION. However, in the following it is marking **reason**-RESULT: "She felt sick *so* she took some medicine." The nonskewing form would be "*Because* she was sick, she took some medicine," or "She was sick, *therefore*, she took some medicine."

EXERCISES – Logical Relations

A. Go through this chapter translating each of the sentences (given
    at the end of the description of a relation) into a language other
    than English. (There are four or eight sentences for each relation.)
    Are there several receptor language forms which could be used
    to translate the sentence and still encode the same relation? What
    are the receptor language forms which signal each relation?

B. Study the following, and then fill in the labels which show the
    relation between the two propositions.

1. ⌐   -Joe practiced a lot.   By practicing a lot,
   ⌐   -Joe won the race.   Joe won the race.

2. ⌐   -I am hungry.   Although I'm hungry,
   ⌐   -I will not eat.   I'll not eat.

3. ⌐   -I stopped eating sweets.   I stopped eating sweets
   ⌐   -I got thin.   in order to get thin.

4. ⌐   -The door is ajar.   John must be here because
   ⌐   -John must be here.   the door is ajar.

5. ⌐   -Peter painted the fence.   Peter painted the fence
   ⌐   -The fence was rusty.   because it was rusty.

6. ⌐   -I came.   I came to help you.
   ⌐   -I will help you.

7. ⌐   -Mother scrubbed the floor.   Mother scrubbed the floor
   ⌐   -You keep it clean!   so keep it clean.

8. ⌐   -They kept the thieves away.   They kept the thieves away
   ⌐   -They bought a dog.   by buying a dog.

9. ⌐   -Were I not so tired.   If I weren't so tired
   ⌐   -I would play tennis.   I'd play tennis.

10. ⌐   -John drank some water.   Because John was thirsty,
    ⌐   -John was thirsty.   he drank some water.

C. Study the following text. Underline each form which you feel is
encoding a logical relation. Identify the two propositions by
rewriting them. Identify the relation by labeling the role of each
proposition as done in B above.

Example: *in order that* is encoding HEAD-purpose

    ┌─HEAD────────We can do many things

    └─**purpose**────in order that the city parks will be
                clean.

There are many things that we can do in order to clean
up the city parks. But, first, people must be convinced that it
can be done. Although everyone says that they want a clean
city they don't get involved in making it happen. We need to
clean up the parks because the children need clean places to
play, families need places for recreation, and we will all be
healthier. If we all work together it will be easy. If not it will
not happen. Although the mayor talks about it he does very
little. Nevertheless, if the rest of us agree to work together,
then it could happen.

In Singapore, the government punishes those who litter
by having them do community service. Sometimes they also
impose fines because this makes people more careful. But it
doesn't stop all littering. Some people still throw paper on
the sidewalk, and if someone sees them do it they are
ashamed.

Let's clean up our city so that we can be proud of it and
so that the children have a clean and safe place to play!

Chapter 28
Stimulus-RESPONSE Roles

Narrative and dialogue discourse primarily consist of chronological sequences of EVENTS. One thing happens and then another. One person speaks and then the other replies. However, narrative and dialogue discourse may have additional structure beyond that which can be described as chronological (sequential and simultaneous, see pages 304–5). The units of the discourse have relations to one another which are called **stimulus**-RESPONSE relations. In expository discourse, the structure of the discourse is based on logical relations as described in the previous chapter. But in a narrative or a dialogue there are different kinds of relations. A **question** is the **stimulus** for an ANSWER, or a **problem** is the **stimulus** for a RESOLUTION. The **stimulus** EVENT gives rise to or elicits the RESPONSE EVENT.

However, these relations are also different from those discussed in previous chapters in that they are not fixed pairs. **Reason**-RESULT is a fixed pair. The two always occur together. The relation is called **reason**-RESULT relation. The **stimulus**-RESPONSE roles are more flexible. For example, a **question** is paired with an ANSWER, but it might also be followed by a COUNTERQUESTION, or an EVALUATION, or even a REACTION. Because of this flexibility, it is easier to talk about the **roles** of the units than the relations between them. In this chapter, the **stimulus**-RESPONSE relations will be pointed out, but emphasis will be given to the role of each part.

The **stimulus**-RESPONSE roles divide into two main groups–those which are **narrative roles** and those which are **speech roles**. The **narrative roles** are characteristic of **narrative discourse**. The **speech roles** are characteristic of **dialogue**.

Narrative roles

A narrative text is one that recounts EVENTS. It recounts EVENTS which are either real EVENTS which occurred in the past or imaginary EVENTS which occur in sequence in the mind of the narrator. The text is usually told in either the first or third person. Time, location, and participants are important in a narrative text. The backbone of the story or happening being told usually consists of a series of incidents occurring one after another in sequential order. These incidents are related to one another by **stimulus**-RESPONSE roles.

The narrative roles within a discourse often form a plot structure. Narrative roles include those listed in Display 28.1.

STIMULUS	RESPONSE
occasion	OUTCOME
problem	RESOLVING INCIDENT
complication	RESOLUTION
	SEQUEL

Display 28.1

The narrative roles are not paired, except in the sense that one is the **stimulus** of another which is the RESPONSE. For example, one incident may be the **occasion** for a following incident which leads to a **problem** which then leads to an EVENT which is the RESOLUTION. A narrative is more than just a series of EVENTS in most cases. It may, however, simply consist of such a series of propositions in sequential relation to one another as in Display 28.2.

┌─**occasion₁** ──────────── Mary went to town.

├─**occasion₂** ──────────── Mary bought some groceries.

└─**occasion₃** ──────────── Mary came home again.

Display 28.2

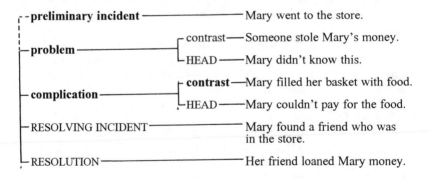

┌┈**preliminary incident** ──────── Mary went to the store.

│   ┌ contrast── Someone stole Mary's money.
├─**problem** ──────────┤
│   └ HEAD ── Mary didn't know this.

│   ┌ **contrast**── Mary filled her basket with food.
├─**complication** ─────┤
│   └ HEAD ── Mary couldn't pay for the food.

├─RESOLVING INCIDENT ──────── Mary found a friend who was
│   in the store.

└─RESOLUTION ──────────── Her friend loaned Mary money.

Display 28.3

Most narrative texts are much more complicated than this and consist of EVENTS which are related to one another in more than a simple sequential way. They form a plot structure. For example, notice the relations in the narrative shown in Display 28.3.

The narrative roles are used to classify the main EVENTS; that is, the backbone of the narration. There will be many other EVENTS in the text which are not on the mainline of the narration. They are background information which is used to support the main EVENT (note the logical relations in the example above). Units such as propositions and propositional clusters which provide background information may be related to the main EVENT by any of the orientation, clarification, or logical relations described in the preceding chapters. Certain EVENTS are simply background and not part of the sequence which makes up the narrative structure. They help to orient, clarify, or, in some way, add information but are not mainline EVENTS.

Stimulus-RESPONSE roles are different from, but not unrelated to, the **cause**-EFFECT roles. The **stimulus**, like the **cause**, precedes the RESPONSE in time. Just as there can be no EFFECT without a **cause**, so there can be no RESPONSE without a **stimulus**. This similarity is strengthened in that there is a natural prominence on the RESPONSE just like there is a natural prominence on the EFFECT in the **cause**-EFFECT pairs. In narrative there is a chaining of **stimulus**-RESPONSE so that a **stimulus** leads to a RESPONSE, and then that RESPONSE may serve as the **stimulus** for another RESPONSE. The chain continues until the final RESPONSE. Often the final RESPONSE will be either an OUTCOME or RESOLUTION (Beekman 1978a:8). The **setting** is simply an orientation relation and not one of the **stimulus**-RESPONSE relations.

Definitions of narrative roles

The **occasion** is an event or a series of events which leads up to or stimulates a certain OUTCOME. The OUTCOME is an event or sequence of events which comes about as a RESPONSE to the previous incidents (**occasions**). See Display 28.4.

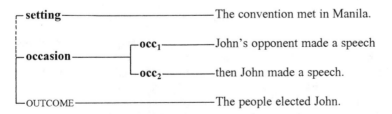

Display 28.4

Problem is a rather generic label which is intended to include any type of "imbalance" such as lack, stress, loss, disaster, threat, tragedy, accident, challenge, crisis, and so forth. The **problem** is the stimulus which leads to a RESOLUTION. Therefore, **problem**-RESOLUTION is a relation in which one unit is the **problem** and the other unit the RESOLUTION (see Display 28.5).

```
┌ setting ───────────────── John and Mary were in Manila.
│
├ problem ───────────────── John became ill.
│
└ RESOLUTION ───────────── Mary quickly drove him to the hospital.
```

Display 28.5

Complication is an incident or sequence of incidents which increases the **problem** and moves it further away from RESOLUTION. RESOLVING INCIDENT is an incident or sequence of incidents which moves towards RESOLUTION of a **problem** or **complication** but does not fully resolve it (see Display 28.6).

```
┌ setting ─────────────────────────── Mary and John were in Manila.
│
├ problem ─────────────────────────── John became sick.
│
│                         ┌ CONCESSION ─── Mary gave John some aspirin.
├ complication ──────────┤
│                         └ CONTRA-      ─── John became even more sick.
│                            EXPECTATION
│
├ RESOLVING INCIDENT ──────────────── Mary rushed John to the
│                                      hospital.
│
└ RESOLUTION ─────────────────────── The doctor cured John.
```

Display 28.6

RESOLUTION consists of an incident or a sequence of incidents which resolves a **problem** or a **complication**. This generally involves a return to normality; that is, the imbalance is stabilized, the need met, and so forth. A **problem** reaches its RESOLUTION when it no longer exists.

When talking about a particular unit, it is identified by its role. That is, a propositional cluster may be the OUTCOME, another may be the **problem**, and so forth. In this sense, we are talking about the role of the particular propositional cluster. However, if two propositional clusters are related to one another, the first being the **problem** and the second being the RESOLUTION, then we can say that these two propositional clusters are related to one another by a **problem**-RESOLUTION relation. In other words, when talking about any one unit, the name used for that unit identifies the role. When talking about two units that are related to one another, the name of the role of each is used, hyphenated to show that it is a relation between the two which are being identified.

SEQUEL refers to a unit which may occur following the OUT-COME or RESOLUTION. It relates back to the preceding (usually large) unit to simply add more information about what happened later. When a large text is being analyzed, it may well be thought of as an epilogue.

Speech roles

The **speech roles** are parallel to the three illocutionary functions of a proposition – statement, command, and question. As **speech roles**, they are called **remark, proposal,** and **question.** These are the three **stimulus** roles. Each has a corresponding RESPONSE role – EVALU-ATION, REPLY, and ANSWER. The **stimulus**-RESPONSE pairs are:

> **remark**-EVALUATION
>
> **proposal**-REPLY
>
> **question**-ANSWER

Notice the RESPONSE is used both as a specific role paired with **proposal** and as the generic term for all RESPONSES in the **stimulus**-RESPONSE relations.

There is a chronological ordering of EVENTS inasmuch as one speaker makes a **remark**, and the next speaker responds with an EVALUATION. Or one speaker asks a **question** and another speaker gives an ANSWER. The speeches are in sequential order. In addition to the relation of one speech to another, there is the internal structure of **orienter**-CONTENT discussed in chapter 26. That is, a **remark** consists of an **orienter**-CONTENT unit. Note Displays 28.7, 28.8, and 28.9.

1.

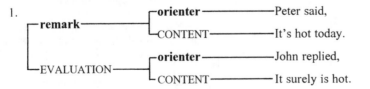

Display 28.7

2.

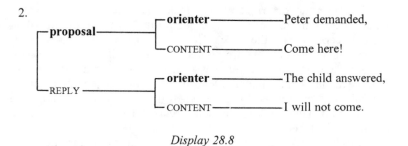

Display 28.8

3.

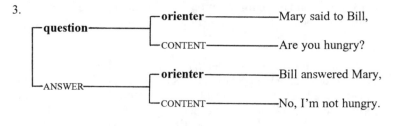

Display 28.9

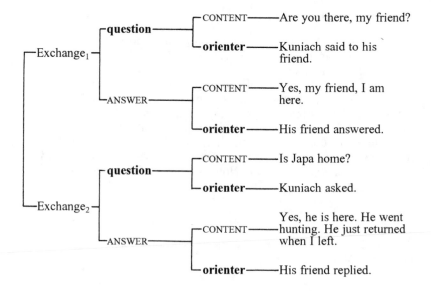

Display 28.10

The **orienter** which occurs as part of the speech role unit is a speech event which often indicates the role classification of the CONTENT. That is, *he asked* will be the **orienter** for a CONTENT which contains a **question.** The orienter plus the CONTENT act as a unit which has the role of **question** in relation to the other speech events. The speech event, in this case *asked*, is often part of the narrative structure as well. That is, the event *ask* is one of a series of events, some of which are speech events and some of which are narrative events.

Display 28.10 shows an example of speech exchange taken from an Aguaruna text. In this example, only two exchanges are included. In both exchanges, the **stimulus** is a **question**, and the RESPONSE is an ANSWER.

The speech roles can be defined as follows (Beekman, Callow, and Kopesec 1981:86):

> A **remark** is any type of **statement** that may be made, such as a rebuke, an accusation, a compliment, etc.

> A **proposal** is any type of **command** such as exhortation, invitation, offer, prohibition, suggestion, directions, challenge, and so forth.

> A **question** refers to any type of **question** such as an interrogation on a witness stand, in contests, in school, or any inquiry for direction or for information.

In a speech exchange, the response to the three roles listed above are EVALUATION, REPLY, or ANSWER. These three roles are defined as follows:

EVALUATION is a statement made in connection with a prior speech stimulus in which the speaker gives his assessment or interpretation of what was said. He evaluates it as good or bad, wise or foolish, helpful, inappropriate, etc. Notice the following examples:

> **remark**: He is really a grumpy person.
>
> EVALUATION: I think so too.

REPLY is a statement made in connection with a prior speech stimulus which gives a positive or negative reaction to a proposal. The speaker says whether or not he is in agreement. Note the following:

> **proposal**: Let's go to town this afternoon.
>
> REPLY: I'm sorry, I'm too busy to go today.

ANSWER is a reply which is directly relevant to a question which was asked. For example:

> **question**: How do you get to the shopping center?
> ANSWER: You go three blocks east from here.

The next speaker will not necessarily give the expected EVALU-ATION, REPLY, or ANSWER. The second part of the exchange may be a **counter-remark, counterproposal,** or **counterquestion.** These roles may be defined as follows:

A COUNTERREMARK is any statement that another speaker makes in connection with a prior **remark,** and that does not express agreement or disagreement but makes an alternative or substitute **remark.**

A COUNTERPROPOSAL is a response to a **proposal** which offers an alternative **proposal.** If the second speaker does not make a **counterproposal,** he generally responds with an agreement or rejection of the original **proposal.**

A COUNTERQUESTION is a response to a **question** with an alternative **question.** The examples in Display 28.11 show how a COUNTERQUESTION comes into the dialogue.

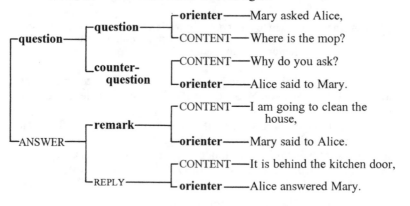

Display 28.11

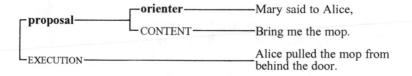

Display 28.12

Notice that when a COUNTERQUESTION occurs then the exchange no longer matches the **question**-ANSWER relation. The first exchange is a **question** and a COUNTERQUESTION. The second exchange answers the COUNTERQUESTION first, and then the initial **question.**

Sometimes when one speaker makes a **proposal,** the second person will not respond but, rather, simply do what was proposed. This role is called EXECUTION. It is the role of the event which was done because of the **proposal** (see Display 28.12).

The **stimulus**-RESPONSE roles for speech events include those listed in Display 28.13.

STIMULUS ROLES	RESPONSE ROLES
remark	EVALUATION
	COUNTERREMARK
proposal	REPLY
	COUNTERPROPOSAL
	EXECUTION
question	ANSWER
	COUNTERQUESTION

Display 28.13

Notice, in Display 28.14, how the COUNTERQUESTION is a REPLY to **question-1** and, at the same time, has a stimulus role in relation to the following speech which is its ANSWER.

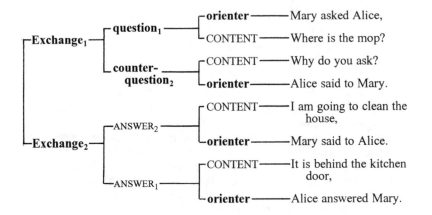

Display 28.14

In the examples above, the exchanges are simply labeled as Exchange-1, Exchange-2, etc. However, such exchanges are usually part of a dialogue text in which there is a combination of narrative and speech exchanges. The speech events, then, are part of a narrative discourse, and the narrative and speech roles occur simultaneously. Both the narrative and speech structures need to be considered in the analysis. If the dialogue is part of a longer narrative, it is usually most helpful to label the display by narrative roles. The speech roles may be put in parentheses when this seems helpful. Notice Display 28.15.

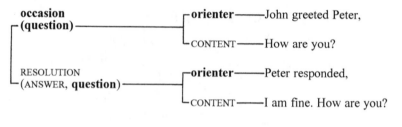

Display 28.15

Functions of quotations

The primary function of the quotation form is to recount speech acts, to report that a certain person expressed a certain idea in spoken words; something was said by someone. The form will have a quotation and one or more quote margins indicating who did the speaking and to whom. *John said to Bill, "I am hungry."* The semantic structure would be as follows:

```
┌─orienter─────────John said to Bill.
│
└─CONTENT──────────I am hungry.
```

When the **orienter** is encoded in the quote margin and the CONTENT is encoded as a quotation, there is no mismatch.

In many languages, quotations have many secondary functions. In some languages of South America and also in Papua New Guinea, the grammatical form of a quotation sentence is used to encode cause-effect relations. When the relation is **purpose**, the quotation is an imperative sentence, and the quote margin is a dependent form of the verb *say*. Notice the following (the actual Aguaruna is not given but, rather, a literal back-translation into English):

1. ┌─MEANS─────── He hangs it up

    └─**purpose**─────── in order that it get dry.

Aguaruna: He hangs-it-up, "*Let it get dry*," *saying.*

English: He hangs it up to dry./He hangs it up in order that it get dry.

2. ┌─MEANS─────── He carves it a little bit more.

    └─**purpose**─────── in order that the prow will be a bit higher

Aguaruna: A little-bit-more he-carves-it, "*Its prow that-risen let-it-be*," *saying.*

English: He carves it a little more so that the prow will be a bit higher.

When the relation being encoded is **reason** rather than **purpose**, the quote margin will consist of the nominalized form of the verb *say* and the dependent form of the verb *be*, rather than the dependent form of the verb *say*. For example:

┌─RESULT─────── I lay down

└─**reason**─────── because I was tired.

Aguaruna: I lay down "*I am tired*," *one-who-says I-being.*

English: I lay down because I was tired.

Notice the contrast in the following forms:

PURPOSE:

Aguaruna: I will go, "*That he stay*," *I-saying.*

English: I will go in order that he stay./I will go so that he will stay.

REASON:

Aguaruna: I will go, "*That he stay*," *one-who-said I-being.*

English: I will go because I want him to stay.

Other languages may use quotations to encode other relations.

Thought as speech

There is a sense in which what we think takes the form of direct speech in our minds. Perhaps it is because of this, that in many languages, THOUGHT processes take the form of *verbs of saying* and the CONTENT, the form of **direct quotations.** In chapter 26, the relation **orienter**-CONTENT was presented. This relation was used to describe not just speech but also perceptual, emotional, cognitive, and volitional EVENTS as well (see pages 321–23).

In English, **quotation forms** are used almost exclusively for speech, but in many Amerindian languages, **quotation forms** are also used for THOUGHT processes. Notice the following examples in which Aguaruna (Peru) uses a **quotation**, but the natural English form would not be a **quotation**. In translating, the form must be adjusted. In going from English to Aguaruna, **quotation forms** must be used, and in going from Aguaruna to English, the **quotations** must be changed to nonspeech forms. (The Aguaruna examples are modified literal translations. They are taken from Larson 1978.)

THOUGHT

1. **Aguaruna**: *"Bird will it maybe appear?" I saying,* again I went.

   English: Thinking that another bird would surely appear, I went.

2. **Aguaruna**: *"Just how I-help?" I saying,* I say.

   English: I say it wondering how I can help.

COGNITION

1. **Aguaruna**: I thank you *saying, "Was it not because he really helped me that I did like this?"*

   English: I thank you knowing that I was able to do this because you really helped me. (The pronoun *he* in the Aguaruna quotation refers to the person spoken to and so is the translated *you*.)

2. **Aguaruna**: Since the things made by the Incas are well preserved, *"Like that were they those who surely worked?" saying we know.*

   English: We know how the Incas did (made) things because the things which they made are well preserved.

BELIEF

1. **Aguaruna**: The ancestors are those *who say, "A person who eats big pieces of food will never be able to cut trees well."*

   English: The ancestors believed that a person who eats big pieces of food would never be able to cut trees well.

2. **Aguaruna**: If an owl hoots, *"A person will die,"* they are those who say.

   English: If an owl hoots, they believe that someone will die.

DESIRE

1. **Aguaruna**: *"Down river I will go," also saying,* I wait.

   English: Wanting to go down river, I am also waiting.

2. **Aguaruna**: I also desire *"That he be a teacher," saying.*

   English: I also want him to become a teacher.

If the receptor language uses **quotation forms** to represent **orienter**-CONTENT relations other than direct speech, it is also important that the translator know the form of the **quotation** to be used. Different sentence types may be used in different languages to contrast various processes. For example, in the Aguaruna examples above, the Aguaruna forms would be as follows:

thought	a question in the subjective mood
cognition	a question which is hypothetical
belief	a statement which is in the declarative mood
desire	a statement which is future declarative or an imperative (command) form

When translating from English into a language which uses **quotation forms** to encode most **orienter**-CONTENT relations, the translator will want to use these natural **quotation forms**, not literal English forms.

Rhetorical functions of quotation forms

Quotations in many languages are used for rhetorical effect. They may be used to highlight a part of a story or some main event. The use of the grammatical quotation form to highlight certain EVENTS or PARTICIPANTS is found in many languages. The quotation often consists of a **question, proposal,** or **remark** with no corresponding **answer, reply,** or **evaluation.** That is, only the **stimulus** is given and a **response** never occurs.

In Aguaruna, dialogue form is used to highlight description and events having to do with the major character. In a story about a visit to a lake where there was a boa; all the facts about the boa are encoded in quotations by the other participants. The first description of the boa is encoded in the following paragraph as a **remark.**

> When it began to quake like that, since there were
> three of them, they said to one another, "There is a
> boa here and he is angry and wants to eat us. That's
> why it is quaking like that. Also, the buzzards which
> are here are spying for the boa, and so seeing us,
> they called telling the boa that we are here."

Notice that no particular person is credited with making this speech. The three talk to one another. It is simply a way of highlighting the description of the boa, who is the main character. No **reply** occurs in the text.

In a language in which quotations are not used to encode a description of the main participant in order to introduce him into the story, the translation might need to use a descriptive paragraph such as the following:

> Then the earth began to quake where the three stood.
> There in the lake lived a boa. If he became angry he
> would grab them. There were some buzzards nearby
> who had made a promise to the boa to let him know
> if someone came. When the buzzards saw the men,
> they began to make noises.

Throughout the Aguaruna story about the *boa*, there are many quotations. They indicate actions of the main PARTICIPANTS and highlight the main EVENTS of the story. Only by reading the content of the quotations can the main story line be followed. At the peak of the story, the information about the *boa* is given in the form of a **question** as a quotation rather than a **remark.** At the peak of a narrative, the **question** may also be **answered** for emphasis. At the same time, a great deal of repetition is included at the peak. The following is the peak of the boa story:

> ...it became dark although it was not raining. When
> it became like that, he said to himself, "Why has it

*become dark like this? Surely the boa has done it in
order to grab me." Running and running, he arrived
where his friends were and said, "How has it been
here? Over there where I was fishing it became dark.
I said to myself, 'The boa has done it in order to grab
me,' and running and running I came." When he said
that, they answered, "Here it did not become dark.
It was light like it is now. It is surely the boa who
did it in order to grab you."*

The Aguaruna examples above illustrate how the quotation form
is used for highlighting in one language. Each language will have its
own special forms for highlighting. The important thing is for the
translator to be aware of the **rhetorical** nature of some **quotations** and
not translate literally, i.e., with a quotation form, unless the receptor
language uses **quotations** in the same **rhetorical** manner.

Direct and indirect quotations

In order to translate well, the translator must first determine if a
given quotation in the source language is being used to encode
something that was said, and is, therefore, a **real speech**, or whether
it represents a **secondary function**, or perhaps is being used
rhetorically.

In addition, there is an added problem which effects translation.
This is the fact that there are two kinds of grammatical forms which
encode speech events in languages. These are called **direct** and
indirect speech. In **direct speech**, the speaker is quoted more or
less exactly. In **indirect speech**, the exact words may or may not
be used.

Many languages do not have an **indirect speech** form. If the
English source text is to be translated into these languages, all **indirect
speech** will need to be cast in the forms of **direct speech**. For example,
to say *You promised to come* in the Waiwai language of Guiana a form
would be used which says literally *"I will certainly come," you said*
(Hawkins 1962:164). In Navajo, spoken in the western United States,
only direct speech occurs.

Many languages do not have special words like *ask* and *answer*
to signal the **question**-ANSWER, **remark**-EVALUATION, and **proposal**-RESPONSE relations; rather, *say* is used for reporting all speech
relations, and the context or form of the quotation lets the audience
know if it is being *asked* or *answered,* etc.

Another matter which makes the translation of speech difficult is
the change of tense and mood, and the shift of person. Notice the
following:

```
┌─orienter────────He said
│
└─CONTENT────────I will give it to you.
```

These two propositions, related by **orienter**-CONTENT relation, can be translated into English by either of the following sentences. Notice the change of tense and person.

> 1. He said, "*I will* give it to *you.*"
> 2. He said that *he would* give it to *me.*

Very few Papua New Guinea languages have both **direct** and **indirect speech** forms to express CONTENT. **Direct speech** is used almost exclusively. This requires adjustment of pronouns. The Gahuku form for the above propositional cluster would be *He said I will give it to me.* The first person subject pronoun of the verb *give* refers to the original speaker of the utterance, and the first person indirect object pronoun refers to the one citing the quote (Deibler and Taylor 1977:1066).

When languages do have both **direct** and **indirect quotations** (speech) there is usually a special function for each. That is, there may be a preference but, in addition, there will be some contexts in which one is more appropriate than the other. For example, **direct quotations** may be used when the quotation is the CONTENT of a main EVENT of the story. However, when the quotation is the CONTENT of an EVENT which is filling a support role, such as **reason, purpose,** etc., the indirect form will be chosen. The main warning to translators is not to assume that **direct speech** should be translated by **direct speech** and **indirect speech** by **indirect speech**. The important thing is to use the natural forms of the receptor language and not translate literally the forms of the source text.

Many more examples of mismatch could be given, but each translator needs to find the appropriate grouping, order, and relation markers for the language into which he is translating. They will not match the grouping, order, or relation markers of the source language nor be isomorphic with the semantic structure. They will be unique.

Quotation margins

Languages have different ways of expressing the information about the situation of a particular speech – who said it, to whom was it said, when and where, etc. This kind of information is normally given in the **quotation margin**. In the following examples the **quotation margin** is in italics:

1. *Peter said to John yesterday* that he would not be back.

2. "I'll not be back again," *he said to his brother.*

Both direct and indirect speech have **quotation margins**, the part of the sentence which identifies the speaker, hearer, time, etc.

The problem arises in that the source language and the receptor language often do not have the same grammatical forms or the same usage of **quotation margins.** Sometimes the source text will not include information about the situation in which a speech was made because the circumstances are obvious to the original audience. However, because the new audience may be uninformed, it may be necessary to be more explicit in the translation to avoid confusion.

Another matter which needs to be watched carefully by the translator has to do with where the **quotation margin** occurs in relation to the quotation itself. Some languages will always give the **quotation margin** first, others at the end of the quotation and some medially, breaking into the quotation to add the **quotation margin** information. Some, like Gahuku of Papua New Guinea (Deibler 1971a:102), for example, regularly require the quotation margin both preceding and following the quotation, especially if the quotation is more than one short sentence. Notice the following:

...laga	**loko**	**limoq:**	*Guivahaniqnemaka,*
thus	saying	he-said	My-Lord

gizapa	*lamanoq*	*oketanogo*	*uve.*
watch	well	them-surely	I'll

Laqa	**loko**	**lokago**
Thus	saying	after-he-said

Translation: ...he said, "My Lord, I will surely watch over them well." After he said that...

Some languages will use all three types of **quotation margins** for different but for special situations. For example, Headland (1979) presents the following information on **quotation margins** in Tunebo (Colombia):

Opening quotation margins may be omitted:

1. before a negative response to a previous proposal,
2. before a very emotional response,
3. following a verb of command, or the verb send, and
4. where the quotation is very closely related to the previous action.

Medial quotation margins are used:

1. to mark a change of topic or a new phrase of the same topic within a speech,
2. between each argument for a course of action in order to soften the request, and
3. between each reason for a negative response in order to give emphasis to the reasons.

Final quotation margins occur regularly with all quotations but may be omitted between speeches in a dialogue under the following circumstances:

1. the quotation is a question,
2. there is a speech verb within a quotation, and
3. the response is very emotional.

There may be a **total absence** of any **quotation margin** in a Tunebo narrative when dialogue is used to mark the peak. The series of question-answer exchanges occur with no opening, medial, or final **quotation margin.**

The above description of Tunebo is given to emphasize the fact that each language will have its own rules for the use of **quotation margins. Quotation margins** should not be translated literally. They may need to be shifted to a different position, and there may not be the same number of them as in the source language. Only the natural forms for the receptor language should be used. Notice the following translation from Tunebo:

Tunebo:	*Wiquir*		*esar*	*canor*	*ruway*	*áyjacro.*
	Having-returned		there	work	to-do	sent

	"Erara	*ítuwi,"*	*wajacro.*	*"As*	*owar*	*ituwi,"*
	There	live	said	me	with	live

	wajacro.	*"As*	*ac*	*yahra*	*tihw̃i*	*Owa,"*	*wajacro.*
	said	Me	for	potatoes	weed	weed	said

English translation: When I returned there he sent me out to work saying, "Live here with me and weed my potatoes."

Notice the following example where the quotation margin is divided by the quotation:

Tunebo: *Isat*   *"Barjau,"*   *waquita,*   *"Asa*   *requin*   *áhajira*
          We   let's-go   when-said   I   still   yet

          bitiru,"   *w'acuayra.*
          go-not   said

English translation: When we said, "Let's go!" he answered, "Not yet." or When we said, "Let's go!" he said, "I'm not going yet."

There may also be a difference from language to language as to the forms which are used in **quotation margins**. Often there are fixed forms. Only certain verbs may be used. The number of verbs which may occur in verb margins may be small or large. In English, it is very large. In many Amerindian languages, *said* is most often used and the content of the quotation carries the added components found in such English words as *ask, refuse, rebuke, beg,* etc. In Surui (Brazil), **quotation margins** contain no verb at all, only nouns and pronouns. Jamamadi (Brazil) uses one basic verb for all types of quotations (data from Robert Dooley).

Another problem may arise in translation when the person speaking is not indicated. It may be necessary in some languages to include this information in the **quotation margin**. Sometimes the source text will contain quotations within quotations. These may become quite complicated. Note the following three English forms for the same information:

1. The students said that the teacher had told them to go to see the headmaster.
2. The students said that the teacher had said, "Go and see the headmaster."
3. The students said, "The teacher said, 'Go and see the headmaster.' "

Adjustments may need to be made involving changes from direct to indirect quotations, or vice versa, and changes in the quotation margin forms as well. A semantic display of the above English sentences can be seen in Display 28.16.

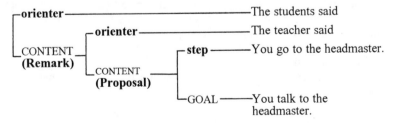

Display 28.16

It may be helpful for the translator to diagram the levels of quotations within a quotation, stating the orienter, as above, before translating. Then the natural forms of the receptor language will need to be used to show the relationship of the quotations to one another.

Vocatives

A **vocative word** or **phrase** is a form used for direct address to a person or group of people, usually using a personal name, a title, or a kinship term. The vocative usually occurs within a quotation. It has various functions in a text. However, the function of **vocatives** in the source language will often not match the function of **vocatives** in the receptor language.

Vocatives are not usually found in quotations which are rhetorical quotations or quotations functioning to encode a meaning other than a speech act. They only occur when real speech is being reported.

Barnwell (1974:9-10) describes the following functions for **vocative phrases** in English. Other languages may have some of the same or some additional functions.

1. To show the attitude of the speaker towards the addressee;
2. To make a personal appeal by focusing attention on an individual or group of individuals;
3. To focus on certain qualities of an individual or group;
4. For rhetorical or stylistic effect; and
5. To mark off sections of an argument (the beginning of a new topic).

Once the translator has identified the function of the **vocative**, he will be prepared to decide if a different form would be more appropriate in the receptor language.

The **vocative** sometimes occurs at the beginning of the sentence, sometimes at the end. In Greek it also occurs medially with the quotation. This will also vary from language to language. There may be a fixed position, or the position may change to indicate a special function. In most languages of Papua New Guinea, the **vocative** coming first in the sentence or paragraph is the more natural form; and is used to signal the beginning of a new topic or to simply open the conversation. But when used to show the attitude of sympathy, the **vocative** often comes at the end. Note the following:

1. "*My brother*, let's go fishing tomorrow."
2. "Why are you crying, *my brother*?"

Some languages allow for long descriptive **vocative phrases** and others do not. A nonvocative form may be needed. Note the following:

> **Source language**:   "You hypocrites! How did you deceive me?"
>
> **Receptor language**:   "What hypocrites you are! How did you deceive me?"

The choice of term often depends on the communication situation. For example, the appropriate term may be determined by factors such as whether the situation is formal or informal, whether the person is an old acquaintance or a new acquaintance, etc. Each language will have its own standards of appropriateness for using various terms in **vocative expressions.**

In some cultures, kinship terms are used almost exclusively as means of addressing a person; in others, names are more common for addressing family members and others. The translator may need to make some adjustments in translating **vocatives**. For example, when translating an English dialogue containing a quotation, where two brothers call each other by name, the more correct receptor language translation might use *brother*. This would be true in Papua New Guinea where names are not used by relatives.

> **English**:   "*John*, I'm sorry but I can't go with you today."
>
> **Receptor language**:   "*My brother*, I'm sorry I can't go with you today."

No information is lost since the context has already identified the participants as *brothers* and the name of one as *John*.

In some cultures, it is improper to use direct address in some situations. It may be considered unacceptable for a man to use a **vocative form** in speaking to a woman. Some adjustment in the translation will be needed. The function of the **vocative** needs to be identified and handled in some other appropriate way.

For example, **vocatives** are used in English to show the attitude of the speaker to the addressee. In a given text, a man might be quoted as saying, "*Daughter*, may I help you?" The purpose of the **vocative** is to establish an attitude of kindness. If this quotation were to be translated into a language where this would be inappropriate, the **vocative** might need to be deleted and something added to the quotation margin to indicate the purpose: "May I help you?" he said kindly.

When translating **vocative phrases** the translator would:

1. study the function of the **vocative** in the source text and try to communicate the same meaning in the translation;

2. use the grammatical forms which are natural to the receptor language; and

3. use an appropriate form, bearing in mind the speaker, the addressee, the content, and the communication situation (Barnwell 1974:13).

In Aguaruna of Peru, for example, vocative forms are used at the beginning of each paragraph of a letter. They function to indicate that one topic has been finished and another topic is going to be discussed. A letter of five paragraphs will have at least five vocative forms. Therefore, when translating a letter from English, it was necessary to introduce into the translation vocatives at each point where there was a major change of topic. Also, if a letter contains direct commands, the vocative is used to soften these commands so that they do not seem harsh to the readers. For these two reasons, i.e., to mark a new topic and to soften the commands, a translation into Aguaruna may contain several more vocatives than the source text. Not to use these vocatives in the translation would be unnatural and give a wrong meaning.

Great care must be taken in the translation of quotations. First, the source text will need to be analyzed to see if the quotation is really encoding a speech act which is a part of the narrative or if it is used in a secondary function or for rhetorical effect. Depending on the function of the quotation, adjustments will need to be made in the translation. Careful attention will need to be given to a choice between direct or indirect quotations, to the use of quotation margins, to the choice of grammatical forms such as pronouns, tense, and mood within the quotation, and to vocatives. The goal is to use the natural forms of the receptor language to communicate the author's intended purpose for the quotation. Likewise, it may be necessary to introduce quotations in the translation which are not quotations in the source text in order to correctly translate secondary functions and rhetorical usages in the receptor language.

EXERCISES – Stimulus-RESPONSE roles

A. Go back through the section on narrative roles (page 353–57) and find the examples which are given in the form of semantic displays. Study each display and translate the meaning into the natural forms of a language other than English. You should expect the form to be quite different from the semantic displays and from the English translations.

B. Assume that you are translating into a language that uses direct quotations to express **purpose.** Rewrite the following in English using a quotation.

1. John went to the doctor to get some medicine.

2. The people watched to see if he would get up again.

3. He sent a servant to get some of the fruit from the tree.

4. He climbed to the top of the hill in order to watch the sun go down over the ocean.

Express each of the above naturally in a language other than English. Would a quotation be needed to express **purpose?**

C. Assume that you are translating into a language that uses direct quotation to express **thought** and **cognition.** Rewrite the following in English using a quotation.

1. He thought that he could make some money if he kept working on the book.

2. John knew that it was too late to get into school the next semester.

3. Mary thought she would rather go later.

4. The people knew their president was ill.

Express each of the above naturally in a language other than English. Did you use a direct or indirect quotation form?

D. Speech verbs sometimes cannot be translated directly into other languages. Instead of the italicized word, use the verb *say* and a quotation which indicates the meaning of the italicized word and rewrite.

1. He *exhorted* him to go to the doctor.

2. He *commanded* him to go back and get his uniform.

3. He *promised* to give her whatever she might ask for.

4. I *commend* you for your good work.

5. He *asked* him where his father was.

6. I *suggested* that she could help with the class.

Express each of the above naturally in a language other than English. What changes did you make?

E. Rewrite the following **indirect quotations** as **direct quotations**. Change the pronouns, verbs, or order, as necessary, for natural English. Then translate each sentence into a second language you speak. Did you use a **direct** or **indirect quotation** in the translation?

1. He said that he was sick.

2. He said that he had been sick.

3. He said that he was going.

4. He asked her when she would give it to him.

5. He said that he would do it tomorrow.

6. He said that you would give it to her.

7. He said that I would give it to him.

8. He said that they were his friends.

F. There are also languages in which **indirect quotations** are preferred to **direct quotations**. Sometimes quotations of the source language will need to be translated in a more indirect form. Change the following **direct quotations** to **indirect quotations** in English. Then translate into the second language you speak with either the **direct** or **indirect form**, depending on which sounds more natural.

1. Then he said to them, "Let's go to the next town."

2. Finally they said to him, "Who are you?"

3. John told his brother, "I don't know where the book is."

4. They said to each other, "If we say, 'We can't come,' he will be angry, but if we go he will say, 'Why did you come?' "

5. Then someone asked, "How do we get there from here?" The guide replied, "You will have to go back to the village and say to the inn keeper, 'Give us a map.' "

G. The following is part of a Tunebo text (from Headland). Notice that the **medial quotation margin** is expanded to reiterate the setting. Both **initial** and **final quotation margins** also occur. First translate the Tunebo into natural English. Then translate the same information into another language which you speak. Is the natural form of this second language you speak more like Tunebo or more like English?

Tamri	*erar*	*as*	*quin*	*rioát*	*táyocuano:*	*"Bahan*	*sasá*
Town	there	me	to	white	asked	you	children

jica?	*Bahan*	*wacjí*	*jica?*	*Bahan*	*wiya*	*jica?"*	*wacárora.*
have?	you	sons	have?	you	wife	have?	said.

Waquít,	*ajat*	*wánora:*	*"Chero,"*	*wánora,*	*ajat*	*Tamri*
When-said	I	said	Have	said	I	Tame

erara.	*Eyta*	*wacárora*	*rioát*	*as*	*quin.*	*Ajat,*	*"Eyta*
there.	Like-that	said	white	me	to.	I	like-that

chero,"	*wánora.*	*"As*	*sasa*	*jiro.*	*Wacjí*	*jiro.*	*Wiya*	*jiro,"*
have	said.	I	children	have.	Sons	have	wife	have

wánora.
said.

H. Write ten sentences in a language other than English, so that each sentence contains a vocative word or phrase. Try to use as wide a variety of types (name, kinship, role, description, etc.) as is natural. Then think about and analyze the function of each of the vocative phrases. Do the vocative phrases occur at the beginning, in the middle, or at the end of the sentences?

TEXTS

Chapter 29
Groupings

In chapter 25 the hierarchy of semantic **groupings** was discussed briefly. As the translator begins working on a particular text, one of the first things he will want to do is study the **groupings** within the text. He will ask himself how the text is divided. He will want to know how many major sections there are, or how many episodes. And then, as he works in more detail, paragraph boundaries and propositional clusters become important. In this chapter, the **groupings** which will be useful to the translator are discussed. Examples are given of some short texts showing the semantic analysis of the **groupings** and the relationships between the units. Examples are also given of the mismatch of **groupings** between languages.

Propositional clusters

A **propositional cluster** consists of more than one proposition. The propositions are related to one another by **communication relations** discussed in section IV. One proposition is the **central (HEAD) proposition** of the cluster, and the other propositions have various relationships to the **HEAD proposition** or to one another. Together they have one illocutionary function (to state, command, or question).

First, let us consider the first six propositions of the paragraph analyzed at the end of chapter 24. These six propositions group together. They form a **propositional cluster** and are encoded by a single grammatical sentence (see Display 29.1).

Number 2 is the content of what was *pretended*, and so 1 and 2 are closely related and form a pair. Number 4 is the reason for number 3, and so 3 and 4 are closely related and form a pair. Number 6 is the means of accomplishing 5, and so 5 and 6 are closely related and form a pair. So within the unit 1-6 there are three smaller units or **clusters** (more than one proposition).

But again there is grouping. Unit 5-6 is an **amplification** of unit 3-4. So the four propositions 3, 4, 5, and 6 are also a **cluster**. This **cluster** (3-6) is a unit which relates to the unit 1-2. The relation between **cluster** 1-2 and **cluster** 3-6 is called **concession**-CONTRAEX-PECTATION. It means here that *Although Shasta pretended to lead (one would have expected him to lead, but he didn't) Bree really led.* So the unit 1-2 and the unit 3-6 are also related in a special way. The result is a **propositional cluster** made up of smaller **clusters.**

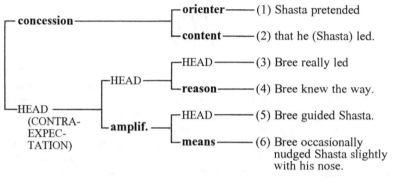

Display 29.1

We see that 1-6 is a **propositional cluster**. A new **cluster** begins after proposition 6. We will talk more about finding boundaries between units later. Notice that the **propositional cluster** 1-6 is equal to the grammatical sentence in English: *Shasta was pretending to lead, but it was really Bree who knew the way and kept guiding him by little nudges with his nose.* Other languages might not use a single sentence. As a matter of fact, the same information could be presented in English in more than one sentence. For example: *Shasta pretended to lead, but Bree really led. He was the one who knew the way. He kept guiding Shasta by little nudges with his nose.* The order might also be changed in English, or in some other language: *Bree really led although Shasta pretended to lead. Bree guided Shasta by little nudges with his nose. He led because he was the one who knew the way.* The six propositions might be translated into the receptor language by one sentence or by three or four. They might have the same order as the semantic structure, or they might be reordered because of the grammatical structure of the receptor language. One proposition might even be repeated in the receptor language, like the repetition of *Bree led* in the example above. *Bree really led* is stated at the beginning, and *He led* is repeated again in the last sentence.

But this group of propositions is also related to those which follow in the story. Any discourse is a complex **configuration of propositions** grouped into larger and larger groupings. Display 29.2 gives an idea of how these groupings might be for some texts. Propositions unite to form clusters, and these unite in larger units which unite into still larger units. [Abbreviations are used for **Proposition** (Prop), **Propositional Cluster** (ProCl), **Semantic Paragraph** (Para), **Episode** (Epis), **Episode Cluster** (EpCl), and **Discourse** (Disc).]

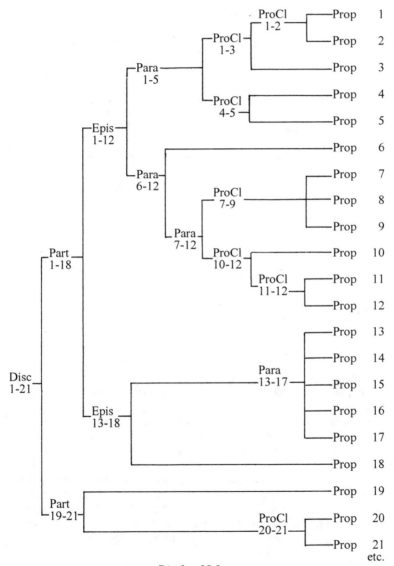

Display 29.2

Propositional clusters have the same illocutionary function as propositions. They can express **statements, questions,** or **commands.** For example, **propositional cluster** A (Display 29.3) is a **statement**; B (Display 29.4) is a **question**; and C (Display 29.5) is a **command.**

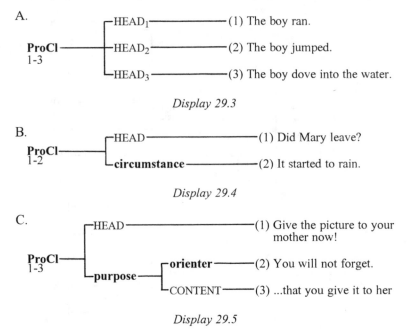

Display 29.3

Display 29.4

Display 29.5

When the propositions which make up a **propositional cluster** are simply in sequence, one added to the other, as in A, all of them have the same illocutionary function as the **propositional cluster.** In A, all three propositions are **statements,** and the **propositional cluster** is also a **statement.** When there is only one HEAD proposition, it carries the illocutionary purpose as in B and C. In B, proposition 1 is the HEAD of the cluster, and since this HEAD proposition is a **question,** the cluster is also a **question;** similarly in C, since the HEAD proposition is a **command,** the propositional cluster is also a **command.**

Notice that in C, the content of *forget – that you give it to her –* is part of the meaning, so is included in the propositional analysis. However, it is left implicit in the source text. If it were included in the English form, one would probably say *Give the picture to your mother now so that you won't forget to do it.* This illustrates the fact that there is also skewing between the grammatical sentence and the propositional structure. A part of the **propositional cluster** which can be left implicit in one language may need to be made explicit in another and vice versa. In many languages, there will be pro-verbs which will substitute for a proposition within a **propositional cluster** when the EVENT mentioned in a previous proposition within the **cluster** is repeated in another proposition later in that **cluster.**

In English, we may say *John is here. We saw his car.* The grammar has just two simple sentences. However, the semantic structure is a **propositional cluster** of three propositions (see Display 29.6).

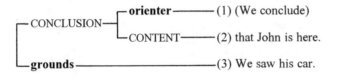

Display 29.6

The proposition *we know* is left implicit in the English source text. It is the **orienter** of the CONTENT *John is here*, that is, the total meaning is *we know that John is here*. The **grounds** is given, that is, *we saw his car*. However, the relationship between the **grounds** proposition and *we conclude* is left implicit. The propositional cluster could be translated in full into English by saying *We know John is here because we saw his car*. A translation of the original English sentences into some receptor languages would need to include the information left implicit in the source text and use a form which includes all three propositions and the natural forms to indicate **grounds** in the receptor language.

Semantic paragraphs (episode part)

Propositional clusters unite to form **semantic paragraphs.** The term **semantic paragraph** is used to distinguish it from a grammatical paragraph. Sometimes there is no mismatch of semantic structure and grammatical structure. However, as in all parts of language, there may also be skewing of semantic paragraphs and grammatical paragraphs. For this reason, the term **semantic paragraph** is used to distinguish it from grammatical paragraph, which is the more common usage. In narrative text, the semantic paragraph is often a unit in an episode.

A **semantic paragraph** consists of propositional clusters and propositions which are related to one another by **communication relations.** One propositional cluster will be the central (HEAD) cluster, and the others will have various relationships to the HEAD cluster or to one another. There will be a unity of semantic content. The **semantic paragraph** will center around a particular **theme.**

The following **paragraph** is analyzed below to illustrate how the propositions unite to form propositional clusters and how these unite to form a **paragraph**. The relations between the propositional clusters are labeled to show how **communication relations** also unite these clusters. The **paragraph** is taken from a text which describes a certain rare disease. It says:

> *(1) Checking upon gene frequencies for rare diseases is at present no easy task. (2) In most areas of the world lacking hospital facilities and diagnostic skills, population comparisons are impossible. (3) Even in the great medical centers, rare hereditary disorders may erroneously be considered race-limited or population-limited in their stead. (4) Obviously, even elementary data on the comparative frequencies of the rare gene-determined disorders are to a large extent lacking today.*

In this particular **paragraph** the propositional clusters match the grammatical sentences (numbered 1, 2, 3, and 4). Display 29.7 shows the relations between the propositional clusters which make up this **paragraph,** only the HEAD proposition of the cluster has been given, the dots indicating that there are several other propositions related to it within the cluster.

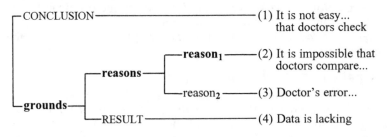

Display 29.7

The **paragraph** contains two **reasons** (clusters 2 and 3) which tell why data is lacking...(cluster 4). Clusters 4 and 2-3 unite to form another larger cluster which is the **grounds** for the initial CONCLUSION (the theme) of the **paragraph** (cluster 1), that *it is not easy to check.*

The paragraph structure of other languages will not match English. Some may put the **reasons** before the RESULT or the **grounds** after the CONCLUSION. This paragraph could also be rearranged in English, the order of the clusters being changed. Notice the following in which the propositional clusters are numbered to match the above diagram.

(2) In most areas of the world lacking hospital facilities and diagnostic skills, population comparisons are impossible. (3) Even in the great medical centers, rare hereditary disorders may easily be missed, while other disorders may erroneously be considered race-determined or population-limited in their stead. (4) Therefore, even elementary data on the comparative frequencies of the rare gene-determined disorders are to a large extent lacking today. (1) Checking upon gene frequencies for rare diseases is at present no easy task.

(1) Checking upon gene frequencies for rare diseases is at present no easy task. (4) It is obvious that even elementary data on the comparative frequencies of the rare gene-determined disorders are to a large extent lacking today. (2) This is because in most areas of the world lacking hospital facilities and even diagnostic skills, population comparisons are impossible. (3) Even in the great medical centers, rare hereditary disorders may easily be missed, while other disorders may erroneously be considered race-determined or population-limited in their stead.

The important point to notice here is that the relations between the propositional clusters remain the same even if the order is changed and different forms are used to signal the relations. Just as the concepts within a proposition may be realized by different orders and forms in the clause of a language, and propositions which make up a proposition cluster may occur in various orders and forms in a sentence, so also the propositional clusters within a **semantic paragraph** may be arranged in various orders and use different forms in the grammatical paragraph. The three grammatical paragraphs are different, but the **semantic paragraph** is the same. Each language will have different arrangements. Some languages will always have the **reason** precede the RESULT. Other languages allow both orders. The translator will look for the most natural and easily understood arrangement of the units of the paragraph as he translates.

Although the **semantic paragraph** and the **grammatical paragraph** often match, there are many examples of languages where they do not match. The translator needs to be aware of this possibility and not just translate source language paragraphs as if they were always the same as receptor language paragraphs.

An extreme example of this kind of skewing occurs in an Aguaruna composition (Larson 1978:201-03) by a sixteen year old telling about the things he did with his father when he was younger. There are several **semantic paragraphs** in the discourse; however, they are encoded in a single grammatical sentence. This text is given below simply as an example of this kind of skewing. This long sentence begins with *my father* and ends with *he was* (see the bold italics in the text). Between this subject and predicate, in Aguaruna, is a long series of events and speeches. But all are in the one grammatical sentence. (In the text the speech exchanges are marked with a double bar to help the reader see the structure. Verbs are marked with **same subject** (ss) and **different subject** (ds).) The important thing for the reader to notice is that this one long sentence is then translated into English by eight grammatical paragraphs, and that most of the paragraphs are made up of several sentences. In the English translation below, the paragraphs more closely match the semantic groupings.

Augmattsatjai	*machik*	*uchuch*	*asan*	*nuni*
I-will-tell	a-little	little-child	I-being-ss	like-that

wajukmaun.
what-it-was-obj.

	Mina	*apag*	*chichagtak,*	*"Namakan*
	my	father	speaking-to-me-ss	river-obj

epenkui		*wemi,"*	*tujutkui,*		*senchi*
when-they-fence-ds		let's-go	saying-to-me-ds		very-much

tsetsemakun,	*"Maake,"*	*tai//*	*apag*	*"Untsu*	*amek*
I-being-cold-ss	it-is-enough	say-ds	my-father	rather	you

pujuumata,	*kashin*	*iik*	*mijakui*	*maami,"*
stay-imper	tomorrow	we	they-washing-ds	let's-kill (fish)

takui	*pujai//*	*kashi*	*namaka*	*epenak*	*tseketai*
saying-ds	I-stay-ds	night	river	fencing-ss	jumping-ds

waka	*"Uchuchi,"*	*tujutkui,*	*kanajan*	*tepaun*
coming-up-ss	little-child	saying-to-me-ds	I-sleeping	lying

"Jaa,"	*tai//*	*"Nantakta,"*	*tujutkui,*	*"Wagka*	*tame,*
ho!	say-ds	get-up	saying-to-me-ds	why	you-say

apawa?"   *tai,*   *"Nantakim*   *taata,*   *namak*   *tsekama*
my-father   say-ds   you-getting-up-ss   come   fish   jumping-ds

nu   *kanu*   *minantua*   *maami"*   *takui,*   *"Ayu,"*
that   canoe   those-who-jump-into   let's-kill   saying-ds   okay

tusan//   *nantakin*   *wenu*   *namaka*   *jegan*
I-saying-ss   getting-up-ss   I-going-ss   river   I-arriving-ss

"Apawa,   *wamkek*   *wakitkitag?"*   *tai,*   *apag*   *"Atsa,*
father   quickly   will-I-return   say-ds   my-father   No

machik   *asa*   *wemi,"*   *takui,*   *kanu*   *buku*   *asamtai,*
a-little-bit   being-ss   let's-go   saying-ds   canoe   dry   being-ds

nuwi   *tepesan*   *kanaja*   *ai//*   *kagka*   *tsekeak,*
there   I-lying-down-ss   sleeping-ss   being-ds   fish   jumping-ss

kagkajui   *tugkugmatai,*   *tsetsekai*   *jakun*
on-my-leg   it-hitting-me-ds   cold-instrument   I-being-sick-ss

shintajan,   *"Apawa*   *senchi*   *tsetsemajai,"*   *tai,*
I-waking-up-ss   my-father   very   I-am-cold   say-ds

apag   *chichak*   *"Wakitkimi,"*   *takui,*   *"Ayu,"*   *tusan//*
my-father   speaking-ss   Let's return   saying-ds   okay   saying-ss

"Apawa   *wajupa*   *kagkash*   *maume,"*   *tai,*   *"Ipak usumat*
father   how-many   fish   you-killed   say-ds   four

maajai//   *wakitkimi,"*   *takui,*   *"Ayu,"*   *tusan*   *jega*
I-kill   let's return   saying-ds   okay   I-saying-ss   house

wakan   *shiig*   *kanaja*   *tsawaja*   *tepai//*   *dukug*
I-going-up-ss   good   sleeping-ss   dawning-ss   lay-ds   my-mother

"Nantakim   *amesh*   *kagka*   *yuwata,"*   *takui,*
getting-up-you-ss   you   fish   you-eat-imper   saying-ds

yuwan//   *"Apawa*   *kagkash*   *nijattamek?"*   *tai,*   *"Ehe,*
I-eating-ss   father   fish-maybe   will-you-wash   say-ds   yes

nijattajai	ajum	etsa	tajimai,"	takui//	"See,
I-will-wash	later	sun	it-stands-ds	saying-ds	thank-you

chah,	Ajum	matjai,"	tai,	apag	"Ajum
wonderful	later	I-will-kill	say-ds	my-father	later

nijakui	maata,"	takui,	"Ayu,"	tusan	pujai//
washing-ds	you-kill	saying-ds	okay	I-saying-ss	stay-ds

apag,	"Tikich	aents	ainaujai	weajai,	wawasapa
my-father	other	people	they-are-with	I-go	harpoon

jukita,"	tujutkui,	"Ayu,"	tusan,	jukin
bring-imper	saying-to-me-ds	okay	I-saying-ss	I-taking-ss

jega	ai//	"Jasta,	timu	dekagtajai,"	tus
arrive-ss	be-ds	wait	poison	I-will-pound	he-saying-ss

dekeakui	pujusan	dii	pujai//	timu	dekamu
pounding-ds	I-staying-ss	see	stay-ds	poison	those-who-pounded

ashimak	"Nijajai,"	takui,	mijan	kagka	niya
finishing-ss	I-am-washing	saying-ds	minnow	fish	he-first

jakui,	supu	supu	wajatuan	wegai,	kagka	nantakui
dying-ds	splash	splash	I-standing-ss	go-ds	fish	rising-ds

pusut!	ijun	jukitakaman	shiig
wham	I-hitting-ss	I-trying-to-grab-ss	well

ijuchmau	asan	kagka	ukuinak	wematai
one-who-does-not-hit	I-being-ss	fish	they-leaving-ss	going-ds

pempenkin	wegai//	nuishkam
I-wavering-back-and-forth-ss	go-ds	there-also

nanatun	maatakamin	aweman
those-that-surfaced-obj	I-trying-to-kill-ss	I-sending-away-ss

waja wajakuan	jau	megkaekamtai	apajun
I-standing-and-standing-ss	sick-ones	being-lost-ds	to-my-father

jegantan,	*"Amesh*	*maumek?"*	*tai,*	*"Ehe,*	*machik*
I-arriving-ss	you-perhaps	did-you-kill	say-ds	yes	a-few

maajai,"	*takui//*	*"Wika*	*machujai"*	*tai,*	*apag*
I-killed	saying-ds	I	I-did-not-kill	say-ds	my-father

chichagtak,	*"Maanchuchuitme*	*awis*	*aikamtai,"*
speaking-ss	you-are-very-small	therefore	it-happened-like-that

tujutin	*ayi.//*
one-who-said-to-me	he-was

The following is one possible English translation:

I am going to tell you a little bit about what it was like when I was a child.

My father said to me, "When they put the fence in the river, let's go fishing." Since I was very cold I said, "I don't want to." My father said, "All right, you stay here. Tomorrow, when they put the poison in the water, we'll go and kill some fish." And so I stayed home.

That night they put a cane fence into the river. When the fish began jumping, my father came up and called, "Son!" I was lying sleeping and said, "Ho!" He said, "Get up!" I said, "Why do you say that, father?" He said, "Get up and come! The fish are jumping and we'll kill those that jump into the canoe." I said, "Okay," and getting up went to the river. I said, "Father, will we go back right away?" Father answered, "No, we'll be here a little while."

Since the canoe was dry, I lay down and fell asleep. A fish jumped into the canoe and hit my leg, and woke me up. I was very cold. "Father, I'm cold," I said. My father said, "Let's go back." "Okay. How many fish did you kill?" I asked. He said, "I killed four. Let's go home." I said, "Okay," and I went up to the house. I slept well, and when I woke up, I just lay there.

My mother said, "Get up and eat some fish!" As I was eating, I said, "Father, are you going to put poison in the river to kill the fish?" He said, "Yes, I'll put it in about noon." "Oh, good! Then I'll kill some fish," I said. And my father said, "Later, when they put the poison in, you can kill some fish!" I said, "Okay," and waited at our house.

At last my father said, "I am going to go on ahead with the other people, you bring the harpoon!" I said, "Okay," and getting the harpoon went to the river. My father said, "Wait while I pound the poison." I stood and watched him.

When they finished pounding it, they said, "Let's put it in the water." The poison made the minnows sick first. I said to my father, "The fish are sick." And he answered, "Kill them!" So I went splashing along. When a fish came up to the surface, I hit him, splash. I tried to hit them, but I went this way and that way. I tried to kill those that came up, but instead I drove them away.

So I just stood there and when the sick fish were all gone, I went back to my father and said, "Did you kill any?" He said, "I killed a few." I said, "I didn't kill any." He answered, "You are very little, that is why." That's how my father taught me.

Units larger than a paragraph

We have already said that paragraphs unite to form larger units and that these units group into larger and larger units until the discourse itself is the largest. How many levels of inclusion there will be in a given discourse, and how these may best be labeled, will depend on the text that is being analyzed. A discourse may consist of only one **episode.** Or it may consist of many **episodes** grouped in many **episode clusters** and **parts** and **sections** as in the case of a novel or autobiography. However many units there are, the relations discussed in chapters 27 and 28 will still apply, but different names are sometimes used for larger units.

When a whole discourse is being considered, there are usually three major parts; that is, the **opening**, the **BODY (HEAD)**, and the **closing.** Sometimes it is more appropriate to call the opening **introduction, setting,** or **preliminary incident. Opening** is a generic term. That is, the **opening** might be a **setting,** an **introduction,** or a **preliminary incident**, or a combination of these. In addition to being characteristic of a total discourse, the roles **opening, BODY**, and **closing** are also often found as parts of a paragraph, episode, episode cluster, or part of a discourse.

Setting is a narrative counterpart of **circumstance.** It provides information in time, location, participants, and background events or states. It often consists of state propositions. The **setting** of a narrative may be an embedded descriptive discourse or a minor nonproblem narrative. In discussing the structure of Wobé of Ivory Coast, Link (in Grimes 1978:226) says: "In the orientation of narrative discourse, settings are given concerning time, place, and topic. Participants are introduced, and background information is added, if there is any.... There is a tendency to give time before place and both of them before participants." Other languages will have different ways of organizing the information in the setting. For example, Aguaruna of Peru puts the participant identification first and observations about location later in the **setting.**

The **introduction** is characterized by the fact that it states the theme of what is to follow. For example, in Aguaruna, the appropriate **introduction** to a legend is *I'm telling the story about such and such.* This initial proposition is not a **circumstance**, but simply an **introduction** or **opening**. For certain discourse types, these may have a fixed form. In a large text, the **introduction** may be quite long. For example, in a book it might be a whole chapter. Some **introductions** may be called *prologue* or *preview.* The **introduction** includes some information on the theme of the discourse. In Amahuaca (Peru, data from Margarethe Sparing), a story often begins with an introduction which consists of a summary sentence telling what the story is about. For example, *In the old days grandmothers ate their grandchildren,* or *Our ancestors received fire from squirrels.*

Preliminary incident is an event, or sequence of events, relevant to those which follow but, like the **setting**, not part of the stimulus-RESPONSE relation between the other events or episodes. Although **setting** may involve an event, it functions primarily to "set the stage" for the events of a narrative unit. It is more concerned with which participants are involved before the events take place and what is going on at the time of the opening of the narrative. The **preliminary incident**, however, presupposes the **setting.** It actually gets the events of the unit under way. But the **preliminary incident** is not an integral part of the BODY of the discourse. The following is the **preliminary incident** of a Denya (Cameroon) story (Abangma 1987:32). See chapter 34, exercise B, for the rest of the story.

Gebé	*gefɔ́*	*gébɔ́*	*gelu*	*eyígé*	*meshu*	*anene*
Time	certain	it-contr	it-was	when	Elephant	he-the-one-who

épaá.
invited-a-feast

There was a time when Elephant invited people to a feast.

Closing is also used in a very generic way. Different types of discourses will have different types of **closings.** An expository discourse will likely have a **conclusion** unit as a **closing** unit. A **summary** may be used where the content is paraphrased using more generic predicates and substitutions like "that's all they did." Certain kinds of texts will have a **moral** as the **closing** unit.

Openings and **closings** should be noted very carefully by the translator. These are the units of the discourse which most clearly define the theme or purpose of the entire discourse. A careful analysis of these parts of the discourse will be very helpful in correct interpretation of the main **BODY** of the text. One of the first steps a translator should take when looking at a text is to isolate the section which is the **opening (setting, introduction, preliminary incident)** and the part that is the **closing.** These need to be looked at apart from the text as well as in relation to it.

Openings and **closings** often have very special forms in the grammatical and lexical surface structure of languages. These forms may signal the purpose of the text. They may simply be fixed forms which are an indication of the genre of the text. For example, in English, a text which begins *once upon a time* is clearly going to be a fairy tale. In some African languages *long ago* is used to begin a story of this type. Since such fixed openings and closings will differ greatly from language to language, they cannot be translated literally. The translator must use the appropriate form of the receptor language in order to signal the correct genre and the theme of the **BODY** of the text. Concerning fixed patterns in the Mumuye language of Nigeria, Peter Krusi (in Grimes 1978:267) says:

> Every narrative starts with an **introduction** which gives the topic of the story or the main characters of the story. Folk tales and made-up stories are introduced with *ru gmaa'gmaa' tan* (story free now) 'The free story I am telling now...' followed by the identification of the characters: *yí pu'n yí ti'nbmoo'li* (hold Fly hold Wormcast) '...is about Fly and Wormcast.' Fly is the main character because he is mentioned first. The form of introduction in such tales can vary considerably; sometimes only the main character is mentioned there.

It should also be noted that not all units of the **BODY** of any text are of equal importance. Some will, for example, be major events, others minor, and so forth. Most discourse types will have some part of the structure which will be the **peak** or most significant part. The matter of **prominence** will be discussed in chapter 32.

Skewing of groupings

At the beginning of chapter 25 a chart was given displaying the groupings in the semantic structure and in the grammatical structure and showing the match and skewing possibilities. It was pointed out that a proposition is encoded by a clause (or simple sentence), a propositional cluster by a sentence, a semantic paragraph by a grammatical paragraph, etc., when there is no skewing. However, not all language structures have the same grammatical groupings. A translator might expect that surely every language will have the grouping called a **sentence**. However, in some parts of the world, such as in Australia (see K. Callow 1974:20), there is no clear unit between the clause and the paragraph in some discourse types. The text simply goes along with clauses following one after another to form a paragraph. The fact that there are groupings in the semantic structure, and what these groupings and the relations between them are, is communicated in the information content of the clauses, rather than by another level of structure. In many Papua New Guinea languages, there is no clear distinction between sentence and paragraph in the grammar (see Longacre 1972a:2, 25).

Above, an example from Aguaruna was given in which one **sentence** encoded what, in the semantic structure, was eight paragraphs. It is characteristic of Aguaruna structure that narrative will group what is semantically a paragraph into a single long **sentence**. **Sentences** may be extremely long in narrative discourse. On the other hand, in expository and hortatory discourse the groupings which are **sentences** (indicated by an independent verb) are very short and often encode a single propositional cluster, thus matching more closely the semantic groupings. This difference between discourse types is also reported for other languages, for example, Waffa of New Guinea. K. Callow (1974:20) reports:

> In Waffa the sentence is clearly marked in explanatory and hortatory discourse, and sentences build up into paragraphs equally clearly. In third person narratives, however, the sentence is nowhere to be found, or rather, the distinction between sentence and paragraph disappears; one may only say that all narrative paragraphs consist of one sentence, and the sentence can be quite long.

The translator must give special attention to using the grammatical groupings which are natural to the receptor language. He will not just literally translate a source language **sentence** with a receptor language **sentence**. After grouping the information content into semantic units he will look for the most natural groupings of the receptor language grammar. For example, in the translation of English texts into Aguaruna it was found that the shorter **sentences** in narrative discourses had to be grouped into very long **sentences** in Aguaruna, and the very long **sentences** used in the expository English texts had to be translated into Aguaruna with many short **sentences.**

Longacre (1976a:291) also reports that in Fore of Papua New Guinea, a text was found in which what was clearly four **episodes** in the semantic structure was encoded by a single paragraph in the Fore grammatical structure.

The grammatical structures of one language will not match those of another. The fact of this mismatch of groupings in a number of languages is described by Longacre (1976a:277) as follows:

> ...Three Australian aboriginal languages (Walmatjari, Mantjiltjara, and Wik-munkan) and one New Guinea language (Bahinemo) which I studied...seem to involve one less level in the upper range, i.e., we do not need the three levels, paragraph, sentence, and clause, but only two levels.... The lower of the two levels is much like a simple sentence in European languages. Its nucleus has only one clause but subordinate clauses may occur in the periphery of the construction. The higher level takes up all other sentential functions.... In brief the two levels found in these languages distribute the functional load in a way not parallel in any close manner to paragraph and sentence versus clause or to paragraph versus sentence and clause in a European language.

EXERCISES – Groupings

A. Look again at the analysis of the **propositional cluster** about *Shasta* and *Bree* at the beginning of this chapter. Translate the six propositions into a second language which you know. Then, using this information translate the **propositional cluster.** Make three different translations, arranging the order differently or using different ways of expressing the **relations.** When you have finished, you should have three translations of the source text which is the English sentence *Shasta was pretending to lead, but it was really Bree who knew the way and kept guiding him by little nudges with his nose.* Reread your three translations. Is each one communicating the same meaning as the source text? Is each one natural, receptor language form? Which of the three do you think is the best style, that is, which sounds the best to you as a speaker of the receptor language?

B. Look again at the analysis of the three **propositional clusters** on page 370. First do A. Translate the three propositions into the second language which you speak. Think about how they would go together in the receptor language. Would you want to use one sentence or two or three? Then find more than one way of translating the **propositional clusters.** Be sure your translation is accurate in content and natural in style. Do the same with B and C.

C. Above (page 371) the English sentences *John is here. We saw his car*, were analyzed. Look at the analysis again. The semantic structure has three propositions in the **propositional cluster.** Translate this **cluster** into the second language which you speak, using more than one receptor language form.

Chapter 30
Discourse Genre

One of the first things a translator will want to do is to identify the discourse genre of the document to be translated. In most languages, there are many formal differences between a **narrative**, for example, and an **expository** text. Different discourse types are appropriate for writing about different subjects. If the author is recounting an adventure, he will normally use **narrative structure**, perhaps with some dialogue mixed in and, occasionally, some **description**. The discourse structures used to recount an adventure will not be the same as those used to explain how one can best raise chickens, for example. Every language has a variety of discourse surface forms. The author will choose the discourse type which best communicates his purpose in writing. If he wants to recount a series of events, he will normally use **narrative discourse**. If he wants to teach someone else how to do something, he will use the forms of a **procedural discourse**. There are also many subtypes. Languages will have special forms for legends, first person narration, short stories, prayers, argumentation, newspaper reports, scientific papers, political speeches, "how to do it" books, etc. Some languages have highly stylized forms for poetry, ceremonies, and children's stories. In Aguaruna, the form used for telling a dream or vision includes repeating every clause twice (see Larson 1978:390, 394–99).

Basic to finding the groupings within a discourse is an understanding of discourse genre and how they contrast in the semantic structure. Six basic contrasting genre will be discussed: **narrative, procedural, expository, hortatory, descriptive,** and **repartee.** The differences between these genre can best be seen by thinking of the purpose of the writer. In **narrative discourse**, the author's purpose is to *recount*; in a **procedural discourse**, to *prescribe*; in **expository discourse**, it is to *explain*; in a **descriptive discourse**, to *describe*; in **hortatory discourse**, to *propose, suggest,* or *command*; and in **repartee discourse** to *recount speech exchange*. When **narrative** and **repartee** are found intermingled in the same discourse, the result is **dialogue discourse** which is a special surface structure form.

The groupings within discourse genre are different for each discourse genre. Deep structure **narrative discourse** is characterized by plot structure (see chapter 28). The units consist of chronologically ordered and related past events. In **procedural discourse**, however, the constituents are *procedures*. *Procedures* consist of sequentially ordered and closely related steps. In **expository discourse**, the constituents are logically related *points* about a theme. *Points* consist of a theme plus comments. **Descriptive discourse** is like expository discourse, but the *comments* are usually State Propositions rather than Event Propositions. The theme, rather than being a proposition, is a THING or an EVENT. In **hortatory discourse**, the constituents are logically related proposed or obligatory *injunctions*. *Injunctions* consist of proposed ACTIONS plus supporting reasons, purposes, etc. In **repartee discourse**, the constituents are sequential *exchanges*, and *exchanges* are related to one another in a structure which Longacre (1976a:193–94) calls game structure. In addition, all languages have **dialogue discourse. Dialogue** is a combination of **narrative** and **repartee** structures rather than a distinct discourse genre and so it is not listed. It consists of chronologically ordered and related past events, some of which are speech events.

The SUMMARY CHART (Display 30.1) shows the main characteristics of the discourse genre. (For more discussion of discourse genre see Grimes 1975, Longacre 1976a, and Larson 1978.)

SUMMARY CHART — characteristics of discourse genre				
genre	**person orientation**	**time (illocutionary function)**	**backbone**	**primary structure**
NARRATIVE	first / third	past / (statements)	main-line events	stimulus-response
PROCEDURAL	unspecified	(commands)	procedures	steps-goal
EXPOSITORY	third	(statements)	themes	logical (cause-effect)
DESCRIPTIVE	third	(statements)	topics	topic-comments
HORTATORY	second	(commands)	injunctions	grounds-exhortation
DRAMA	depends on the discourse within the exchange			exchanges

Display 30.1

For each discourse genre, a short text of each of these types is given to highlight the contrast in the deep structure, and to show the skewing that may occur between the semantic and the grammatical structures.

Narrative discourse

The purpose of a **narrative discourse** is to *recount events*, usually in the *past*. The backbone of the **narrative** is a series of events which are usually ACTIONS. The agent of the events is usually THIRD PERSON or FIRST PERSON, that is, either the narrator tells about the things which happened to someone else or to himself. The presence of participant, time, and location spans are involved in determining groupings (see chapter 31). That is, an episode usually has a unity of participants, location, and time. The structure is that of plot structure (stimulus-RESPONSE).

The following Aguaruna text is the opening episode in a **narrative discourse**. Following the text and its gloss is an idiomatic English translation followed by Display 30.2.

Makichik	*aents*	*aagsean*	*ajuntak,*	*etsa*	*akagaig,*
One	person	fish-hook-obj	throwing-in	sun	going-down-ds

namakaa	*weauwai.*	*Nunik*	*etsa*	*wamak*	*akaikimtai,*
to-river	he-went	Doing-so	sun	quickly	went-down-ds

kiimpag	*waketak*	*kawau*	*shinutai,*	*jii*	*ekeematuk*
getting-dark	returning	frog	croaking-ds	fire	lighting-for-himself

diikmaa	*makichik*	*kayanmak*	*kuwau*	*majamjajai*
trying-to-look-for	one	on-a-rock	frog	toad-with

tsanian	*ekeemas*	*shinu*	*ekeemtatman*
being-together	sitting	one-who-croaks	one-who-desired-to-sit-obj

wainak,	*kuwaun*	*achika*	*juwak,*	*majamjan*	*tiwiki*
seeing	frog-obj	after-grabbing	taking	toad-obj	brushing-off

ajugka	*ukukiuwai.*
after-throwing-him-into-the-water	he-left-him

*Once upon a time there was a man who went down to the river
one evening to fish. While he was fishing the sun went down quickly
and it got dark. As he was returning home he heard a frog croak.
So he lit a fire and began looking for the frog. Suddenly he saw a
frog and a toad sitting together on a rock singing. Grabbing the
frog he took it with him. However, he brushed the toad into the
water and left it....*

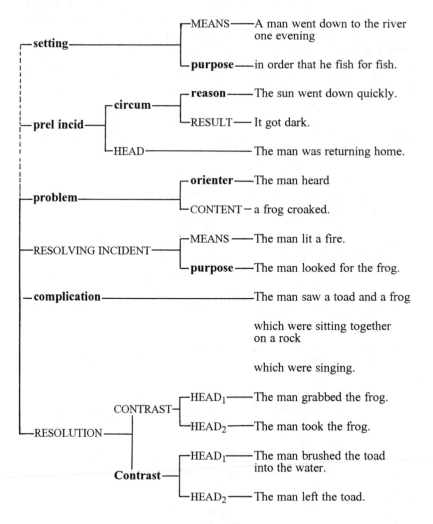

Display 30.2

(The story has an additional **episode**. In the second episode the toad comes to the man's house at night and scolds the man. Then in the **closing** the man agrees never to accuse the toad of being a "toad" again.)

Notice that the main events of the episode are *returned, heard, lit (a fire), saw, took, left*. The other events are simply supporting these main events. These events form the backbone of the episode. They are the **preliminary incident, problem, RESOLVING INCIDENT, complication**, and **RESOLUTION** of the narrative structure.

Notice that there are only two sentences in the Aguaruna surface structure. The first matches the **setting** of the semantic analysis. The second sentence includes all the rest of the information in the **episode**. There is only one main verb, at the very end, which means *he left him*. However, there are groupings within the sentence in Aguaruna which are marked by a suffix *-k* on the verb. Notice the ending of the words for *return, light, see,* and *take*. These are marked as main events, along with the final main verb, *left*. Other verbs are subordinate to these verbs, reflecting the support roles of the events in the semantic structure.

The narrative plot structure is shown in the stimulus-RESPONSE roles on the far left. Notice that logical, orientation, and clarification relations also occur in a narrative, but they are supporting the main events which form the backbone structure of narrative discourse.

As we noted before, the Aguaruna form has only two sentences. However, notice that in the English translation seven sentences are used. Another language may use a form with more sentences, or with less sentences. In the deep structure, there are sixteen propositions. There are six units in the narrative plot structure as indicated on the far left of the display. If the grammatical forms matched the semantic structure, there would be a sentence for each propositional cluster, which would equal one for each narrative role. The English translation given above comes close to matching the grammatical sentence with the semantic propositional clusters. However, the Aguaruna sentence includes a number of propositional clusters.

Narrative structure in Aguaruna tends to have long sentences with many dependent verbs and one final independent verb. The propositional clusters are reflected in the use of the *-k* mentioned above. That is, there is a grouping in the grammatical structure between the clause and the sentence, which might be called a mini-sentence, and which is marked grammatically by *-k*. In other languages, the groupings of the narrative structure will be still different. A translator will not expect to translate sentence for sentence. He will express the semantic structure of the narrative with the natural sentence length of the receptor language.

Procedural Discourse

The purpose of a **procedural discourse** is to *prescribe*, to give the **steps** in how to do something. Each procedure is a unit and the discourse consists of a sequentially related series of steps within each procedure. Very often the event being talked about will be a PROCESS, or an ACTION which is a PROCESS ACTION. The AGENT is not usually specified, and it is characteristic of procedural discourse that most of the ACTIONS will have an AFFECTED. The propositions often contain an INSTRUMENT or MANNER concept. The groupings in the semantic structure will parallel the steps and the procedures.

The following Aguaruna discourse tells *how to cure scorpion bites*. First the text is given in Aguaruna with the English gloss, then the semantic analysis is displayed, and finally, an idiomatic English translation is given. Notice how much information is implicit in the Aguaruna text but is made explicit in the semantic Display 30.3. Some information which is implicit in Aguaruna is also explicit in the English translation (following the display).

Titig	*ijuujatmataig*	*Chiyag*	*tegai*
Scorpion	if-it-bites-someone	(name of a tree)	scraping

nijayi	*juki*	*ejapchiijiya*	*awi*	*taumi,*	*shiig*
its-trunk	taking	from-its-little-middle	there	digging	well

tujukasua,	*juki*	*ujuchnum*	*pepejet*	*ijika*	*chukuut*
making-smooth	taking	in-cotton	wrapping	tying-up	squeezing

chukuut	*ijuja*	*kujatia*
squeezing	wringing-out	one-drinks-it

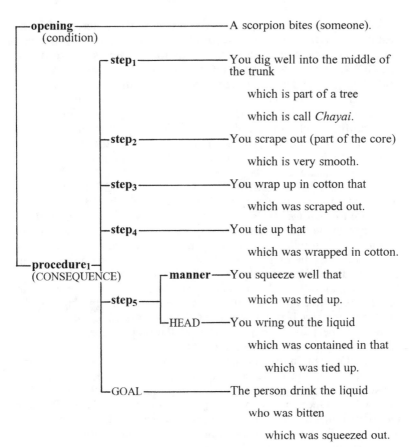

Display 30.3

The text continues with other **procedures**, including drinking hot pepper and afterwards taking ginger as a laxative. It concludes with a closing **summary** statement *and so that is how he will get well.*

If a scorpion bites someone prepare a drink from the Chiyag tree. First dig well into the very middle of the trunk and scrape out the very smooth part of the core. Then wrap the scrapings in cotton, tie the bundle up and squeeze it very hard in order to wring out the liquid. Then the person who was bitten should drink this liquid.

Notice that the structure of the procedure is a series of **steps** leading to a final **GOAL**, the drinking of the liquid by the one bitten. The structure is simple, an **opening**, a series of **steps** and the **GOAL**. If there were no skewing between the semantic structure and the grammatical structure, each **step** would be a sentence. However, in Aguaruna, the entire procedure text is given in one sentence with a single main verb *that-he-drink-it*. The main verb has a suffix which indicates imperative; however, it is an imperative used only in teaching. All the other verbs, with the exception of the opening *if-it bites-someone* are simple verb stems with no tense or person markers.

Although, in the semantic structure, the AFFECTED has been indicated in each proposition, there are no nouns in the surface structure for *that which was scooped out, that which was wrapped up*, etc., or even the *liquid*. That is clearly understood from the verbs used, and leaving it implicit adds to the cohesion of the text.

Notice that the English, however, has had to be a bit more explicit and includes some of the objects of the verbs. Also the text is grouped into four sentences in the particular translation given above. It might be grouped differently and the same meaning kept. In English, the opening is clearer if it includes the **GOAL**, that is, *drink the liquid*. It would not be natural to wait until all the **steps** were given, as in Aguaruna, before indicating the **GOAL**.

The Denya (Cameroon) language also includes the **GOAL** in the opening part of a procedural discourse. Abangma (1987:54) says that the speaker states the **GOAL** which is in primary focus in the opening of the text. Once stated in the opening, the **GOAL** is hardly ever mentioned again until the conclusion when the **GOAL** is finally attained. This **GOAL** is encoded in a hypothetical conditional clause at the beginning of the text in Denya.

Expository discourse

The purpose of **expository discourse** is to *explain* or to *argue*. The nonchronological communication relations (orientation, clarification, logical) are typical of expository and also of hortatory discourse. **Expository discourses** consist of information logically related about a theme.

The following Denya text (Abangma 1987:69–70) (Display 30.4) is an exposition on the theme *poverty is bad*. Following the text and its gloss, an idiomatic English translation is given, and finally, the semantic structure is displayed (Display 30.5).

gekpo	genó,	yi gé	ákúu	ńnó	gekpo,	genó	gebo.
poverty	thing	which	they-call	that	poverty	thing	it-bad

ɔbegé	gekpo,	ɔbɛɛ	bɔɔ́	ame	fúú,	né	ɛcomele	ɛwĩɛ	meo
if-you-are	poor	you-are	people	eyes	open	in	gathering	your	speech

muú	áfyɛɛ́	mekpo	wiɛ.	muú	gekpo,	andé	ákii
person	he-put-not	head	there	person	poor	woman	they-love-not

ji,	mendé	alu	mbɔ,	akɛlege	ŋka,	akɛlege	mandeé
him	woman	she-is	like-that	she-wants	money	she-wants	clothes

akɛlege	ndé ndé	ɔbegé	gekpo,	ɔkágéfyé	maá	ne
she-wants	what-not	if-you-are	poor	you-know-not-put	children	in

mwɛ,	nwɛ	akɛlege	ŋka.	maá	abɛgé	wɔ	nwɛ,
school	schooling	it-requires	money	child	if-he-be	you	school

ɔcyɛɛge	ji	ŋka,	nwɛ	ɔcyɛɛge	ji	mandeé	ɔcyɛɛge	ji
you-give	him	money	school	you-give	him	clothes	you-give	him

ŋka	meyɛɛ́.	ɔlápɔ	ne	ŋka,	ɔ̌pyéé	ébina.
money	food	you-not	with	money	you-do-not	these

Display 30.4

The discourse continues with several more **themes** and ends with a **closing**. The following is a possible English translation of the portion of the text given above:

> *What people call poverty is a bad thing. If you are poor you are worthless in the eyes of other people. At meetings they don't pay any attention to what you say. Also women do not love a man who is poor. Women want to have money, clothes, and lots of other things. Also, if you are poor you will not be able to send your children to school. But if you have money then you are able to send them. If you have a child who goes to school, he will need fees for school, clothes and money to buy food. If you don't have money, you can't pay for these things.*

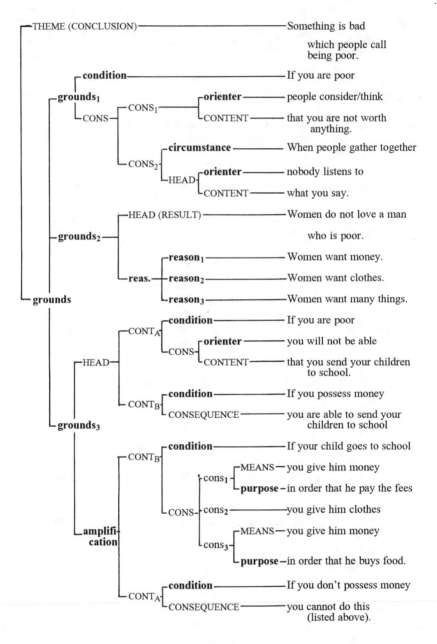

THEME (CONCLUSION) ——————————— Something is bad

which people call being poor.

—condition ——————————————— If you are poor

grounds₁

CONS₁ —orienter ——————— people consider/think

CONS— CONTENT ——————— that you are not worth anything.

CONS₂ —circumstance ——————— When people gather together

HEAD —orienter ——————— nobody listens to

CONTENT ——————— what you say.

—HEAD (RESULT) ——————————— Women do not love a man

grounds₂

who is poor.

reason₁ ——————————— Women want money.

reas.— reason₂ ——————————— Women want clothes.

reason₃ ——————————— Women want many things.

grounds

CONTₐ —condition ——————————— If you are poor

CONS— orienter ——————— you will not be able

HEAD— CONTENT ——————— that you send your children to school.

CONT_B —condition ——————————— If you possess money

grounds₃ CONSEQUENCE ——————— you are able to send your children to school

CONT_B —condition ——————————— If your child goes to school

cons₁ —MEANS — you give him money

purpose — in order that he pay the fees

CONS— cons₂ ——————————— you give him clothes

amplifi-
cation

cons₃ —MEANS — you give him money

purpose — in order that he buys food.

CONTₐ —condition ——————————— If you don't possess money

CONSEQUENCE ——————— you cannot do this (listed above).

Display 30.5

Notice that the **opening** states the **theme** of the discourse. Then there are three **grounds** which prove the **theme**. Denya groups the material into six sentences, each made up of from three to six clauses. The **theme** is stated at the beginning of the presentation of points 1 and 3, and at the beginning of point 2 it is indicated only by *person poor*. In the semantic display, it is included at the beginning of each point.

In the English translation, nine sentences are used. The English sentences consist of only one or two clauses. For example, the Denya repeat *she-wants* three times—*she-wants money, she-wants clothes, she-wants what-not*. The English uses the verb only once and makes a single clause *wants to have money, clothes, and lots of other things*.

The translator should not expect the groupings to match between the receptor language and the source language. The source language is used to determine the meaning, the underlying structure, and then that meaning needs to be expressed in the natural grammatical groupings of the receptor language.

Descriptive discourse

Descriptive discourse has often been included in **expository discourse**. They are the same in that they are not basically chronological. Rather, a **topic** is developed. An **expository discourse** consists of logically related points about a theme. In **descriptive discourse** the points related to the theme are most likely to be state propositions rather than event propositions (see chapters 19 and 20). Delimitation relations occur frequently within the propositions. ATTRIBUTES are common in the propositions. The **topic**, rather than being a proposition, is often simply a THING, i.e., some PLACE, PERSON, ANIMAL, etc., although it may also be an EVENT.

The following text in Aguaruna is a description of a *woodpecker*. Following the text and its gloss, the semantic structure is shown in Display 30.6, and finally an idiomatic English translation is given.

Tatashmak   *makichik* *pishak* *takauwai.*
Woodpecker-topic one   bird   is-one-who-works

Pujuuwai   *numinum.* *Taumnai* *numin.*
Is-one-who-lives   in-a-tree.   Is-one   who-digs-holes

Juka   *pishak* *ekeemchauwai*   *ayatak*
That-topic bird   is-not-one-who-sits   rather

peemnai   *ujuken.*
is-one-who-fastens-against-side-of   with-his-tail

Tatashmak   *yaigchi*   *iyashig,*   *tujakush,*
Woodpecker-topic   is-very-small   his-body   but

chichigmai.   *Yuuwai,*   *dukuchin,*   *shunin,*   *datunchin,*
is-strong.   Is-eater   grubs-obj   larvae-obj   insects-obj.

Kaninai   *waanum.*   *Nanamnai*   *atushat*   *yaki.*
Is-one-who-sleeps   in-a-hole   Is-one-who-flies   far   high

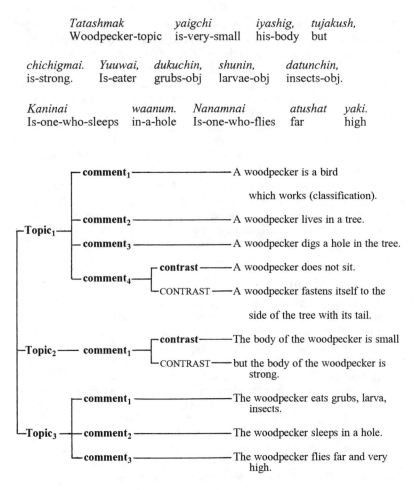

Display 30.6

The woodpecker is a bird which works. It lives in a tree in which it digs a hole. It does not sit like other birds, but rather it fastens itself against the side of the tree with its tail.

The woodpecker has a very small body, but nevertheless its body is very strong. The woodpecker eats grubs, larvae, and insects. It sleeps in a hole in a tree. It flies long distances and very high.

Notice that the description has three parts. First it tells the characteristics of a woodpecker which distinguishes him from other birds. Then the body of the woodpecker is described and finally its living habits. These are labeled topic 1, 2, and 3. The first and last topics have several comments.

The Aguaruna surface structure marked the topic, *woodpecker*, at the beginning of the two paragraphs. The suffix -*k*, which marked the main events in narrative discourse, marks the topic in descriptive discourse. Notice the word *tatashmak* at the beginning of both paragraphs. In the English translation, *The Woodpecker* occurs at the beginning of each paragraph indicating a new paragraph, that is, a new grouping.

In both languages, each **point** is encoded in a separate sentence. The Aguaruna sentences are equative sentences, i.e., the verb has been nominalized and then the equative suffix -*i* added – *is-one-who-lives, is-one-who-digs, is-one-who-sits,* etc. In English, the finite verb is used – *lives, digs, sits,* etc. In both languages, the surface structure groupings more closely match the deep structure than in the other genre already discussed. In Aguaruna, **descriptive discourse** the sentences often are equivalent to a single semantic proposition and contain only one clause. This is very different from Aguaruna **narrative** structure where a sentence contains many clauses and often is equal to a paragraph, as discussed above.

Hortatory discourse

The purpose of **hortatory discourse** is to *propose, suggest,* or *command*. The backbone of the structure is a series of ACTIONS which are commands. The SECOND PERSON **agent** throughout is characteristic of this genre. In **hortatory**, there are also some actions which are not in the main event line, or backbone, but rather are background and related to the main event line by the nonchronological communication relations discussed in chapters 27 and 28. The **manner role** often occurs in the propositional cluster, and the propositions themselves often contain a concept which is the **affected**. **Instrument** is not uncommon in the propositions. The groupings are not so much dependent on a chronological ordering of events as on logically related **injunctions**. An **injunction** is given with the arguments supporting the **injunction**.

The following Denya (Cameroon) text is an exhortation to study (adapted from Abangma 1987:73–5). The semantic structure is presented (Display 30.7) followed by the text and its English gloss (Display 30.8) and, finally, an idiomatic English translation is given.

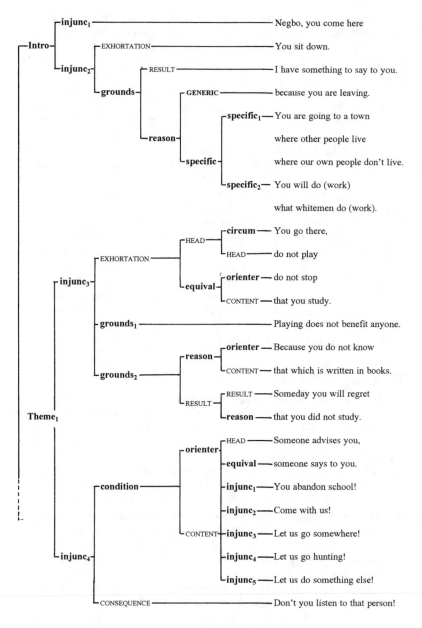

Display 30.7

Negbo,   *cwɔ́*   *wi,*   *jwɔ́lé ka,*   *mbɔ́*   *ɛkɛ́kɛ́*   *mecɔ́*
     come   this-way   sit   down   I-took   little   speech

maá   *áŋjɔ́c*   *gé*   *wɔ*   *mbɔ*   *ɔ́jyɛ́ɛ*   *malɔ*   *bɔ́*   *cácá*
to   say   see   you   like-that   you-who-going   towns   people   other

muú   *se*   *wiɛ*   *apɔ́* .   *utɔɔ́*   *mekálá*   *ne*   *ɔ́jyɛ́ɛpye.*
person   our   there   he-is-not   work   whiteman   that   you-going-is-do

   ɔ́jyɛgé,   *ɔ́jyagé,*   *ɔ́nɛ́rɛ́*   *mekpo*   *né*   *metu*   *ɔ́líá*
   you-went   you-dare-not   you-placed   head   on   play   you-left

nwɛ   *máángi.*   *metu*   *ácyɛ́ɛ́gé,*   *muú*   *geno*   *gefɔ́*
book   to-study   play   it-gives-not   person   thing   some

ɔbɛgéraŋkáa   *nwɛ,*   *gébé*   *gékwɔnege*   *nyíɛ,*   *ɛyigé*   *ɔlali.*
you-remained-know-not   book   time   it-reach   fut,   that   you-cry

   Muú   *acyɛɛ́gé*   *wɔ*   *majyɛɛ́,*   *aké,*   *"líá*   *nwɛ*   *cwɔ́,*
   person   he-gave   you   advice   he-said   abandon   school   come

débɛ́   *fa,*   *déŋmégé*   *gentómé,*   *dépyégé*   *ndé*   *ndé,"*   *ɔ́wugé.*
we-be   here   we-short   hunting   we-do   what   what   do-not-listen

Display 30.8

    *Negbo, come over here and sit down. I have something
to talk to you about. You are going to leave and go to a town
where none of our people live. You'll learn to do the thing
that the white men do.*

    *While you are there do not waste time playing around.
Keep at your studies, because it never helps anyone to play
around. If you don't keep at your books and learn all you can,
someday you will regret it.*

    *If your friends suggest skipping school to go and do this
or that, like going hunting, or anything else, don't pay any
attention to them.*

The text continues with **injunctions** on other themes.

    Notice that the introductory paragraph has three sentences in
Denya and four in English. The first theme, *study and don't play
around*, includes two injunctions, encoded in two paragraphs in both

languages. The first paragraph has four sentences in Denya and three in English. And the second has a single sentence in both languages.

Repartee discourse

The purpose of **repartee discourse** is to *recount speech exchanges*. The surface structure form is usually called "drama." The structure is that of a series of speech exchanges. Each speech is a small discourse and can be analyzed as such. However, these small discourses are related to one another. The interrelation of the speech exchanges can be rather complicated because of the changes of tense and mood, and the shift of person.

The content of the exchanges may be narrative, expository, hortatory, procedural, or even dialogue or drama if the speaker is recounting another set of speech exchanges. In chapter 28, a number of examples were given. Note the following additional example. First the Aguaruna forms with the English gloss is given (Displays 30.9, 30.10, and 30.11), then the semantic (Display 30.12), and finally, an idiomatic English translation is given.

Ex_1
  1. *Pujamek, kumpaju?*
     Do-you-stay my-friend

  2. *Ehe, pujajai, kumpaju.*
     Yes I-stay my-friend

Display 30.9

Ex_2
  1. *Yakumash pujawak?*
     Monkey-doubt does-he-stay

  2. *Ehe, pujawai. Wakaegak weu. Yama*
     Yes he-stays hunting he-went Now

     taun   ukukjai.
     one-who-returned I-left-him

Display 30.10

Ex_3
  1. *Wajina maame?*
     What-obj did-he-kill

  2. *Wakemkachmae.*
     He-did-not-find-anything

Display 30.11

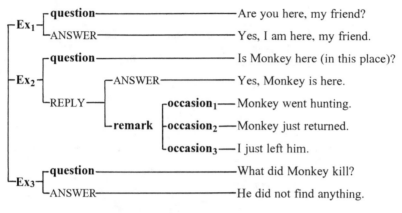

Display 30.12

"Hello, are you home?"
"Yes, I'm here."

"Is Monkey home?"
"Yes, he's back. He went hunting but had just
 returned when I left his house."

"Did he kill anything?"
"No, he didn't find a thing."

Because of the change of speaker, there is no skewing between
the semantic groupings **exchanges** 1, 2, and 3 and the grammatical
units in Aguaruna and English. Notice the difference in the way the
embedded narrative of **exchange** 2 is encoded. In Aguaruna, it consists
of two sentences *hunting he-went* and *now one-who-returned
I-left-him*.

Dialogue discourse

Dialogue discourse is a combination of **narrative** and **repartee**.
The purpose is to *recount* events, usually in the past, as for **narrative**.
The difference is that many of those events are **speech events**; that is,
there is **repartee** structure also. So the characteristics of both genre
must be kept in mind. Examples were given in chapter 28. The
following **dialogue discourse** is given first in Aguaruna with an
English gloss, then the semantic structure is shown in Displays 30.13a
and 30.13b, and finally, an idiomatic English translation is given.

Atashu   Amichjai   augmattsatjai.
Rooster   Fox-with   I-will-tell

Atash   pegkejan   ashinu   pujaun,   wainkau   Amich.
Rooster   good-obj   crow-er   stay-er-obj he-saw   Fox

Nunik   "Kumpaju,   amek   pegkeg   shinamu   nu   imatam?"   tusa,
Being-so   my-friend   you   good   crow-er   that   are-you   saying

tama   "Wii   kumpaju   shinajai,"   tusa,   tama
having-said-ds   I   my-friend   I-crow   saying   having-said-ds

"Ayu   kumpaju,   yamaish   shinukta,   wisha   antuktajai,"   tusa,
okay   my-friend   now   crow-imper   I-also   I-will-listen   saying

tama   "Ayu,"   tusa,   shinau.
having-said-ds   okay   saying   he-crowed

Nunitai,   "Kumpaju,   ame   pegkeg   shinam.
When-he-did-so-ds   my-friend   you   good   you-crow

Imatai,   ashi   pishak   aidaush   shiig   anenawai.
Being-like-that-ds   all   bird   they-are   very   they-are-happy

Tuja   yamai   pusam   shinukta,"   tusa,   tama
And   now   you-closing-eyes   crow-imper   saying   having-said-ds

"Atsa,"   tutai   "Atsa   kumpaju,   ame   nunitai   ashi   pishak
no   when-said   no   my-friend   you   when-do-so-ds   all   bird

aidaush   shiig   aneastinme,"   tusa,   tama   "Ayu,"
they-are   very   they-be-happy-imper   saying   having-said-ds   okay

tusa   pusa   shinutai   yuwau.
saying   closing-eyes   when-crowed   he-ate-him

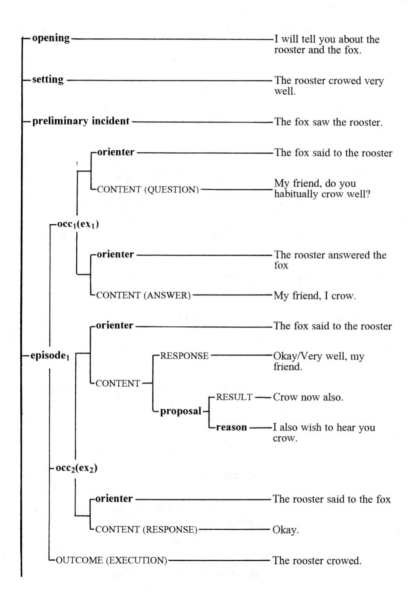

Display 30.13a

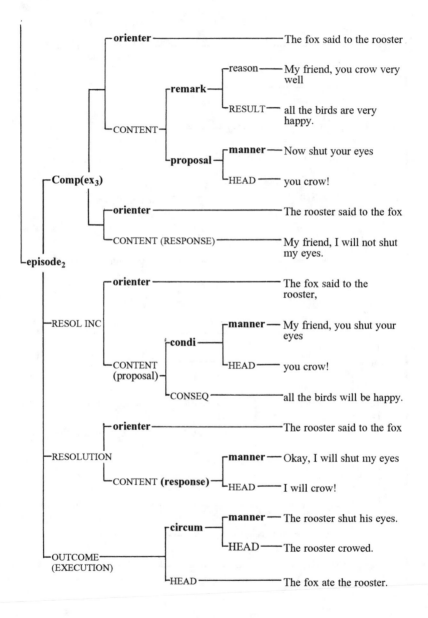

Display 30.13b

Once upon a time there was a rooster who crowed very well. One day Fox saw the rooster going by. He said to him, "My friend, is it really true that you crow very well?" The rooster replied, "I crow." Then Fox said, "Good! Crow right now so that I can hear you too." So the rooster said, "Alright," and crowed.

After the rooster crowed the Fox said, "You crow very well indeed! Because you crow so well all the birds are delighted. But now shut your eyes and crow!" But the rooster refused. So Fox said, "But if you crow with your eyes shut it will make all the birds very happy." And so the rooster agreed. He shut his eyes and crowed. And the Fox ate him.

In Aguaruna, the **opening** is encoded in a separate sentence and the **setting** and **preliminary incident** in a second sentence. However, in English, the setting is included in the first sentence with the opening and the **preliminary incident** is a separate sentence, but part of the paragraph encoding episode 1. Notice also the special forms used in each. The word *I-will-tell* is the characteristic **opening** for an Aguaruna legend. *Once upon a time* is a characteristic **opening** for English.

Notice that the Aguaruna encodes an entire episode with a single sentence. The only independent verb in Aguaruna is the one at the end of the paragraph, *he-ate-him*. English, on the other hand, uses several sentences in both. The **preliminary incident** is included in the same paragraph with the first **episode**. Each of the quotations and the quotation margin which goes with it are separate sentences, in English, with the margin preceding the quotation. In Aguaruna, the quotations are strung together by dependent *saying* verbs. The first goes with the previous quotation and the second series as linkage between the quotations. The grouping of clauses into sentences and sentences into paragraphs is very different in English than in Aguaruna.

Mismatch of discourse structure

The order in which information is introduced may need to be changed for some languages in the process of translation. For example, in many languages of Papua New Guinea, it is necessary to give the full setting before describing any sequence of events. This setting must include the participants, location, and any background information. Once this is all presented, then the sequence of events may follow. For example, the following story would need to be restructured:

A man was walking along the shore of a lake. He saw two fishermen, George and his brother Burt, who were catching fish in the lake with a net. The man said to them, "Do you have any fish for sale?" The two brothers stopped fishing and sold a few fish to the man....

In the translation into some languages, the information might need to be restructured as follows:

Two brothers named George and Burt were catching fish in the lake with a net. A man was walking along the shore of the lake. He came to where the brothers were fishing and said to them, "Do you have any fish for sale?"....

Sometimes information which is given much further along in the source text will need to be moved into the setting and, thus, put early in the receptor language text. It may be necessary to set the stage carefully before beginning the narrative sequence. In current American English, a narrative often begins with a peak of high action and then later goes back and fills in background information and previous episodes. The chronological order is badly skewed. When translating it may be necessary, in some languages, to introduce the background material before jumping into the story.

In earlier sections of this text, we have repeatedly mentioned the fact that when a structure is used in its primary function there is usually little problem in translation. However, when a secondary function occurs there will probably need to be a change of form. This principle also holds for discourse type. If a narrative discourse is encoded by narrative in the source language, then narrative is also used in the receptor language translation. However, this is not always so. Part of what makes writing interesting is a skewing between the semantic structure and the grammatical forms used. So a narrative told in dialogue form may be more "interesting" than a straight narrative. A description told as hortatory will catch the readers attention better. The problem comes in that a second language, the receptor language, may not use the same skewing to add the feature of interest to a text. Therefore, the translator needs to be conscious of skewing, recognize the deep structure genre and translate with the appropriate receptor language forms.

In English short stories, as we all know, the narrative may be carried by dialogue. In fairy tales, however, it is the description which is carried by the dialogue. For example, in *Little Red Riding Hood*, the description of Grandmother is all in the dialogue. On the other hand, Grimm's tales from German have much description which is not inside the dialogue. Some English speakers have said that translations into English do not seem like fairy tales, that is, they are not told like fairy tales are supposed to be told. It is this element of description outside the dialogue that makes them sound foreign. Could they not be told in English with the description in dialogue, as fairy tales original to English are told?

Aguaruna is the opposite of English in this matter. In English, short stories use dialogue to carry the narrative, and fairy tales use dialogue to carry the description. In Aguaruna folklore, it is the narration that is often carried by the dialogue, and stories of present-day events use dialogue for description and highlighting. For example, in the story of a visit to a lake where there was a boa, the description of the **setting** is all in dialogue.

The story, translated more or less literally, is given below:

> *When it began to quake like that, since there were three of them, they said to one another, "There is a boa here and he is angry and wants to eat us. That's why it is quaking like that. Also, the buzzards which are here are spying for the boa, and so seeing us, they called telling the boa that we are here."*

In a language in which dialogue is not used to encode the setting of the story, the translation might need to be more like the following:

> *Then the earth began to quake where the three stood. There in the lake lived a boa. If he became angry he would grab them. There were some buzzards nearby who had made a promise to the boa to let him know if someone came. When the buzzards saw the men, they began to make noise to let the boa know they were there.*

Each language has a primary form appropriate for each genre and for the many subtypes. A narrative told in narrative style is easily translated into the narrative style of another language, since there is no mismatching. But a narrative story told by the dialogue forms of English may not necessarily be best translated by dialogue into an Amerindian language, for example. The narrative may have to be told in Amerindian narrative style, with long narrative sentences, using dialogue only to highlight peak and certain major events or to add description. So the form may need to be drastically changed.

James Marsh (see Longacre 1972a:155) reports that in Australian Aboriginal languages, a text which semantically is procedural genre often uses the grammatical form of dramatic discourse. Drama hardly seems an appropriate grammatical form for English procedural discourse, but may be quite appropriate in languages.

Robert Longacre drew my attention to a text which has the English grammatical form of a procedural discourse but, in fact, is semantically a description. While the material in this discourse is essentially descriptive, it is given in a procedural form, i.e., the discourse is given as if one were on a guided tour through the regions and towns which are mentioned. It is told in second person which is the normal English procedural form. Notice the following:

> *Leaving charming, tourist-ridden Cuernavaca, you continue your journey southwestward through a beautiful region of picturesque villages, rugged mountains, small streams, and dense vegetation....*

> *...turning your eyes upward, you get a wonderful view of the great long stalactites....*

> *...After seeing this underground fairyland, you get into your car again, travel back to the main highway, and start for Taxco, the most picturesque village in central Mexico.*

> *Now your upward climb grows more and more exciting, for your driver is taking a series of breathtaking curves at what seems to be dangerously high speed. Although he sounds his horn at every turn, you find yourself in a state of fear. Yet mingled with your fear is a feeling of sheer delight....*

Another example (from Longacre 1976a:208) occurred in the *Dallas Morning News* (Davenport 1973). The reporter was giving a first person account of an apartment fire, but the story is cast in the form of procedural discourse, i.e., the pronoun *you* and the present tense: *you go to bed, you wake up, you smell smoke*, etc. To translate this as a story in many languages, the procedural discourse would have to be changed to narrative style, i.e., first person pronoun and past tense: *I went to bed, I woke up, I smelled smoke.*

At all levels of language structure there are primary and secondary functions of grammatical forms. The procedural form, in the above, is being used in a secondary function to add vividness to the description or narrative. All secondary functions present possible adjustments of form in the receptor language translation. What is in the form of a dialogue in the source text might need to be translated by narrative; what is a source text drama might need to be translated as a procedural text; etc. The translator will want to identify semantic genre to see if the source text matches this genre or not. If not, is the source text form an appropriate form for this genre in the receptor language, or will some adjustment need to be made in form? A literal translation of the discourse type of the source may lead to misunderstanding or distortion of meaning.

A translator should also be aware of the fact that *almost any long text will be a mixture of genre*. A narrative will have some repartee, often with hortatory or expository genre in the quotations. An expository discourse may have narrative discourse embedded as illustrations. The embedded discourses will need to be translated as a special unit within the larger discourse, using the appropriate receptor language forms.

EXERCISES – Discourse Genre

Go back through the chapter and translate the texts given as examples into a language other than English. Translate from the semantic display. Is your translation more like Aguaruna or Denya or English? What difference of sentence and paragraph groupings did you make? Did you make any other major changes?

Chapter 31

Cohesion

Groupings are primarily hierarchical in structure. In grammar, a group of clauses make up a sentence, and a group of sentences make up a paragraph. Several paragraphs make up a section, and so forth. **Cohesion**, *on the other hand, is linear, running through the discourse, weaving it together.* Notice Display 31.1, where three short sentences make up a paragraph. The groupings are shown on the left. Lines are drawn to show the **cohesion** which is indicated by the pronouns *he*, by the past tense of the verbs, and by *it* referring back to *car*. Lines of **cohesion** run down through any text holding it together in various ways.

As can be seen by the example above, **cohesion** does not stop at

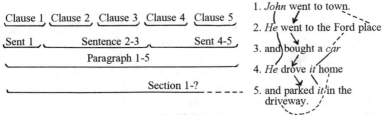

GROUPINGS   COHESION

Display 31.1

the boundaries of **groupings**. Rather, it binds the units together. In addition to the marking of participant line by the use of *John, he*, and the absence of subject (in 3 and 5), and the cohesion between *car* and *it*, there is also some lexical cohesion between *Ford* and *car* and between *town* and the *Ford place* which was in *town*. In the same way, there is some minor cohesion between *home* and the *driveway* which implies the *driveway at home*. If one were to draw in all the possible lines of cohesion, they would indeed be numerous in any text. We are concerned here with those which are signaled by special devices of a given language and used to give cohesion to the text.

425

There is a close relationship between **cohesion** and **groupings** in that the **cohesion** within a unit will be much tighter than at boundaries. The very lack of **cohesion** at certain points in a text indicates a boundary between two units. The devices for **cohesion** within a sentence will often be different from those within a paragraph or episode, etc.

Cohesion in the semantic structure

The **relational structure** itself is a cohesive element of the discourse. This is especially true within the propositional cluster and episode or semantic paragraph. However, the **relational structure**, including plot structure, is an important cohesive element. We have looked at these in the displays presented in previous chapters, especially in chapter 29.

In addition to these **relational structures**, however, there are a couple of other features of a discourse which are important to the cohesion of the discourse. These are **spans** and **semantic domains**. We will now look at these two features.

Span is a very important feature to be studied when analyzing the cohesive elements of a text. By **span** we mean the continuation of a given participant, setting, or event through a part of the text. For example, if a major participant is named *Peter*, as long as *Peter* continues as the major participant there would be a **participant span** related to *Peter*. Or if a certain episode took place *inside the house* and then the following episode took place *outside*, there would be two separate **location spans**. The first **span** would have to do with the location of *inside the house* and the second with the location of *outside the house*. In the same way, there will be **temporal spans, setting spans**, and **spans** related to a particular **event** or **happening**. However, the **spans** will not always be clearly marked, in that there may be some **overlap**. For example, the **participant span** for *Peter* may **overlap** partially with the **participant span** for *John*. It is often helpful to the translator to be able to chart out the **spans** of a particular text that he is planning to translate. This will help in identifying carefully new participants, locations, times, etc., and will help to make sure that changes of location, time, and participants are adequately indicated. Since languages have quite different surface forms for handling the indication of change of participants, time, location, etc., it is important to know, and to consciously think about, where these change points are.

If the translator is making a semantic display, like those in the previous chapters, he may want to mark the various **spans** on the display with different colors for each **span**. If he does not make a semantic display, he can mark **spans** on the source language text or make special charts to show the **spans**. In one way or another, it will be very helpful to him if he takes the time to look carefully at these matters. (For more detail on charting of **spans**, see Grimes 1975:82–96.) The boundary of these different **spans** will not always coincide, but when they do, it usually signals a major division in the text.

Notice the following displays. In the first, the **spans** have been marked alongside the source text. In the second, the **spans** have been marked on the semantic propositions and charted at the right.

SPANS

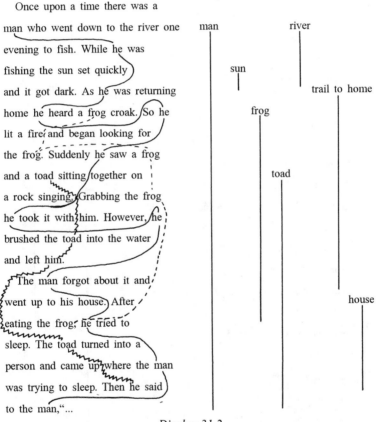

Display 31.2

Notice that it is much easier to plot the **spans** on the propositional display than on the surface structure text. It is best to make the display first, that is, list all the propositions and then to mark the participant spans. The second display shows quite clearly that the *man* is the agent throughout the first part, and then there is a change over, and the *toad* becomes the agent in the last part. These kinds of shifts do not show up so easily if the lines for **spans** are simply drawn on the source text itself.

The purpose of drawing in the **spans** is to alert the translator so that he will then use the appropriate surface structure signals of the receptor language to mark the cohesion which these **spans** bring to the discourse.

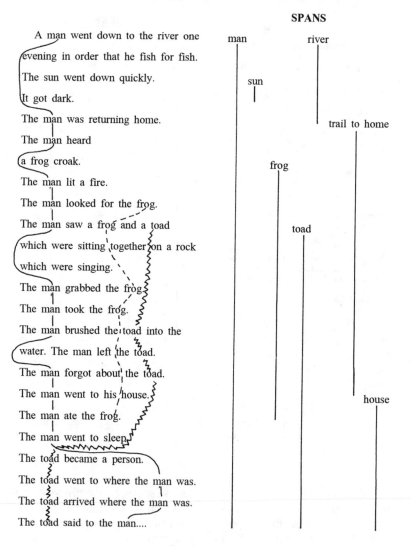

Display 31.3

In the story given above, the device for showing the cohesion in English is the use of the noun *man* at the beginning of a paragraph and the change to the pronoun, or the use of no subject, throughout the paragraph. This may not be the correct device for the receptor language. On the semantic display, all of the information is given, and the translator can then use this in selecting the appropriate receptor language forms. He may signal the participant **span** by verb affixes or by using the noun more frequently than in English. What forms he uses should not depend on the English forms, but on the natural way of signaling participant **spans** and cohesion in the receptor language.

Semantic domain is another feature of structure which adds cohesion to a text. One of the things which will help a translator in the analysis of the source text is a study of breaks in **semantic domains. Semantic domain** does not refer to using the same form or referring to the same specific item over and over (this would be concordance), but rather to the fact that the things being referred to are from the same **domain,** i.e., center around the same topic or have certain semantic components in common. For example, *sea, casting nets, lake, fisherman, boat, fish,* etc., all belong to the same **domain**. When there is a break in the **semantic domain**, there is usually a boundary between semantic units. Sameness of content is also an important criteria. The reoccurrence of the same referent would often indicate that one is still within the same unit.

In any discourse that one might be analyzing, there will be the presence of various cohesive features at the same time. For example, in a narrative discourse there will be the event-line and also the participant spans in addition to the time spans, location spans, and semantic domain. All of these things work together to give cohesion. Breaks in several of these cohesive features would indicate a boundary. The more breaks at one point, the larger the grouping being indicated will be.

We turn now to a brief summary of the characteristic cohesion features of each discourse genre. This will help the translator know what to look for in the analysis of a given genre.

In **narrative** discourse, the first or third person participant span indicating the main agent of most of the actions is crucial. Location span, temporal span, and mood span are also relevant in narrative. The relatedness of contiguous and ordered events also adds cohesion to the narrative. The semantic domain of concepts which are used will be an additional cohesive feature.

In **procedural** discourse, coherence is based on GOAL and AFFECTED spans and on the sequential ordering of related processes. Sometimes the time span may be important when certain processes are to be done at a stated interval. The overlap in the semantic domain of the concepts used also adds cohesion, as for all discourse types.

In **expository** discourse, coherence is based on the theme span and the overlap of semantic domain of concepts and their relation to the theme. As mentioned above, the logical relationships between the propositions and propositional clusters also adds cohesion to any unit.

In **descriptive** discourse, cohesion is based on the topic span, that is, the thing or event which is being described. Within each topic span there will be overlap of semantic domain which will give further cohesion to the unit.

In **hortatory** discourse, the coherence is based on the proposed activity span. The second person agent participant span often goes throughout the body of the text. Logical relations between the central and supporting propositions and propositional clusters also add coherence. Again semantic domains give further cohesion.

In **repartee** discourse, the coherence is based on the ordered sequence of speakers. The reference to the same person from speech to speech can also add cohesion. The particular characteristics of cohesion will depend on the discourse genre of the speeches being made. Dialogue discourse will be a combination of the cohesive features of **narrative** and the cohesive features of **repartee**. In analyzing the semantic structure of a discourse, one must give careful attention to the surface structure markers of the source language. Each language will have its own devices for indicating boundaries between units and for giving cohesion within the unit.

Surface structure devices

There are many devices which give **cohesion** to a text. The particular devices which are used, and even the ways in which they are used, will vary from language to language. Such **cohesion devices** as pronouns, substitute words, verb affixes, deictics, pro-verbs, conjunctions, special particles, forms of topicalization, and so forth, if translated one-for-one from the source language into the receptor language, will almost certainly distort the meaning intended by the original author. It is, therefore, very important that a translator be aware of **cohesive devices** and recognize them as such. He will then look for the appropriate devices of the receptor language for use in the translation.

The encoding of participant spans is usually closely related to the use of pronouns, generic substitution words, verb affixes, switch reference devices, and, in some languages, implicit participant reference. The encoding of time spans may be by special time words, deictics, verb affixes, and by lack of time indication when it is still the same time span. Location spans are also often indicated by deictics or simply by not mentioning location until there is a change. Change in time and/or location is often an indication of the beginning of a new unit.

In narrative, procedural, and dialogue discourse the chronological ordering of the event-line adds **cohesion** to the discourse. However, in addition, there may be pro-verbs, conjunctions, chaining, linkage, back reference, tense, and aspect markers, or special particles.

In expository, descriptive, and hortatory discourse, where themes are being developed, **cohesion** will come through the theme-line and through devices such as lexical cohesion, topicalization, nominalization, and old information being left implicit. Special forms such as sandwich structures and parallel forms may also occur.

Although certain devices were listed above as characteristic of a certain discourse type, any of these devices may be found in any discourse type. However, it is helpful to think of some of these in relation to the discourse types in which they occur most frequently. Several cohesion devices are discussed below, in order to make the translator more aware of the variety of surface structure devices which encode deep structure spans, event-lines, and theme-lines.

Lexical cohesion

Without a doubt, the selection of vocabulary items from a common semantic domain adds greatly to the cohesion of a text. When the words in a paragraph, for example, come from the same semantic domain this adds a unity to the paragraph. This, of course, is a direct reflection of the semantic domain cohesion in the deep structure discussed above.

However, in addition to this more general lexical cohesion, there may be surface structure lexical ties which the author brings about by using **synonyms, antonyms, substitution** of more generic words for specific words, **parallel expressions,** and so forth. Most of the devices which will be discussed below include some element of lexical cohesion. For example, a **pronoun**, since it includes a part of the meaning content of the noun for which it stands, adds lexical cohesion.

Expectancy chains provide a special kind of lexical cohesion. For example, if someone says, *"He aimed his gun, and he _____,"* the hearer will most likely fill in the blank with the word *shot/fired*. Or if someone says, *"He killed it, cooked it, and _____,"* most everyone would fill in the blank with *ate it* (Longacre 1977:12). Lexical **expectancy chains** of this type add cohesion at the sentence level. One might expect that all such **expectancy chains** would match between the languages, but this is not necessarily so. Events which can be left implicit in one language may need to be made explicit in another, since they are part of the **expectancy chain**. For example, in English we can say *He went to town* and no further event is needed. However, in many languages it is expected that the event *arrive* will also be included. That is, the sentence would need to include both *He went to town* and *He arrived*. Since such **expectancy chains** are a very important cohesive device, the natural form of the receptor language should be used including making implicit events explicit. **Expectancy chains** usually operate on a sentence level.

At paragraph level a common lexical cohesive device is that of **substituting generic vocabulary** for more specific vocabulary. For example, notice the following conversation where the **substitute words** are italicized (Nida 1964:73):

> The *machine* broke.
> Where did you buy the *old thing* anyway?
> I bought *it* at the discount house.
> Then toss the *stuff* out.

The substitute *it* is a normal pronominal cohesive element. *Thing* is a more generic way of referring to *machine*. The combination *old thing* and the word *stuff* are **substitute words** which add cohesion and color to the conversation.

Synonyms and **antonyms** may also be substitute vocabulary. They add cohesion to a paragraph. Note the following examples:

1. *John had been a **policeman**.... He was a good **cop** and well-liked by the people.*
2. *There was nothing **slow** about that game.... It moved so **fast** it made my head swim.*

Between sentences within a paragraph, there are many languages which use repetition of the verb as a cohesive device. That is, one sentence ends in a verb and then the same verb is picked up at the beginning of the next sentence. This will be discussed in more detail under **chaining** later in this chapter. However, notice the following Aguaruna paragraph in which *say* (forms in bold type) is used as a cohesive device between sentences within the paragraph.

Dutika	*ai,*	*"Waji*	*wakejagme?"*	***tujutme.***
Do-so-ss	being-ds	what	do-you-want?	she-said-to-me

Tujutkui		*"Namakan*	*wainkatasan*	*wekaejai,"*
When-said-to-me-ds		river-obj	in-order-to-see-ss	I-walk

timajai.	*Taai*	*ataktuu*	*"Tuwyia*	*ainagme?*
I-said	After-said-ds	again	from-where	are-you

Takanchmawaitjume.	*Juwiya*	*aentsuk*	*atumea*	*anin*
you-are-strangers	From-here	people-topic	you	like

ainastsui,"	***timae.***	*Takui*	*"Tikich*	*aentsuitjai,"*
they-are-not	she-said	When-said-ds	other	people-I-am

tusan	*ukukmajai.*
I-saying-ss	I-left-her

Sandwich structures also bring about a kind of lexical cohesion. The same thing is stated at the beginning and the end of a unit, thus identifying the unit, and at the same time adding **cohesion**. Note the following example (the sandwich structure is in bold type):

> *I was afraid and dared not oppose them. I knew that if I were discovered I would be taken to prison. I hid out wherever I could find a place to stay. I looked for food at night. **I was always afraid.***

Pronouns

A great deal has already been said about **pronouns**. However, it is important to discuss **pronouns** as a cohesive device of discourse, particularly because they do not function in the same way from language to language. It is quite common in English, for example, to introduce a new participant with a noun phrase and then refer to this participant by a **pronoun** throughout the rest of the paragraph. In fact, the **pronoun** is used to show that this particular participant is the topic of the entire paragraph. Below, two versions of the same text are given. The one at the left uses the natural pronominal system of the source text. (The text is a modified literal English translation.) At the right the same text is given, but adjustments have been made to use the more natural forms of English. The participant reference has been italicized to show the difference.

LITERAL ENGLISH

They say that *Oriole* took *Nighthawk* up high to his nest. *He* put *him* in it in order that *he* sleep in the nest. However, *he* was not able to sleep because, when the wind blew, the nest moved, and *he* was afraid. *He* said, "My brother-in-law, I will fall. Take me to the ground." When *he* said that, *he* said, "No, you will not fall. Do not go out lest you die of the cold."

And so *he* woke up without sleeping because of fear. *He* returned home. As *he* left *he* said, "I will also return to take you to my house to sleep." *He* said "Okay."

NATURAL ENGLISH

Once upon a time the *Oriole* invited the *Nighthawk* to his nest which was high up in a tree. *Oriole* put *him* in the nest so that *he* could sleep there. However, *Nighthawk* was not able to sleep because when the wind blew it made the nest move, and this made *him* afraid. So *he* said to *Oriole*, "Brother-in-law, I will fall. Take me to the ground." But *Oriole* said, "No, you won't fall. Don't leave the nest, or you will die of cold."

So *Nighthawk* was not able to sleep because *he* was so afraid. As *he* left to return home *he* said to *Oriole*, "I will come back another day and take you to my house to sleep." *Oriole* said, "Okay."

There are some languages in which it would be inappropriate to use **pronouns** in the translation of the paragraph above. Once the participant has been mentioned, the cohesion of participant reference would simply be handled by having no overt subject in the clauses which follow. The lack of an overt marker adds the cohesion. This would be true, for example, in Aguaruna, where the translation would include verb affixes of person but no free **pronoun**. For the Bororo of Brazil, however, the appropriate form would be to explicitly repeat the name of the participant several times before changing to pronominal forms (K. Callow 1974:32).

Each language will have special devices for introducing **major participants** which may be different from those which introduce **minor participants**. Also, as the discourse flows along, forms might be quite different when talking about **major** versus **minor participants** in the story. In languages which make a clear distinction between **major** and **minor participants**, the translator will, of course, have to use the proper devices, even though these are not present in the source language text. In many languages, there are special formulas for introducing **major participants** which help to distinguish them from **minor participants** which appear in the story as well.

Even though the noun may be used for back reference in English, often either the article or some modification will need to be used with the noun. The following example (Longacre 1977:4) shows how, when it is first introduced, the phrase *a dog* is used; then in referring back *the dog* is used; and on the third repetition *that dog* is used.

> *As I stepped out of my front door, I saw **a dog** coming down the sidewalk. Before I knew what was happening **the dog** bit me. **That dog**, I learned later, had bitten three people before I came on the scene.*

Not all languages have articles, and even those which do may not use them in the same way. Different devices will need to be used to add the cohesion which is indicated by the English *a dog, the dog, that dog*. Back reference which has to do with time or location often includes deictic pronouns as in *at that time* and *in that place*. Any and all kinds of back reference add cohesion to the text. However, since these devices are different for each language, they cannot automatically be translated into another language. In some languages, lack of overt back reference linkage produces cohesion, since it is understood that there is a unity until a new time, a new location, or a new participant is introduced. Translating back references literally could be very confusing to the receptor language audience.

Role

Some languages, including Amuesha (Peru), refer to participants other than the one who is the topic under discussion by relationship to that main participant. For example, if there are two participants *John* and *Peter*, and *John* is *Peter's father*, then if *John* were the topic of the paragraph, *Peter* would be referred to as *his son*, not as *Peter*. But if *Peter* were the topic, he would be referred to as *Peter*, and *John* would be referred to as *his father*. The relationship might be kinship, as above, or perhaps a role relationship like *his servant, his king*, or whatever.

In Pame (Mexico), role also is very important in referring to participants. Role is sometimes used, rather than pronouns, as a cohesive device. In a story about a man named *Paul* who was taken prisoner, notice the change from the pronoun *him* to the word *prisoner*:

English: *The police arrested **Paul** and as they were about to take **him** into the jail...*

Pame: *The police arrested **Paul** and as they were about to take the **prisoner** into the jail...*

In some Amerindian languages (Wise 1968:4), the villain must be introduced first in a myth. The order in which participants are introduced may be very significant in setting up major versus minor participants and in clearly identifying the role of the participants. In a language where the villain of a myth is introduced first, any change from this norm would need to be clearly signaled. Lack of awareness of such matters could result in a very distorted translation into another language in which the hero is always introduced first.

Conjunctions

Conjunctions are linking words. They may join together a series of clauses, sentences, or paragraphs. Some languages have many **conjunctions**, whereas, others have almost none. For example, in Indo-European languages, we have many **conjunctions** such as *and, but, then*, and *however*. Many of the **conjunctions** in Indo-European languages are encoding deep structure relations. Pidgin English of New Guinea has a very limited number of **conjunctions** in contrast to standard English. Some Papua New Guinea languages have only two **conjunctions**.

Temporal **conjunctions** usually encode the relations between semantic structures which are related to one another by chronological sequence. In English, this would include such **conjunctions** as *then, later, before*, and *and* (meaning *and then*), among others. Other

conjunctions encode nonchronological semantic structures. Some English **conjunctions** of this nature are *but, therefore, because,* and *nevertheless.* There are many more in English. However, in other languages, such relations may not be encoded by **conjunctions** at all, but by verb affixes. For example, in many Amerindian languages, there are few **conjunctions** but complicated verb morphology which shows the relations and adds the cohesion which the **conjunctions** add in English. This is discussed in more detail under **chaining** below.

Notice the cohesive **conjunctions** in the following text. The source text is Manobo (from Dubois 1973:21–2). The conjunction *yan* occurs four times adding cohesion to the paragraph. The English translation is a modified literal translation showing the structure of the source text. The following data is taken directly from Dubois.

The conjunction **yan**, for example, is a general logical connective ranging in meaning from "therefore" or "as a result" to "and so," "and then," or "next." For example,

> *Kage se qinayen din, Penayit kaw man.* **Yan** *nenayit dan.* **Yan** *migqindanqindan se sebad diyaq te qemayen din kagi din. Doton kay kenami qontoq kay qegkepuluk so wedad doma day.* **Yan** *qonaq dan qimpekaqen kidoqen, qaw qontoq neqidowan dan te kedomaqan dan.* **Yan** *minikagi siqyan, Siqak, qemayen, qibeg ko mengognam den. Kagi, Meqakay man qatoq, meneng seqini qoloq se kelimahan qaw wedad tinanem no.*

> Their aunt said, "Come up." **Then** they came up. **Then** the one fellow told his uncle saying, "There at our place we are very sad because we have no wives." **Then** the relatives first fed them there and were very kind to them. **Then** the one said, "For myself, uncle, I now want to get married." He (the uncle) said, "That's fine, boy, but there's just one difficulty if you have planted no permanent crops."

Just as **yan** introduces what would most reasonably follow, likewise **meneng** 'but' introduces what in the opinion of the narrator, would not ordinarily be expected to follow. The text just quoted continues,

> **Meneng** *minikagi se qotaw siqyan. Doqen bag deqitek tinanem ko niyog, qaw qebaka qeleg doqen, qaw menge qayamqayam heman qeleg man doqen.*

Yan kagi se qemayen din siqyan, Meqpiya man kediq.

But that fellow said, "There are a few coconuts I've planted, and also abaca (Musa textilis), and some domestic animals also." **Then** his uncle said, "That's surprisingly good."

Chaining

In many languages there is cohesion by **chaining**. In **chaining**, some part of the preceding information is repeated at the beginning of the new unit. For example:

> *John **ate** all he could. Having **eaten** so much he **went** to town. While he was **going** he had a flat tire....*

This kind of **chaining** is another kind of back reference. In **chaining** between sentences, the predicate of the old sentence is often repeated in the new sentence.

Chaining does not always repeat the exact words of the preceding unit, but may use a more generic word. For example, in Aguaruna, pro-verbs are used which refer back to the previous action. The verb *nuni-* is used when referring back to an intransitive action and the verb *duti-* when referring back to a transitive action. Verbs of motion and verbs of saying, however, are more often repeated with the same verb stem. Notice Display 31.4 in which the **chaining** is marked by the archs.

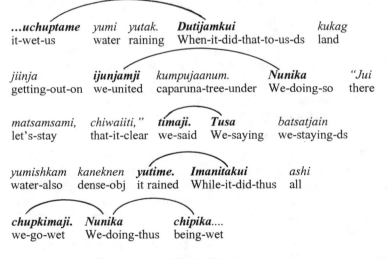

| *...uchuptame* | *yumi* | *yutak.* | ***Dutijamkui*** | | *kukag* |
| it-wet-us | water | raining | When-it-did-that-to-us-ds | | land |

| *jiinja* | ***ijunjamji*** | *kumpujaanum.* | ***Nunika*** | *"Jui* |
| getting-out-on | we-united | caparuna-tree-under | We-doing-so | there |

| *matsamsami,* | *chiwaiiti,"* | ***timaji.*** | ***Tusa*** | *batsatjain* |
| let's-stay | that-it-clear | we-said | We-saying | we-staying-ds |

| *yumishkam* | *kaneknen* | ***yutime.*** | ***Imanitakui*** | *ashi* |
| water-also | dense-obj | it rained | While-it-did-thus | all |

| ***chupkimaji.*** | ***Nunika*** | *chipika....* |
| we-go-wet | We-doing-thus | being-wet |

Display 31.4

Notice that sometimes both the pro-verb and the previous verb are included as in the last sentence *we-doing-thus being-wet*. Also notice that some of the **chaining** verbs have a *ds* included in the meaning. This stands for **different subject** and keeps the participant back reference clear without the use of any nouns or pronouns.

Same versus **different subject** is a crucial feature of **chaining** in Papua New Guinea languages. The following example (from Longacre 1972a:5–6) shows how the Kanite language uses this device to show clearly who the subject is in each clause. The clauses are numbered serially. The example and discussion are from Longacre.

(1) *hi-s-u'a-**ke**-'ka*
do-int-we-tr-you

(2) *naki   a'nemo-ka   hoya   ali-'ka*
so   women-you   garden   work-you

(3) *naki   ali   ha'noma   hu-ne'atale-'ka*
so   work   finish   do-compl-you

(4) *inuna   kae-'ka*
weeds   burn-you

(5) *popo   hu-'ka*
hoe   do-you

(6) *inuna   kae-'ka*
weeds   burn-you

(7) *naki   ha'no   hu-tale-te-**ke**-ta'a*
so   finish   do-compl-cons-tr-we

(8) *naki   viemoka-ta'a   keki'yamo'ma   ha'noma   nehi-s-i-ana.*
so   men-we   fence   finish   do-int-it-conj

"If we do this, you women work the garden, when it is finished hoe and burn the weeds, when that is finished we men will finish making the fence."

The example has a series of eight clauses, of which the verbs are the most important structure in each clause. The last clause, number 8, ends with a conjunctive marker *-ana*, which binds it into the broader framework of a paragraph. The subject of the first clause is *-u'a* 'we'. This morpheme is followed by *-ke*, a transition marker which tells us that there will be a different subject in the clause which is to follow. The final morpheme of the first form *-'ka* tells us that there will be a second person subject of the following clause. This second person subject is the subject of clauses 2 through 6; in each verb the suffix - *'ka* tells us that the next clause will also have a second person subject. In number 7, again we have occurrence of the transition morpheme *-ke* which tells us that there will be a different subject in the following clause, and the person and number of this subject is indicated in the final morpheme *ta'a* 'we' of the verb form in number 7. So we find that in clause 8, "we-men" is the subject of the clause. It is important to note, however, that even in this example the eight clauses do not compose a simple linear string of eight clauses, in spite of the chaining of clause to clause by means of the indication of same (unmarked) subject versus different subject in the following clause. Thus, it is evident that there is a cluster of clauses 4 through 6, and that 6 is a repetition of 4.

Verb morphology

The fact that a series of clauses or sentences have the same tense, mood, or voice adds a feature of cohesion to the unit in which they occur. Several languages have already been mentioned in which a narrative will be told in past tense, and then there will be a switch to present tense at peak. The peak unit gains cohesion as a unit through the use of tense. If an entire text is narrated in one tense, past for example, this fact adds cohesion to the text. If there is a change of tense and the tense span is broken, there is a boundary and lack of cohesion.

Many languages have affixes on the verbs which carry tense, mood, voice, and person. These affixes are very important in adding cohesion and in showing the boundaries. Some examples were given above.

The contrast in affixes on the independent verbs, and the dependent verbs in some languages add cohesion to the main event-line which is found in the independent verbs. At the same time the dependent verbs are often marked with some concordance to the independent verb, adding cohesion in that way.

In many languages, there is a kind of double accounting. That is, for example, a participant may be referred to by a noun while there is also agreement in the verb as to person and number. There may be a pronoun and a verb affix in the same clause accounting for the person and number. Many languages have systems of concord in which there is agreement between nouns and adjectives or nouns and verbs. This kind of double accounting also adds cohesion to the unit.

Order

It seems almost too obvious to mention, but the chronological and logical order also add cohesion to the text. The ordering of main events or main procedures is expected. If they are out of order, then there is a signal needed to indicate that the chain has been broken and to account for the information which is being introduced out of order.

Each language will also have special devices for signaling that a unit is out of order, that the chain has been broken. For example, in English *after* is used in this way: He ran across the street *after* he finished parking the car.

Larger units may also be presented in nonchronological order. Each language has devices for indicating **flashback** and **foreshadowing**. These interrupt the order and, therefore, cause some lack of cohesion. How they are indicated will depend on the language. Concerning Toura folk tales, Ilse Bearth (in Grimes 1978:211) says:

> **Flashback** and **foreshadowing** are represented by short sentences here and there in the story, giving a quick view either into past or future, with past and future aspects respectively. They stimulate the hearer's attention, expectation, and apprehension. An example of flashback: *É nuu fóó, ke woõ bala lã a si be, gwiline ké wei' ye: Bala é* ...(it be-past long-before-that, that they race reidentification it take exist, king unmarked-information say-past he: Race it...) "Namely, long before they started the race, the king had ordered: 'This race...' "

EXERCISES – Cohesion

A. Write a short story in a language you speak other than English. After you have written the story study it carefully, identifying all the cohesion devices you can find. Are there conjunctions? Is there chaining? How often are pronouns used, and what is the function? Go through the devices mentioned in this chapter and see which occur in the story you wrote.

B. Now write down in a language other than English the directions of how to go to another house in the village or city where you are living. After you have written the directions, study them carefully, identifying all of the cohesion devices you can find. Are they the same as for the story you wrote first? What is the difference?

C. Translate the story you wrote for A and the directions you wrote for B into English. Use the natural pronouns and conjunctions of English and whatever other cohesion devices you need. If English is not your first language, check your translation with a native English speaker, and ask him or her to correct your translation so that it will sound natural and use the correct cohesion devices.

Chapter 32
Prominence

Prominence is the feature of discourse structure which makes one part more important, i.e., more significant or prominent than another. Surface structure devices used to mark **prominence** are many and varied. For the translator, the first step is to discover which parts of the source text the author intended to make **prominent**. Once he has successfully analyzed the intent of the author in this matter, he must consider the proper devices in the receptor language which will reconstruct the same **prominence** in the receptor language. Therefore, we will first consider **prominence** as a feature of semantic structure, then discuss kinds of **prominence**, and finally, look at some of the devices used to indicate the different kinds of **prominence**.

Prominence in semantic structure

Every semantic unit has natural prominence. The organizational center of the unit is the naturally prominent part. For example, in an event proposition the EVENT concept is the central constituent and the other concepts relate to it. Therefore, the EVENT is the most prominent constituent, unless some other constituent is made especially prominent. In a propositional cluster, the main (HEAD) proposition is the most prominent. In the preceding discussion of relations, capitalization has been used to show which role is more prominent in a relation. For example, in **reason**-RESULT the RESULT is more prominent than the **reason**. In the **complication**-RESOLUTION relation, the RESOLUTION has more prominence than the **complication**. Within a paragraph, the HEAD proposition of the HEAD propositional cluster will be the most prominent proposition, etc. If some naturally less prominent unit is to be prominent, it must be "marked."

In looking at a discourse, prominence varies with the discourse genre. In **narrative**, prominence is related to the **major events**, to the major participants, and to certain units of the plot structure. These **major events** form the mainline or backbone of the narration. In the structure of a narrative some **episodes** will be more important than others. For example, the PROBLEM and the RESOLUTION are often the most prominent units. They are certainly more prominent than **setting** or **preliminary incident**.

In **procedural** discourse, prominence is related to the major **steps** which form the backbone of the discourse. The GOAL is more prominent than the **steps** leading up to it. When a number of **procedures** are involved, some may be more important than others.

In **expository** discourse, prominence is related to the theme and the comments which are more important in the development of the **theme**. These main **comments** form the backbone of the discourse with the other support **comments** as background. The central **theme** is the most prominent element. In the logical structure which makes up the discussion of the themes, CONCLUSIONS are more prominent than the **grounds** which support them, and the RESULTS are more prominent than the **reasons**, unless the **reason** is "marked" for prominence.

In **descriptive** discourse, prominence is related to the **topic** and the **comments** which are most important in describing the **topic**. The central **topic** has natural prominence.

In **hortatory** discourse, the major **proposed activities** form the backbone of the discourse and are most prominent, with reasons, purposes, etc., as background.

In **repartee** discourse, the **speaker exchange** is prominent, while stray remarks are setting or background. The actual prominent elements in the speeches will depend on the discourse type of the speech.

In **dialogue** the prominent characteristics of narrative and repartee both apply.

It should be evident that the relationship between groupings, cohesion, and prominence is very close. Matters of prominence and cohesion are interrelated with the boundaries of units. On the other hand, for each unit, both the features of prominence and the features which add cohesion help define the unit. Many times these are very similar features. The translator will be taking all of these matters into consideration at once as he analyzes the source text and translates into the receptor language.

Kinds of prominence

There are many devices which signal prominence in a given language. Also, the variety used in the languages of the world is great. However, before discussing some of these devices, it is important to distinguish between three kinds of prominence (material from K. Callow 1974:49–69). These three kinds of prominence are closely related to the domain over which the prominence extends. For this discussion, the three types suggested by Callow are used. There are many other ways of classifying and looking at this matter. Callow distinguishes these three types: **thematic, focus**, and **emphasis**.

Thematic prominence has the largest domain. It says to the hearer, "This is what I am talking about." **Thematic prominence** has to do with the information which is prominent because it contributes to the progression of the narrative or argument of the text. The major events, major procedures, and major themes are all part of thematic prominence. In contrast, there is the nonthematic material, support material, which adds information, but is not crucial to the development of the event-line, theme-line, etc. Another way of talking about **thematic prominence** is in terms of foregrounding and backgrounding. That which the author wishes to be the foreground material has **thematic prominence**.

The information which is essential to the development of the discourse is thematic. The rest of the information, which may be removed or put at a different place in the discourse, is background and nonthematic. **Thematic prominence** occurs at various levels. A paragraph will have material which is thematic. An episode will likewise have material which is foreground and that which is background. How this information is marked as **thematic** is different for each language. It is obviously important that the translator be aware of which material is **thematic** in the original in order to appropriately translate it as the thematic material in the receptor language. Examples of some devices used to signal **thematic prominence** are given in the next section of this chapter. (See also K. Callow 1974:53–60.) Mismatch of usage between languages is also discussed.

Focus is distinct from thematic prominence. **Focus** says to the hearer, "This is important, listen!" It acts as a spotlight. It will choose some part of the material, and say, "This is of special importance!" It highlights one thematic event as more important than another. It marks the peak of a narrative, for example. It marks one participant as more important than another at certain points in the narrative or one procedure as the crucial one in a procedural text. **Focus** does not carry over a long portion of text. For example, if a participant is in focus, this **focus** may need to be renewed periodically throughout the text. **Focus** prominence has a more limited domain than thematic prominence does.

There is often a natural **focus** which would require special devices to change. For example, the participant which is the AGENT has natural **focus** in English narrative. But if, at a certain point in the discourse, a participant who is the AFFECTED were to be thrown into **focus**, special devices, such as change of order, would be needed to indicate this change of **focus**. (See K. Callow 1974:60–3.)

Emphatic prominence, called **emphasis**, is the kind of prominence which is more closely related to the communication situation.

Emphasis involves the speaker-hearer relationship in some way. It has to do with emotion or expectation (K. Callow 1974:63). **Emphasis** makes prominent an item of information which the narrator thinks will be surprising to the hearer, or it may warn the hearer that the emotions of the speaker are quite strongly involved. A translation which simply transfers the information, and does not also transfer the emotion of the author, will be dull and unnatural. The full meaning of the author will not have been communicated.

To translate well, the translator must study the prominence of the source text from the point of view of (1) what type of prominence there is, (2) the domain of that prominence, and (3) the intensity of the feelings of the author about the prominent information. The signals of the source language should help the translator do this. Then he must find the best devices by which to signal this prominence in the receptor language. We turn now to a review of some devices which have been found to signal prominence.

Devices used in surface structure

Prominence may be either **natural** or **marked**. For example, in the sentence *John shot the tiger with an arrow* the **natural prominence** is on *shot* as the EVENT. But in the English sentence *It was John who shot the tiger with an arrow*, there is **marked prominence** on *John* as the AGENT. Prominence is **marked** by putting the nonprominent material into a relative clause and *John* as the complement in a stative clause with a dummy topic *it*. To put the prominence on *tiger*, the AFFECTED, *tiger* would come in the stative clause, and *John* would be part of the relative clause, *It was the tiger that John shot with an arrow*. In each case, prominence is **marked** by a special device, a surface structure grammatical form.

The devices which **mark prominence** – whether **thematic, focus**, or **emphasis** – are many and varied as mentioned before. We can only present some examples here, which will hopefully encourage the translator to look for the prominence signals in the source text, and then, match this prominence in the receptor language, not by using the same signals, but by using the different signals peculiar to the receptor language.

Change of order is a common device for showing prominence in many languages. **Forefronting** is especially common. The natural **order** will have natural prominence for some element in the construction, but by changing to an unexpected or unusual **order** prominence is added. Within the clause in English, prominence may be given by moving the AFFECTED into subject position at the beginning of the sentence and using a passive as in *Peter was hit by the car*. *Peter* is **forefronted**. Putting a unit at the beginning of a clause or paragraph often marks prominence in English. Cromack (1968:309) says that in Cashinahua (Peru) the first word of the body of the text is crucial. It is "in primary focus for a paragraph or series of paragraphs." In Muyuw (Papua New Guinea) the usual **order** in a clause is subject-verb-object, but if the object rather than the subject is in focus then the **order** is object-subject-verb.

In Oksapmin (New Guinea), independent verbs normally occur in sentence final position. Any nonevent information occurring sentence final, therefore, is unexpected and carries significance within the discourse; it is marked for prominence (Callow 1974:63).

In order to mark thematic prominence in a text, some languages use a kind of a **theme statement** at the beginning. McArthur (1981:10) cites an example from Aguacatec (Guatemala) where such a **theme statement** occurs both at the beginning and end of the unit, in a sandwich structure. He says, "one group of paragraphs was found to be headed by the clause: *c'ulutxum Lu'* = *'Peter (was) obedient.'* The following material consisted of three paragraphs that developed the theme of Peter's obedience. This unit ended with a verbatim repetition of the phrase *'Peter (was) obedient.'* A statement of theme often occurs first in the unit and may be repeated at the end of the unit."

Nominalization is also a device used to indicate prominence in some languages. But in others it is used in the opposite way, as a device for backgrounding material. Literal translations of nominalized verbs can greatly distort the intended prominence. For example, Longacre (1977:14) gives the following discussion on **nominalization**.

> ...in an English discourse sometimes the purpose of nominalization is to shunt something off the event line or to in some way push it away from the spotlight. Thus, we have a sentence such as "The arrogance of his assertion completely offended me." Presumably, here the spotlight of the sentence is on the verb "offend." The sentence also tells us in a more indirect way that an assertion has been made by somebody and that the assertion was characterized by arrogance. To stop and to express the latter two concerns by means of full verbs, each in its own clause, would have detracted considerably from the fundamental thrust of the sentence, which is on the word "offend."

The function of **nominalization** in the Tucanoan languages of Colombia is very different, however. In these languages, **nominalization** is not as common as in English, and when it does occur its function is not to shunt an event away from the spotlight but to spotlight it, i.e., to put it in focus.

In Aguacatec (Guatemala, data from McArthur), **nominalization** is also a device for putting an event in focus or making it more prominent. Note the following example in which *selling* is in focus:

Ja	*chi*	*ben*	*in*	*c'ay-il.*
aspect	them	went	my	selling

'I **sold** them.'

We have already mentioned **passive voice** which often occurs when some participant other than the AGENT is the subject of the sentence. **Passive voice** is a device which is used in some languages to mark prominence. In English, the AGENT is often put in focus by using a **passive** verb and putting the AGENT in a prepositional phrase after the verb. *The tiger was shot by John* makes *John* more prominent than the form *John shot the tiger.*

Verb morphology is a common device for foregrounding and backgrounding within a text. Languages have special **tense** and **aspect affixes** which indicate the main line of the narrative or the theme line of a discussion. Aguaruna (Peru) has a **suffix** *-ka* which marks main line verbs in narrative and procedural discourse, the topic in descriptive discourse, and theme in expository discourse. Similar **affixes** are reported for many Amerindian languages. Examples from Aguaruna were given in the preceding chapter.

It is not uncommon to find a **change of tense** as a marker of major units such as the peak of a narrative. In English, a story may go along in the past **tense** and then suddenly shift to present **tense** at peak. The Foré language in New Guinea starts in the remote past **tense**, shifts to recent past as the story gains momentum, and to the present **tense** at the peak of the story – only to drop back to the remote past at the story's end (Longacre 1977a:12). Such usage of **tense** to show prominence is not uncommon. The translator will want to use the natural forms of the receptor language even when it means **changing the tense** of the source language text if the two languages do not use this device in the same way.

In Cuaiquer (Colombia), both progression (thematic prominence) and focus (highlighting of participants) are marked. The **suffix** *-ne* marks the progression by highlighting the main events. Henriksen and Levinsohn (1977:45) give the following description of the use of *-ne*:

> The suffix *-ne* is attached to linkage elements, dependent clauses, and nouns. Linkage elements unite paragraphs together, giving cohesion to the discourse as a whole. Dependent clauses unite together sentences and embedded paragraphs within a paragraph. Nouns, referring to either the agent or the

patient of an action, may be marked with *-ne* when a major participant is the referent, both in paragraphs forming the backbone of the discourse and in embedded paragraphs which do not constitute the backbone.

Notice the following example taken from Henriksen and Levinsohn (1977:60) which shows the major participant *ulam* 'armadillo', marked with the **suffix** *-ne*.

Pilgulta	*quiritne*	*manaz*	***ulamne***	*manaz*
To-cave	as-it-dug	then	the-armadillo	then

	ca	*quiriguatmis.*
	this	dug-and-went

Suasne	*manaz*	*ahuane*	*chicihtpa*	*guinguinguatmis*
Then	again	people	dug-quickly	doing

	pilne'.
	the-dirt

Pilayucman	*tailltahuane*	*sun*	***ulamne***	*ca*
Inside-dirt	after-falling	this	armadillo	this

	quillnaguatmis...
	said

"As it dug the dirt, the armadillo entered the hole. Then the people quickly dug into the dirt. After falling inside, this armadillo said..."

Tunebo (Colombia) uses a combination of **forefronting** and a **suffix** *-a* to mark the thematically prominent participants. The Tunebo language overtly marks the thematically prominent participant in a story, both for the whole story (global theme) and for each of the individual paragraphs (the local themes). The global theme is marked by occurring in a **fronted position**, preceding the dependent clause(s) which gives the setting of the discourse. In the **fronted position**, both a noun (or name) and the pronoun *ey* are used to introduce the global theme. Both are also marked with the **suffix** *-a* in narrative discourse. Note the following example (Headland and Levinsohn 1977:135):

Eya	**Utacaya**	*sisbur*	*bawoy*	*cohwyata,*	*bar*	*sucuir*	*bijacro.*
He	(name)	chicken	third	crowing	at-that-moment	bathing	went

"As the chicken crowed the third time, Utacaya bathed and went."

Special particles, or **words**, are another device for marking prominence. In Hausa, the **words** *ne* and *ce* are normally used to express identity: "It is a...." When coupled with certain grammatical changes, however, these **words** form a system of prominence. Koop (1983:11–2) gives the following examples in which location, time, goal, and actor are shifted to the front of the sentence and followed by *ne* or *ce*. In each case the prominence is on the **front-shifted item**.

Neutral form with no marked prominence			**Marked for prominence**				
1. *sun*	*zo*	*daga gifa*	*daga*	*gida*	***ne***	*suka*	*zo*
they	came	from home	from	home		they	came
			(location prominent)				
2. *ta*	*tafi*		*ita*	***ce***	*ta*	*tafi*	
she	went		she	it was	she	went	
			(actor prominent)				
3. *mun*	*zo*	*jiya*	*jiya*	***ne***	*muka*	*zo*	
we	came	yesterday	yesterday	it was	we	came	
			(time prominent)				
4. *malami*	*ya*	*fada*	*malami*	***ni***	*ya*	fada	
teacher		spoke	teacher	it was	he	said	
			(actor prominent)				

The domain of this prominence is the grammatical sentence.

Koop (1983:13) states that **particles** such as *dal, fa,* and *kam* are regularly used to highlight participants in Hausa (Nigeria). These **particles** may be used with events or with whole sentences. For example, *ina son wannan fa* meaning "I want this one, really!"

Sentence length is another device which is used in some languages to highlight the peak of a narrative. Some languages will shift to very **short sentences** at the peak of the story and the action moves very quickly. In others, the peak is marked by **extra long sentences. Extra long sentences** at peak are reported for Wojokeso (Papua New Guinea). This **extra length** at peak occurs in both narrative and procedural texts in this particular language (Longacre 1976a:223). By contrast, Aguaruna, which normally has **long sentences** in narrative, shifts to a series of one-word or two-word clauses moving very rapidly at peak (Larson 1978:69).

The **clause** or **sentence type** chosen may be a device for signaling thematic material. Independent **clauses** are usually more prominent than dependent ones. In Kuteb (Nigeria), theme is indicated by the use of independent rather than relative or embedded **clauses**. Nonthematic material appears in relative **clauses** introduced by *ti* and *ta*. This is one of the major features of Kuteb requiring restructuring in translation from English according to Koop (1983:17). Languages which have few independent **clauses** with long chaining of dependent **clauses** will have some other feature to indicate which of the dependent **clauses** are on the main-line.

In direct contrast to the Kuteb mentioned above, one function of the **relative clause** in Greek discourse is to mark thematic material. It carries information which is on the theme-line. The function of the **relative clause** would need to be determined in order to translate correctly. One would translate some Greek **relative clauses** into Kuteb with **independent clauses**.

In Mezquital Otomí (Mexico), a **rhetorical interrogative sentence** is used to reinforce a proposition already stated. A **paraphrase sentence** may also be used in this way to add significance to the previous proposition (Wallis 1971:19).

In Hausa (Koop 1983:13) whole sentences are emphasized by putting them into the form of a **negative interrogative sentence**:

ba	*na*	*ce*	*zan*	*zo*	*yau*	***ba?***
neg.	I	say	I'll	come	today	neg.

"Didn't I say I'll come today?" meaning, "I said I'd come today."

Rhetorical questions are used in many languages to signal the start of a new subject or some new aspect of the same subject. They tell what the theme of the following information is going to be. For example, in Korku (India), a **rhetorical question** is used to direct attention to the main theme being developed. A sentence like the following would draw attention to the theme: *No money left! And now in the end what was their condition? They had no money left* (Kirkpatrick 1972:30).

If one is translating from a language which frequently uses **rhetorical questions** to introduce the theme or topic of the text or section of the text, and the receptor language does not have this device for marking theme, the natural receptor language sentence type for stating theme should be used. For example, Trique of Mexico does not use **rhetorical questions** as a device for prominence. **Rhetorical questions** are used to indicate negative emotions such as rebuke or ridicule. So a statement with proper thematic markings would be substituted for the **rhetorical question**.

Source text: Who made you better than anyone else?

Receptor language: You weren't made any better than anyone else (adding the correct device to put emphasis on *you*).

Quotations, the form of direct address, is also a device used in many languages to highlight main events, including the peak of the discourse. These **rhetorical quotations** are sort of pseudo-dialogue whose function is to highlight a part of the plot structure or the main procedure or main theme (see Larson 1978:chapter 3). The function of such **rhetorical quotations** in Aguaruna (Peru) is primarily one of adding vividness and highlighting the major events. This has already been discussed somewhat on pages 257–61. **Quotations** used for highlighting are often **questions, remarks,** or **proposals** which occur without the expected ANSWER, EVALUATION, or REPLY.

In an Aguaruna story, "How the hummingbird brought fire," the two major events of the story are encoded with a **remark quotation**. There is no participant to do the speaking, just an indefinite *someone*. The two major events are the hummingbird's contact with fire and his giving it to man. They have the following form in Aguaruna (Larson 1978:66):

1. *"Tsetseaje. Jinum anagtajai," tusa itau jega.*
It-is-cold By-fire I-will-warm-it saying brought-it house

   Saying, "It's cold. I'll warm it by the fire," someone brought it into his house.

2. *...wajakii wetai tuinau, "Jempe jiin juawai.*
it-rising it-going they-said Hummingbird fire-obj is-taking

   Jempe jiin juawai."
   Hummingbird fire-obj is-taking

   ...when it rose and flew away, they said, "The hummingbird is taking fire. The hummingbird is taking fire."

The agent of *said* is never identified. An indefinite *they* is introduced in order to use a direct **quotation** to highlight this event.

Dialogue is often used in order to highlight certain episodes. But if this device is not used in the receptor language, care must be taken not to translate the **dialogue** literally with **dialogue** and thus lose its purpose, that of highlighting. Notice the further prominence signaled by the repetition inside the **quotation** of the second **quotation**, in the Aguaruna example above.

The **absence of quotations** may mark peak in a dialogue discourse. For example, in Aguaruna (Peru) a story about a *sandpiper* is almost entirely dialogue. Then at the peak, by way of contrast, there is a sudden change of rapid events **without quotations**. One verb follows another in rapid succession. (See Larson 1978:69–70 for the full example).

Rhetorical underlining occurs when the author wants to be sure that an important point is made prominent. This is done by extra words. He may employ a paraphrase which repeats the information, as mentioned for Otomí earlier; or he may use a parallelism or various other forms of repetition. **Rhetorical underlining** may occur at any level of structure, varying in usage from language to language. For example, in Hausa (Africa), the verb may be repeated for emphasis:

a	***byinn***	*wu*	emphasis:	*a*	***byinn***	*wu*	***byinn***
they	hit	him		they	hit	him	hit

In Otomí (Mexico), when the location is crucial to the development of the plot, there is repeated locative reference. In a single sentence there may be an anaphoric locative, a locative aspect in the verb affix, and a postclitic which stands for the adverb "there" (Wallis 1971:20).

Tucano (Colombia) uses embedded **paraphrase** paragraphs at the peak of a legend narrative. **Paraphrase** is a restating of the same information in another way, sometimes with the addition of some bits of information. Notice the following Tucano paraphrase paragraph (Welch 1977:244) in which *wijawʉ* and *piracuarapʉ* are restated:

Ʉsa	*tore*	*wijawʉ.*	*Naniacã*	*cinco*	*de*	*la*	*mañana*	*nicã*
We	there	we-left	Morning	five	in	the	morning	be-when-ds

ta	*wijawʉ*	*tore.*	*Ʉsa*	*bʉrʉaa*	*te*	*Piracuarapʉ.*
precisely	we-left	there	We	going-down-river	until	Piracuara

Piracuarapʉ	*ta*	*ejawʉ*	*tja.*
Piracuara	precisely	we-arrived	rep.

Emphatic pronouns are used in many West African languages. There are two **pronouns** for the same person, one emphatic and one nonemphatic (Barnwell 1975:167). Specifically in Kuteb (Koop 1983:14), there is a short and a long form of the **pronoun**. When emphasis is desired the long form is used. For third person the short form is *u* and the long form is *awu*. Notice the following sentences:

			emphasis:	*awu*	*ti*	*ku*	*ba*
u	*ku*	*ba*		he	it	is	coming
he	is	coming					

"It is he who is coming."

	emphasis:	*awu*	*ti*	*risu-wu*	*ku ba*
		he	with	head-his	coming

"He himself is coming."

In English, the use of the **pronoun** preceding the main noun (or name) is used to show the thematic nature of the participant. Notice the following example from Longacre (1977b:5):

1. When *he* came to power, *Augustus*...

2. When *Augustus* came to power...

The meaning is the same. However, in the first, *Augustus* is clearly thematic. The information to follow will be about *Augustus*. In number two, there is no indication of thematicity. The clause may simply be encoding circumstance, which is background material. By presenting the clause first with a **pronoun** and then the name, the thematicity is marked.

Pronouns are used in some languages to mark the participant line clearly in the discourse. Presence or absence of **pronouns** may be closely related to major participants versus minor participants.

Bacairi (Brazil) is also reported to have certain third-person forms which are thematic and others which are nonthematic (Wheatley 1973:105–16). Focus on the major participants in Bacairi is obligatory, and only one participant can be in focus in a given paragraph or episode. Notice the third person **pronouns** in Bacairi (Wheatley 1973:106) in Display 32.1.

	THEMATIC		**ATHEMATIC**
Nondeictic	*inara* (animate)		*mangue*
	ila (inanimate)		*manrin*
Focal	*maca*		*mau(a)nca*
	mara		*mau(a)nran*
Nonfocal	*auaca*		*uanca*
	auara		*uanran*
Deictic	*mira*		
	xira		

Display 32.1

In his article on "Nominal Elements in Bacairi Discourse," Wheatley (1973:107) states:

> *Maca* 'he (focal, thematic)' is the pronoun used first in a discourse, generally to introduce the main character. *Maca* is also used for any new character who is placed in focus later. If a change of actor is desired once focus is established, one uses the nonfocal thematic pronoun *auaca* 'he' for the new actor. This is true whether the other actor is being introduced for the first time or whether he is being referred to after having been introduced elsewhere, as long as in that part of the discourse he is not the focal character.

Another aspect of focus is that it has to be reestablished periodically. From the point in a text where *maca* is used identificationally to tag a character as focal, that identification applies only over a limited span before the same character is again referred to as *auaca*. The span, which may be from two to about twenty clauses, depends upon whether other possible elements that have only a focal status (such as sickness or medicine) have occurred in the text meanwhile. It is as though main focus status were like a static electrical charge that leaks away into the atmosphere unless reestablished.

In English, the **pronoun** serves to keep the topic clearly in focus throughout the paragraph. It may mean using a passive in order to keep the same **pronoun** as subject. Note the following:

> *John went into town to do some shopping.* ***He*** *went by the library and picked up some books also. Then as **he** was coming home **he** was run into by a car and was taken to the hospital.*

Notice that the subject of every sentence is *he* once John is introduced as the subject and topic in the first clause. This is to keep the topic clear. To say *a car ran into him* and *someone took him to the hospital* would break into the topic line of English. Therefore, the **pronoun** *he* keeps *John* in focus, and the last two clauses are passive.

The **alternate use of nouns and pronouns** is also often related to the matter of major participants versus minor participants. In many languages it is assumed that the participant functioning as AGENT is in focus, and this is expressed grammatically in the subject of the clause. Cakchiquel (Guatemala) sometimes uses the passive construction to maintain focus on the major participant throughout a section of the text.

Greek, however, may have several participants as AGENTS in the same paragraph. Notice the following statement (K. Callow 1974:62) concerning problems encountered in translating from Greek into Cakchiquel:

> ...Greek may have several different participants all functioning as agents (and sometimes all as grammatical subjects) in the space of one verse. A literal translation here would cause the readers considerable confusion as focus was apparently shifted rapidly from character to character. In Cakchiquel it is natural to keep one participant in focus for several clauses, and therefore verses sound extremely unnatural if they switch focus from one participant to another and then back to the first again. In these cases Cakchiquel sometimes uses a passive construction so as to maintain focus on the first participant throughout.

In Aguaruna (Peru), a **noun** form or name is used when a new participant is introduced. As long as that same participant remains the major participant, no **noun form** is used to refer to that person, only verb affixes. If the **noun** were repeated it would mean some other person by the same name had come on stage as the major participant. A special **noun phrase** with a back reference form may be used, however. **Pronouns**, in Aguaruna, function when contrast needs to be shown between participants, but not as a way to mark the participants throughout a paragraph or discourse. If translating into English, **pronouns** would need to be used when there are none in the Aguaruna text. Notice the contrast in the two following versions of the story about the oriole and nighthawk. The **nouns** and free **pronouns** which refer to these two participants are in bold print (nouns and pronouns referring to other THINGS are not in bold print).

AGUARUNA

Tuwajame	**Chuwi**	**Sukuyan**	*iwakiu*	*yaki*	*pasugken.*
They-say	Oriole	Nighthawk-obj	caused-to-go-up	high	to-his-nest

Egkeau	*kanajattus*	*egkemau*	*pasugnum.*
Put-him	in-order-that-he-sleep	that-put-in	in-nest

Kanumain	*dekapeachu*	*pasug*	*buchittai*	*dase*	*urnpuam,*
One-able-to-sleep	did-not-feel	nest	when-moved-ds	wind	blowing-ds

ishamak	*tau,*	*"Saiju*		*iyagtatjaj.*	*Akankita*	*nugka."*
fearing	said	my-brother-in-law		I-will-fall	take-me-down	to-ground

Tutai	***Chuwi***	*tiu,*	*"Atsaa,*	*iyagchattame.*	*Jinkiipa*
Saying-ds	Oriole	said	no	you-will-not-fall	do-not-go-out

tsetsekai	*jakaim."*
from-cold	lest-you-die

ENGLISH

They say that the **Oriole** took the **Nighthawk** up high into **his** nest. **He** put **him** in it so that **he** could sleep there. However, the **Nighthawk** wasn't able to sleep. When the wind blew and moved the nest **he** was afraid. **He** said, "My **brother-in-law, I** will fall! Take **me** to the ground." The **Oriole** answered, "No, **you**'ll not fall. Don't go out or **you**'ll die of the cold."

Notice the difference in the use of the **pronouns** in English and in Aguaruna. In English, the main participant, Oriole, is named and then continues as the topic with the **pronoun** *he* as the subject of each sentence. Then Nighthawk becomes the major participant, and again the subject of the following sentences is *he*. When the *Oriole* becomes the major participant again the name, *Oriole*, is again used. In Aguaruna, the two participants *Chuwi* and *Sukuya* are named at the beginning. No **nouns** or **pronouns** occur until *Chuwi* occurs in the margin of the quotation. The AGENT of each verb is clear from the semantic content of the verbs. They are not marked. Props, such as the *nest* and the *wind*, are marked in Aguaruna by a different subject(ds) marker on the verb. This marker also occurs on the verb *say* in the quote margin. The important thing to see is that the use of **nouns** and **pronouns** to mark the participant line is very different in these two languages. If translating from Aguaruna to English, many **pronouns** and **nouns** need to be added to keep the topic clear. In translating from English to Aguaruna, **nouns** and **pronouns** will not be transferred into the receptor translation, but the verb content and verb affixes showing same and different subject will be used.

Phonological devices are used to indicate prominence in oral material. There may be special intonation patterns, stress on certain words, a change in tone, etc. Sometimes these can be indicated by punctuation in the written text, but other devices may need to be added to make the prominence clear. In Vagla (Ghana) there are special tone perturbations which draw special attention to certain elements in the clause (K. Callow 1974:60).

Ideophones in Hausa (Nigeria) and in most other African languages are a device for emphasis of the action or state signaled by the verb (Koop 1983:13).

Sometimes a **performative** will be used to give prominence to the theme or add emphasis to a particular point. The author states overtly, with a clause such as *I say to you*, before giving the point. In the Greek New Testament, a commonly used form inside the quotation is *Truly, truly, I say to you....* It is important that a translator translating from the Greek recognize these **performatives** as statements meant to add prominence and not as content statements. The purpose is not to inform the audience that one is speaking, but to add prominence to the statement which follows. In Kasem (Ghana), *I say to you* would either mean "I'm talking," which is so obvious that it would not usually be stated, or that a statement which was made previously was misunderstood, and the speaker is patiently repeating himself. Neither of these functions fit the Greek function. The translator translating into Kasem would need to look for the device most appropriate in Kasem and use that in the translation, rather than literally translating *I say to you* (K. Callow 1974:65). However, when **performatives** are stated overtly, it can be of great help to the translator in identifying the theme of the source language.

Translating prominence

We have looked at many devices which are used to indicate prominence. There are many more. Each language will have its special forms to show what is thematic, what is in focus, and what is emphasized. How, then, does the translator handle this complicated problem? In addition, cohesion and grouping are closely related to prominence in many languages.

As the translator studies the source text, he must be asking himself, "What grammatical and lexical signals indicate the main theme of a discourse in this language, and what grammatical and lexical signals indicate background or supportive material? How are focus and emphasis signaled? Who are the major participants?" A study of participant, time, and location spans, as well as theme spans, will help answer these kinds of questions.

As he analyzes a particular text, the translator must clearly answer these questions in order to make a clear statement of the meaning. Once he has identified the prominence of the source language, then he will ask the same questions about the receptor language and apply the answers to the translation.

The greatest amount of mismatch between languages probably comes in the area of devices which signal cohesion and prominence. Only the correct receptor language devices will result in a natural and easily understood translation. A misrepresentation of prominence in the translation can distort the meaning intended by the author, as well as make the translation sound very unnatural.

EXERCISES – Prominence

A. While doing the exercises for chapter 30, you wrote a short story in a language other than English. Go through the story carefully identifying all the prominence markers you can find. Look for ways theme, focus, and emphasis are indicated. Review the devices listed in this chapter. Which occur in the story you wrote? What do they mark?

B. Write about a trip you took. Write in a language other than English. First write it with the theme of how beautiful the scenery was. Then rewrite it with the theme of how difficult it was to travel as you did. Now rewrite it spotlighting one particular difficulty. Finally, rewrite it putting emphasis on some unexpected incident that occurred. What kind of changes in form did you use to give prominence in each case?

Chapter 33
The Communication Situation

In the overview, chapter 4, three kinds of meaning were discussed briefly – **referential, structural**, and **situational**. Most of the book has dealt with the referential and structural meaning of the text. It was mentioned in chapter 4 that the **situational meaning** has to do with the relationship between the author and the addressee(s), where the communication took place, when it took place, the age, sex, and social status of the speaker and hearer, the relationship between them, the presuppositions which each brings to the communication, the cultural background of the speaker and of the addressee(s), and many other matters which are part of the context in which the discourse was spoken or written. A text may be completely unintelligible to someone who does not know the culture of the original document, for example. It was also mentioned that some of the information from the **communication situation** may be left implicit. Both the author and the audience have the information in common and so it need not be stated.

In chapter 13, lexical items were looked at from the point of view of the **situational context.** (It would be good for the student to review this material before reading the rest of this chapter.) In this present chapter, we will look at the text as a whole and how it must be understood and translated in light of the communication situation.

In order to interpret a text correctly, it is necessary for the translator to know certain things about the **communication situation**. The meaning is determined in part by who the author was, the purpose he had in writing, for whom the document was written, the relationship between the author and his audience, the culture of the source text, how much common information is shared by the audience who reads the source text and the audience for whom the translation is being prepared, and other factors of the **communication situation**.

The author

The goal of the translator is to communicate to the receptor audience the same information and the same mood as was conveyed

459

by the original document to the original audience. To do this, he must have the **author's intent** firmly in mind as he translates. The translator should read the source text several times asking himself, "What was the **intent** of the author as he wrote this particular text? What information does he want to communicate, what mood, and what response did he expect from the readers?" A translator who is oblivious to such questions will not be able to produce a faithful translation. Any author must deal with such choices before he begins to write at all. In the same way, the translator must also deal with them.

An author must decide what the content of his text will be; what he wants to talk about. This choice may well be restricted by social and cultural factors. He must answer, at least in his mind, what his purpose or **intent** is. Is he simply telling a story to entertain his audience, or is he recounting some specific events in order to prove someone guilty of a crime? Is he telling a mystery and, therefore, hoping to keep his audience in suspense until the very end? Or is he supplying information which will be important in understanding how some program is operating? What is the primary purpose of the text he is going to write? Just as the original author had to answer these questions in order to write, so the translator must answer them in order to translate well. He must put himself into the shoes of the original author.

Once an author has established his **intent**, he chooses a particular discourse type for his text. Normally, if his **intent** is to entertain or to relate events of the past, he will choose to use narrative or dialogue discourse. Drama (repartee) is often used to entertain as well. If his purpose is to instruct, it is likely he will choose procedural discourse structures. If he wants to convey information about a theme, he will usually choose expository discourse structures. Sometimes, in order to develop a certain mood or liven up the text, he will choose a discourse type which is not the one expected. He will purposefully choose skewing of discourse genres for special effect. He may use procedural to recount an event as illustrated on pages 420–22. But it is important to the translator to consider why the author chose to use an unexpected discourse type. Will this same skewing be equally effective if carried over into the receptor language, or should other features be used to bring about the same effect of mood or to liven up the text?

The **intent** of the writer is stated overtly in some texts and left implicit in others. The word **performative** is used to refer to the part of a discourse which indicates the author's **intent**. A **performative** statement may also indicate the author's source of information or clarify something within the discourse. We have already given some examples of an author indicating the source of his information. Some languages will begin each discourse with a **performative statement**.

In Aguaruna, a narrative almost always has an opening which includes the word *augbauttsatjai* 'I will relate/tell' when telling a story. But if he is telling something which he saw happen, he will use *etsegkatjai* 'I will tell.' The difference has to do with the source of the information. If he did not witness it, he will use the first; if he did witness it, he will use the second **performative**. Similarly, there are special **performatives** for each discourse type (Larson 1978:41–53).

In translating from a language which is very explicit in the matter of using **performatives** to a language which leaves this information implicit, it may be that the translator will need to use a different form of opening. If he is translating from a language which does not make the **performatives** explicit into one which does, he may need to be more explicit and include this information in the opening. The translator's goal is to use the natural form of the receptor language to indicate the author's **intent** and, at times also, the author's source of information.

The author normally has full information about the culture and other situational matters related to his audience. He knows what his audience will be able to deduce without making it explicit in the text. The author's own identity, prestige, etc., will effect how he writes. In addition, he can decide to highlight some participants and background others in recounting an experience. He can make some events very important and omit others.

Certainly, the speaker's **intent** or purpose, as well as the society's purpose for a given discourse, enters into the choices made, especially in the choice of discourse type. In discourse subtypes such as fairy tale, mystery story, legend, short story, etc., the matter of the speaker's intent becomes even more crucial.

It is possible that the content of the discourse and the **intent** of the speaker may be quite different. For example, a narrative may have for its content the recounting of a journey. The **intent** or purpose in telling it may be to inform someone else, to simply entertain the audience, or to shame someone who was involved. This difference in purpose will effect the choices of the author. He will use different grammatical structures and make different choices of lexical items depending on his purpose. These choices lead to what is normally called **style**. **Style** is a patterning of choices of grammatical structures and lexicon in order to create a certain effect to carry out the intent of the author.

The author can choose the groupings he will use. He can choose to use a certain style so that the material will be easy reading and entertaining or hard to read and rather dull. He can choose the order in which the information is presented. He can choose to use highly emotive words rather than less emotive words. The choices are made because of his purpose.

   Style can be very important in certain discourse subtypes such as poetry, short story, and fairy tales. The more specific the discourse type, the more the detailed matters of **style** become relevant. And these details will not be the same from language to language. For example, the correct **style** for telling a dream in Aguaruna is for the words of the *Being* appearing in the dream to be repeated throughout. Notice the following:

| *Waimakbau* | *kaja* | *atiamu.* | | *Chah,* | *dii* | *diit* |
| Vision | sleep | that-which-touches | | Oh, | see | see-much |

| *wainmashchabaijai* | *imaa* | *imaanikbaijai.* | | "*Mantuau,* |
| I-saw-a-vision | great | I-felt-the-greatness | | He-who-killed-mine |

| *mantuau* | *etusaayaa,* | *etusaayaa* | *tuigki,* | *tuigki,* |
| he-who-killed-mine | keep-doing-to-me | keep-doing-to-me | where | where |

| *iika,* | *iika,* | *jiyakbau* | *jiyakbau* | *ataja,* | *ataja,* |
| revenging | revenging | one-who-kills | one-who-kills | I-will-be | l-will-be |

| *bashi,* | *bashi* | *jintanum,* | *jintanum* | *dawen,* | *dawen* |
| abandoned | abandoned | on-the-road | on-the-road | tracks | tracks |

| *yututkunua,* | *yututkunua.* | *Mina,* | *mina* | *pataajukes,* |
| I-covering | I-covering | Mine | mine | perhaps-my-own-family |

| *pataajukes;* | | *aawa,* | *aawa;* | *nunake,* | *nunake,* |
| perhaps-my-own-family | | it-is | it-is | to-just-that-one | to-just-that-one |

| *juaknua,* | *juaknua* | *dekaske,* | *dekaske* | *etegkeaknua,* | *etegkeaknua* |
| I-taking | I-taking | truly | truly | I-choosing | I-choosing |

| *nuiya,* | *nuiya.* | *Bashi,* | *bashi* | *jinta,* | *jinta* |
| from-that-one | from-that-one | Abandoned | abandoned | road | road |

| *akinkunua,* | *akinkunua.* " |
| I-changing | I-changing |

   Translation: This is about a vision which I saw while sleeping. Oh, I saw a powerful vision and I felt its greatness. The spirit being said, "Where someone is always killing my relatives, right there I will kill in revenge, wiping out his tracks and leaving an abandoned trail. Perhaps it will be my relative. Yes, I might actually choose a relative. I will change his trail into an abandoned trail."

The translator will ask himself why the original author chose the forms he used. What intent led to these choices? And then he will ask how the same intent can be created in the receptor language translation.

In some texts, the author will clearly state his **intent**. There may be formulaic ways of indicating intent as in such statements as, "Now I am going to tell you the story about..." which is a clear marker of narration and may in some languages indicate a myth, for example. The author may take a whole paragraph at the beginning, or at the end, or both to state his intent and explain the purpose of writing the discourse.

In a general way, the purpose of each discourse genre can be summarized (Larson 1978:144–45). A **narrative discourse** is usually told to entertain or to inform about past events, whether actual or legendary. It further has the intent of teaching group norms and values in a covert and interesting way. A **procedural discourse** clearly has the purpose of teaching or instructing how to do something. **Expository discourse**, on the other hand, is concerned with teaching or informing about a certain theme. **Descriptive discourse** gives information about a certain item or event. It describes the item or event in order to convey information to the listeners. Also, there is often an aesthetic purpose, a desire to please by choosing words which will create a visual picture in the mind. **Hortatory discourse** has as its purpose to persuade, exhort, ridicule, discipline, or command. It may include overt teaching of the norms and values of the society. The author will choose quite different forms and lexical items to persuade than to ridicule. **Drama** (repartee) is most often intended to entertain or to add vividness when embedded within a narrative and also, to affect the emotions. **Dialogue** is a combination of narrative and repartee purposes. As we have noted before, an author may choose **dialogue** to highlight major parts of a narrative. What is important is that the translator establishes firmly in his mind the intent of the author and his reasons for choosing a certain surface structure discourse type before beginning to translate at all.

In many ways, the **emotional tone** of a passage is the key to real communication effectiveness. The author may wish to create a feeling of urgency, persuasiveness, tentativeness, exuberance, or despondency. Whatever the **tone** of the source text, built into it by choices of tense, mood, voice, and choice of the main action verbs, it is important that this same emotion be communicated in the translation. For an effective transfer of the **tone** of a text, the translator must be well acquainted with both the source and receptor language and culture.

Understanding the **attitude of the author** is very important in a correct interpretation of a text. The speaker has a certain **attitude** towards the information he is communicating, the source of the information, and its reliability. He will also have a certain **attitude** toward the audience. Each language will have special ways of communicating this **attitude** of the author. It may be by a direct statement of some kind about the source of the information – *I say..., so and so told me..., I suppose that..., I conclude that..., it is rumored that..., apparently such and such happened.* The author may consider the information reliable and use such expressions as *undoubtedly* or *undeniably.* On the other hand, he may put the responsibility on someone else for the reliability by something like *so and so says.* The author may also indicate his approval or disapproval of the information.

Some languages have lexical signals to indicate the **attitude** of the author towards the information. For example, notice the following comments by Grimes (1975:235–36):

> ...in Nambiquara of Brazil, declarative statements and possibly questions require the speaker to specify one or another category of *verification.* This distinguishes eyewitness statements from statements based on deduction or conjecture, on the one hand, and from statements of what is common knowledge in the society, on the other. For example, "the tree fell over" could be stated in such a way as to assert that the speaker saw it fall and is reporting what he saw, that he came across it lying on the ground and concluded that it got that way because it fell or that he and everybody else is aware that it fell because someone else reported it first.

If the source text does not indicate where the author got his information, the translator may need to deduce this as best he can in order to fulfill the requirements of the receptor language to indicate the author's point of view on this matter. There will, without doubt, be some clues in the source text, even though they are not overt as in the receptor language.

The author may choose to be neutral about the characters in a story he is writing, or he may choose to stand alongside one of them. He "adopts the viewpoint of that character as his vantage point" (Longacre 1976:210). Notice the following quotation from Longacre:

> Vantage point is morphologically marked in the structure of Oksapmin (New Guinea). In one sort of Oksapmin narrative, one can single out one person or one set of persons as the vantage point of a story in the third person. All verbs

which refer to these people as agents must have one type of verb morphology while all verbs which refer to other people as agents must have a different type of verb morphology. The hearer is made certain by the very verb morphology at whose side he is standing in the course of the story. This device also serves for keeping participants straight in the course of the story so that fewer proper nouns or other ways of explicit reference must be used, once the reference of the morphological categories is established.

Audience

The author's attitude towards the **audience** also plays an important part in the communication situation. Every good writer writes with his **audience** in mind. He writes to a certain person or group of people. The translator must be aware of for whom the original text was written. But he also has a further factor; who is his translation intended for? Both of these **audiences** will come into play as he works on the translation. In analysis of the source document, he will be considering the original **audience**; in the restructuring into the receptor language, he will be taking into account the **audience** which will read the translation.

> ...the speaker adjusts the form of his message and its expression to the intellectual and emotional composition of his receivers, to the historical, social, economic, and other determinants of the world in which he himself and the receivers of his message live, to the aims that he has set himself to achieve with this message, etc. (Ivir 1975:206)

In describing Denya (Cameroon) discourse, Abangma (1987:28–46) shows how the introduction of a narrative text often includes establishing relationship between the speaker and the hearers. Certain formulaic expressions are used. In oral discourses, this relationship is kept through the discourse in a number of ways including "cry and response, songs, repetitions, digressions, rhetorical questions, evaluations, and other ways."

If a communicator wants to communicate the same message to several different groups of people, even within his own culture, he might very well write it differently for different groups. It is not likely that the message would be stated the same way for two different communication situations; therefore, it is important to ask questions about the group to whom the original author was communicating and about the group for whom the translation is being made.

Ivir (1975:208) goes so far as to say that:

In addition to the requirements concerning the translator's knowledge of the two languages and two cultures, there is one more procedural requirement that he should meet: he should try to establish the state of social interaction in which the original message was expressed and then, adjusting his own expression of the message in translation to the characteristics of the social interaction in which he is involved with his audience, he should try to replicate with his audience the process of communication that the original author had gone through with his audience.

This underlines the importance of a conscious research of the original communication situation by the translator before he translates. It also emphasizes the importance of his thinking about the **audience** for whom he is translating. There will be some differences in the communication situations of the source text and the translation. The translator should be aware of these differences and find ways to compensate for them so that the original message is communicated in the new context.

One of the main differences will be in general information known to the author and **audience**. The author has his store of knowledge, all that he has learned and experienced. He writes from that knowledge bank. Since no two people have the same set of knowledge, the readers of the discourse will not have the same knowledge bank as the writer. This is why a writer must know to whom he is writing. As he writes, he is thinking about the **audience**, filling in details that he thinks the **audience** does not know, but leaving implicit other information which he expects they do know. Perhaps the most extreme example is people telling folk tales to one another. Everyone knows the story. The information is all familiar, who did what and what they said. The purpose of telling it at all is usually to entertain. And so, if the speaker decides to leave out some part, the audience does not lose the thread of the story. In fact, they may supply it. In an oral situation, they may remind the narrator that he left something out.

The problem for the translator comes from the fact that he is often translating a document containing information which is not part of the knowledge and experience of the receptor **audience**. The translator himself may not have the same knowledge as the original author. So he will have to study other documents of the time, read commentaries of various kinds, use dictionaries and lexicons, encyclopedias, and various reference books in order to increase his knowledge before he can translate the document. But he must also keep in mind that the **audience** for whom he is translating does not have this information either.

An author usually has in his mind an overall structure of the discourse – the story he wishes to tell or the theme he wishes to expound. How much detail he will include depends on how important it is to the main overall purpose or theme of the discourse. He adds more details at certain points because he wants to highlight a particular event or procedure. He may add evaluative comments as he moves along. He will add some collateral material if he feels his **audience** needs that or a flashback to some previous episode.

Because of the lack of sameness between the knowledge bank of the original **audience** and the knowledge bank of the receptor **audience**, the translator will feel the need to make a good deal of information explicit which the original author left implicit because his **audience** already knew this information. At the same time, he must be very careful that by adding this information he is not changing the intent of the original author. The addition of a great deal of material, at a certain point in the text, may leave the impression on the receptor **audience** that something is a very important point, when, as a matter of fact, it was quite incidental in the source text. (This will be discussed in more detail in chapter 34.)

The educational level of the **audience** also affects the restructuring of the text. If the original audience and the **audience** for whom the translation is intended are of the same educational level, there will be little problem. However, if the translation is for persons with less education or for newly literate people, the translator will need to make appropriate adjustments. If the translator wants the translation to be read by the well educated, and also the newly literate, it will be necessary to present the translation in a "common language" which will overlap between the two and be acceptable to both (Wonderly 1968).

There may actually be dialects according to class system, according to education, or according to the amount of bilingualism. The translator will need to decide on dialectical matters before beginning his work. If written in the dialect of the bilinguals, with many borrowings from another language, it may not be understood by the less bilingual. These matters are complicated. The translator must decide who his **audience** is going to be.

Other aspects of the communication situation

A communication which is treated as an event abstracted from the **social context** of which it is a part becomes nearly unintelligible. The **social relationship** between the original author and his audience affects the content and form of the original document. These **relationships** may have to do with such matters as age, status, and the culture's ideas of superiority and inferiority. There may be special forms of politeness used when addressing the socially superior and special forms for addressing young people or children.

If, in the analysis of the source text, the translator becomes aware of the fact that such special forms are being used, he will not simply translate the forms literally, but rather, he will identify the **social relationship**. Then he will use appropriate forms in the receptor language for addressing persons in that same social class or age bracket. However, his task is more complicated if he is translating for a different social level or age level than that for which the original author wrote.

Notice, for example, the following differences in the usage of Japanese personal pronouns depending on the social relationship (from Tobita 1971:54–5):

> *Abrupt-Vulgar (male)*: (...very often used among young men, espe-cially students, in a very friendly conversation, but it can be rude in certain situations...)
>
> *Familiar (male)*: (...used by men, but currently a small but increasing number of girl students, young mothers, female school teach-ers, and young female TV entertainers use...when they talk to their boy friends, sons, boy pupils, and fellow performers...)
>
> *Familiar (female)*: (Young women often use...in familiar conversation...)
>
> *Polite (male or female)*: ...
>
> *Honorific Very Polite*: ...

The **location** of the original writing may also affect the translator's job. If the original document was written in and about a desert environment and is to be translated for people who are unfamiliar with such an environment, such as tropical forest people, the translator would be likely to experience some difficulty in his search for vocabulary, as discussed in chapter 13. However, if the receptor audience was acquainted with desert cultures and geography through visiting other areas or through previous reading and education, the problem would not be so great. Matters of climate, topography, flora, and fauna all enter into the problem. The original author assumed a common knowledge of this kind of information. For example, the word *harmattan* would immediately bring with it many memories and experiences for the desert dwellers of Africa. Even when explained, it would have only a very superficial meaning to people who had lived all their lives in the tropical forest or in northern Europe.

The **time** of the writing of the source document will affect the translation. If one is translating a text written only last week, the gap which must be spanned will not be as great as if one is translating a text written a thousand years ago. The knowledge bank for the author and translator will be more or less the same and that of the two audiences also will be overlapping when translating a current document. But in translating a document of some antiquity, the gap between the original author, the translator, and between the two audiences will be much greater.

The translator should make every effort to be faithful to the historical facts and information of the source text. When translating a document written in a different period in time, the translator should not remove it from its time setting but find ways to communicate the historical information in natural, present-day linguistic forms. A natural and clear translation is not dependent on familiar information. New information, even historical facts, can be presented in a natural and clear manner. But if a translator ignores this difference of **time**, distortion may enter in.

The following are two translations of a document written several thousand years ago describing a dinosaur. In the second, there is a phrase used which is not appropriate for a translation of a document set in a **time** long before *steamrollers* existed.

1. His undersides are jagged potsherds, leaving a trail in mud like a threshing sledge.

2. His belly is covered with scales as sharp as shards; he drags across the ground *like a steamroller*.

The **occasion** for the writing of a document may also be crucial to understanding the intent of the author. The translator asks himself, "What was the **occasion** of the writing of this text?" A text written to be read as a political speech will be quite distinct from a speech written to be delivered as a sermon at a funeral. The choices will be more than just vocabulary differences. There will be appropriate openings and closings. A particular genre may be more appropriate for one than for the other. The audience may be addressed by quite different vocative forms. An awareness of the **occasion** for the writing of the source text will help the translator choose the forms to be used in the translation.

Culture

Throughout this book, reference has been made many times to the relationship between culture and language and the effect this has on the translation process. The reader might want to review these references at this time. In chapter 4, the importance of implicit cultural information in determining the meaning of a text is discussed. The importance of cultural considerations in finding adequate vocabulary for the translation is considered in chapters 9, 13, 16, and 17.

Language is a part of culture and, therefore, translation from one language to another cannot be done adequately without a knowledge of the two cultures as well as the two language structures. Ivir (1975:208) says, "The translator must know the subject matter which he is translating. He must know the culture from which the message originally came as well as the culture for which it is being translated." Translation is "the transference of meaning from one patterned set of symbols occurring in a given culture...into another set of patterned symbols in another culture..." (Dostert 1955:124).

All meaning is culturally conditioned. And the response to a given text is also culturally conditioned. Each society will interpret a message in terms of its own culture. The receptor audience will decode the translation in terms of its own culture and experience, not in terms of the culture and experience of the author and audience of the original document. The translator then must help the receptor audience understand the content and intent of the source document by translating with both cultures in mind.

Culture is a complex of beliefs, attitudes, values, and rules which a group of people share. The writer of the source document assumed the beliefs, attitudes, values, and rules of the audience for which he wrote. The translator will need to understand them in order to adequately understand the source text and adequately translate it for people who have a different set of beliefs, attitudes, values, and rules.

It is inevitable that the author's **worldview** will come through in what he writes. Each individual is shaped by the sociocultural patterns of his society. A person's patterns of thought are those considered natural in his culture. Often he is not overtly aware of them and yet they do influence his writing in many ways. The language itself reflects various aspects of the culture. For example, a culture which has social levels that are highly developed will often have whole sets of pronouns to accommodate these levels. The culture affects the vocabulary which is present in the language (pages 148–49).

Wheatley (1970) reports that the Bacairi people of Brazil believe that each person should do as he himself pleases. No one can coerce or discourage anyone from doing anything he wants to. This practice extends to children as well. It is an egalitarian society, and no one wants to stand out. The chief has no real authority over anyone else. Some members of the society gain respect because of knowledge or age. The shaman probably has the most unofficial authority in the group. If a translator were translating into this language, a text from a language belonging to a culture with a highly developed political authority structure, some care would need to be taken. It would be easy to produce a text which would not be understood at all by the

Bacairi. Somehow the cultural information about political authority would have to be communicated for the translated text to make sense to the Bacairi audience.

Throughout Melanesia, the **worldview** of the people includes the basic concept of powers which influence a person. These powers "...can be felt behind any major event. The source of the power lies in spirit beings, creative and regulative deities, and particularly in the ancestral spirits. Power is everywhere..." (Ahrens 1977:143). Most westerners do not share this notion of power as a part of reality. When translating from a Melanesian language to English or English to a Melanesian language, this difference can be crucial in the understanding of what is communicated by the translation. These differences of cultural **viewpoint** cannot be ignored.

In a culture such as that of Japan, levels of social status are very important and must be indicated in translating into Japanese. On the other hand, if one were translating a document from Japanese into English, it would not be appropriate to try to keep all of the distinctions of Japanese social status in English. In Japanese, there is a choice of imperative ranging from abject humility to imperial decree (Hoffer 1980:168). When translating into English, these distinctions would not be kept, although there are certain forms that are more formal which would be used with those in authority and less formal ones for ordinary people. The translator needs to be aware of the differences so that he can adequately handle them in translating.

In Africa, a friend might come and put down a couple of dishes of food on one's doorstep and say, "Eat!" To a person of some other culture, such as American, it might sound very harsh, and the person would feel they must obey. But, as a matter of fact, that is not the intent in the African culture. The friend has cooked supper and is simply inviting the other person to share it. That person is free to eat a full meal or just take a few mouthfuls and then say that they are satisfied. If in a text being translated from an African language and culture into English, such a situation were a part of the story, the translator would not use the English imperative "Eat!" The translator should rather say, "Would you like some?" or "Help yourself, if you would like." The words *would like* give the attitude and cultural information which was communicated by the command "Eat!" in the African story.

Many times there are THINGS or EVENTS which at first glance might seem to be identical but which have a very different **value** or significance in a second culture. Notice, for example, the following contrast described by Franklin (1979). The **value** in Western cultures is compared with the Papua New Guinea culture:

gift:

> **Western**: Given to friends, often in exchange, not always voluntary and frequently with reciprocal, but nonequal gift in return.

> **Papua New Guinea**: Given to those in particular exchange or kin relation. Given to seal a relation. Larger (more valuable) gift given to put the recipient in an obligatory relationship.

forgiveness:

> **Western**: Based on a person first of all admitting guilt. Then as a compassionate feeling to the one who is socially ashamed.

> **Papua New Guinea**: A cancellation based on mutual agreement and understanding. Viewed as a legitimate payment to compensate for something.

And so, we see that although the *giving of a gift* and the *forgiving of someone* are common to both cultures, the **values** and implications are different.

Headland (1974:416), in discussing **cultural values** and the differences between cultures, gives the following example from Manobo:

> For example, in a Manobo language in the Philippines, the translator correctly rendered the words "Your daughter is dead," as "Your daughter is very sick." This complies with the deep-set Philippine value of using euphemistic speech to convey a message. This is the actual phrase one would use in Manobo society to tell a man his child had died; and this phrase, rendered in a culturally appropriate way, is correctly understood by the Manobo readers.

Notice also the following illustration from Newman (1977:402–3):

> But the problem of translating does not in any sense end with solving the problem of language structure. We must also pay close attention to the differences in the cultural backgrounds between the readers of the original and the readers of the translation. What is meant here may be illustrated to some degree by using a paragraph from the Malay short story *Kau Mesti Sunat, Kata Bapa* by A. Samuel Ismail. What follows is a fairly literal rendering of the Malay.

> *Mother told Jabar who lived behind my house to take me to the tomb of Habib Noh to ask safety from that shrine. I took along flowers, incense, a comb of bananas, and some yellow glutinous rice to the shrine. And in return, I was given some fine yellow cloth to be made into a bracelet and a belt.*

Everything in this text is clear to the Malay reader, because he is familiar with this custom. Nothing of the emotional value is lost for him either, because he knows the significance of each event and object mentioned. But several problems exist for a reader like myself.

(1) *who lived behind my house.* This expression reflects the structure of the Malay village, something unknown to Western readers. In my own culture such a statement would carry quite bad feelings about the situation; it would imply that Jabar was a poor man and couldn't afford a place of his own, and so he just lived out back, behind my house. In American English the proper cultural equivalent would be something like "our next door neighbor," or "who lived nearby."

(2) *to ask safety from his shrine.* At least two problems exist for the English reader. Firstly, the Malay word *selamat* (here rendered "safety") covers an area of meaning different from the English word "safety." What is really meant is more precisely conveyed by the word "blessing" in English. Then, secondly, it is clear to the Malay reader that this blessing is asked from Habib Noh, not from his shrine. He is considered a saint, and in popular thought his departed spirit can provide the seeker with certain benefits. So then, for the English reader who does not know this cultural background, it will be helpful to translate "to Habib Noh's tomb, to ask for his blessing."

(3) *a comb of bananas.* This is, to be sure, a small matter, but in English we speak of a "hand of bananas."

(4) *yellow glutinous rice.* I tested this expression on some rather well-educated people in the United States, and every one of them had a negative reaction. I could have said, "yellow sticky rice," and for some people I did use this term, with an even worse reaction. It is possible to keep the

technical term *pulut kuning* and use a footnote, but this is a short story, and readers don't like to have to shift back and forth from text to footnote in reading this kind of story. On the basis of these observations, it would seem best to me to use some terms in English that express clearly and concisely the function and value of *pulut kuning* in the Malay context, because neither component of meaning, "glutinous" or "yellow," is really essential in the context. I would propose something like "some choice rice" or "some specially prepared rice" as an approximate cultural equivalent.

(5) *I took along...to the shrine.* Perhaps the purpose of his taking along these objects to the shrine is clear, but most English readers whom I tested had no clue as to the significance of this act. For the Malay reader the meaning comes out from the text, without an additional comment; but for the poor, ignorant English reader it is helpful to add the information: "as an offering."

(6) *and in return I was given.* Once again there is a custom that is clearly known and appreciated both by the writer and by his original readers. But I am forced to ask, "was given by whom?" His father? Mother? Or someone else? The problem is easily solved in translation by changing the passive "was given" to an active and then stating the subject of the verb clearly: "And in return, *the keeper of the shrine* gave me..."

The cultural setting of the source document must be understood by the translator if he is to give a correct interpretation of the text he would translate. If the original document is from a culture other than his own, he will need to make a special study of the source language cultural context. For example, in some Waurá (Brazil) texts, participant identification is by cultural clues. All members of the tribe know the culture and so, for example, in the description of a certain ceremony, the participants are not identified. The audience knows who did what. The mention of certain cultural items serves to clarify and identify the participants. Notice the following example (Richards 1979:32):

Punupa	*amunau*	*patakata*	*kamalupihi*
See	chief	sit-cause	clay-pot

Then the chief places a clay bowl (on the ground).

In the narrative, two participants have already been identified as *chief*. The question then is to which *chief* is being referred. But there is no ambiguity for those who know the culture. Richards (1979:33) says:

> ...only the Waurá make *clay bowls*. Thus, it has to be the Waurá *chief*, and not the Kalapalo *chief*, the latter would be selling *belts and necklaces, not clay pots*. Moreover, it is the visitors and not the host of the festival, who put down trade items to be bought in the trading session which is a part of all such festivities.

In discussing the narrator's use of cultural information, Richards (1979:33) further comments that:

> ...with a certain background knowledge of the culture, the listener can understand who did what even when this is left implicit. The result of this is that the narrator has the possibility of using this freedom in how he identifies his participants, to highlight some, and leave others as minor characters.

In other texts in Waurá, the clues for participant identification are found in the linguistic forms of the text rather than in the cultural knowledge. The use of linguistic clues versus cultural clues will vary depending on the information being communicated and the audience to whom it is being communicated.

Obviously, a translator translating from Waurá into another language, say Portuguese, would not be able to count on clues from the culture to identify participants. His audience does not know these clues. He will rather use the natural forms (the linguistic clues) from the Portuguese language. This may mean that he will need to be much more explicit in introducing participants and keeping track of them throughout the discourse.

One might wonder if it is possible to translate the document of one culture and language into another effectively. We have talked mostly of the areas where problems may arise. But on the other side, we must be encouraged by the fact that there are underlying bases for human communication whether within a language group or from one group to another. Nida (1964:53–5) lists four basic factors which make communication possible and, therefore, make possible the translation of a message from one language and culture to another. These are: (1) the similarity of mental processes of all people, (2) similarity of somatic reactions (similar physical responses to emotional stimulus), (3) the range of common cultural experience, and (4) the capacity for adjustment to the behavioral patterns of others.

The specific details may vary from culture to culture, but the mutual humanness which gives us the factors listed above, allows people to accept that there are differences and to grasp the difference and understand the message. The important thing for the translator is to know what information must be made explicit in the translation in order for the receptor audience to encode the correct intended meaning of the author. That will keep him from assuming that by simply saying in the text *he smiled* (a common somatic reaction) that the receptor will interpret it as *a friendly smile* and not *ridicule*. The function of *smiling* to indicate friendliness is not universal.

The primary criterion for the translator is that he must constantly think about what his translation is communicating. He keeps watching for anything that would give a wrong meaning or could be misunderstood. He is also alert for places where the translation is ambiguous and needs to be clarified. He certainly does not want to include information that carries no meaning at all. So his question is, "What do the receptors understand from this translation? Is it as close as possible to what the original author intended to be understood?" A careful translator will check his translation with several people, asking questions to be sure they understand what the source text meant to communicate.

EXERCISES – The Communication Situation

A. Write, in your mother tongue, an account of a trip you took recently. Then rewrite the same account to each of the following (idea for this exercise is from Stine 1972):

    1. to a friend so as to amuse him

    2. to a child five years old

    3. to older relatives at home

    4. to a friend in order to grieve him (make him sad)

B. On page 473, there is a paragraph quoted from a Malay short story by A. Samuel Ismail. Cultural notes are given, quoted from Newman (1977). Study the paragraph and the notes. Translate the paragraph into a language other than English in such a way that it will be clearly understood.

Chapter 34
Information Load

The goal of the translator is to communicate the same information as was communicated by the source text. Information which is thematic in the source will, hopefully, be thematic in the translation. Some information is central, that is, it is crucial, to the understanding of the narrative or argument. It must be kept central in the translation. Other information is background information added for clarification or orientation and should not be made central. These are matters which we have discussed in previous chapters. We have also discussed the fact that the information will have quite a different form and may be distributed differently in the translation than in the source text. In the process of making needed adjustments, the distinction between mainline and support information must be handled carefully.

There is another aspect of how information is handled which has only been hinted at so far. This is the matter of the **information load**, the rate at which information, especially new information, may be introduced into the text. The **information load** is related to the speed at which new information is introduced and to the amount of new information which the language normally incorporates in particular constructions. Some languages introduce information slowly. Others use complicated noun phrases which allow for information to be introduced more rapidly.

Within the same language, there will be a great deal of difference in **information load** for various styles of writing. Technical materials usually have a higher **information load** than novels, for example.

Individuals tend to differ in the rate at which they introduce information in their speech and writing. We all know people who speak very directly and rapidly, including a lot of information in a rather short speech. We also know others who seem to ramble on and on. They use a lot of words, but the **information load** is very slight. Little important information is communicated. So the difference in **information load** may be individual, may depend on the audience being addressed, and may also vary from language to language.

477

Notice the following example. Two texts about the *turbine* are given. The second is easier to read than the first. The **information load** is not as "heavy" in the second. (Example from Barnwell 1980:123):

A. The steam turbine obtains its motive power from the change of momentum of a jet of steam flowing over a curved vane. The steam jet, in moving over the curved surface of the blade, exerts a pressure on the blade owing to its centrifugal force. This centrifugal pressure is exerted normal to the blade surface and acts along the whole length of the blade. The resultant combination of these centrifugal pressures, plus the effect of changes of velocity, is the motive force on the blade. (from E. H. Lewitt: *Thermodynamics Applied to Heat Engines*)

B. The principle of the turbine is extremely simple. If the lid of a kettle is wedged down, when the water boils, a jet of steam will issue from the spout. If this jet is projected against the blades of a fan or any sort of wheel shaped like the old-fashioned water-wheel, it will, obviously, drive it round. In the power station, steam is generated in huge boilers, and very often a temperature as high as 850 degrees Fahrenheit at a pressure of sometimes 1,000 lbs. per sq. in. is built up before the steam is released from the boiler to the turbine jets.

The turbine comprises two parts, the rotor or moving part, and the stator or fixed portion. Instead of a single nozzle with one jet, there are a large number of nozzles... (from: *How and Why it Works*, published by Odhams)

As can be seen by studying the above examples, highly technical words make understanding more difficult. Relating the new information to something familiar makes it easier to understand. Long sentences and complicated grammatical constructions make it harder for the reader to follow what is being said. There are many factors which are involved in the **information load** of a particular text. The translator needs to be familiar with these in order to make a translation which will be easily understood by the receptor language audience.

There are a number of special translation problems related directly to **information load**:

1. There will be information in the source text and culture which is *unknown* to the speakers of the receptor language. (Already mentioned in chapters 13, 16, and 33.)

2. The receptor language will have different ways of handling *old versus new information* within the text itself. The rate at which *new information* may be introduced will vary from language to language as well as the ways in which it is introduced.

3. In each language there are *expectancy chains*, that is, certain words or phrases are expected to follow certain others.

4. *Redundancy patterns and functions* will not match between languages. The redundancy of the source text must not be translated literally, but on the other hand, the redundancy patterns of the receptor language must be fully developed in the translation in order to keep the **information load** from being too "heavy."

5. Some *implicit information* of the source language and culture will need to be made *explicit* in the translation. At the same time, some *explicit information* of the source text will need to be made *implicit* in the translation.

Each of these problems will be discussed below. Although we have separated them for discussion, in a very real sense they are all related to one another. The translator is constantly faced with the question of **information load**. If the translation is too "heavy," that is, the rate of new information is too rapid, the receptor audience will not be interested in reading the translation. A well-educated audience will read a "heavier" text more easily than will a newly literate person. The **information load** and the rate of introducing new information must be appropriate to the audience for whom the translation is intended.

Known and unknown information

In chapter 16, the matter of finding lexical equivalents, when the CONCEPTS are **unknown** to the receptor language audience, was discussed. Solutions included using a generic word with modification, modification by comparison, or using a loan word with modification. These solutions do help to communicate the meaning of the source language CONCEPT. At the same time, however, they may add to the information load. Such equivalent expressions do not easily bring to the mind of the reader a clear idea of what the THING or EVENT being described is like. He has never seen it. Even with the descriptive phrase, he must use his imagination, rather than relating the phrase to a **known** object or action. If many **unknown** CONCEPTS are introduced in a short amount of text, such descriptive expressions can make it hard for the reader to understand. After the descriptive phrase has been used several times, it becomes familiar and is no longer **unknown**.

Just as unfamiliar phrases add to the information load, so technical terms and unusual combinations of words add to the load. Ordinary everyday language is the easiest to understand and carries the least information load, because it is familiar. In the same way, familiar themes or topics make for easier understanding. If the text is about a completely new idea or an **unknown** event, it may be necessary to stretch out the translated text, that is, to tell it more slowly, with added redundancy and some added information to clarify. A good example is the translation of the Bible done by Judson into the language of Burma. This Bible is a third longer than the Bible in English. Before printing it, he checked it with Buddhist monks to make sure that they could understand it. For clarity, the text had to be expanded considerably. But after over a hundred years, it is still understood and used by the people.

If one is translating a historical document, that is, a text which tells about events which happened and were written about many years ago, special care will need to be given to the information load. The translator will want to be faithful to the historical setting. He will want the facts to be as they were represented in the source text. It is often necessary, when dealing with a historical document, to add introductory material to describe the setting and historical facts before beginning the actual translation. This helps the reader to become acquainted with much of the **unknown information** apart from the translation itself. The translator will not want to make the translation sound to the hearers as if the events had just happened recently in their own village. Pictures and footnotes help make the **unknown** CONCEPTS of the source text easier to be understood and lighten the information load (see Barnwell 1983a:24).

All meaning is culturally conditioned. The receptor language readers will interpret the message in terms of their own culture. They cannot draw on the experiences of the source text writer, but only on their own. The translator must make it possible for the reader to understand the message in light of the source text background. To do this he must supply, at some point, the information needed. Some can be woven into the translation, when appropriate, but much of this background will need to be given in introductions, notes, or glossaries.

If a text is highly predictable, it will be easy for the reader to follow. If it is less predictable, it will be more difficult. Because of this, special care must be taken by the translator when referring to unfamiliar objects and to activities which are **unknown**. The translator must try to introduce new objects and events in such a way that the reader will not be distracted from the main theme of the text.

For example, the sentence, *The president, wearing a grey suit, left the plane*, would carry a lot of **known** information in some countries where it is expected that the president will wear a suit when traveling. Even the color *grey*, although not predictable, is one of a small range of choices that would fit the circumstance (example from Geoffrey Hunt). However, if translating for a culture unfamiliar with *presidents, suits,* and *planes*, this rather simple sentence would contain a lot of

unknown information. (There are few places in the world today where this would actually be true.) When the information is **known**, and, therefore, more or less predictable, the load is not "heavy." But a translator might want to include all the information with something like this: *The man who was the chief for the whole country came out of, and left, the machine that flies. He was wearing cloth the color of ashes which covered his whole body.* All of the unknown information is spelled out in descriptive phrases. But the result is an **overload** of new information. The whole point of the narration is lost in the mass of detail used to present all of the information of the source text and culture. If *the president* has already been identified and described, a shorter form could now be used for *president*, such as, *the chief.* The same may be true for *the plane.* Perhaps only *machine* would be sufficient. What he was wearing may still present a problem. If a lot of attention is given to what in the original is a small detail, the focus of the sentence could be changed or lost. Instead of describing the suit in detail, some generic phrase, indicating that he was "dressed up," might be sufficient. The result would be something like *the chief, who was dressed up, left the machine* or *the chief, dressed in fine clothes, left the machine.*

Another example concerning **known** and **unknown** information is given by Wonderly (1968:40):

> ...a handbook on automobile maintenance written for the mechanic may use the normal technical language of the trade; but if the same information were to be translated adequately into language suitable for a history professor, many technical concepts would have to be expressed by descriptive phrases and explanatory sentences, and the resulting material would be much longer. The professor's channel capacity, for automotive subject matter, is more limited and thus calls for a slower rate of information flow and hence a longer form of the message.

Every message includes some information which is **known** and some which is **unknown**. If there is a great deal of **unknown** information, the rate of presentation of the information will need to be slower. If the rate is too fast, the reader will not understand, or part of the information will be lost. The information flow will depend on the receptor language speaker's background knowledge of the subject matter being presented. Sometimes the form of the message will need to be "stretched out" in order to communicate clearly.

Known and **unknown** information has to do with the relationship between the source text and the receptor language and culture. It is based on the differences of experiences and culture. The information being presented in the source text may be completely foreign to the receptor audience.

Old and new information

We turn now to a different matter, that of **old information** and **new information** in a given text. **Old information** is that which has already been introduced in the text. **New information** is that not previously referred to in the text.

At the beginning of a text the main topic or the main participants are usually introduced. Each language will have grammatical forms which do this. Once the topic or the participants are introduced, they then become **old information**. The reader knows this information, and it can be referred to throughout the text by special devices of the language which indicate **old information** (also called **given informa-tion**). As the text moves on, more **new information** is presented, and once presented, becomes part of the **old information** of the text. In English, the definite and indefinite articles serve to indicate **old** and **new** information. The phrase *a boy* or *some boys* would indicate that some **new information** is being introduced into the text. But the phrases, *the boy* and *those boys*, would only be used if *boy* and *boys* were **old information.**

Welch (1977:229) says that in Tucano (Colombia), information that is both new and primary typically occurs in the independent clause. Concerning the discourse as a whole, she says that:

> In a Narrative Discourse, Paraphrase and Explanatory Paragraphs frequently are embedded within the Narrative Paragraphs to slow down the speed at which new information is introduced. The information speed also slows down con-siderably at places where the speaker is slowing down before launching himself into new material. (Welch 1977:238–9)

Welch also mentions that in oral speech this slowing down is often accompanied by a lowering of intonation and by slowing down the actual rate of speech.

A direct translation of nouns and pronouns from English into Adamawa Fulani (Africa) would be very confusing to Fulani speakers. In Adamawa Fulani, there are five ways to refer to participants. They are introduced and dismissed from the text by what Stennes (1969:51) calls **basic identification**. This may be general, as in "a person" or very specific, as with the name of the person. **Substitute identification** may be used to refer to the participants in order to indicate the role the participant plays in the story as a whole, in contrast to the role in a particular event (Stennes 1969:52). Pronominal forms are used to refer back to the basic identification. There are three classes – **regular class pronouns, secondary focus pronouns**, and **topic pronouns**. How these are used in the handling of old information is described in Stennes. He says that "the full range of choices is never available at any one appearance of a participant since there are many complex factors to consider." This means that a person translating into Adamawa Fulani will need to be very careful to use the correct form in introducing new participants and in referring back to those already introduced. When translating from Adamawa Fulani into English, care will need to be taken not to translate literally the nouns and pronouns of that language, but to use the natural forms of English. If the rules of the receptor language are not followed, there will be confusion in the minds of the readers of the translation.

Each language will have its own way of indicating **old** and **new information** in its surface structure forms. Concerning this, Chafe (1970:233) says:

> ...Word order and intonation seem to play the major role in such representation, perhaps in all languages. It is impossible, however, to make a general statement of this kind with much assurance, since the matter has been so little studied. Other devices, certainly, are found. In Japanese, for example, we find the surface structure particle *wa*, reflecting old information, and *ga*, reflecting new.

The important thing for the translator is that he not translate literally the devices of the source text, but use the natural forms for handling **old** and **new information** in the receptor language. Some questions which he will need to ask include the following: "How are new participants introduced into a text?" "How are new events introduced?" and "How are change of location or time indicated?"

In some languages, **new information** occurs only in main clauses. Some languages have a special form or topic sentence to introduce the topic of the text. There are rules in each language for introducing new participants, new locations, change of time, etc. For example:

> Mundurukú (Brazil) distinguishes new and known participants by mentioning them in different positions in the clause. If the subject of the verb refers to a participant being introduced for the first time, it precedes the predicate; if the subject refers to a known participant, it occurs following the predicate. (Sheffler 1970:31; Callow 1974:83)

Callow (1974:73) points out that:

> *Affixation for gender, case, etc.*, is also a common way of relating new to known material. In some languages, certainly, affixes may provide new information. But much more commonly, affixes refer to something already known in the discourse. Thus, nouns, adjectives, and demonstratives may carry affixes which signal both their relationship with each other and their relationship with the verb. Verbs may carry affixes which indicate the relationship with preceding and following verbs, as well as with certain nouns in the sentence.

The languages of Papua New Guinea use a great deal of linkage and overlay. This is **old information** and helps to keep the **information load** from becoming too "heavy." It slows down the **information rate**. There is overlap (redundancy) at the beginning of each sentence. In their statement about this, Deibler and Taylor (1977:1065–66) call this **recapitulation**. Note the following statement about the use of **recapitulation** in Papua New Guinea languages.

> It is typical in the non-Austronesian languages of Papua New Guinea to express a series of chronologically successive events by a long succession of clauses, all but the last of which occur with verbs in a dependent temporal form whose morphology is quite different from that of the verb in the final clause. In translating narrative passages into these languages, then, one does not necessarily make sentence breaks as frequently as they occur in the source text. When there is a sentence break, however (following a sentence-final independent clause), the succeeding sentence typically begins with a recapitulation of the same verb in a dependent temporal form. Thus in the Gahuku translation of *The Farmer* (Havenhand 1963), in one paragraph one sentence ends with 'he plants it,' and the following sentence begins with 'As he plants it....' Further on in the same paragraph one sentence ends with 'he spreads on medicine' (insecticide), and the following sentence begins with 'After he has spread on medicine....'

(For more details and examples of **old** and **new information** see chapter 5 of K. Callow 1974. Notice that Callow uses **known** to refer to **old information**, i.e., she does not distinguish **old** and **new information** from **known** and **unknown** information.)

Expectancy chains

Another feature of languages which is closely related to known information is **expectancy chains**. Certain words or phrases are expected to follow certain others. There is a predictable order which is well known. The **expectancy chain** is usually clearly tied to well known cultural experiences. Longacre (1976a:151) says:

> Around the world, we find **expectancy chains** which involve actions which customarily occur in sequence such as: *leave (some place)...go...arrive; search...find; waste away...die; fall down...smash; take out a corpse...bury; eat a quantity of food...be satisfied; get...bring/take...dispose of.* Some expectancy chains are especially conditioned by the particular culture area in which they are found. Thus from New Guinea, Bougainville, New Hebrides, and Aboriginal Australia, we find such expectancy chains as the following: *see a pig...catch/kill it; kill...cook...eat; dig...cook...eat* (referring to sweet potatoes); *go with hooks...tie hooks...catch fish...bring fish...eat; cook in leaves... put into container...bring to the canoe...come down; tie up...put into canoe; climb a log...see at a distance.* Expectancy chains may involve succession with different actors (reciprocity) as in the following: *shoot...die; hit...die; call...answer; give (to someone)...appreciate; give (to someone)...cook (it).*

The translator uses **expectancy chain** patterns to decrease the information load, i.e., to make the information flow naturally. For example, the English text may simply say *John went to town.* To translate literally would be very confusing to receptor language speakers where there is an **expectancy chain** of *leave...go...arrive* as in Aguaruna (Peru). It would be more natural to say *John leaving, going, arrived at the town.* English *went* clearly implies he *left* and he *arrived.* Making this explicit and filling out the **expectancy chain** for Aguaruna makes the translation natural. In English, one says, "He bought the rice to eat," but the Colorado Indians of Ecuador would add *cook* before *eat.* Without mentioning the expected action of *cooking,* the hearer would understand that it was to be eaten raw (data from Bruce Moore).

Expected information which occurs according to expectation causes no problem for the reader. The problem arises when there is a difference in **expectancy chains** between the source language and the receptor language. Sometimes information which is strongly expected in the receptor language is not part of the explicit source language form. As the receptor language reader reads the translation, he will expect certain information to be next. When it does not occur, he is confused, and the information load becomes "heavy." For example, if in translating *John went to town* into Aguaruna, only the verb *went* were used in the translation, it would leave the Aguaruna reader confused, wondering if John *arrived* or not. The **expectancy chain** requires the addition of *arrived* in the translation.

In West African languages (K. Callow 1974:87) "any motion that took place must be stated." Motions implied in the source text must be made explicit in the receptor translation. Motion is not left implied in these languages, but stated. It is **expected information** and, if left out, will cause confusion. Callow cites the example of the translation of Exodus 2:3 about Moses in the bulrushes. The rather literal English says, "She took for him an ark...and put the child therein; and she laid it in the flags (plants) by the river's brink." The motion of *going from the house to the river* is not in the original text. Many languages would need to add the **expected information** shown in italics below: "She made an ark...and put the child in it. *Then she went to* the river's brink and laid the ark among the flags." When certain motions or other items are **expected** in the receptor language, the information load will be increased if they are not included in the translation. Also, if events are **expected** to take place in a certain order, a change of order will add to the information load.

Redundancy

All languages have patterns of **redundancy**. **Redundancy** is a repetition, but it is more than just saying the same thing twice. Sometimes the exact words, phrases, or clauses are repeated. More often the exact words are not used. However, the words which are used refer to the same THING or EVENT or to the same proposition or episode. A pronoun is **redundant** in that it refers to the same THING as the noun for which it stands. There are many ways in which languages build in **redundancy**. Some languages have a greater amount of **redundancy** than others, but according to Nida (1964:126), there is a **redundancy** of about fifty percent in most languages.

One of the differences in amount of **redundancy** has to do with the speed at which new information is introduced into a text. Some languages have a high information rate. Others have a comparatively low information rate. Some discourse types will have a slower rate than others. A great deal of **redundancy** slows down the information rate. Notice, for example, the following text from Mamainde (Brazil) (data from Kingston 1973:15, italics his):

Long ago, when our forefathers were many, a meteorite was
 chopping for honey.

The *chopper* was *chopping* to meet a certain species of honey.

As he *chopped*, they *met* him.

As they *met* him, he was *chopping*.

Chopping away, he was there *chopping*.

As he was *chopping*, he said: "I'm *chopping* for honey."

When they *met* him, he wanted to give them the axe, but they
 said, "You *chop*, yes, you *chop*," I suppose they said.

"I'll *chop*", he said.

And *chopping*, he hit the honeycomb.

This example is a case of extreme **redundancy**. In addition to the
repetition of *chopping* and *met*, in italics in the text, there is also
redundancy of participant reference, of *honey*, of words like *said*, etc.
The information rate is very low. Most languages will have a higher
information rate. However, the more **redundant** the forms are the
easier it will be for the readers to guess what is coming next. This will
often make reading and comprehension easier. Increasing **redundancy**
sometimes improves the communication. However, only the natural
patterns of **redundancy** should be used.

When a lot of unknown information is being introduced because
of difference in source and receptor culture, it may be necessary to
use a great deal of **redundancy** in the translation to slow down the
rate of information so that the audience can absorb all the new
information. But this must be done by using the natural forms of
repetition. If this is not done, the communication flow may be
overloaded and the readers confused.

Tunebo (Colombia) (data from Headland 1975:5) introduces several bits of information in the first sentence of a narrative text, including
the participants and main event. However, in the following sentences
only one new bit is added per sentence, keeping the main very constant.
Headland says, "The **repetition** of the main verb is particularly evident
at the beginning of a narrative discourse or episode where a lot of new
information is necessary to get the action going." She gives the
following example (only the literal English translation is given below):

There *I went* out in the forest.

I went hunting.

I went to the area of the Sarari River.

I went to Cutuji.

When *I went* to the forest, I got lost.

In the above example, there is exact **repetition** of the pronoun and verb throughout the paragraph.

There are also other ways of referring back to an action. In Aguaruna (Peru) exact **repetition** is sometimes used but the use of a pro-verb is also very common. When the **repetition** is of a verb of "saying" or "motion" the exact verb is repeated as in "*He said...having said...*" or "*He went...having gone...*" For referring back to other verbs, there are two pro-verbs. *dutik-* refers back to transitive verbs, and *nunik-* refers back to intransitive verbs. This **repetition** not only slows down the rate of information, but is one of the main devices for sentence and paragraph linkage in Aguaruna. In the following piece of Aguaruna text, these forms are in bold (*ds* means different subject than subject of the main verb):

Jaguar and Armadillo by Arturo Paati

1. *Ikamyawa   wekama   wainkau   Shushuin.*   2. *Igkug,*
   Jaguar   walking   he-saw   Armadillo   Meeting

*"Yamai   kumpajuh,   yuwatjame,"   tusa   **tama***
Now   my-friend   I-will-eat-you saying   having-said-ds

"Ayu,   tujash,   mina   yujuata   tusam   wakegakmek,
okay   but   me-obj   eat-me   you-saying if-you-desire

duka   pegkeg   ichinkachu   jukim   imanum
leaf   good   that-not-torn   you-taking   in-that-good-one

aepjuasam   yujuata,"   tama   "Ayu,"   tus
roasting-me   eat-me   having-said-ds   okay   saying

wegai,   nugka   niishkam   machik   tainu.
going-ds   ground-obj   he-also   little-bit he-dug

3. ***Nugka   dutikai,***   *Ikamyawashkam*
   Ground   after-doing-so-ds   Jaguar-also

wakau   duka   juki.   4. *"Paii,   yamai*
he-came-back   leaf   bringing   Okay   now

yuwatjame,"   tama   niishkam   duka   nanchikia
I-will-eat-you   having-said-ds   he-also   leaf   scratching

ichigku.   5. *"Atsaa,   pegkegchawai,   ichinkauwai.*
he-tore-it   No   it-is-not-good   it-is-torn

Tikich	*utita,"*	*tima*		*ataktu*	*weu*	*dukan*
Other	you-bring	having-said-ds		again	he-went	leaf-obj

juwak.
bringing

	6.	**We**	**juki**	*wakau.*	7.	*"Paii,*	*dekas*
		Going	bringing	he-came-back		Okay	truly

yamai	*yuwatjame,"*	*tama*		*Shushuishkam.*
now	I-will-eat-you	having-said-ds		Armadillo-also

"Ayu,	*juwi*	*tepestajai,"*	*tus*	*waan*	*mamikis*	*duka*
Okay	here	I-will-lay	saying	on-hole	right-above	leaf

ainak	*tepeau.*
they-are	he-lay

	8.	**Nunik**	*Shushui*	*tiu,*	*"Amek*	*dekas*	*yaki."*
		Doing-so	Armadillo	he-said	you	truly	high

There are many kinds of **redundancy**. Most of them have been referred to previously in this book. There is full repetition of a word, clause, or larger unit; there may be partial repetition with some amplification; there may be a kind of paraphrase or restatement; or a positive and then a negative restatement; linkage of events by repeating the verb; back reference to participants or props by pronouns and substitute words; etc. Larger units may also be redundant as with previews, summaries, flashbacks, expansions, overlays, etc. Although **redundancy** does slow down the information flow, that is not its only function in discourse. It is also a device which signals groupings, cohesion, and prominence as discussed in chapters 29, 30, 31, and 32.

Redundancy is helpful in identifying the units of a discourse. Where **redundancy chains** stop, there is usually a major break, such as a paragraph boundary or episode closing. For example, as long as a series of pronouns in English refers back to the same referent, the same unit is being developed. When there is an introduction of new information, and the series of **redundant** pronouns stops, a new unit has begun. In some languages every sentence in a paragraph will begin with a verb which is **redundant** and refers back to a previous action. When there is no **redundancy**, a new unit, i.e., a new paragraph, has begun.

Openings, closings, previews, summaries, etc., are **redundant** in that they usually include some part of the body of the text. They supply information, which by being **redundant**, will help to decrease the load of new information. There is often an overlap of information in the opening and closing or in the preview and summary. This **redundancy** ties the text together as a unit. There may be an overlap of information at the beginning and ending of an episode or a paragraph, signaling the boundaries of this unit.

Almost all of the devices mentioned in chapter 31 on cohesion involve a certain amount of **redundancy**. This **redundancy** has the primary function of adding cohesion, but at the same time is very important to the information rate of the text.

Prominence is also indicated by **redundancy**. For example, the theme may be repeated several times, in the opening, closing, and throughout the text. **Redundancy** may be used for emphasis, in order to make a stronger emotional impact on the hearer. Notice the following (Barnwell 1980:193):

1. *Take heed and beware.*

2. *I was dumbfounded, flabbergasted, and amazed.*

3. *Be good and don't get into trouble.*

4. *Have courage, don't despair.*

5. *My memory is terrible, I just can't remember things.*

In larger units, such as a total discourse, **redundancy** is often used to mark the peak or main event of the discourse. Longacre (1976a:217–18) calls this **rhetorical underlining**. He says:

> ...The narrator does not want you to miss the important point of the story so he employs extra words at this point. He may employ parallelism, paraphrase, and tautologies of various sorts to be sure that you don't miss it.... The importance of rhetorical underlining must not be underestimated. It is one of the simplest and most universal devices for marking the important point not only of a narration, but of other sorts of discourse as well.

We have already discussed using the appropriate forms to indicate grouping, cohesion, and prominence in the translation. That is, the forms of the receptor language are to be used, and the forms of the source language are not to be reproduced literally. Nevertheless, this needs to be reemphasized because translators tend to carry over the **redundancy** features of the source text into the translation. If they do this, the style of the translation will be unnatural. Some **redundancy** is found in all languages. But there are specific kinds with special functions. **Redundancy** is very important if the information load is not to be too high. But

redundancy cannot be just added here and there as one might sprinkle salt on one's food. It must be used only when appropriate in the receptor language. It must be omitted from the translation, even though it occurs in the source text, if putting it in the translation produces an unnatural form in the receptor language.

The following are examples taken from actual translations into English. In each case the translator left in **redundancy** of the source language which is not appropriate in English.:

1. Translation: The *earnings received* for this period amounted to a hundred dollars.

   Natural English: The earnings for this period amounted to a hundred dollars. ("Received" is redundant since "earnings" are always "received.")

2. Translation: The chairman has always placed construction of a new building in the *highest position of priority*.

   Natural English: The chairman has always given highest priority to the construction of a new building.

3. Translation: The conference was attended by the members of *the Communist Party* of the Soviet Union, *the Socialist Unity Party* of Germany, *the Communist Party* of Romania, *the Communist Party* of Italy, *the Communist Party* of Spain, *the Communist Party* of Bulgaria, and *the Communist Party* of France.

   Natural English: The conference was attended by the members of the Communist Party of the Soviet Union, the Socialist Unity Party of Germany, and the Communist Parties of Romania, Italy, Spain, Bulgaria, and France.

4. Translation: In the past two years the U.S. has raised its tariffs on a number *of imported items from the countries of West Europe goods*.

   Natural English: ...tariffs on a number of imports from Western Europe.

As can be seen in the above examples, reducing the amount of **redundancy** may make for easier understanding. Adding **redundancy** is not necessarily equal to ease of reading or naturalness. The natural patterns of the receptor language will be the least "heavy" in information load and the easiest to read and understand.

Each language has ways of making clear what is new information and what is old. Each language has ways of controlling the information rate and the amount of **redundancy**. The translator will need to study the natural text material of the receptor language in order to observe patterns used for introducing new information and referring back to old information. He will also want to observe the ways in which the rate of information flow may be slowed down in the language and the ways in which **redundancy** is used.

Implicit and explicit information

The matter of **implicit** and **explicit information** was introduced in chapter 4. The student would benefit from rereading that chapter before continuing. Since **implicit information** and **explicit information** are closely related to the information rate and "heaviness" of the text, more details concerning this matter are given here.

As pointed out in chapter 4, all communication is based on shared information. Every text that one may wish to translate will have some information which is **implicit**. It is not stated in any **explicit** form in the text itself. However, it is information which the author and readers of the text have in common, or it is old information already mentioned elsewhere in the text. Since it is clearly understood by both the author and the readers, it is **implicit**, that is, it is clearly implied but not stated.

A number of matters related directly to **implied information** have already been discussed previously. In chapter 21, a number of constructions which have **implied information** were analyzed and the **implied information** made **explicit**. These included passive constructions, abstract nouns, and genitive constructions. The following examples are given as review. **Implicit information** is added in parentheses in the rewrite.

Passive to active:	*The door opened.*
	(Someone) opened the door.
Abstract noun:	*forgiveness*
	(someone) forgave (someone)
Genitive construction:	*pitcher of milk*
	pitcher (containing) milk

In rewriting a text semantically, it becomes necessary to make many implied CONCEPTS **explicit**. Whether they will be **implicit** or **explicit** in the translation will depend on the natural forms used in the receptor language.

In chapter 23, the **implied information** which is often found in a metaphor was discussed. Sometimes the comparison is left **implicit** and sometimes the topic. The following examples are given as review. **Implicit information** is added in the restatement in parentheses:

Metaphor:

He's a pig.	A pig (is dirty). He (is likewise dirty).
John is a bean pole.	A bean pole is (tall and thin). John (is likewise tall and thin).
The tide turned against the government.	(Like) the tide turns (its force against the land), (the people) turned against the government.

Throughout parts 3 and 4 earlier, in rewriting the surface forms as semantic structure, the **implicit information** often had to be made **explicit**. Many examples are given. In chapter 33, the need to make situational information of the source text **explicit** in the translation was discussed also. We turn now to a discussion of how the translator handles the matter of **implicit** and **explicit information** in the translation.

Beekman and Callow (1974:45–57) suggest that there are three types of **implicit information** – derived from (1) the immediate context in the document, (2) the remote context in the document, and (3) the cultural context. If information is to be included in the translation, it must be clearly **implied information**, not just something the translator decides he would like to include. Therefore, these three types serve as helpful guidelines.

Information **implied** in the immediate context is most easily identified. Grammatical ellipses are common in all languages, but the forms will not match between languages. For example, if someone asks, "*How many dollars do you have?*" the answer would simply be "*Ten.*" All the rest of the information (*I have...dollars*) is left implicit. But in Aguaruna it would be necessary to say "*Ten they-are.*" Or one might even say "*Mine ten they-are.*" The Aguaruna makes **explicit** the information in the context that is in the preceding sentence. No information is added, it is only made **explicit**.

Occasionally, whole clauses are left **implicit** in the source text. In some languages these **implicit** clauses will need to be made **explicit**. For example,

> **Surface form**: *The king called his servant and asked him to check on it.*

> **Semantic rewrite** (implicit information in parentheses): *The king called his servant and (when the servant came to the king,) the king said to the servant, "You find out (if the guest has arrived.)"*

Notice that the first **implicit** proposition is simply the logical event which occurs between *called* and *said to him*. In some languages, it is more natural to include this event, or it may even be expected (an expectancy chain). The second proposition, *Has the guest arrived?* comes from the immediately preceding part of the text, which is not reproduced here. No new information has been added. It has simply been made **explicit**.

The matter of grammatical constructions which have **implicit information** was discussed above – passives, abstract nouns, genitives, etc. The immediate context often supplies the information needed, if a different grammatical structure which leaves information **implicit** is to be used. But in addition to this, the receptor language may require that certain information be made **explicit** because of special grammatical requirements of certain words. For example (Beekman and Callow 1974:55), in Zapotec (Mexico) the word meaning *to choose* always requires the addition of a purpose clause. This information must be supplied if the word is to be used. Some words require an *object*, and other words require that the *location, direction, result*, etc., be given. The information needed to be supplied is usually found in the immediate context. Certain verbs in English require an object. *Made* and *saw* require an object. If no specific object is named, then *it* or *something* may be supplied: *I made it, I saw something.* In other languages, different words may require that the *object* be stated.

The information which needs to be supplied in the translation may not always be found in the **immediate context**, that is, in the part of the text just preceding or following the passage in question. Sometimes this information can only be supplied by looking at the more **remote context** or at the **communication situation** itself. In translating literary works, especially if they are historical, it may be necessary to look at the sections which come earlier or later in the work itself or even in other books written during the same period in history. It may be necessary to look at other literature of that time in order to find out what is being referred to in the text to be translated.

Whether historical or contemporary, it is often necessary to look to the **communication situation** as the source for **implied information**. It is sometimes almost impossible to be sure what the author means without knowing such things as the relationship between the author and the audience, the political, social, or religious setting, and other aspects of the culture described in the text. A good translator will make use of good dictionaries, encyclopedias, atlases, commentaries, and other books which will give him sufficient background to interpret the text he is working on correctly. Some of this background information may need to be made **explicit** in the text. Some may better be handled in introductory notes and some in footnotes or glossaries. How this is done will depend on the needs of the audience for whom the translation is being prepared.

One of the most crucial questions facing every translator is, "When may *implicit information* become *explicit* in the translation?" Decisions must constantly be made. There are two extremes – making too little **explicit** and leaving the readers confused or unable to understand the translation, or making too much **explicit** and overloading the information rate by introducing too much information too fast. There are a few guidelines which will prove helpful. In the most general terms, the rule is that **implicit information** should be made **explicit**, if the receptor language necessitates it in order to avoid a wrong meaning or in order to present the material in natural forms and pleasing style.

Four more specific guidelines may also be helpful. **Implicit information** may be made explicit

1. when required by the *grammar* of the receptor language,

2. when necessary for correct and clear expression of the source text *meaning*,

3. when needed for *naturalness of style* or to create the same emotive effect as the source text, and

4. only if *truly implied* in the source text.

The danger is that the translation may become unduly free. The fourth principle needs to be emphasized. Information may not be added at the whims of the translator. It must be truly implied in the source text and needed for correct meaning and naturalness.

Notice the following example (data from Catherine Rountree). First, the literal translation into English from Saramacan (Suriname) is given, then a modified literal, then an idiomatic translation, and, finally, an unduly free translation. The unduly free translation errs primarily in that information is added which is not truly implicit in the source language.

Literal: ...But he must be careful (must remind himself) that the living of the family of ours hasn't changed at all from how he knew it here.

Modified Literal: ...But he must remember that the ways of our family have not changed at all from the way he knew them.

Idiomatic: ...But I do want to remind you how the family feels about it. They expect you to come care for her as they always have. (In the letter, third person is used in Saramacan where second person would be used in English. The information about "come care for her" is clearly stated in the previous sentence of the text and is all right to make explicit here.)

Unduly free: ...But you know how the rest of the family is. They really feel you should come *and if you don't, they are going to hold it against you, I know*. (The part in italics is not implied anyplace in the text and thus is added information, not implicit information made explicit.)

No information should be added which is not clearly a part of the source text linguistic or cultural context and needed for **grammatical, semantic,** or **stylistic** reasons.

In this chapter, we have been talking about the information load. Since some of the **implicit information** which is made **explicit** is new information, it must be treated as such in the translation. A further caution is needed lest this new information distort the theme or focus intended in the original document. It is very important that the translator who is introducing information new to the receptor audience, but not new to the original audience, does not use forms that will make it seem like mainline or thematic material. The discourse could become distorted or too much emphasis given to something which is not that important to the original author. Such information should be presented in such a subtle or natural way that the intended prominence of the source text is not distorted.

As has been stated several times already, one of the things which makes a translation sound nonidiomatic to the receptor language reader is the heavy load of information. In many languages the information needs to be introduced more slowly and the number of bits of information in a clause or sentence reduced. The problem is that as a translator makes **implicit** source language information **explicit** for correct meaning, he often adds to this load. In order to reduce the load, in other places he should also make some **explicit** information of the source language **implicit** in the translation (see Larson 1969).

The guidelines for doing this are very similar to those given above but are the converse. They also have to do with the requirements of the receptor language **grammatically, semantically**, and **stylistically** (points 1-3 stated earlier). The main caution is to be sure that it is indeed a change from **explicit** to **implicit** and not deleted. Notice, for example, the following text. First, the source text is given with an English gloss. Then the idiomatic English translation. All information which is **explicit** in the source text but left **implicit** in the translation is italicized in the gloss. No information is lost. Some is moved in order to make the story more natural. It is still retrievable from the total context.

SOURCE TEXT (Aguaruna, Peru)

Tuwajame	*Chuwi*	*Sukuyan*	*iwakiu*	*yaki*	*pasugken.*
They-say	Oriole	Nighthawk-obj	caused-to-go-up	high	to-his-nest

Egkeau	*kanajattus*	*egkemau*	*pasugnum.*
He-put-him	in-order-that-he-sleep	*that-put-in*	in-nest

Kanumain	*dekapeachu*	*pasug*	*buchittai*	*dase*	*umpuam.*
One-able-to-sleep	he-did-not-feel	nest	when-moved	wind	blowing

ishamak	*tau.*	*"Saiju*	*iyagtatjai,*	*akankita*
fearing	he-said,	*My-brother-in-law*	I-will-fall	take-me-down

nugka."	*Tutai*	*Chuwi*	*tiu,*	*"Atsaa,*	*iyagchattame.*
to-ground	Saying	Oriole	he-said,	*No*	you-will-not-fall

Jinkiipa	*Tsetsekai*	*jakaim."*
do-not-go-out	from cold	lest-you-die

IDIOMATIC ENGLISH TRANSLATION

Once long ago Oriole took his brother-in-law, Nighthawk, with him high up into his nest to sleep. But he couldn't sleep because the wind was blowing and the swaying of the nest frightened him. He said, "Oriole, please take me down so I don't fall." Oriole answered, "You'll not fall. If you go out now you'll freeze to death."

Some information which is required **grammatically** by the source language may be left implicit in the translation. Certain grammatical items are present in the source text because they are obligatory categories of that language. For example, when translating from Japanese into English, the translator will not try to keep the distinctions which are indicated in Japanese pronouns having to do with levels of honor. He will let that information remain unexpressed and use the natural forms of English which do not carry this information.

In Aguaruna of Peru, masculine and feminine are not distinguished in the grammar. Distinctions such as *he* and *she* of the English source language are simply left **implicit** in the Aguaruna translation.

Nouns and pronouns of the source text may be replaced by affixes or absence of person markers in the receptor language, when that is the appropriate receptor language form.

Some languages use rather complicated noun phrases, whereas others do not. For example, a source text which says *The man who stood up and read from the newspaper* might be referred to as *the man who read, that man*, or may be referred to simply by a pronoun in the receptor language, where complicated noun phrases would be "heavy" or unnatural. The information has already been given and so is indicated in *that man*.

Some information which is required **semantically** by the source language may be left implicit in the translation. Components of meaning in words do not match between languages. Not all the semantic components of a word in the source language are necessarily found in a corresponding word in the receptor language. Some components may be left implicit in translation. For example, in Ticuna (Peru), as well as in many other South American Indian languages, the receptor language does not make a distinction between *governor, king, emperor,* etc. The general word for *chief* is used for all of these, and the translation makes the semantic distinction only if the distinction is in focus. Otherwise, rather complicated descriptive equivalents would be needed, since these words are not distinguished in the semantic structure of Ticuna.

In Siriono (Bolivia), where lakes and sailboats are unknown, and therefore, there are no lexical items referring to them, the phrase *we should sail to Italy* was translated simply as *we should go to Italy*. The component of going *by water, with sails* was left implicit, although in the total context it was made clear that the trip was made on water.

Some information which is required **stylistically** by the source language may be left implicit in the translation. Redundancy is a matter of style. Some languages use more redundancy than others. If all of the redundancy of the source language is translated literally into the receptor language, the information load will be too high. Some of this information may be left implicit. For example, a source text which repeated the location several times in a short number of sentences was translated into Aguaruna mentioning the location only once. This was much better style in Aguaruna; it was more natural. In Aguaruna the location is not usually repeated until there is a change of location.

Sometimes the source text will have a redundancy of semantic elements which also may be unnatural. For example, the sentence *She was an elderly woman, about 84 years of age* was translated into Aguaruna by simply saying *she was 84 years of age.* The fact that she was an elderly woman is still clearly implied and retrievable, and the Aguaruna is more natural.

Some information of the source text which is **implicit** will need to be made **explicit** and some which is **explicit** will need to be made **implicit**. This is perhaps one of the most difficult aspects of the translation process. One of the things which most often makes a translation sound nonidiomatic or unnatural to the receptor language reader is the "heavy" load of information. As the translator makes **implicit** source language information **explicit** for correct meaning, he adds to this load. In order to balance the load, there will be other places where some **explicit information** of the source language will need to be made **implicit** in the translation. The goal of the translator is to be accurate in representing the meaning of the source text, and, at the same time, to use the natural idiomatic forms of the receptor language.

As in all of the translation processes, the translator should constantly be looking for the receptor language form which will accurately represent the meaning of the source text, and, at the same time, present this meaning in a clear natural way. He should be faithful to the source text meaning and to the receptor language structure. Above all, he must avoid incomplete, extraneous, or different information. It will be necessary to make **explicit** many details that were obvious to the original readers when dealing with a text from a different culture or situation. He must not add to the total message, but simply present the message to the receptor more slowly, in less concentrated doses, so that it can be understood clearly.

EXERCISES – Information Load

A. The following story (contributed by Lee Ballard, taken from Barnwell 1983:92) is a fairly literal translation of a story in the Ibaloi language, spoken in the Philippines. First read the story through.

> ...One of those who found (some of the buried money) was Juan Bejar.... They arrived with it at night to his house, and he did-*kapi*-for-it that night at his house at Salakoban. Yes, it was at his house where he did-*kapi*-for-it.

The next morning, as they were eating the head, the new jaw bone fell-down. And it was not tilted when it fell, but rather it was upright and it was pointing east. When the old women saw it, they said, "Do-it-a-second-time. Perhaps they have regarded-it-as-insufficient." And yes, Juan did-*kapi*-for-it a second time.

Can you answer the following questions? Answer as best you can.

1. Why did they do *kapi*?

2. Who was eating the head?

3. The head of what?

4. What fell down?

5. The jaw bone of what?

6. Where did it fall from?

7. What is the significance of the jaw bone's pointing east?

8. What was the old women's reaction to what happened?

9. Why did they react in this way?

10. How do you understand the sentence, "Perhaps they have regarded it as insufficient?"

Probably there are many things which are not clear to you. This is because the writer of the story was writing for fellow Ibaloi people. There are many background cultural facts which he assumes his audience already knows, and so he does not explain them.

Now read another translation of the same story:

...One of those who found (some of the buried money) was Juan Bejar.... They arrived with it at night to his house, and he celebrated the *feast of kapi* with a pig as payment to the ancestral spirits that night at his house at Salakoban. Yes, it was at his house where he celebrated the *feast of kapi* for it.

The next morning, as they were *having the traditional community breakfast following feasts*, the jaw bone *of the pig which had been sacrificed the previous evening* fell down *from the eaves of the house where it is traditionally hung*. And it was not tilted when it fell but rather it was upright, and it was pointing east *where the ancestral spirits are said to live*. When the old women saw it, *they regarded it all as a bad omen and* said, *"Celebrate kapi* a second time. Perhaps *the ancestral spirits* have regarded *the pig you sacrificed* as insufficient *payment."* And yes, Juan celebrated *kapi* for it a second time.

For non-Ibaloi people, this version of the story is more meaningful. The unknown cultural information has been included. Now see if you can answer the questions given above.

B. The following represents the source text. It is the English gloss of a text in Denya (Cameroon) from Abangma (1987:93–7). Go through the text marking the old and new information. *Underline* the **new information** and *circle* the **old information**.

Source Text

Story listen. Hear. Time certain it was, when elephant he entertained occasion. He said. They went, they cleared farm his. They cleared farm a lot. Farm is big. They left. They returned home.

Elephant he prepared food. He gave. He said. They ate. They ate good for long. He divided food. He gave Crab not. Crab he was certainly stream. However Crab he went put bottom with person, who he cooks food. He said. He put pepper much.

Papa elephant...

C. Below is a *literal* English translation of the above source text. Then follows an *idiomatic* English translation. See the instructions following these texts.

LITERAL ENGLISH TRANSLATION

Listen to a story! There was a time when Elephant invited people to a feast. He asked people to go and clear his farm. They went and did clear a very big farm. The farm was really big. Then they left and came back home.

Elephant prepared food. He gave it to people and asked them to eat. They ate lots of food. He shared the food but he did not give any to Crab. Crab was then in a small stream. However, Crab went and conversed with the man who cooks food and serves it to Elephant. Crab told him to put a lot of pepper in the food.

Having eaten, Papa elephant sent...

IDIOMATIC ENGLISH TRANSLATION

Once upon a time Papa Elephant gave a party. First he invited a lot of people to go and clear his land. It was a big farm but they cleared it all. Then they returned home again.

Because they had worked for him. Elephant prepared a feast and invited all the people who had cleared the land. He served food to everyone except Crab who was in the stream at the time. Because he didn't get any food, Crab was angry and went and talked to the cook. He asked him to put lots of pepper in Elephant's food.

After Papa Elephant ate his food he sent...

1. *Circle* every item in the Literal Translation which has been made more **explicit** than in the Source Text. Has any information been left **implicit** in this Literal Translation? If so, put a *wavy line* under it in the Source Text.

2. Compare the Literal Translation and the Idiomatic Translation. The Literal Translation consists of correct English sentences. However, it does not sound like natural English because too much information is left **explicit**. *Draw a box around* every lexical item in the Literal Translation which is made **implicit** in the Idiomatic Translation.

3. *Put an x* over any lexical items in the Idiomatic Translation which have been made more **explicit** than in the Literal Translation.

4. Translate this story into another language other than English. Is your translation more like the Source Text, the Literal English Translation, or the Idiomatic English Translation as far as amount of information made **explicit** is concerned?

D. In any text, there are certain words or phrases which the reader will be expecting to occur following certain other words. In the following sentences, the second member of the **expectancy chain** is left blank. See if you can fill in the blanks. (Some sentences are from Longacre 1976a:151.)

1. I went to look for it but I couldn't _____ it.

2. He fell out of a tree but some low lying limbs broke his fall and he didn't _____ very badly.

3. He wasted away to a mere eighty-five pounds but the doctor arrived in time and he _____.

4. I called to her but she was angry and didn't _____ me.

5. It fell down but didn't _____.

6. They left for Paris but didn't _____.

7. I ate five slices of bread but was still _____.

8. He killed and cooked his game and then they _____ it.

9. Mary became very sick so we called the _____.

10. They took the corpse out and _____ it.

11. The poor animal wasted away and _____.

12. John went fishing and _____ three big ones.

E. The following is a story told by an Australian Aborigine (data from Ted Furby). This is a semi-literal back translation from Garawa into English. Go through the text and underline all the **redundancy** using a different color for each lexical item. Then study to see what patterns of **redundancy** occur in the language. Translate the text into the second language you speak, using only the natural redundancy of that language. Do not translate literally the **redundancy** patterns of the Aborigine language. Make an idiomatic receptor language translation.

They fought together in the east place. In the east place they fought. That spearing one, he killed many strangers in the east place.

They put that spearing one, he to look after the camp. At night he looked after the camp in the east. He heard them coming from the north. They came quietly in the bush from the north. Quietly they came. They were strangers, and they came quietly through the bush. They were strangers. But that spearing one, he heard them coming from the north.

He shot his shooting-stick. Again he shot, and again. He killed many of the strangers. Many strangers he killed with his shooting-stick. With his shooting-stick he killed many strangers.

The others, they stopped. They were frightened. Very much they were frightened. Quietly they returned through the bush. They were frightened. They returned to the north quietly.

That spearing one, he successfully hit many strangers, killed. In the east place he killed them. They came from the north.

F. In each of the following translations into English, the italicized words have been translated literally from the source language. Evaluate the italicized words as translations. Improve upon them if you can, substituting other words, deleting a word or words, or changing the grammatical structure. Look especially for **redundancy** which is not natural in English.

1. He studied that in *a course of the French language*.

2. Our exports in 1970 amounted to 1.3 *million dollars* but in 1972 to 15.5 *million dollars*.

3. With this kind of international assistance the *least developed developing* countries are able to receive favorable conditions of credit.

4. This means that one adult in 13, and one is six *of all the toilers employed in the national economy of the country*, belong to it.

5. The shoe factory *of the name of* Armando Gamboa is a curious enterprise.

6. The earnings *received* for this period amounted to a hundred dollars.

7. His brother committed suicide *by drowning himself to death* in the river.

8. The Directorate *still up to now* has not supplied the names of students who are scheduled to come.

9. He is *absolutely, positively* sure.

10. The situation has prompted us to *this, that we should* take action.

THE TRANSLATION PROGRAM

Chapter 35
Establishing the Project

In chapter 5, the various aspects of a translation program were discussed briefly. The purpose of the following section is to elaborate on the matters discussed there.

Before any translation work is begun, the project must be defined. What is to be translated? For whom? By whom? With what resources? Or, using the terms introduced in chapter 5, the **text**, the **target**, the **team,** and the **tools** must all be decided upon. One of the greatest hindrances to producing a good idiomatic translation is lack of adequate planning before the actual translation begins. In this chapter, we will discuss the four aspects of planning listed above. In chapter 36, translation procedures themselves will be discussed; in chapter 37, the testing of the translation and the final manuscript preparation will be discussed.

The text

Before any work on a translation is undertaken, the feasibility of the project and the desirability of the translation should be clear. What **text** is to be translated? Why has the particular **text** been chosen? Some translations are undertaken simply as a job. This is often true with technical translators. They are asked to translate a certain document for their employer. But many literary translators simply decide on a certain project which interests them and then pursue it. Why is a certain piece of literature chosen?

The questions which translators need to ask are questions like the following: Will it be read? By whom? What effect will it have on the audience? How long will it take to do the project? Are there people available to handle all aspects of the project? Is there money available? Who will publish it? Many translation projects have never been completed because these questions were not asked early in the program.

Texts are chosen to be translated for various reasons. Most often the reason is to communicate the information content of the source

509

text to people who speak a language other than that of the source text. It may be information which is historical, political, religious, or which tells people how-to-do-it, a travelogue about distant places, or facts important to the economic development of a country. The form of the source **text** may be that of a scientific article, instructions for the use of some medicine, business correspondence, a textbook, some folk tales, or one of many other possible **text** types.

However, the information content is not always foremost in the mind of the person planning to translate. Sometimes the reasons are based on the person's enjoyment of the **text**. It is pleasing aesthetically—a poem, a novel, a mystery story, an essay. It captures the attention of a translator, and he wants to see it in another language, perhaps his own mother-tongue. He wants others to enjoy it also, others who do not know the language in which it is written. Whatever the reasons for desiring to translate a given **text**, the choice is closely related to questions about the **target audience**.

The target audience

No translation should be undertaken without a clear understanding of who will use it. It is not simply a matter of knowing that there are those who will use it. A good deal must be known about those who will use it. Questions of dialect, educational level, age level, and bilingualism affect the form of the receptor language which will be chosen for the translation. One does not write with the same complexity of language for children, for example, as for highly educated adults. So, before the translation project begins, these matters should be carefully evaluated.

Once it has been determined that there is a need or desire for a given document to be translated into a given language, the question of **dialects** arises. A **dialect** is a speech variety within a language. There may be social dialects, dialects which vary because of the geographical spread of the language, and other differences based on educational level, age, occupation, and degree of bilingualism.

If a language is spoken by a large group of people scattered over a wide area, there will be several **dialects**. When one of these is the mother tongue of the prospective translator, he will probably want to translate into his own **dialect**. Nevertheless, he should consider whether or not this choice will serve the larger number of people, if widespread usage is desirable. Is one **dialect** more central geographically, is it understood more easily by speakers of the other **dialects**? Is there a "common-language" (see Wonderly 1968:1–3) form which is understood by speakers of the various dialects? (For more details on dialect surveys see Grimes, Joseph E. 1995. *Language Survey Reference Guide*. Dallas, TX: Summer Institute of Linguistics).

In addition to these dialect differences, there will be differences related to **social levels**. These **social levels** will depend on various factors in the society – level of education, occupation, or even based on the class into which one is born. **Social levels** are often accompanied by a difference in language forms and usage. The people for whom the translation is intended may be well educated, or they may be new readers. What percent of the population reads? Will the translation be aimed at the educated only or the new readers? Will it try to bridge the gap and be acceptable to both? Choices throughout the translation process will depend on the answer to these questions.

Is the **purpose** of the translation for personal reading, to be used in school, or for oral reading in church and home? The style appropriate for silent study in school may be different than that for oral reading in the church. Perhaps the translation is only for a small part of the population. It may be an article of interest to medical doctors. This would not be translated the same way as if it were for the general public, in which case less technical words would need to be used. A folk tale being translated for inclusion in a linguistic journal may not be the same as a translation of the same folk tale for inclusion in a book of stories to be read for entertainment.

The **age** of the audience will also affect the form of the translation. This was discussed in chapter 33, but needs to be mentioned here again. Will the translation be for children, for adolescents, or for adults? If it is aimed at a part of the population, rather than the public in general, this will affect many decisions in the translation process. The translator must have his audience in mind at all times as he translates.

The degree of **bilingualism** can also make a difference. Are most of the people who will use the translation bilingual in the source and receptor languages? If so, some key words may well be borrowed from the source language. If they are all monolinguals in the receptor language, great care will need to be taken in the selection of equivalents for key words. If there is a kind of mixture, in which people use both languages, but do not keep them clearly separate, again, this may affect the forms chosen for the translation.

The relative **prestige** of the receptor language (or of different dialects within it) may affect the acceptance of the final product. If people have a negative feeling about a given language they may not want materials in that language, but prefer the language which has more **prestige**, even though they do not understand it as well. On the other hand, sometimes the production of materials in writing in a language may add a new **prestige** to that language. Will the translation enhance the use of the receptor language and its acceptance as a vehicle of communication? Are there government language policies which need to be taken into consideration?

What is the **function** of the receptor language? Is it used primarily as a personal language for thinking, dreaming, praying, and speaking to one's immediate family, or is it used by the entire speech community for discussing whatever topic they might wish to discuss in the home, school, community, in correspondence, and on the radio?

Another matter of great importance is the **target audience's** attitude towards the **alphabet** to be used. In many translation projects a great deal of effort must be expended in arriving at an agreement on an **alphabet** for the project. It is crucial that this be done early, before much translation has been done. There have been cases where a book has been boycotted in a particular area because it contained spelling conventions that were unwelcome by the people there. It was impossible to sell the books. There are records of heated debates over orthographic systems which were tied to political or denominational groups. Very excellent books have been rejected by a community because the words were not "spelled right." Gudschinsky (1969) says,

> Unfortunately, the problem of orthography is one of the most explosive in the world. Differences about alphabets have frequently caused shooting wars, riots, and serious political division. In some languages, competing groups using different orthographies have actually perpetrated large competing literatures.

For some programs, the **alphabet** will already have been determined. If not, there are some basic principles which can be followed in deciding this important matter. First of all, an **alphabet** should be *easy to read* with a minimum of ambiguity. It needs to be well tested to be sure that it is indeed readable. It should also be *socially acceptable*. If the people reject the **alphabet** they will reject the book that is being translated. Social antagonism may come from members of the society who are bilingual or from people of status outside the linguistic community or even from government agencies. These matters should be checked out before the **alphabet** is finally decided upon. But there is also no point in modifying an **alphabet** to the point where it cannot be easily read.

Another important matter to consider in deciding on the **alphabet** is the *practical matter* of which keys are on typewriters and typesetting machines. If a letter or two need to be added to the typewriter or typesetting machines, this needs to be planned in advance and provision made for the adjustment.

Once the **alphabet** is settled on, there will still be the question of how individual words are spelled. There may be dialectical differences. Which spelling is to be used? When borrowed words are used, such as names of people and places, will the words be spelled with the official language spelling, or will it be adapted to the language of the translation? If the translation is from a vernacular language into the official language, will the vernacular spelling be used, or will it be modified to conform to the spelling forms of the official language? This needs to be planned ahead of time in order not to have to spend a lot of time later correcting inconsistencies. (For more detail on alphabet design see Smalley 1963 and Gudschinsky 1969.)

The translation team

Some translation projects are done completely by one person. More often, a project involves a number of people who contribute at some stage in the project. Even if the project is basically the work of one person, the results will be better if there are others available for evaluation and consultation. Before the project is begun, those responsible for the project will need to assess the personnel available and the skills which they will bring to the project. Additional personnel may be needed.

Some member of the team, hopefully the **translator**, must be able to read, write, and speak the source language. He must have a good understanding and ability to determine the meaning of the source text. He must also understand the source culture. If the **translator** is not able to determine the meaning of the source document, there is little hope that the translation will be of good quality.

If the **translator** has only a fair knowledge of the source language and culture, he may still do a good translation, if he has an advisor or **consultant** with whom he can discuss those parts of the document which he himself cannot interpret. In some translation projects such as Bible translation, there will be commentaries written about the source text which he can consult in order to find answers, but he must be able to discover the meaning of the source text. These are skills which can be acquired, but they are essential before the project is undertaken. Some member of the team must provide skill in interpreting the source document.

A **translator** will, of course, understand the receptor language and culture. He needs to be able to read, write, and speak his language well. Someone who has lived outside the language area for some time may have difficulty making a good translation. He will certainly need to do extensive testing with people who speak fluently.

The above statement applies to cases in which the **translator** is translating from a second language he has learned into his own language. However, sometimes **translators** are translating from their own language into a second language, for example, the official language of their country. In this case, it is very important that there be speakers of the receptor language available to help with the testing and evaluation. These should be persons whose mother tongue is the receptor language. Even when a **translator** is translating into his mother tongue, he will want to check with other speakers of the language to be sure the translation is communicating well the meaning of the source text.

In addition to a good knowledge of the source and receptor languages and cultures, the **translator** must have skills in cross-language transfer. He must understand translation principles and be able to apply them. He must understand the structural differences between the two languages. If he has had enough linguistic training to compare the two languages, this will help him in the transfer process.

A good **translator** must be willing to receive help and criticism. He will want to test the translation with other people. When they don't understand or when they make suggestions, he needs to be able to accept their ideas without anger or resentment. Otherwise, he will not be able to test the translation adequately and improve the quality.

So far, we have talked mostly about the translator(s). There will be other people involved as well. Sometimes it is well to have **testers**. The translator himself may do the testing, but often it is an advantage to have others do this. A **tester** takes the draft of the translation to other people in the community to see if it can be understood clearly, and whether or not it communicates the right message. The person who does the testing must also understand translation principles and know the receptor language well. A **tester** needs to be a person who relates well to other people and knows how to listen carefully and record what is said to him. He will need to make notes of the comments made by those with whom he is testing. His goal is to be sure that the intended audience is able to understand well.   He will make suggestions which often make the translation more accurate, clearer, or more natural.

In addition to **testers**, sometimes it is also good to have some **reviewers. Reviewers** do not need to have had extensive training in translation principles. They are simply people who are interested in the translation and willing to help. They should, however, have an understanding of the concept of idiomatic translation, a good sense of style, and of grammatical structures. Their responsibility is to read through the translation and make comments or ask questions. Their comments are returned to the translator for his use in revision. It is good, if possible, to have a number of **reviewers**, representing a cross section of the audience. For example, if the translation is intended for a majority of the people, then some **reviewers** who are well educated, some of average education, and some new readers could be included on the team as **reviewers**. Both men and women should be included.

The purpose is to be sure that the whole range of prospective readers understands easily the message intended in the translation.

In some translation projects there will also be technical people to help such as **keyboarders** and **proofreaders**. Often the translator does his own manuscript preparation. However, if technical people are also included on the team it is important that they bring the skills needed and that they know how they fit into the project. It is important that technical people be very accurate and available to work when needed. The **keyboarder** can expect to prepare the preliminary drafts, often making stencils and duplicating material, so that copies can be sent to **testers** and **reviewers**. The **keyboarder** will need to make the corrections for each revision and will eventually prepare the final manuscript. It is important that, before becoming involved in the project, the **keyboarder** be aware of the work that is involved and have a willingness to make corrections several times — as many times as necessary to get a polished copy for the publisher.

In many translation projects there will also be an **advisor** or **consultant**. Even when a translator is completely bilingual and bicultural in the source and receptor languages and cultures, he may want someone with whom he can discuss both the exegesis of the source text and the translation equivalences which he has used. Many translators, who are translating from a source text which is written in their second language, will want a **consultant** to help solve especially difficult problems. Sometimes a person with more linguistic training can be of special help in comparing the two languages, following some of the ideas set up in the previous chapters of this book. To be of real help a **consultant** should have advanced knowledge of linguistics, of translation principles, and of the source language and culture. In addition, it is helpful if he is familiar with the receptor language or some related language with similar structures. His role is to help by discussing problems and to assist any members of the team who will need more training before the project can begin. There will be less frustration further on in the program, if each one is adequately trained for his job and if the responsibilities are carefully worked out ahead of time.

The **publisher** can also be considered part of the team, since without a **publisher** who is willing to publish the manuscript, the translation would not be completed. The important thing is to plan about publishing before starting the project. Each **publisher** has special regulations concerning format and supplementary information. The translator will save himself a lot of time later, if he knows from the beginning what format he is to use. Also, if he knows how the **publisher** likes to handle footnotes, glossaries, bibliography, and illustrations, it can be done that way from the beginning. It will save time later, not only for the translator, but especially for the keyboarder and others helping with the manuscript.

The **distributors** are also important people in the project. Sometimes the **publisher** is also the **distributor**. Other people may also be involved. If the translation is to be distributed widely, someone needs to organize publicity and distribution.

And finally,   but most important, every project must have a **coordinator**.   It may be the same person as the consultant, or the translator, or one of the testers.   But one person must take on this responsibility, with the rest of the team knowing clearly who is doing this important job.   The **coordinator** must help each member of the team do his part of the project well, advising and assisting in many ways.

In some projects, instead of a lot of individuals doing specific jobs, there will be a **committee** or **committees**.   Nida (1964:247–251) lists three types of committees which are sometimes a part of a translation project. These are the **editorial committee**, who do the drafting of the translation, a **review committee**, who provide special expertise in either the source or receptor language, and the **consultative committee**, who often simply give their approval to the translation, depending on the situation.   If **committees** are to be used, these should be carefully chosen and the work outlined as part of the establishing of the project. (For more on committees see Nida 1964:247–251).

In addition to deciding on the people who will be involved in the project and outlining the responsibilities for each member, it is helpful to work out a suggested time table for the project. This will help the members of the **team** and/or **committee** to know what their commitment is. It usually takes longer than planned, however, and this needs to be considered lest the translation never get finished. There needs to be commitment on the part of all members of the team. When there is a clear understanding of the goals and agreement on responsibilities and timing, the project is most likely to succeed.

The tools

We turn now to the materials needed for a successful project. **Tools** is used to refer, not just to the books that will be needed, but to the equipment, work space, and finances as well, that is, all the material aspects of the program. These matters need to be planned before the work gets under way.

First of all, plans should be made for where the work is to be done. A translator working by himself needs a **place** where he can work free from interruptions. If there is a team working on the project, each member will need a **place** to carry on his or her part of the work. And if there is a committee planning to work together it is very important that a special meeting **place** be planned. This may seem obvious. But the frustration of interruptions because of lack of a work area has often discouraged the completion of a translation. The best work will be done under good working conditions. This will need planning ahead of time and perhaps some financial outlay as well.

What **equipment** will be needed? Typewriters, computers, printers, and a duplicator or photocopy machine are a must. Are these available for the project?

It is especially important that the translator(s) have available the **books** they will need for **reference** in studying the source text and culture. A good translator will make use of dictionaries, lexicons, grammars, cultural descriptions, other **books** written during the same historical period, and any other materials which will help him to have a full understanding of the source text and the culture. These **books** should be chosen and accumulated at the place where the translation work will be done before the work begins. There may also be **books** written on the receptor language and culture which will be helpful, including a good dictionary.

Those planning the project must also consider the **financial resources** available for the program. What will be the source of such income? Who will disperse the funds? What will the salaries be for each member of the team (if salaries are to be paid)? How much will the supplies cost, the books, the training? The main expenses for a translation project (Barnwell 1983a:17) include:

a. Salary for the translator(s).

b. Salary for the keyboarder.

c. Expenses for the translator to attend training courses and sometimes special workshops. This would include the travel expenses.

d. Expenses for those who are testing the translation, including travel expenses and cost of attending training courses or committee meetings.

e. Sometimes equipment may need to be bought: typewriter, computer, duplicating machine, desk, etc.

f. Stationery: paper, stencils, ink, carbon paper, paper clips, etc.

g. Cost of duplicating and circulating the trial copies to testers and reviewers.

h. The expense of publishing. It needs to be determined ahead of time who will be paying for the publishing and distribution.

A translation program has the greatest hope of being successful when the four T's (text, target, team, and tools) are arranged far before the project is begun. Whoever wishes to establish a project must take a careful look at the **text** to be sure it should be translated. He should think carefully about who the **target audience** or readers will be and what effect this will have on the style of the translation. He needs to be sure that people are available to form a **team** that can work together and complete the work. He must have available the **tools** needed to do the work, including the funds for paying expenses. Once these matters are in order, the translation work can begin.

EXERCISES – Establishing the Project

A. If you are planning a translation project, write up that project according to the matters discussed in this chapter: the text, the audience, the alphabet, the team, and the tools. Give a careful description of each aspect of your proposed program, with names, dates, and other details, if possible.

   If you do not yet have a specific program in mind, think of one in which you might be interested and write it up in the same way, even if it is only imaginary.

B. If the above program was for translating into your mother tongue, write up a similar program for translating into your second language.

Chapter 36
Translation Procedures

Throughout this book, translation has been presented as a process which begins with the source text, analyzes this text into semantic structure, and then restructures this semantic structure into appropriate receptor language forms in order to create an equivalent receptor language text. This is a very general way of looking at the translation process. Translation is actually much more complicated than such an overview might indicate. In actual practice, the translator moves back and forth from the source text to the receptor text. Sometimes he will be analyzing the source text in order to find the meaning, then restructuring this meaning in the receptor language, and moving back once again to look at the source text or the semantic analysis which he has done. All three are repeatedly looked at as he works. Below, we will discuss the steps or procedures which the translator follows as if they were done in a given order. But it must be kept in mind that, in practice, there will be this moving back and forth. At times, even while he is working on the final draft, the translator will go back and reread things he looked at in his preparation. He should, as a matter of fact, often refer back to these materials.

The steps to be discussed below include (1) preparation, (2) analysis, (3) transfer, (4) initial draft, (5) reworking the initial draft, (6) testing the translation, (7) polishing the translation, and (8) preparing the manuscript for the publisher. (Numbers 6-8 are discussed in chapter 37.)

Preparation

There are two kinds of **preparation**. First, there is the **preparation** which the translator should have before beginning the translation task and, secondly, there is the **preparation** which he undertakes as he begins work on a specific translation project. The first kind of **preparation** should have included training in writing, in linguistics, and in translation principles. (**Preparation** in writing and some linguistic studies have been assumed for students using this book.)

519

The translator should have had practice in writing the receptor language. Unless he has done some **creative writing**, other than translation, it will be hard for him to write naturally in the receptor language. Good writers make good translators. They are used to putting the forms of the language on paper. Attending a writers workshop may be excellent preparation for translation. Such a workshop would also give help in matters of manuscript preparation and publishing. It is also helpful if the translator has had enough **linguistic study** so that he can discover the features of the receptor language which indicate the groupings, cohesion, and prominence in that language. He needs to be able to make comparisons between the lexical structures of the two languages, as done in Part II of this book. It is assumed that he will have had training in **translation principles**.

The above matters should be cared for before the project is begun. Once the project is underway, then the translator begins the second kind of **preparation – preparation** related to the text to be translated. He will first want to become well acquainted with the text. To do this he will **read the entire text through several times**. As he reads through he may want to mark any sections which seem unclear. His purpose is to understand the message intended by the author, as well as to get a feel for the style and the emotional tone. He asks himself, "What is the information that is being communicated?" and also, "What feelings or impact is the text intended to have on the readers?"

Next, the translator will want to **study the background material** which is available. This will include finding out about the author, about the circumstances of the writing of the text, the purpose for which it was written, the culture of the source text, and for whom the text was written. If the text is historical, a study should be made of the period of history in which the events took place and in which the text was written. If the text is about a culture unfamiliar to the translator, special attention should be given to studying the cultural background of the source text. History books, anthropological descriptions, encyclopedias, and commentaries about the text may be helpful. If there is more than one version of the source text, these should be compared.

The study of background material should also include the **study of linguistic matters** related to the text. In some cases, it may be very helpful for the translator himself to do a comparison of texts in the source and receptor languages. He may be able to do this in a special workshop where he can study the texts of the receptor language with some guidance. Special attention should be given to studying texts of the same genre as the one to be translated. The discourse features of the particular genre in focus should be looked at carefully. The analysis of the various grammatical matters discussed previously in this book will also be of benefit to the translator.

During the reading and rereading of the text, the translator will want to make notes. For example, he will note the key terms and the sections which seem obscure and will need added research. There may be cultural matters which immediately strike him as potential problems. He will want to do added study on these. As he researches, he should take notes for later use. When he feels acquainted with the text he is ready to begin the analysis.

Analysis

As the translator reads through the text, he should write down any lexical items which seem to be **key words**. These will be words which are crucial to an understanding of the text. One of the first steps in **analysis** should be a careful study of these **key words**, in order to find a good lexical equivalent in the receptor language. Often it will be necessary to consult dictionaries and encyclopedias for more information. The components of meaning which are crucial and need to be transferred should be identified (principles to be followed are found in Part II above). The translator may want to start a notebook or file for these special words. When a decision is made about a lexical equivalent, he should write this down to refer to when it reoccurs. Later, when he begins transferring into the receptor language, he must be careful, however, that he does not slavishly follow the material in the notebook and end up with pseudo-concordance. This preliminary study is to help focus attention on words which are going to be important and must be given special attention in the transfer process, but each context must be considered separately when such **key words** are used in the translation (see chapter 10).

If the text is a very long one, the translator will need to divide it into smaller units and work on one of these at a time. Therefore, it is important to **study the groupings** of the text next. If the text is divided into sections or chapters, this may be helpful. But if, as in the case of the Bible, there are chapter divisions marked which do not actually coincide with the grammatical and semantic units of the source text, the translator will need to be very careful as he looks for boundaries of units. Most texts will be marked for chapter divisions only if there is a real semantic break. Particular attention should be given to **identifying** the **opening** and the **closing** of the text. They will give clues concerning the theme. In addition, they may be written in a special style and will need to be considered carefully in the drafting of the translation. **Groupings** will depend on the genre of the text (review chapter 30). The translator will also need to note the **relations** between various units, discover what the **cohesive devices** used are indicating (see chapter 31), and also identify the units which are most prominent. Unless matters of **prominence** (see chapter 32) are carefully analyzed, the meaning of the text may be distorted when the drafting is done.

Although the principles of analysis in this book are taught beginning with the smaller units and moving up to the whole discourse, the actual analytical process is the opposite. The translator analyzes the larger units first, identifying the units and the relations between them, deciding which are more prominent, etc. Then he studies the smaller units, such as paragraphs and sentences. The analysis of the source text, as well as the transfer into the receptor language, is a dynamic process. Although the translator begins with the larger units and moves down to smaller ones, he will also be constantly moving back to look at the larger units and to reevaluate his analysis on the basis of the analysis of smaller units. This moving back and forth between larger and smaller units is very important. If a translator simply translates sentences, without keeping the episode structure in mind, for example, the translation will contain distortions of meaning. On the other hand, it is impossible to keep clearly in mind a very large unit. The paragraph is probably the basic unit which the translator should focus on, while at the same time moving up to higher levels and down to detail.

Once familiar with the larger units and how they relate to one another, the translator is ready to begin smaller units. He may decide to work on a given episode, but even so, he will have to do the actual detailed work on an even smaller unit. He may analyze all the paragraphs of a given episode into some form of semantic representation before beginning the initial draft. He should go through a given paragraph, identifying all of the EVENTS and all of the PARTICIPANTS, including any that may be implicit in the source text. All secondary senses, figurative senses, and rhetorical functions of words, phrases, clauses, or sentences should be noted. In fact, any of the many potential adjustments discussed in Parts 2 and 3 should be considered. Many translators find it helpful to **rewrite** in the source language the part of the text they are working on **in propositions, eliminating the skewing** between the deep and surface structure of the source text. (How to do this is described in chapter 24.) Relationships between propositions or propositional clusters should also be indicated as discussed in Parts IV and V.

How detailed the analysis will be will vary with the difficulty of the text. The more difficult the text, the more need there will be for a careful rewrite into semantic structure before any transfer is begun. The translator should not become burdened with making extensive semantic displays. They are a tool to help in his analysis. Some find it most helpful to simply rewrite the text in a near semantic presentation like the following:

SOURCE TEXT

There are no sure ways to avoid having your pocket picked. But there are some common-sense points everyone should remember. Carry with you only what money you need, and don't flash it. If you're a woman, don't let your handbag dangle; hold the bag itself with your hand over the clasp. For a man, an inside pocket is the easiest picking. Above all, be suspicious in crowds. Move instantly when jostled.

REWRITE OF THE TEXT

There is nothing you can do in order to be sure that no one will steal your money from your pocket or purse. But there are some things you should remember which will make it less likely to happen. These are common sense things which you can do. You should carry with you only the amount of money which you need. You should not display the money in such a way that others can see it. You, women, should not let your handbags dangle, but rather you should hold the bag in your hands with a hand over the clasp so that the bag cannot be easily opened. You, men, should not put your money in the pocket which is inside your coat. Thieves can very easily steal it from this pocket. When you are in a crowd, you should always be suspicious that someone is trying to steal your money. Therefore, you should move instantly when someone jostles you.

This kind of a semantic rewrite can be very helpful since *most of the implicit information is made explicit and the secondary and figurative senses eliminated.* However, when the translator uses this rewrite to translate, he should not make a literal translation of the rewrite. Rather, he should use it as a base and draft a translation of it which is clear and natural in the receptor language. The rewrite is an exegetical tool.

Concerning the importance of analysis, Nida (1981:98) says that the most satisfactory approach to translation consists:

...in the syntactic and semantic analysis of the source language text. This means essentially determining the underlying semantic structure both of the linguistic units and of the various combinations. Once this has been done thoroughly, one is then in a much better position to transfer from the source to the receptor language, for the underlying structures of language are formally and semantically closer together than are the surface structures of languages.

Transfer

Transfer is the process of going from the semantic structure analysis to the initial draft of the translation. The **transfer** takes place in the mind of the translator. The semantic analysis will have eliminated most of the skewing between the deep and surface structure of the source text. After this is done the translator is faced with **transferring** this meaning into the second language and introducing the appropriate receptor language skewing. A literal translation of the semantic structure display will not be a good translation. In the **transfer** process, the translator is producing a receptor language equivalent. In carrying out this process, he will look for good lexical equivalence for concepts of the source language and culture, he will decide whether or not the figurative and rhetorical devices of the source language will be transferable or if some adjustment will need to be made, he will consider what grammatical forms to use to best communicate the correct meaning, and he will consider how to signal cohesion and prominence. The kinds of adjustments that will be made have been illustrated throughout this book. Without an adequate study on translation principles the **transfer** process can be very difficult and the results unsatisfactory. The transfer process will result in an initial draft.

Initial draft

The work of analysis, transfer, and **initial drafting** are not independent the one of the other. As Nida points out (1981:99):

> ...in analyzing the meaning of a text in a source language, one bears in mind the kinds of problems which one will inevitably face in the transfer of the meaning into the receptor language. Analysis of the rhetorical structure inevitably involves some consideration of the relationship of the rhetorical devices to equivalent devices in the receptor language. In a sense, the translator is engaging in analysis, transfer, and restructuring more or less all at the same time.

Once again, there will be this moving back and forth from the source to the receptor text. As soon as the translator begins making his **initial draft**, he may find that he needs more information, as far as analysis is concerned, and may need to go back for more background reading or check again in the dictionary. As he transfers the meaning, he will not ignore completely the forms of the source text, for there may be times when the best equivalent will be identical to the form used in the source text, but at other times very different forms will be used.

As the translator begins the initial draft, he should be working at paragraph level. Once he is sure what the paragraph is to communicate, he should compose the draft as naturally as possible, without looking at the source language or even the semantic rewrite. He should just let it flow naturally, expressing the meaning clearly. It is easier to polish a draft which is natural, even if it does not include all the information, than rework a text for naturalness later. Once he has a natural draft of the paragraph, he can check for any missing information, for accuracy, etc. A good translation is based on good analysis. If the analysis was well done and the meaning is clear, the translator will not find it difficult to express the meaning in the receptor language.

However, there are a number of things which the translator should keep in mind as he does this **initial draft**. First of all, he should be thinking clearly about who will use the translation, their level of education, and other matters discussed in the previous chapter on establishing the project (chapter 35). The audience should be like a backdrop to all of the **drafting**. He should also have in mind the author's purpose, since this also will affect decisions in **drafting**. The topic of the paragraph should be clearly in the translator's mind, as well as the theme of the larger unit to which it belongs. The semantic structure analysis will help him know which propositions are on the main line of the discourse and which are background, and also, what the relations are between them. There are many things to keep in mind as one translates. It is the combination of all of these that will make for an accurate and natural **draft**.

Reworking the initial draft

The **reworking of an initial draft** should not be undertaken until a larger section is completed. It is best if the **draft** has been left untouched for a week or two. In this way the translator comes with a fresh look at it and is able to be more objective in his evaluation and **reworking** of it. The **reworking of the initial draft** includes checking for naturalness and for accuracy.

The first thing the translator will do is to **read through the manuscript** of this larger unit which he is checking. Sometimes it helps to **read it out loud** or to **read it into a tape recorder and listen to it.** In doing this, he should be looking for (1) wrong grammatical forms or obscure constructions, (2) places that seem too wordy, (3) wrong order, awkward phrasing, (4) places where the connections do not seem right and it does not flow easily, (5) collocational clashes, (6) questionable meaning, i.e., it seems strange now that he hears it read, and (7) style. Anything at all that makes it sound unnatural and foreign should be marked and then reworked. He will need to read through several times, concentrating on one potential problem at a time.

The second thing the translator will need to do is to check for **accuracy of meaning**. He can only do this by a careful comparison with the source text and the semantic analysis. Some of the problems he may find are (1) something omitted, (2) something added, (3) a different meaning, or (4) a zero meaning, that is, the form used just does not communicate any meaning at all. When checking for meaning, he will look not only at the meaning of the words, but also of the sentences and especially the relations between the sentences and the paragraphs and larger units. He must ask himself, "Do the grammatical forms chosen in the initial draft clearly communicate the relations intended in the source text?"

A third thing the translator will need to check is whether or not the **theme** comes through clearly. Not having looked at the draft for a while, he may be able to evaluate this. This may be one of the things that will be more easily evaluated through the comprehension testing which will be done a bit later in the procedures.

The draft should also be read through concentrating on the **information load**. Is the amount and kind of redundancy natural in the receptor language? Is there such a heavy load of explicit information that it is hard to follow the main ideas? Should some information be made implicit? Or should some be made more explicit because lack of certain information is obscuring the communication?

Keeping all these things in mind, the translator will make adjustments in the **initial draft** and do a **second draft** in order to care for any matters that need changing. It is good to do a **second draft** even if no serious errors were found. Most writers **rework** a document they are preparing for publication several times before the **final draft** is ready. In **redrafting**, one tends to make the style more natural and eliminate awkward wordings. A translator must be willing to **reword the draft** several times before the **final draft** is prepared.

After the translator himself has done this **second draft**, he is ready to have it tested with others. Sometimes he does this testing himself. Sometimes there are members of the team who are trained to be testers. They will do the testing and bring the results back to the translator for consideration in the next (third) draft. Testing procedures and manuscript preparation will be discussed in the next chapter.

EXERCISES – Translation Procedures

A. Translate the following text into a language other than English. Follow through with the steps as outlined in this chapter. First, do whatever preparation is needed, then analyze the text and transfer the meaning into an initial draft. Check this carefully with the source text, read it for naturalness, and do a second draft. Your audience consists of adults who have finished no more than primary education and are not bilingual in the source language. (This text is from *Universal History of the World*, Volume 2 [Ancient Greece] by James L. Steffensen, 1966, Gulden Press, New York.)

During the Dark Age, the large kingdoms of Homer's Achaean heroes had disappeared. The Greek world was now dotted with dozens of little countries. They had begun with fortresses set on hills and crags. Soon each fortress was surrounded by a village, as farmers abandoned their huts in the fields and built new homes close to the walls. In times of danger, they could take refuge behind the walls. A market place was built, and a few metalsmiths and potters opened shops. When temples were set up inside the fortress, the castle hill became an acropolis, a "high-town," sacred center of a kingdom as well as a place to hide from attackers. The village chief began to call himself a king.

In a kingdom not much bigger than a town, everyone could keep an eye on the king and his friends, the noblemen. The people watched their rulers carefully, for life in Greece was changing, and not always for the better. Food was scarce, and there was meat only on holidays. The rest of the year, the people ate mostly barley porridge, and sometimes fruit and olives. Even wheat was expensive, and no one had much money. The little kingdoms did not have enough olive trees to make them rich. Besides, the groves belonged to the noblemen, who never shared their profits.

These new noblemen were not knights. They managed the kingdom's business, like a town council, and they kept a tight hold on their land. But when it came to war, they were perfectly willing to give everyone a share in the fighting. Noblemen no longer rode to battle in chariots and fought in single combat. Battles were now fought by long lines of men who formed a deadly wall of swords and shields. All armies used the new formation, and to be effective it required every man in the kingdom.

That meant more problems for the king. The citizen-soldiers began to ask why, if they were so important in battle, they should not be just as important at home. They made angry speeches at the Citizens' Assembly, to which all the men of the kingdom belonged. The Assembly had always had the right to vote on peace or war, but the citizens began to demand the right to vote on other things. They wanted land, new laws, more food, and lower taxes. The king promised to see what he could do, hoping that this would be enough to satisfy them.

Chapter 37
Testing the Translation

A translator is concerned that the result of his work be a good quality translation. How can the translator know if he has succeeded or not? He must be willing not only to check it carefully himself, but also to expose it to testing of several kinds. A translation which does not effectively communicate the message of the source text is of limited value. The translator has wasted his time. Even if someone publishes it, people will not buy it and use it. And so the procedures involved in **testing** the translation are a very important step in the total project.

Testing should be begun early in the project. After the first section, episode, or chapter is completed, it should be **tested**. If early materials are **tested**, this will give feedback to the translator which will point out his weaknesses and help him to do better and better as he moves along. He will not keep making the same kinds of mistakes over and over. Also, the **testing** will be more adequate if done on smaller units. If it is left until there is a great volume of work, it may not be done as carefully. In addition to the checking of each part, when it is all finished, it will need a final revision (review or polishing), looking at it as a total discourse as well.

Four aspects of testing will be discussed below: (1) **why** test the translation, (2) **who** does the testing, (3) **how** the testing is done, and finally, (4) **how the results are used** in polishing the final manuscript.

Why test the translation

There are three main reasons for testing a translation. The translator wants to be sure his translation is **accurate, clear,** and **natural**. These three features are important throughout the translation, so the entire translation must be checked for each one. In any sentence, there may be need for improvement in **accuracy, clarity,** or **naturalness**. It is very easy, as one is translating, to inadvertently omit some piece of information. Sometimes in restructuring, the translator is working hard at getting across the meaning and in so doing adds information which was not really in the source text. This information will need to be deleted. Sometimes mistakes are made in the analysis of the source text or in the transfer process and a different meaning results. It is because all translators make these kinds of mistakes, that a careful check for **accuracy** is needed. Note the following examples of inaccurate translation (sentences are numbered for convenience in discussing the text):

SOURCE TEXT (Saramacan, Suriname)

1. De   fisi   de   kai gede a   de baaku ku   weti.   2. Basu
　The fish they call gede it is black and white   Under

bee   feen   noo tade wetiweti. 3. Nusu buka   feen   tade
stomach of-him only is   white   Nose mouth of-him is

baaibaai. 4. A   taabi   bia   a   buka. 5. A   tade a   sitonu
broad   It has   whiskers on mouth   It is   in   stone

baaku. 6. A nango a   kakisi. 7. Ma de   tasuti en ku   goni.
holes   It goes   in trap   But they shoot   it   with gun

8. Fisi da di   soni   di   a   tanjan. 9. De   taa   a   suti
　Fish is the thing which it eats   They say   it   sweet

tumisi.
exceedingly

AN ACCURATE ENGLISH TRANSLATION

There is a kind of fish called Gede. It is black and white except for the belly which is all white. It has a flat, broad nose, and whiskers on its mouth. Gede fish live in rock crevices and feed on other fish. People catch them in traps or shoot them with a gun. They are delicious.

AN INACCURATE TRANSLATION

The fish called Gede is striped. The stripes are black and white except on the stomach where it is solid white. Its nose is very long and it has whiskers. It lives in the holes in rocks. People catch Gede in traps and they also shoot them with guns. The people eat this fish which is very delicious.

The above translation is inaccurate in the following ways:

1. The addition of *striped* is not justified by the text. It would need to be checked in the background information, but it looks like extraneous information.

2. The source language word *baaibaai* is glossed as *broad*. It refers to the width, not the length of the nose. This is a wrong meaning.

3. The location of whiskers has been omitted.

4. The information about what the fish eats, that is, that it eats fish, has been omitted also. (Or perhaps there is a wrong analysis of sentence 8.)

The second reason for testing a translation is to be sure that it is **clear**. A translation may be accurate but still not communicate to the people who are to use it. The forms of the language used should be those which make the message of the source text as easy to understand as the source text itself was to understand. As we will discuss in detail later, the only way to check for **clarity** is to test it with persons who are not familiar with the source text and ask questions which will show what they understand. Notice the following example in which the information is the same as in the text above, but the message does not come through clearly in English.

UNCLEAR TRANSLATION

There is a fish called Gede, black and white and white stomached. It is broad mouthed with whiskers on it. It is in holes of rocks. It goes into traps. People shoot it with guns. What it eats is fish. People say, "It is very sweet."

It is unclear if *Gede* is a single fish by that name or the name of a type of fish. It is unclear where the whiskers are. The sentence about *holes of rocks* is unclear. It is unclear why it *goes in traps*, although the reader might be able to guess. The word *sweet* is not normally used about fish. Is it really *sweet,* or does it mean something else? The above is an unclear translation of the source text.

The third reason for testing the translation is to be sure that it is **natural**. A translation may be accurate in that the translator understood correctly the source text and is attempting to communicate that information, and it may even by understandable, and yet the forms may not be the natural idiomatic forms of the receptor language. The translation must be tested to see if the grammatical forms used are those normally used. Does the translation "flow" easily? Does it "sound right" to the speakers of the language, or does it sound "foreign?" When we hear foreigners speak our language, we can often understand them. The message is accurate and clear, but at the same time they sound strange. The translator does not want his translation to sound "strange" or "foreign." He wants it to sound **natural**, as if it were not even a translation, but an original composition in the receptor language. The following is an unnatural translation of the text given above in Saramacan about the Gede fish:

AN UNNATURAL TRANSLATION

There is a fish called Gede. It is black and white and white stomached. It is broad mouthed with whiskers on it. It lives in the holes of rocks. It goes into traps and gets caught. People also shoot it with a gun. It eats fish. People say it tastes good.

In the above English translation, the individual sentences are correct English. The information is accurate and can be understood. However, the style is very unnatural and monotonous. The information is not told in an interesting way. The same forms are used over and over. It does not "flow" as a coherent paragraph. It is an unnatural translation.

Who tests the translation

The translation will be of better quality if several people are involved in testing. Of course, the **translator himself** will do a lot of careful checking and testing. He will need to be responsible for what are called **self-checks**. (See **comparison** and **back-translation** later.) He may also do the **comprehension testing**. That is, he may go out and ask various people to help him by reading the translation or listening to it and then answering questions about it (details will be given later). He will do some **naturalness checking**, too, by comparing his translation with texts in the receptor language, and by having people read the translation, or by reading it over and over to himself. Some kinds of **self-checks** were discussed near the end of chapter 36, under "reworking the initial draft."

If a **translation consultant** is available, he can be of tremendous help in checking the translation, especially for possible inaccuracies and for the correct use of translation principles. The consultant can also train the translator in how to do other kinds of testing, and in the final manuscript preparation, he can answer the many questions which come up. It is especially advantageous for the translator to have a working relationship with a consultant from the beginning of the project. In that way, the consultant can encourage the translator throughout the project and help him learn how to apply the principles he has learned. A consultant can often help with difficult exegetical questions.

It is good if each translation project has some **testers**. If not, the translator also will need to be the **tester**. But someone needs to test the translation with people who are unfamiliar with the source text in order to see if it communicates clearly. This is done by using comprehension questions. The method will be outlined later. The qualifications of **testers** were discussed in chapter 35.

There will also be **reviewers**. They are people who are willing to read through the translation and make comments about clarity and naturalness. If they are familiar with the source text, they may also raise questions about accuracy. Reviewers' qualifications were also discussed in chapter 35.

The **translator(s), consultants, testers,** and **reviewers** will all need to work together with one goal – to make the translation as **accurate, clear,** and **natural** as possible.

Ways of testing a translation

There are several ways of testing a translation. There is some overlap between them, in that the same person may be involved in several kinds of tests, and the tests may give similar information about the translation. The following ways will be discussed: (1) comparison with the source text, (2) back-translation into the source language, (3) comprehension checks, (4) naturalness and readability testing, and finally, (5) consistency checks.

Whatever kind of checking is being done, it needs to be done systematically, and notes need to be taken carefully. A "hit-or-miss" kind of checking will not lead to a quality translation. The one who is checking must know for what he is checking. Randomness in testing is ineffective because a person cannot think about many things at once. Each kind of check should be done separately, with specific goals, and with notes recorded for the translator to use in revision. The notes are important, not just for improving the translation which was checked, but also for evaluating the errors which are repeated again and again. By studying the notes, the translator will be able to identify his weaknesses and overcome them in future work. The content of the notes will depend on the kind of check which is being done. It is often helpful to have a chart and tick off the completion of each kind of test, section by section, throughout the translation. At the time they are marked as completed, the results should be filed in a place where they will be readily available for revision work.

Comparison with the source language

A careful **comparison** with the source text will need to be made several times during the translation process. We have already mentioned the importance of this kind of check when doing the second draft (see chapter 36). The translator will want to do a careful **comparison** at several points in the total project. Also, when he considers the translation completed, he will go back and do one more careful comparison. It is easy to make mistakes at any step in the translation process. One of the main purposes of the **comparison** is to check for equivalence of information content. This check is done to be sure that all the information is included – nothing omitted, nothing added, and nothing different. The **comparison** is a self-check; that is, it is done by the translator. It could, of course, be done by someone else who knows both languages well and knows translation principles.

After checking to be sure that all of the information is there, the translator will make another **comparison** of source language and receptor language texts, looking for any problems or potential problems. He will note anything he wants to rethink or check with other people. He needs to be as objective as possible and look at his own work critically. At the same time, he should be cautious and not just change things without carefully thinking about it.

The best way to do **comparison** checks is to have a draft of the translation which is typed with double spacing and wide margins so that ideas can be written in the margin and so that alternatives can be written above the line for later evaluation. The purpose is not to conform the translation to the forms of the source language. We have already discussed in great detail the need to use the natural forms of the receptor language. But it is important to be constantly checking to be sure that the meaning and the dynamics of the source text are indeed communicated by the translation.

Back-translation

A second way to check a translation is by having someone else, who is bilingual in the source and receptor languages, make a back-translation of the translated text into the source language. This person takes the translation and writes out the meaning he gets from it back into the source language. He should do this without having read the source text used by the translator. This **back-translation** will let the translator know what is being communicated to this person.

A **back-translation** is not meant to be a polished idiomatic text in the source language. Rather, it is a literal rendering of the translation to be used for checking purposes. It should have each lexical item rendered literally. The sentences used in the **back-translation** may, however, be in the normal form of the source language grammar. Translating and **back-translating** are very different. In translating, one uses natural and clear forms; in **back-translating**, literal forms are used in order to show up the structure of the translation being **back-translated**.

Notice the following example of a source text, translation, and **back-translation**. (The Aguaruna was written by Silas Cuñachi. Sentences are numbered in order to make the comparison with the **back-translation** easier.)

SOURCE TEXT

The Orphan Boy

There once was a man who lived alone with his wife. They had no children. He said to his relatives, "Please have pity on me. I want a child to raise so that I will have someone to go with me when I go to work." Then one of his relatives named Wampukus answered, "There is a child at my house who has no parents. He is nearly grown up. I will give him to you, but be careful. He will pester you all the time asking to go and swim across the river. On the other hand he is an obedient child." Then he went and brought the child to the man....

TRANSLATION INTO AGUARUNA

1. *Makichik Uchi   Bitaik   Tsakapagbou*
   One   child orphan   that-which-was-brought-up

2. *Aishmag nuwentin uchigmachu jimagchik pujus   pataayin*
   Man   married childless just-two   staying his-relatives-obj

iniasu, "Waitjuktajum, wi uchijiimainun   wakejajai uchin
asked   have-pity-on-me I able-to-have-child-obj I-want   child-obj

tsakapagtasan,   'uyuntusat   wi takamunum' tusan."
in-order-that-I-raise that-he-accompany-me I while-working I-saying

3. *Tutai   Wampukus aiku,   "Mina jegajui   pujawai uchi*
   He-saying-ds Wampukus answered Mine at-my-house lives   child

dukugtuchu ashi tsakaje.   Nuna   amastajai,   tujash
motherless all he-has-grown-up That-obj I-will-give-to-you but

kuitamakata,	*waitkagmastatui*		*namaka*	*yukumak*
be-careful	he-will-cause-you-to-suffer		river	swimming

wekeenuwe	*amain*	*katigtatus,*	*tujashush*	*chichaman*
one-who-desires-to	across	in-order-to-cross	however	word-obj

uminuwe. "	4.	*Akatjamak*	*imatiksag*	*itauwe...*
he-is-one-who-obeys		Advising	doing-like-that	he-brought-him

BACK-TRANSLATION OF AGUARUNA TRANSLATION

(1) An Orphan Child which was Brought Up.

(2) A married man who was childless, just the two of them living together, asked his relatives, "You (pl) pity me, I want to be able to have a child in order to raise the child, in order that he accompany me while I am working." (3) He saying that, Wampukus answered, "At my house there lives a child who is motherless, almost grown-up. That I will give to you, but be careful, he will cause you to suffer, being one who desires to swim in the river in order to go across. However, he is one who obeys what he is told." (4) Advising like that he brought him....

A **back-translation** makes it possible for the translator and a consultant to make a careful comparison with the source text, looking for differences in meaning and for inadequate application of translation principles. It gives the consultant access to the translation, even when he does not know the receptor language.

Care should be taken, however, in the use of a **back-translation**. Like most other checking methods, it has some potential weaknesses. If the person who did the **back-translation** lacks fluency in one or the other of the languages or becomes careless, the **back-translation** might be a poor **back-translation** of a very good translation. **Back-translations** do not test naturalness. The translation may be less idiomatic than it seemed from the **back-translation** or more idiomatic. These matters need to be checked by other methods. The **back-translation** focuses on meaning equivalence rather than naturalness.

But, at the same time, a **back-translation** is an important tool. It is especially helpful if the translator wishes to consult with someone who does not speak the receptor language. The **back-translation** can then be used by the consultant to understand what is being communicated by the translation. On the basis of the **back-translation**, he will be able to ask questions about analysis of the source text and the application of translation principles. In an extended translation project, it is usually good to have someone trained as the back-translator. A person who is truly bilingual and trained to do **back-translation** can be of great help in improving the quality of the translation.

Comprehension tests

Good **comprehension testing** is the key to a good translation. The purpose of this test is to see whether or not the translation is understood correctly by speakers of the language who have not seen the translation previously. It is designed to find out what the translation is communicating to the audience for whom it is intended. This type of test involves having people retell the content of the translation and answer questions about it. The results of such testing will help the translator improve the translation so that it says what it is meant to say and so that it is clear and uses natural receptor language form.

Comprehension testing may be done by the translator himself or by some other person especially trained to do this type of testing. If the translator himself does the testing, he will need to be very careful not to be defensive of his work, but to want to really know the truth of what is being communicated by the translation. Ideally, someone else will do this testing. This is better because someone else takes a new look at the translation. Also, it may be hard for the translator to be objective about his own work. Whoever does the testing should be trained in translation principles and understand the goals of an idiomatic translation. He should be trained in how to do the testing, be a person who relates well with people, and knows how to listen well and record accurately.

Comprehension testing is done with persons who are fluent speakers of the receptor language. These people should be ordinary people from various segments of the society. Testing should be done with young people, middle aged, and older people. It should be done with the more highly educated and with the newly literate, if the translation is intended for all. If the translation is intended for a special group, then a variety of people from that group should be included as respondents. It should be done when the respondents are relaxed and have time. If they are under pressure, they will not give adequate thought to the questions being asked. The respondent should be someone who is positive about helping and wants to be involved in improving the translation. It is important to explain carefully that the test is not to test him, the respondent, but is to test the translation. It is not an intelligence test, nor a test of his memory ability, nor of his ability to formulate fancy answers. It is simply a way of finding out if the translation needs improving in some way. The translation, not the respondent, is being tested, and it is important that the respondent know that. Some people will just naturally be more helpful than others. However, those who are less helpful should not be made to feel that they have failed.

During the testing, the **tester** should be keeping careful records of the responses he is getting. Using a cassette recorder can be very helpful. However, he should also be taking down notes. The **tester(s)** needs to be given a copy of the translation which has wide margins with plenty of room to make notes. Some **testers** have found it helpful to have the questions they wish to ask typed in a column down one side of a sheet of paper, leaving room after the questions for three columns, one for correct answers, one for wrong answers, and one for questionable answers. Then, later the **tester** and translator can evaluate the answers that were given. Each **tester** will work out the system which best helps him record the information. The notes should also include any criticisms or suggestions made by the respondents. All comments about the translation should be recorded even though they may not seem helpful at the time.

Depending on the situation, the **tester** may read to the respondent the material to be tested, or the respondent may read it for himself. The method chosen will depend on the level of education of the respondent. The first testing is for **overview**. The respondent is asked to retell or give a summary of the material read. The **tester** should be careful to choose a section which is a unit and which is not so long that it would be hard to remember the content. The purpose of asking for a retelling of the content is to see if the main event-line or the theme-line is clear. People tend to remember the main events or the main theme of something they read. This will be what they can tell back. If they tell this back correctly, then it is clear the translation is communicating correctly in this respect. If they have trouble retelling the theme, it may be that some revision will need to be done on the discourse structure of the translation.

It is very important that the **tester** not interrupt the respondent as he is retelling the content. Rather, he should simply jot down notes on what is said, or record it on a cassette to refer back to later. He should not break the respondent's train of thought. And he should certainly never correct him. If the respondent gets it all mixed up, that is alright, because it is important to know that he had this problem. But he should not be corrected or intimidated in any way. When the respondent retells what he has read, hopefully, he will recall those points which were the main events of a narrative, the main steps of a procedure, or the main points of an exposition. This is very important in checking for theme and other discourse features.

Sometimes the respondent may want to do a written retelling or summary. He will write a sort of paraphrase in his own words. This can be very helpful and will often suggest some improvements in the form of the translation. A written restating of the text can be especially helpful in testing such features as theme and prominence at higher levels of the discourse.

The second step in **comprehension testing** is asking questions about the translated text. The questions should be prepared ahead of time, not made up on the spot. This gives the **tester** time to think through what he expects the respondent to understand and, also, to decide exactly what he wants to check. In this way he can formulate the questions carefully, so as to obtain the information for which he is looking. It will help him use the time well while working with the respondent. People are more apt to be willing to help if the **tester** is prepared and knows what he wants to ask.

There are several kinds of questions, each with a different purpose. Questions may be asked to give information about the **discourse style**, or about the **theme** of the text, or they may be questions which have to do with **details**. Each of these will be briefly discussed and illustrated. (For more details see Rountree 1983.)

Style questions are concerned with the genre as well as the style of the translation. The purpose is to see if the text is appropriately and skillfully told. The following types of questions are suggested by Rountree:

What kind of talk is this? story? instructions? scolding? advice?

Was the person who told this story young or old, man or woman?

Do you think he tells stories very often?

Do you think he was talking to children or adults, men or women?

Do you think he was in a hurry? Why?

Some possible answers to these questions are:

"I think an old person told it because a young person would not use this vocabulary."

"I think he was talking to children because the vocabulary is so simple."

"I think he was in a hurry because he just gives the facts one after the other without any padding."

These questions and answers tell a great deal about the style of the translation. They show whether or not the translation is at a level of complexity appropriate to the audience for whom it is intended.

Questions may also be asked which are designed to evaluate the translation of the **theme**. These questions focus on the high points of the story or argument. Notice the following examples which might be used to test a translation of the story of the *Tower of Babylon*. (See Rountree 1983:8–12 for further discussion of these questions. The story is first given from the *Good News Bible* and then the questions listed below the story.)

TRANSLATION TO BE CHECKED

At first, the people of the whole world had only one language and used the same words. As they wandered about in the East, they came to a plain in Babylonia and settled there. They said to one another, "Come on! Let's make bricks and bake them hard." So they had bricks to build with and tar to hold them together. They said, "Now let's build a city with a tower that reaches the sky, so that we can make a name for ourselves and not be scattered all over the earth."

Then the Lord came down to see the city and the tower which those men had built, and he said, "Now then, these are all one people and they speak one language; this is just the beginning of what they are going to do. Soon they will be able to do anything they want! Let us go down and mix up their language so that they will not understand each other." So the Lord scattered them all over the earth, and they stopped building the city. The city was called Babylon, because there the Lord mixed up the languages of all the people, and from there he scattered them all over the earth. (Good News Bible, Genesis 11:1-9)

THEME CHECKING QUESTIONS

1. From this story what can you tell me about the language situation long ago?

2. Where did the people live?

3. What were their plans?

4. Why did they want to do that?

5. What did the Lord think about it?

6. What did he do?

7. What happened to the people?

8. What became of the city?

9. Why was it named Babylon?

10. Why didn't the Lord want them to build the city?

The purpose of these **theme** questions is to determine if the main points of meaning are clear in the translation. The **theme** questions are used to begin the discussion. Other questions may arise from them. The respondent should be free to expand his answers in any way. If the answer to the question is direct and correct, there is no problem, but sometimes the answer is not correct. There are many reasons for wrong answers. Sometimes it is culturally strange or even unacceptable to ask these kinds of questions. It may take a bit of training for the respondent as well as the **tester**. As they work together, it will become easier. Sometimes the problem is with the question rather than the answer. That is why it is important to think about them ahead of time. Sometimes the **tester** misunderstands what the respondent intended to communicate. Sometimes the respondent misunderstands the question. Sometimes an answer seems wrong at first but is actually correct when looked at more carefully. For this reason, careful evaluation of the information is necessary before the translation is changed because of the questions. Most of the wrong answers indicate a need to reconsider the translation. The reason for the misunderstanding needs to be found. Is the misunderstanding due to the words used, or the grammar, some special phrase, the connectors, or some rhetorical device which is used wrongly? Such questions will need to be thought through carefully as the translation is polished.

Detail questions are questions about words, phrases, and other matters which the **tester** does not want to ask while he is concentrating on the main points of the text. Detail questions often lead to complicated discussions and would cause the respondent to lose track of the main points, if asked while discussing genre or theme. When doing the detail questions, such matters as the meaning of key words, the implications of symbolic actions and the interpretation of a figure of speech which has been used in the translation are discussed. They may also include questions about facts such as who did what, when, where, and why. The test is to see if the facts are correct, if the choice of lexical equivalents communicate the correct meaning, and if figurative forms of the receptor language are communicating well. The answers to most **detailed questions** should be clearly found in the text unless one is checking to see if implicit information is retrievable. The following are examples of questions which might be asked when checking the details of the *Tower of Babylon* story given on page 540:

1. How many languages did the people speak at first?

2. Where was the plain they settled in?

3. What did the people make?

4. Why did they bake them?

5. How did they hold the bricks together?

6. What did they build inside the city?

7. Who came down to the city?

8. What did he see in the city?

9. What did he do to the people?

10. Why did he do it?

11. Where did the people go?

12. Why did they stop building the city?

13. What was the city called?

Naturalness tests

The purpose of **naturalness tests**, as suggested by the name, is to see if the form of the translation is natural and the style appropriate. This testing is done by **reviewers**. **Reviewers** are people who are willing to spend time reading through the translation making comments and suggestions. It is advantageous if they are persons who have a certain amount of skill in writing the receptor language. Some of them may be persons who are bilinguals in both the source and receptor language and willing to review for accuracy as well as naturalness. However, most **reviewers** simply read the translation looking for ways to improve the naturalness and style. They will need some careful instruction before beginning this kind of checking. Otherwise, they will not make helpful suggestions and their work will not improve the translation. (See Bunkowske 1983 for a detailed discussion of the work of **reviewers**.)

Reviewers need to know enough about translation principles to understand what is meant by an idiomatic translation. They can probably best be trained by having a consultant or translator work through a number of texts with them. The translator prepares a number of "defective texts" for practice. These are texts in which unnatural forms, unclear back reference, collocational clashes, etc., have been introduced. Then, as the translator goes through these texts with the potential **reviewer**, the **reviewer** will see the kinds of things he should look for as he checks the translation. If **reviewers** can be found who already have training or are willing to take extensive training, this will greatly improve their usefulness to the project. However the training is done, the **reviewers** need to clearly understand the difference between a "defective text" and one which communicates naturally. For example, notice the difference between the following texts. The first two are defective, they are not good English. The third is natural English, that is, it is not "defective." The same paragraph has been translated three different ways in the example:

VERSION 1 - DEFECTIVE TRANSLATION

Once there was a man. He wanted a monkey. He wanted to tame it. So he went hunting. He hunted a lot. He saw a lot of monkeys. One had a baby. He killed the mother. He took the baby to his house. He tamed it. He taught it and he kept it at his house.

VERSION 2 - DEFECTIVE TRANSLATION

A man, in order to get a monkey and tame it, went hunting, they say. Then after much hunting he saw a group of monkeys going by. Seeing one that had a baby with it, he killed that one. Taking the baby and taming it, he brought it to his house and kept it there, teaching it, they say.

VERSION 3 - NATURAL TRANSLATION

Once there was a man who wanted a monkey for a pet. He went hunting to see if he could find one to tame. After he had hunted a long time he saw a group of monkeys going by. One had a baby with it so he killed that one and took the baby with him to his house. Then he tamed it and taught it many things.

A **reviewer** should be taught to expect the translation to be meaningful and easy to read. When it is not they should immediately write a comment about it, giving any further reaction which might help the translator improve the translation at that point. Different **reviewers** may be especially good at checking for different matters. Some may be good at reviewing for format problems. These **reviewers** can be especially helpful in reviewing the final draft. Some will be good at checking accuracy by comparing the translation with the source text. All should be looking for ways to improve the clarity, naturalness, flow of the discourse, and the emotive impact on the readers. (See Bunkowske 1983:34–37 for more details.)

The process used by the **reviewer** is first to read through the whole section of the translation at one time. This is important for checking the flow of the translation and the overall meaning of the text. Some **reviewers** like to read aloud. As the **reviewer** reads, he should have a pencil in hand to mark any place where it was hard to read or where it seemed unnatural or unclear. If he hesitated and had to go back and reread to understand, this should be marked. After reading all the way through, he should go back and study carefully the places where he marked the copy. He should write notes either in the margin or on a separate paper to give to the translator. Then he will go through it again looking for any additional suggestions. It is important that his notes be carefully done so that they can be useful to the translator. It is helpful if the **reviewer** tells why he had a problem or why he thinks something needs changing.

After the **reviewer** has checked for clarity and naturalness, he may also check for accuracy, if he knows the source language well. He will compare the translation with the source text looking for omissions, additions, or any changes of meaning. Only a person well trained in translation principles can give helpful suggestions concerning accuracy. Others will tend to be influenced by the source language form and often suggest changes in the translation which will lead away from clarity and naturalness. Once again the **reviewer** should make careful notes for the translator. He should not just be critical but also make suggestions for improvement or further checking. Good **reviewers** are of tremendous help in improving the translation, if the translator is willing to take their suggestions seriously.

Readability tests

The translator(s) and tester(s) alike may do **readability tests**. These tests are done by asking someone to read a part of the translation aloud. It should be a complete section; that is, a unit.

As they read, the tester will notice any places where the reader hesitates. Also, if he stops and re-reads the sentence, this should be noted as it indicates some problem in **readability**. Sometimes the reader will simply look puzzled, as if he did not understand why it was said that way. There will also be times when the reader will actually say something different than what is written in the translation.

The one who is doing the testing should not in any way embarrass the reader. He should simply note on his own copy the problems which occur, including writing in the wording that was substituted. If possible, he should note the reason for the difficulty.

Readability tests do not need to be done in formal sessions only. At any time that someone is reading the translation, the translator, testers, and reviewers who are listening should be aware of any difficulties in reading. These should be noted along with the other information such as answers to comprehension questions, suggested changes for naturalness, etc.

Those checking **readability** should be especially conscious of the possibility of problems of information load. Is there just too much information coming too fast in the translation? Or is the information load so slow that it is boring and for that reason not very readable? A text is readable because it is good writing, that is, it has a pleasing style, a good rhythm, and moves along at an acceptable pace. It should be kept in mind that what is readable for one audience may not be readable for another. A highly educated audience will easily read rather complex sentence structure. A newly literate audience will have difficulty with such complicated structures. This is why it is important that the **readability tests** be done with persons who will be the users of the translation. The style of the translation will be different for different audiences. When writing for children, short, simple sentences and a conversational style will need to be used. For older people, longer sentences and a more direct style which will bring out the feeling or emotion of the original source language text should be used. **Readability tests** can help to see if this has been done. Does the reader show emotional response as he reads? Is it the correct response? (For more on style in translation see Stine 1972:202–6.)

Readability may also be affected by formatting matters. The size of type, punctuation, spelling, size of margins, and space between lines may all affect the readability tests. If these format matters are a problem, that needs to be noted. Reading difficulty should not always be blamed on the content of the translation itself. All of those who are testing the translation should be alert for reading problems related to formatting as well as content.

Consistency checks

As the translation comes near to completion, it is very important that **consistency checks** of various kinds be made. Some of these have to do with the content of the translation, and others have to do with the technical details of presentation. All of those who are testing the translation should be alert for reading problems related to formatting as well as content.

The source text will have had certain key terms which were identified and for which lexical equivalents were found. If the document being translated is a long one or done over a long period of time, it is possible that the translator has been inconsistent in the use of lexical equivalents for some key terms. At the end of the translation project a check should be done of such terms. This will be especially true in technical, political, or religious documents. For example, in translating the Bible, there are a number of key terms such as *prophet, scribe, apostle, angel,* and *sabbath.* If the meaning is the same and there is nothing in the context to indicate that a different term should be used, the translator will want to use the same term in each occurrence. A check should be made of such terms to be sure that the same term is indeed used or that there is a special reason for using a different term in a certain context. There may also be key phrases, that is, phrases which are used over and over and have the same meaning in each occurrence. As was discussed in chapter 17, care should be taken not to set up a kind of pseudo-concordance by a consistent form in the translation when the meanings are different because of the context. **Consistency** is desired only when the same meaning is to be communicated.

Consistency in editing matters requires careful attention. There should be **consistency** in the spelling of the names of people and places, for example. This will require a careful proofreading of the entire text. Any "foreign" words which are borrowed and occur several times, should be checked for **consistency** of spelling. The use of capitals and of punctuation should be checked carefully. Are quotations punctuated consistently? Is the use of question marks, commas, brackets, parentheses, or any other punctuation done consistently? In the final review, the formatting of the text and of any supplementary material like footnotes, glossary, and index or table of contents, should also be carefully checked for formatting style. If a translator is unsure of how to handle these matters, there are books available dealing with matters of spelling, punctuation etc., which can be consulted.

Using the testing results

We have discussed many ways in which the translation may be tested. However, unless this information is incorporated into the translation, that is, unless it is actually used by the translator, the testing is wasted. After all of the tests have been carried out, the results will need to be evaluated and recommended changes accepted or rejected or modified in some way. Many good suggestions will be lost, unless there has been a careful system for recording them, and unless the translator or the translation team have been carefully looking at the suggestions. But not all of the testing results should be left on file until the final draft. Certain results are more beneficial at one time in the process and other results at other times. A look at the steps in the translation project will be helpful in showing how the testing fits into the project.

In the preceding chapter the following procedures were listed: preparation, analysis, transfer, initial draft, reworking the initial draft, testing the translation, polishing the manuscript, and preparing the manuscript for the publisher. After the *initial draft* is completed, it will be very helpful to the translator if he himself does some **readability checks** and **comprehension checks** with various people. This will give him a feel for how the translation is communicating. He will then be able to incorporate this information in the reworking of the *initial draft*. He will also do a careful **comparison** with the source text for accuracy. If he is a new translator, a consultant check early in the process will also be of great help.

The reworking of the *initial draft* results in the *second draft*. This draft is then tested by a careful comparison with the source text. A **back-translation** is prepared which the translator will use for a self-check and for working with a consultant. **Comprehension checks, naturalness checks,** and **readability checks** are also made. The information which the testers and reviewers bring back to the translation desk is carefully filed or copied onto a special master copy which will be used in the next revision. A third draft, the *revision draft*, is then made by the translator incorporating the information into the draft. The translator himself may work on this, or if several people are involved in the project, the *revised draft* may be worked on by the whole team. Each suggestion should be carefully considered and a decision made.

Once the *revised draft* is completed, some **consistency checking** may need to be done again. Additional **readability testing** may be done. It may even be wise to do some more **comprehension testing** or **reviewing**, especially on parts of the translation on which there was disagreement among the members of the team. This will then bring back additional information to be included in the *final draft*. The *final draft* will then need to be checked very carefully for **consistency** in technical matters and proofread a number of times. If a number of people can read through it completely, this will give the best check of the *final draft*.

EXERCISES – Testing the Translation

Take the translation which you did in second draft after finishing the previous chapter, and continue using the testing procedures in this chapter (comparison with source, back-translation, comprehension check, naturalness check, readability check, and consistency check). Do not skip any testing procedure. If possible, have some other person do the back-translation. You will need to instruct them carefully. Your instructor will serve as your consultant. Use at least two reviewers. When all the checks are finished, incorporate what you learned into the revised draft. Do any further checking you need to do and then prepare the final draft.

BIBLIOGRAPHY

BIBLIOGRAPHY

Aaron, Uche Ekereawaji. 1983. *Interpropositional Relations in Obolo.* M.A. thesis, University of Texas at Arlington.

Abangma, Samson Negbo. 1987. *Modes in Denya Discourse.* Summer Institute of Linguistics Publications in Linguistics 79. Dallas, TX: The Summer Institute of Linguistics and the University of Texas at Arlington.

Ahrens, Theodor. 1977. Concepts of Power in Melanesian and Biblical Perspective. *Missiology* 5(2):141–73.

Anderson, John M. 1971. *The Grammar of Case: Towards a Localistic Theory.* Cambridge: The University Press.

Anderson, Stephen R. 1971. On the Role of Deep Structure in Semantic Interpretation. *Foundations of Language* 6: 197–219.

Austin, J.L. 1962. *How To Do Things With Words,* ed. by J. O. Urmson, New York: Oxford University Press.

Ballard, D. Lee, Robert J. Conrad, and Robert E. Longacre. 1971. The Deep and Surface Structure Grammar of Interclausal Relations. *Foundations of Language* 7:70–118. Dordrecht, Holland: D. Reidel.

Banker, John. 1978. Some Aspects of Style in Translation. *Notes on Translation* 72:28–32.

Barnwell, Katharine. 1974. Vocative Phrases. *Notes on Translation* 53:9–17.

———. 1975. *Bible Translation.* Jos, Nigeria: Nigeria Bible Translation Trust.

———. 1977. Testing the Translation. *The Bible Translator* 28(4):425–32.

———. 1980. *Introduction to Semantics and Translation.* Horsleys Green, England: Summer Institute of Linguistics.

———. 1983a. Towards Acceptable Translations. *Notes on Translation* 95:19–25.

————. 1983b. Discovering the Grammar of your Language. ms.

————. 1986. *Bible Translation: An introductory course in transla- tion principles,* third edition. Dallas, TX: Summer Institute of Linguistics.

Barthgate, R.H. 1980. Studies of Translation Models 1: An Opera- tional Model of the Translation Process. *The Incorporated Linguist* 19(4):113–14.

————. 1981. Studies of Translation Models 2: A Theoretical Framework. *The Incorporated Linguist* 20(1):10–16.

————. 1982. Studies of Translation Models 3: An interactive model of the translation process. *The Incorporated Linguist* 21(4).

Beekman, John. 1967. Introduction to Skewing of the Lexical and Grammatical Hierarchies. *Notes on Translation* 23:1.

————. 1978a. Toward an Understanding of Narrative Structure. ms.

————. 1978b. Three Focuses of Consultation Procedures. *Notes on Translation* 81:2–14.

————. 1980. Anthropology and the Translation of New Testament Key Terms. *Notes on Translation* 80:32–42.

————. 1981. Different Working Relationships with a Mother- Tongue Speaker in a Translation Program. *Notes on Translation* 85:2–7.

———— and John Callow. 1974. *Translating the Word of God.* Grand Rapids, MI: Zondervan.

————, John Callow, and Michael Kopesec. 1981. The Semantic Structure of Written Communication. ms.

Bellert, Irena. 1970. On a Condition of the Coherence of Texts. *Semiotica* 2:335–63.

Bendix, Edward Herman. 1966. Componential Analysis of General Vocabulary: The Semantic Structure of Verbs in English, Hindi, and Japanese. Part 2. *International Journal of American Linguis- tics* 32:2:1–190.

Biguenet, John and Rainer Shulte, eds. 1989. *The Craft of Translation.* Chicago: University of Chicago Press.

Bloomfield, Leonard. 1933. *Language.* New York: Henry Holt and Co.

Bolinger, Dwight. 1977. *Meaning and Form.* London: Longman.

Brislin, R.W. 1970. Back Translation for Cross-cultural Research. *The Journal of Cross-Cultural Psychology* 1:185–216.

————. 1976. *Translation.* New York: Garden Press.

————, W.J. Lonner, and R.M. Thorndike. 1973. *Cross-Cultural Research Methods.* New York: John Wiley and Sons.

Brower, Reuben A., ed. 1959. *On Translation.* Cambridge, MA: Harvard University Press.

Bunkowske, Eugene W. 1977. Religious Words! Which and Where? *The Bible Translator* 28:226–31.

————. 1983. Reviewers. *Notes on Translation* 95:31–38.

Callow, Kathleen. 1970. More on Propositions and Their Relations Within a Discourse. *Notes On Translation* 37:23–27.

————. 1974. *Discourse Considerations in Translating the Word of God.* Grand Rapids, MI: Zondervan.

————, Philip Hewer, and Tony Naden. 1975. A Propositional Grammar Outline. ms.

————. *Man and Message* (forthcoming, Lanham, MD: University Press of American, Inc.).

Casagrande, Joseph B. and Kenneth L. Hale. 1967. Semantic Relationships in Papago Folk Definitions. *Studies in Southwestern Ethnolinguistics.* The Hague: Mouton and Co.

Catford, J.C. 1965. *A Linguistic Theory of Translation.* London: Oxford University Press.

Chafe, Wallace L. 1970. *Meaning and the Structure of Language.* Chicago, IL: The University of Chicago Press.

Chau, Simon S.C. 1983. The Nature and Limitations of Shakespeare Translation. *The Incorporated Linguist* 22:16–20.

Cole, Peter and Jerry L. Morgan, eds. 1975. *Syntax and Semantics 3.* New York: Academic Press.

Cook, Walter A. 1971. Case Grammar as a Deep Structure in Tagmemic Analysis. *Languages and Linguistics Working Papers Number 2.* Washington, DC: Georgetown University.

Craig, Hardin, editor. 1951. *The Complete Works of Shakespeare.* Chicago: Scott, Foresman and Company.

Cromack, Robert E. 1968. *Language Systems and Discourse Structure in Cashinahua.* Hartford, CT: Hartford Theological Foundation.

Crowell, Thomas H. 1973. Cohesion in Bororo Discourse. *Linguistics* 104:15–27. The Hague: Mouton.

Crystal, David. 1976. Current Trends in Translation Theory. *The Bible Translator* 27(3):322–29.

Danes, Frantz, ed. 1974. *Papers on Functional Sentence Perspective,* 1–87. Prague: Academia Publishing House.

Davis, Donald. 1974. "Shame" in the Wantoat Language of Papua New Guinea. *Notes on Translation* 54:8–9.

de Waard, Jan. 1971. Do You Use "Clean Language?" *The Bible Translator* 22:107–15.

————. and Eugene A. Nida. 1986. From one Language to Another: Functional Equivalence in *Bible Translating*. Nashville, TN: Thomas Nelson Publishers.

Deibler, Ellis W. 1966. Comparative Constructions in Translation. *Notes on Translation* 22:4–10.

————. 1968. Translating from Basic Structure. *The Bible Translator* 19:14–16.

————. 1971a. Uses of Pro-verb 'to say' in Gahuku. *Kivung* 4:101–10.

————. 1971b. Semantics and Translation. *Notes on Translation* 39:12–16.

———— and A.J. Taylor. 1977. Translation Problems. *New Guinea Area Languages and Language Study* 3:1059–83, ed. by S.A. Wurm. *Pacific Linguistics Series* C. 40.

Di Pietro, Robert J. 1968. *Contrastive Analysis and the Notions of Deep and Surface Structure*. 19th Annual Round Table. Georgetown Monograph series 21:65–82. Washington, DC: Georgetown University Press.

Dik, Simon C. 1980. *Studies in Functional Grammar*. New York: Academic Press.

Dixon, R.M.W. 1971. A Method of Semantic Description. In Steinberg and Jakobvits, 436–71.

Djajanegara, Soenarjati. 1982. On some Difficulties in Translating from English into Bahasa Indonesia. In Ross, 81–9.

Dollerup, Cay and Anne Loddegaard, eds. 1992. *Teaching Translation and Interpretation: Training, Talent, and Experience*. Amsterdam and Philadelphia: John Benjamins Publishing Company.

Dosteft, Leon E. 1955. "The Georgetown-I.B.M. Experiment." *Machine Translation of Languages* by William N. Locke and A. Donald Booth, 124–135. New York: The Massachusetts Institute of Technology and John Wiley and Sons, Inc.

Dry, Helen. 1975. *Syntactic Reflexes of Point of View in Jane Austin's Emma*. Ph.D. dissertation, University of Texas at Austin.

Dubois, Carl D. 1973. Connectives in Sarangani Manobo Narrative. *Linguistics* 110:17–28. The Hague: Mouton.

Elkins, Richard. 1971. The Structure of Some Semantic Sets of W.B. Manobo. *Notes on Translation* 41:10–15.

Figueroa, Paul. 1983. Translation: Art or Science. *The Incorporated Linguist* 22(3):144–47.

Filbeck, David. 1972. The Passive, an Unpleasant Experience. *The Bible Translator* 23:331–36.

Fillmore, Charles J. 1968. The Case for Case. *Universals in Linguistic Theory,* ed. by Emmon Bach and Robert T. Harms, 1–88. New York: Holt, Rinehart and Winston.

―――――. 1977. The Case for Case Reopened. *Syntax and Semantics* 8:59–81. New York: Academic Press.

Firth, J.R. 1968. Ethnographic Analysis and Language with Reference to Malinowski's Views. *Selected Papers of J. R. Firth 1952–59,* ed. by F.R. Palmer. Bloomington: Indiana University Press.

Fleming, Ilah. 1971. Logical Relationships. *Instructions for the Preparation of Data Relevant for the Analysis of Semological Constructions and their Grammatical Realizations.* Mimeographed. Seattle, WA: Summer Institute of Linguistics.

―――――. 1977. Field Guide for Communication Situation, Semantic and Morphemic Analysis. ms.

Forsberg, Vivian. 1977. Workshop for Training Consultants. *Notes on Translation* 91:10–5.

Forster, Keith. 1977. The Narrative Folklore Discourse in Border Cuna. In Longacre 1977b, 1–24.

―――――. 1978. Systematic Translation Checking. ms.

Fox, David G. 1959. How Intelligible is a Literal Translation? *The Bible Translator* 10:174–75.

Franklin, Karl J. 1979. Interpreting Values Cross-culturally. *Missiology* 7(3):355–64.

Frantz, Donald G. 1968. Translation and Underlying Structure I: Relations. *Notes on Translation* 30:22–8.

―――――. 1970. Translation and Underlying Structure II: Pronominalization and Reference. *Notes on Translation* 38:3–10.

Garvin, Paul L., Jocelyn Brewer, and Madeleine Mathiot. 1967. Prediction-Typing: A Pilot Study in Semantic Analysis. *Language 43:* Part 2. Language Monograph No. 27. Baltimore, MD: Linguistic Society of America.

Gentzler, Edwin. 1993. *Contemporary Translation Theories.* London and New York: Routledge.

Gibson, Lorna. 1965. The Use of Role in Translation. *Notes on Translation* 16:3.

Glassman, Eugene H. 1981. *The Translation Debate*. Downers Grove, IL: Intervarsity Press.

Gleason, H.A., Jr. 1964. *The Organization of Language: A Stratificational Approach*. 15th Annual Round Table. 17:75–104. Washington, DC: Georgetown University Press.

————. 1965. *Linguistics and English Grammar*. New York: Holt, Rinehart and Winston.

Glover, Warren W. 1974. *Sememic and Grammatical Structures in Gurung (Nepal)*. Summer Institute of Linguistics Publications in Linguistics and Related Fields 49, ed. by Irvine Davis. Norman, OK: Summer Institute of Linguistics.

Grimes, Joseph E. 1975. *The Thread of Discourse*. The Hague: Mouton.

————. 1978. *Papers on Discourse*. Dallas, TX: Summer Institute of Linguistics.

————. 1995. *Language Survey Reference Guide*. Dallas, TX: Summer Institute of Linguistics.

Gudschinsky, Sarah C. 1951. *Handbook of Literacy*. Norman, OK: Summer Institute of Linguistics and the University of Oklahoma.

————. 1969. Notes on Orthography Preparation and Revision. Appendix II in *Conference on Navajo Orthography*, published by the Center for Applied Linguistics under contract with the Bureau of Indian Affairs, Department of the Interior. Washington, DC.

————. 1973. Orthography and its Influence on the Teaching of Reading. *A Manual of Literacy for Preliterate Peoples*, 116–25. Ukarumpa, Papua New Guinea: Summer Institute of Linguistics.

Guenthner, F. and M. Guenthner-Reutter. 1978. *Meaning and Translation*. New York University Press.

Gumperz, John J. and Eleanor Herasimchuk. 1972. *The Conversational Analysis of Social Meaning: A Study of Classroom Interaction*. 23rd Annual Round Table. Georgetown Monograph Series 25:99–134. Washington, DC: Georgetown University Press.

Gunn, Judy. 1982. A Semantic Structural Analysis of a Buglere Folktale from Panama. ms.

Gutt, Ernst-August. 1991. *Translation and Relevance: Cognition and Context*. Oxford: Basil Blackwell Ltd.

Hale, Austin, ed. 1973. *Clause, Sentence, and Discourse Patterns in Selected Languages of Nepal*. Summer Institute of Linguistics

Publications in Linguistics and Related Fields 40, ed. by Irvine Davis. Norman, OK: Summer Institute of Linguistics.

Halliday, M.A.K., Angua McIntosh, and Peter Strevens. 1968. The Users and Uses of Language. In Joshua A. Fishman, ed. *Readings in the Sociology of Language*. The Hague: Mouton.

————, Angua McIntosh, and Peter Strevens. 1973. Language as Social Semiotic: Towards a General Socio-syntactic Theory. In Luigi Heilmann, Adam Makkai, and Valerie Becker Makkai. *Linguistics at the Crossroads*. The Hague: Mouton.

———— and Ruqaiya Hasan. 1976. *Cohesion in English*. London: Longmans.

Ham, Patricia. 1965. Figures of Speech in Apinayé. *Notes on Translation* 16:2.

Hatim, Baseil and Ian Mason, eds. 1990. *Discourse and the Translator*. New York: Longman, Inc.

Hawkins, Robert E. 1962. Waiwai Translation. *The Bible Translator* 13(3):164–6.

Headland, Edna. 1975. Information Load and Layout in Tunebo. *Notes on Translation* 58:2–24.

————. 1979. Quotation Formulas in Tunebo. ms.

————. 1981. Questions as a Checking Device for Translation. *Notes on Translation* 83:2–9.

Headland, Paul and Stephen H. Levinsohn. 1977. Prominence and Cohesion in Tunebo Discourse. In Longacre, Robert E., ed. *Discourse Grammar Studies in Indigenous Languages of Colombia, Panama, and Ecuador*. Part 2:133–58. Dallas, TX: Summer Institute of Linguistics.

Headland, Thomas N. 1974. Anthropology and Bible Translation. *Missiology* 2:411–19.

————. 1981. Information Rate, Information Overload, and Communication Problems in the Casiguran Dumagat New Testament. *Notes on Translation* 83:18–27.

Henriksen, Lee A. and Stephen H. Levinsohn. 1977. Progression and Prominence in Cuaiquer Discourse. In Longacre, 1977a, Part 2:43–67.

Hinds, John V. 1973. *Japanese Discourse Structure: Some Discourse Constraints on Sentence Structure*. Buffalo, NY: State University of New York.

————. 1976. *Aspects of Japanese Discourse Structure*. Tokyo, Japan: Kaitakusha Co., LTD.

————. 1979. Organizational Patterns in Discourse. *Syntax and Semantics, Vol. 12: Discourse and Syntax.* New York: Academic Press.

Hockett, Charles F. 1956. Idiom Formation. In Halle, Morris et al. *For Roman Jacobson,* 222–29. The Hague: Mouton.

Hoffer, Bates. 1980. Problems in Sociolinguistic Translation. *The Journal of the Linguistics Association of the Southwest* 3(3):165–72.

Hoffman, Rosemary. 1969. *Matias Talks About Government.* Port Moresby: Department of Information and Extension Services.

Hollenbach, Bruce. 1974. Discourse Structure, Interpropositional Relations, and Translation. ms.

Hohulin, Richard M. 1982a. The Quest for Dynamic Equivalence in Translation. In Ross, 15–22.

———— and E. Lou Hohulin. 1982. Problems of Bilingual Lexicography. In Ross, 23–32.

Hohulin, E. Lou. 1982a. Readability and Linguistic Complexity in Translation. *Notes on Translation* 91:14–28.

————. 1982b. Text Grammar in Translation. In Ross, 64–80.

————. 1983. The Semantics of Redundancy. ms.

Hook, Ann. 1980. A Fresh Look at Consultant Procedures. *Notes on Translation* 80:2–21.

Hopper, Paul J. 1979. Aspect and Foregrounding in Discourse. *Syntax and Semantics, Vol 12: Discourse and Syntax* New York: Academic Press.

Hunt, Geoffrey R. 1980. A Logical Development. *Notes on Linguistics* 16:37–40.

Huttar, George L. 1977a. Speech Acts and Translation. *Notes on Translation* 66:29–38.

————. 1977b. World Views, Intelligence, and Cross-Cultural Communication. *Ethnic Studies* 1:3–14.

Hwang, Shin Ja. 1979. The Field Perspective in Translation. Notes for class presentation.

Hymes, Dell H. 1960. Discussion of the Symposium on Translation between Language and Culture. *Anthropological Linguistics* 2:79–84.

————. 1968. The Ethnography of Speaking. *Readings on the Sociology of Language,* ed. by Joshua A. Fishman. The Hague: Mouton.

Ivir, Valdimir. 1975. Social Aspects of Translation. *Studia Ronanica et Anglica Zagrabiensia* 39:205–13. Zagreb, Filozofshi Falultet, Ulica D. Salaja.

Jackson, Ellen M. 1982. Real and Rhetorical Questions in Tikar. Paper presented at the 15th West African Linguistic Society Congress, University of Port Harcourt, Nigeria.

Johnson, Linda and Richard Bayless. 1976. Cohesion in a Discourse-based Linguistic Theory. ms.

Jones, Larry B. and Linda K. Jones. 1979. Multiple Levels of Information in Discourse. *Discourse Studies in Mesoamerican Languages,* Linda K. Jones, ed. Robert E. Longacre, project director, 1:3–28. Dallas, TX: Summer Institute of Linguistics and the University of Texas at Arlington.

Jones, Linda K., ed. and Robert E. Longacre, project director. 1979. *Discourse Studies in Mesoamerican Languages.* Dallas, TX: The Summer Institute of Linguistics and the University of Texas at Arlington.

Joos, Martin. 1958. Semology: A Linguistic Theory of Meaning. *Studies in Linguistics* 13(3–4):53–70.

———. 1962. *The Five Clocks.* Indiana University Research Center in Anthropology, Folklore, and Linguistics Pub. 22. Bloomington: Indiana University.

Keenan, Edward L. 1971. Two Kinds of Presuppositions in Natural Language. *Studies in Linguistic Semantics,* ed. Charles J. Fillmore and D. Terence Langendown, 45–52. New York: Holt, Rinehart and Winston.

Keesing, Roger M. 1979. Linguistic Knowledge and Cultural Knowledge: Some Doubts and Speculations. *American Anthropologist* 81:14–36.

Kilham, Christine A. 1974. *Thematic Organization of Wik-Munkan Discourse.* Ph.D. dissertation, Australian National University at Canberra.

Kingston, Peter L.E. 1973. Repetition as a Feature of Discourse Structure in Manainde. *Notes on Translation* 50:13–22.

Kirkpatrick, Lilla. 1972. Rhetorical Questions in Korku of Central India. *Notes on Translation* 44:28–32.

Klammer, Thomas Paul. 1971. *The Structure of Dialogue Paragraphs in Written Dramatic and Narrative Discourse.* Ph.D. dissertation, the University of Michigan.

Koontz, Carol. 1977. Features of Dialogue within Narrative Discourse in Teribe. In Longacre 1977c, Part 3:11–132.

Koop, Rob. 1983. Prominence in Two Nigerian Languages. *Notes on Translation* 96:10–24.

Lakoff, George. 1971. Presupposition and Relative Well Formedness. *Semantics,* ed. by Danny D. Steinberg and Leon A. Jakobovits, 329–40. Dordrecht, Holland: D. Reidel.

Lamb, Sidney M. 1964a. The Sememic Approach to Structural Semantics. *Transcultural Studies in Cognition,* ed. by A. Kimball Romney and Roy Goodwin D'Andrade. *American Anthropologist* 66(3):57–78.

————. 1964b. *On Alternation, Transformation, Realization, and Stratification.* 15th Annual Round Table. Georgetown Monograph Series 17:105–22. Washington, DC: Georgetown University Press.

————. 1966. *Outline of Stratificational Grammar.* Washington, DC: Georgetown University Press.

Landau, Sidney I., et al, eds. 1977. *The Reader's Digest Great Encyclopedic Dictionary.* Pleasantville, NY: The Reader's Digest Association, Inc.

Larson, Mildred L. 1965. A Method for Checking Discourse Structure in Bible Translation. *Notes on Translation* 17:1–25.

————. 1967. The Relationship of Frequency Counts and Function. *Notes on Translation* 28:14–6.

————. 1969. Making Explicit Information Implicit in Translation. *Notes on Translation* 33:15–20.

————. 1975. *A Manual for Problem Solving for Bible Translation.* Grand Rapids, MI: Zondervan.

————. 1978. *The Functions of Reported Speech in Discourse.* Dallas, TX: Summer Institute of Linguistics and the University of Texas at Arlington.

————. 1979. The Communication Situation and Rhetorical Questions. *Notes on Linguistics* 9:14–18.

————. 1982. Traducción y Estructura Semántica. *Estudios Filológicos* 17:7–21. Valdivia: Universidad Austral de Chile.

————. 1987. Establishing Project-specific Criteria for Acceptability of Translation. *Translation Excellence: Assessment, Achievement, Maintenance,* ed. by Marilyn Gaddis Rose, 69–76 *American Translators Association Scholarly Monographs 1* Binghamton, NY: University Center, SUNY.

————. 1990. Training Translators through Rewriting. *Proceedings of the XIIth World Congress of FIT,* ed. by Mladen Jovanovic,

624–32. Belgrade, Yugoslavia: Fédération Internationale des Traducteurs.

————. 1991. Translating Secondary Functions of Grammatical Structures. *Translation and Meaning* Part 2, ed. by Barbara Lewandowska-Tomaszczyk and Marcel Thelen, 251–58. Maastricht, The Netherlands: Euroterm Maastricht.

————. 1991. Volume editor, *Translation Theory and Practice: Tension and Interdependence,* American Translators Association Scholarly Series, Volume V, New York: State University of New York at Binghamton (SUNY).

————. 1993. Translation and Linguistic Theory. *The Encyclopedia of Language and Linguistics,* ed. by Asher, R. E. and J. M. Y. Simpson, 4685–94. Pergamon Press.

————. 1993. Grammatical Skewing in Translation. *The Encyclopedia of Language and Linguistics,* ed. by R. E. Asher and J. M. Y. Simpson, 4709–16. Pergamon Press.

————. 1997. The Relation of Discourse Genre to Meaning in Translation, to appear in *Translation and Meaning,* Part 4, eds. Marcel Thelen and B. Lewandowska-Tomaszczyk, UPM, University of Maastricht: Hogeschool Maastricht School of Translation and Interpreting.

Lauriault, James. 1957. Some Problems in Translating Paragraphs Idiomatically. *The Bible Translator* 8:166–69.

Leech, Geoffrey N. 1974. *Semantics.* Harmondsworth: Penguin.

————. 1980. *Explorations in Semantics and Pragmatics.* Amsterdam: John Benjamin B.V.

Lehrer, Adrienne. 1974. *Semantic Fields and Lexical Structure.* Amsterdam: North Holland Publishing Company.

Levinsohn, Stephen. 1975. Participant Reference in Inga. ms.

————. 1976. Progression and Digression in Inga (Quechuan) Discourse. *Forum Linguisticum* 1:122–46.

Li, Charles. 1976. *Subject and Topic.* New York: Academic Press.

Lingenfelter, Sherwood G. 1976. The Relevance of the Anthropological Study of Kinship and Local Politics to Linguistics Research and Translation. ms.

Lithgow, David. 1967. Exclusiveness of Muyuw Pronouns. *Notes on Translation* 26:14.

Litteral, Robert. 1975. Lahara Translation Course. ms.

Lockwood, David G. 1972. *Introduction to Stratificational Linguistics.* New York: Harcourt, Brace, and Javanovich.

Loewen, Jacob A. 1964. Culture, Meaning and Translation. *The Bible Translator* 15:189–94.

————. 1971. Form and Meaning in Translation. *The Bible Translator* 22(4):169–74.

Longacre, Robert E. 1958. Items in Context: Their Bearing on Translation Theory. *Language* 34:482–91.

————. 1964. *Grammar Discovery Procedures.* The Hague: Mouton.

————. 1968. *Philippine Languages: Discourse, Paragraph and Sentence Structure.* Summer Institute of Linguistics Publications in Linguistics and Related Fields 21, ed. by Benjamin F. Elson. Norman, OK: Summer Institute of Linguistics.

————. 1971a. The Relevance of Sentence Structure Analysis to Bible Translation. *Notes on Translation* 40:16–23.

————. 1971b. Translation: A Cable of Many Strands. *Notes on Translation* 42:3–9.

————. 1971c. *Philippine Discourse and Paragraph Studies in Memory of Betty McLaughlin.* Pacific Linguistics, Series C, 22. Canberra, Australia: The Australian National University.

————. 1972a. *Hierarchy and Universality of Discourse Constituents in New Guinea Languages: Discussion.* Washington, DC: Georgetown University Press.

————. 1972b. Some Implications of Deep and Surface Structure Analysis for Translation. *Notes on Translation* 45:2–10.

————. 1976a. *An Anatomy of Speech Notions.* Lisse, Belgium: Peter deRidder Press.

————. 1976b. The Discourse Structure of the Flood Narrative. *Society of Biblical Literature Seminar Papers 10,* ed. by George MacRae, 235–62. Missoula, MT: Scholars Press.

————. 1976c. Discourse. *Trends in Linguistics* (Studies and Monographs 1), ed. by Ruth M. Brend and Kenneth L. Pike. The Hague: Mouton.

————. 1981. A Spectrum and Profile Approach to Discourse Analysis. *Text* 1(4):339–59.

———— and Stephen Levinsohn. 1977. Field Analysis of Discourse. *Current Trends in Text Linguistics,* ed. by Wolfgang U. Dressler. Berlin: Walter de Gruyter.

————, ed. 1976d and 1977. *Discourse Grammar Studies in Indigenous Languages of Colombia, Panama and Ecuador.* Parts 1, 2, and 3. Dallas, TX: Summer Institute of Linguistics.

Loos, Eugene. 1961. Capanahua Narrative Structure. *Studies in Literature and Language 4* (1963). Ph.D. dissertation, the University of Texas at Austin.

Lord, John B. 1964. *The Paragraph, Structure and Style.* New York: Holt, Rinehart and Winston.

Loriot, James and Barbara Hollenbach. 1970. Shipibo Paragraph Structure. *Foundations of Language* 6:43–66.

Lounsbury, Floyd. 1956. A Semantic Analysis of the Pawnee Kinship Usage. *Language* 32:158–94.

Lyons, John. 1963. *Structural Semantics.* Oxford: Blackwell.

————. 1977. *Semantics.* London: Cambridge University Press.

Makkai, Adam and David G. Lockwood, eds. 1973. *Readings in Stratificational Linguistics.* University of Alabama: The University of Alabama Press.

Malone, Joseph L. 1988. *The Science of Linguistics and the Art of Translation.* Albany, NY: State University of New York Press.

Mansen, Richard and Karis Mansen. 1976. The Structure of Sentence and Paragraph in Guajiro Narrative Discourse. In Longacre 1976d.

McArthur, Harry. 1981. Theme: How to Translate and Check it. *Notes on Translation* 85:8–13.

Moore, Bruce R. 1964. Second Thoughts on Measuring 'Naturalness.' *The Bible Translator* 15:83–87.

————. 1972. Doublets. *Notes on Translation* 43:3–34.

————. 1973. Symbolic Action and Synecdoche. *Notes on Translation* 49:14–15.

————. 1980. Report of the Translation Consultants Meeting for the Americas. *Notes on Translation* 79:8–23.

Newman, Barclay M., Jr. 1977. Everybody has Black Hair. *The Bible Translator* 28(4):401–4.

Newmark, Peter. 1973. Twenty-three Restricted Rules of Translation. *The Incorporated Linguist* 12(1):9–15.

————. 1974. Further Propositions on Translation. *The Incorporated Linguist* 13(3):62–72.

————. 1980. The Translation of Metaphor. *Babel* 26(2):93–100.

————. 1981. *Approaches to Translation.* Oxford: Pergamon Press.

————. 1982. Translation and the Vocative Function of Languages. *The Incorporated Linguist* 21:29–36.

Newmark, Peter. 1989. *A Textbook of Translation.* Hertfordshire, England: Prentice Hall International (UK) Ltd.

Nida, Eugene A. 1947. *Bible Translating*. London: United Bible Societies.

————. 1951. A System for the Description of Semantic Elements. *Word* 7:1–14.

————. 1954. *Customs and Cultures*. New York: Harper.

————. 1955. Problems in Translating the Scriptures into Shilluk, Anuak and Nuer. *The Bible Translator* 6:55–62.

————. 1961. Some Problems of Semantic Structure and Translational Equivalence. *William Cameron Townsend en el XXV Aniversario de I.L.V.*, 313–25. Mexico, DF: Summer Institute of Linguistics.

————. 1964. *Toward a Science of Translating*. Leiden, Netherlands: E.J. Brill.

————. 1970. Formal Correspondence in Translation. *The Bible Translator* 21:105–13.

————. 1974. Translation. *Current Trends in Linguistics*. Thomas A. Sebeok, ed. The Hague: Mouton.

————. 1975a. Componential Analysis of Meaning. *Approaches to Semantics*. Thomas A. Sebeok, ed. The Hague: Mouton.

————. 1975b. *Exploring Semantic Structures*. Munich: Wilhelm Fink Verlag.

————. 1975c. Semantic Structure Translating. *The Bible Translator* 26(1):120–32.

————. 1981. *Signs, Sense, Translation*. ms. Lectures given at the University of Pretoria in 1981.

————. 1982. Translation Principles and Procedures. *The Bible Translator* 33:208–12.

————. 1982a. Establishing Translation Principles and Procedures. *The Bible Translator* 33(2):208–13.

————. 1982b. Quality in Translation. The Bible Translator 33:329–32.

————, Johannes P. Louw, and Rondal B. Smith. 1977. Semantic Domains and Componential Analysis of Meaning. In Roger W. Cole. *Current Issues in Linguistic Theory*. Bloomington, IN: Indiana University Press.

———— and William D. Reyburn. 1981. *Meaning Across Cultures*. Maryknoll, NY: Orbis Books.

———— and Charles R. Taber. 1969. *The Theory and Practice of Translation*. Leiden, Netherlands: E.J. Brill for the United Bible Societies.

Nishiyama, Sen. 1982. Realities of Translation: A Case Study of the Japanese Experience. In Ross, 123–45.

Ogden, C.K. and I.A. Richards. 1952. *The Meaning of Meaning: A Study of the Influence of Language upon Thought and of the Science of Symbolism.* 10th ed. New York: Harcourt, Brace.

Palmer, F.R. 1981. *Semantics.* London: Cambridge University Press.

Pike, Eunice V. 1967. Skewing of the Lexical and Grammatical Hierarchy as it Affects Translation. *Notes on Translation* 23:1–3.

Pike, Evelyn G. and Rachel Saint. 1988. Workpapers Concerning Waorani Discourse. Dallas, TX: Summer Institute of Linguistics.

Pike, Kenneth L. 1976. *Language in Relation to a Unified Theory of the Structure of Human Behavior.* The Hague: Mouton.

————— and Evelyn G. Pike. 1977. *Grammatical Analysis.* Summer Institute of Linguistics Publications in Linguistics 53, ed. by Irvine Davis and Virgil Poulter. Dallas, TX: Summer Institute of Linguistics and the University of Texas at Arlington.

Popovich, Harold. 1967. Large Grammatical Units and the Space-Time Setting in Maxakali. *Aras do Simpósio sobre a Biota Amazónica* 2:195–99.

Rabadán, Rosa. 1991. *Equivalencia y traducción: Problemática de la equivalencia translemica inglés-español.* Universidad de León.

Reggy, Mae Alice. 1983. Some Thoughts about Testing Texts for Children. *The Bible Translator* 34(2):240–43.

Reid, Lawrence A. 1971. Tense Sequence in Procedural Discourse. *The Archive* 2(2):15–42.

—————. 1970. *Central Bontoc: Sentence, Paragraph, and Discourse.* Summer Institute of Linguistics Publications in Linguistics and Related Fields 27, ed. by Benjamin F. Elson. Norman, OK: Summer Institute of Linguistics of the University of Oklahoma.

Reinfrank-Clark, Karin. 1980. Translation-Craft and Art. *The Incorporated Linguist* 19:55–6.

Reyburn, William D. 1969. Cultural Equivalences and Non-equivalences in Translation. *The Bible Translator* 20:158–67.

Richards, Joan. 1979. Participant Identification in Discourse. *Notes on Linguistics* 10:31–40.

Rose, Marilyn Gaddis. 1981. *Translation Spectrum.* Albany, NY: State University of New York Press.

Ross, Richard B., ed. 1982. *Ten Papers on Translation,* Occasional Papers No. 21 of the Seameo Regional Language Center, Singapore.

Rountree, Catherine. 1984. A Preliminary Guide to Comprehension Checking. *Notes on Translation* 101:3–14.

Roy, Alice Myers. 1981. The Function of Irony in Discourse. *Text.* The Hague: Mouton.

Rupp, James. 1974. Eliciting Metaphors. *Notes on Translation* 53:17–22.

Savory, T.H. 1968. *The Art of Translation.* London: Jonathan Cape.

Sayers, Barbara J. 1980. Christianity Confronts Aboriginal Culture. Supplement of *Alato* 5:7–22.

Schmitt, Christian. 1982. Translating and Interpreting, Present and Future. *The Incorporated Linguist* 21:96–102.

Schramm, Wilbur. 1966. Information Theory and Mass Communication. In Alfred G. Smith, ed. *Communication and Culture* 520–34. New York: Holt, Rinehart, and Winston.

Schulze, Marlene, and Dora Bieri. 1973. Chaining and Spotlighting: Two Types of Paragraph Boundaries in Sunwar. In Hale 1973, 389–400.

Searle, John R. 1969. *Speech Acts.* London: Cambridge University Press.

Sheffler, Margaret. 1978. Mundurukú Discourse. In Joseph Grimes, ed. *Papers in Discourse.* Summer Institute of Linguistics Publications in Linguistics and Related Fields 51,119–42. Dallas, TX: Summer Institute of Linguistics and the University of Texas at Arlington.

Shoemaker, Jack, Nola Shoemaker, and Mildred L. Larson. 1983. *Relaciones communicacionales en la gramática ese ejja.* LaPaz, Bolivia: Instituto Nacional de Estudios Lingüísticos. (Translated from 1978 ms. Communication Relations in Ese Ejja.)

Shuy, Roger W. and Ralph W. Fasold. 1971. Contemporary Emphasis in Sociolinguistics. *Language and Linguistics 24.* Washington, DC: Georgetown University Press.

Simons, Linda and Hugh Young. 1979. *Pijin Blong Yumi, a Guide to Solomon Island Pijin.* Honiara, Solomon Islands: Solomon Islands Christian Association Publication Group.

Smalley, William et al. 1963. *Orthography studies: Articles on New Writing Systems.* London: United Bible Societies.

————. 1976. Questions to be Answered before we Translate. *The Bible Translator* 27:401–6.

Smith, A.H. 1958. *Aspects of Translation: Studies in Communication 2,* preface. London: Secker and Warburg, Ltd.

Steinberg, Danny D. and Leon A. Jakobvits, eds. 1971. *Semantics–An Interdisciplinary Reader in Philosophy, Linguistics and Psychology.* London: Cambridge University Press.

Steiner, George. 1975. *After Babel: Aspects of Language and Translation.* New York: Oxford University Press.

Stennes, Leslie Herman. 1969. *The Identification of Participants in Adamawa Fulani.* Hartford, CT: Hartford Seminary Foundation.

Stine, Philip C. 1972. Let's Make Our Translation More Interesting. *The Bible Translator* 23(2):202–6.

Strange, David and E. Deibler. 1974. *Papua New Guinea Translators' Course.* Ukarumpa, Papua New Guinea: Summer Institute of Linguistics.

Strässler, Jurg. 1982. *Idioms in English.* Tubingen: Narr.

Swellengrebel, J.L. 1963. Politeness and Translation in Balinese. *The Bible Translator* 14:158–64.

Taber, Charles R. 1966. *The Structure of Sango Narrative.* Hartford Studies in Linguistics 17. Hartford, CT: The Hartford Seminary Foundation.

————. 1970. Explicit and Implicit Information in Translation. *The Bible Translator* 21:1–9.

Taylor, John. 1977. Propositions and their Relations in a Tribal Language. *Notes on Translation* 63:14–17.

Tobita, Shigeo. 1971. Levels of Style in Japanese. *The Bible Translator* 22:49–58.

Tosh, Wayne. 1965. *Syntactic Translation.* The Hague: Mouton.

Toury, Gideon. 1995. *Descriptive Translation Studies and Beyond.* Amsterdam, The Netherlands: John Benjamins Publishing Co.

Trail, Ronald L., ed. 1973. *Patterns in Clause, Sentence, and Discourse in Selected Languages of India and Nepal, Part 1, Sentence and Discourse.* Summer Institute of Linguistics Publications in Linguistics and Related Fields 41, ed. by Irvine Davis. Norman, OK: Summer Institute of Linguistics of the University of Oklahoma.

Ullman, Stephen. 1962. *Semantics, An Introduction to the Science of Meaning.* Oxford: Basil Blackwell.

————. 1963. Semantic Universals. In *Universals of Language,* ed. by Joseph H. Greenberg. Cambridge: Massachusetts Institute of Technology Press.

Van Dijk, Teun A. 1972. *Some Aspects of Text Grammars: A Study of Theoretical Linguistics and Poetics.* The Hague: Mouton.

————. 1975. Recalling and Summarizing Complex Discourse. ms.

————. 1977. *Text and Context.* London: Longman.

Wallace, Anthony F.C. and John Atkins. 1960. Meaning of Kin Terms. *American Anthropologist* 62:58–80.

Wallace, Stephen. 1977. *Syntactic Imperialism.* Paper presented at the Annual Meeting of the Linguistic Society of America (December 1977), Chicago.

Wallis, Ethel. 1971. Discourse Focus in Mezquital Otomi. *Notes on Translation* 42:19–21.

Walrod, Michael Ross. 1977. Discourse Grammar in Ga'dang. M.A. thesis, University of Texas at Arlington.

Waltz, Carolyn H. 1977. Some Observations on Guanano Dialogue. In Longacre 1977, Part 3:67–110.

Waltz Nathan E. 1976. Discourse Functions of Guanano Sentence and Paragraph. In Longacre 1976d, Part 1:21–146.

Welch, Betty. 1977. Tucano Discourse, Paragraph, and Information Distribution. In Longacre, 1977, Part 2:229–52.

Wendland, Ernst R. 1981a. Receptor Language Style and Bible Translation I. *The Bible Translator* 32:107–24.

————. 1981b. Receptor Language Style and Bible Translation II. *The Bible Translator* 32:319–28.

————. 1982. Receptor Language Style and Bible Translation III: Training Translators About Style. *The Bible Translator* 33:115–27.

West, Dorothy. 1973. Wojokeso Sentence, Paragraph, and Discourse Analysis. *Pacific Linguistics Series* B, 28. Canberra, Australia: The Australian National University.

Wheatley, James. 1970. Knowledge, Authority, and Individualism among the Cura (Bacairi). *Anthropological Linguistics* 15(8):337–44.

————. 1973. Pronouns and Nominal Elements in Bacairi Discourse. *Linguistics* 104:105–15. The Hague: Mouton.

Whitehouse, J.C. 1973. Translation. *The Incorporated Linguist* 12(2):32–34.

Wiesemann, Ursula. 1980. Events and Non-Events in Kaingang Discourse. *Wege Zur Universalien Forschung.* Tübingen: Gunter Narr Verlag.

Wilson, W. Andre. 1964. But Me No Buts. *The Bible Translator* 15:173–80.

Wilss, Wolfram. 1982a. *The Science of Translation: Problems and Methods.* T"ubingen: Gunter Narr Verlag.

————. 1982b. Translation Equivalence. In Ross, 1–14.

————. 1996. Knowledge and Skills in Translator Behavior. Amsterdam: John Benjamin Publishing Company.

Wise, Mary Ruth. 1968. *Identification of Participants in Discourse: A Study of Aspects of Form and Meaning in Nomatsiguenga.* Ph.D. dissertation, University of Michigan. Published 1971 in Summer Institute of Linguistics Publications in Linguistics and Related Fields 28, ed. by Irvine Davis. Norman, OK: Summer Institute of Linguistics.

Wonderly, William L. 1953. Information-Correspondence and the Translation of Ephesians into Zoque. *The Bible Translator* 4: 14–21.

————. 1968. *Bible Translations for Popular Use.* London: United Bible Societies.

————. 1970. Some Principles of 'Common-language' Translation. *The Bible Translator* 21:126–37.

Woolf, Henry B. et al, eds. 1974. *The Merriam-Webster Dictionary.* New York: G. and C. Merriam Co.

NOTE: *The Bible Translator* is a journal prepared by the United Bible Societies and published by Headley Brothers Ltd., The Invicta Press, Ashford, Kent, TN24 8HH, United Kingdom.

Notes On Translation is published by the Summer Institute of Linguistics, 7500 W. Camp Wisdom Rd., Dallas, Texas 75236, U.S.A.

INDEX

INDEX

573